A THEORY OF DEFERENCE IN ADMINISTRATIVE LAW

In the modern administrative state, hundreds if not thousands of officials wield powers that can be used to the benefit or detriment of individuals and corporations. When the exercise of these powers is challenged, a great deal can be at stake. Courts are confronted with difficult questions about how to apply the general principles of administrative law in different contexts.

Based on a comparative theoretical analysis of the allocation of authority between the organs of government, *A Theory of Deference in Administrative Law* provides courts with a methodology to apply no matter how complex the subject matter. The firm theoretical foundation of deference is fully exposed and a comprehensive doctrine of curial deference is developed for application by courts in judicial review of administrative action. A wide scope is urged, spanning the whole spectrum of government regulation, thereby ensuring wide access to public law remedies.

PAUL DALY is Assistant Professor of Law, Université de Montréal. He has taught property law, administrative law, statutory interpretation and legal history at the University of Ottawa, Canada, tutored in constitutional law at University College Cork and supervised constitutional and administrative law at the University of Cambridge.

A THEORY OF DEFERENCE IN ADMINISTRATIVE LAW

Basis, Application and Scope

PAUL DALY

CAMBRIDGE
UNIVERSITY PRESS

CAMBRIDGE
UNIVERSITY PRESS

University Printing House, Cambridge CB2 8BS, United Kingdom

Published in the United States of America by Cambridge University Press, New York

Cambridge University Press is part of the University of Cambridge.

It furthers the University's mission by disseminating knowledge in the pursuit of education, learning and research at the highest international levels of excellence.

www.cambridge.org
Information on this title: www.cambridge.org/9781107025516

First published 2012

A catalogue record for this publication is available from the British Library

Library of Congress Cataloguing in Publication data
Daly, Paul, 1983–
A theory of deference in administrative law : basis, application, and scope / Paul Daly.
p. cm.
Includes index.
ISBN 978-1-107-02551-6
1. Judicial review of administrative acts. I. Title.
K3412.D35 2012
342′.066–dc23
2011049755

ISBN 978-1-107-02551-6 Hardback

CONTENTS

ACKNOWLEDGEMENTS

My primary debts are to my supervisor, John Allison, who read and commented on my work in great detail, on an ongoing basis, and Adrian Vermeule, who acted as my supervisor during my year as a Visiting Researcher at Harvard Law School. Christopher Forsyth and Jeffrey Jowell, in their capacity as examiners, made pertinent comments. I also consider myself fortunate that Trevor Allan, Mark Elliott and Amanda Perreau-Saussine very generously took significant time to talk with me about my research. In addition, Jeff Haylock read the manuscript in draft and made many incisive comments.

I also benefited from conversations and communications at various times with John Bell, Karole Cuddihy, David Dyzenhaus, Conor Gearty, Bruce Harris, Matthew Lewans, David Gwynn Morgan, Tom Poole, Owen Rees, Eugene Scalia, Kannon Shanmugan, Lorne Sossin, Jason Varuhas, Mark Walters and Peter Wycoff. My ideas benefited from exposure to these other minds – as well as those of my students at Cambridge and Ottawa. The usual disclaimer applies, however, so none of those mentioned should be taken as agreeing with or endorsing any of my views.

I am very grateful to the staff at the Squire Law Library at the University of Cambridge, who provided a warm and professional work environment, in which most of my research was undertaken.

My research was generously funded by a National University of Ireland Travelling Studentship. I was also in receipt of a scholarship from the Modern Law Review.

Finally, I would like to thank my friends and family, for their constant reminders that there is life outside the library, and Marie-France for her love and support.

Montréal

TABLE OF CASES

Introduction

We live in the era of the vast administrative state. Numerous agencies, government departments and officials great and small make rules, distribute benefits, punish rule-breakers and do much else besides. Legislatures delegate power because they cannot possibly fulfil the expectations of the modern citizen through primary legislation. Instead experts are employed as agents to achieve legislators' policy goals, identified in legislation with varying degrees of specificity. Courts, by contrast, lack similar expertise, endure the shortcomings of adversarial decision-making procedures, are removed from the political process and are thus generally not delegated significant administrative powers. At the same time, most modern societies place various limits, policed by an independent judiciary, on government action. Consequently, judges retain a very important role. The difficulty for administrative law lies in the need to ascertain the proper spheres of competence of judges, who assess legality, and expert decision-makers, who choose the wisest policies. The question of the proper means of allocating decision-making authority as between reviewing courts and administrators lies at the heart of my argument.[1] I will argue that a doctrine of curial deference, pursuant to which reviewing courts should defer in appropriate circumstances and to varying degrees to administrative decision-makers, is a necessary feature of the modern legal landscape. A broad and general doctrine of curial deference will be developed by answering three questions: why should courts defer, how should courts defer, and when should courts defer?

[1] In that sense, I train my sights on legal, as opposed to political accountability. As Denis Galligan has noted pithily: 'In the context of delegated powers, accountability branches off in two directions, one towards the political process, the other towards the legal system.' *Discretionary Powers: A Legal Study of Official Discretion* (Oxford: Clarendon, 1986), p. 4.

Exclusions and assumptions

The scope of my argument is ambitious. Nevertheless, I have excluded several topics. I address only statutory powers. I do not address non-statutory powers, or executive or prerogative powers. It is, to my mind, an interesting happenstance that in England the general principles of judicial review are applied to review of statutory, non-statutory and executive or prerogative powers alike,[2] a phenomenon that is not universal. Much effort has been expended in attempting to explain and justify this curious development, much more than on the comparatively neglected question that I consider: whether the general principles of judicial review are or should be affected by statutes which do not refer expressly to the general principles.

My justification for excluding non-statutory and executive or prerogative powers rests on an important simplifying assumption: I assume that judicial review is constitutionally acceptable. I do not aim to reconcile theoretical justifications with judicial practice,[3] and hence I believe, excluding non-statutory powers and executive or prerogative powers is defensible. The assumption is justified because judicial review is generally accepted as legitimate in common law jurisdictions, where commitment to the rule of law requires that judicial review be available to prevent abuses of power and arbitrary uses of power.[4]

In respect of non-statutory powers, a particular difficulty lies in justifying judicial review of their exercise in the first place.[5] Because of the disagreement as to the justification of judicial review of non-statutory powers, it is difficult to propose that non-statutory powers should be included in a doctrine of curial deference designed for statutory powers. Some justifications will simply be incompatible with any

[2] See e.g. *R* v. *Panel on Takeovers and Mergers, ex p. Datafin* [1987] QB 815; *R (Bancoult)* v. *Secretary of State for Foreign and Commonwealth Affairs (No. 2)* [2008] UKHL 61; [2009] AC 453.

[3] Unlike, for example, Mark Elliott, *The Constitutional Foundations of Judicial Review* (Oxford: Hart, 2001).

[4] See generally Christopher Forsyth (ed.), *Judicial Review and the Constitution* (Oxford: Hart, 2000). See also Jeffrey Jowell, 'The Rule of Law and its Underlying Values' in Jeffrey Jowell and Dawn Oliver (eds.), *The Changing Constitution*, 6th edn (Oxford: Oxford University Press, 2007), p. 5, p. 24.

[5] Compare Christopher Forsyth, 'Of Fig Leaves and Fairy Tales: The *Ultra Vires* Doctrine, the Sovereignty of Parliament and Judicial Review' (1996) 55 CLJ 122, 124–7 with Dawn Oliver, *Common Values and the Public–Private Divide* (London: Butterworths, 1999), pp. 37–54.

doctrine designed for statutory powers; others would require significant modifications to any proposed doctrine. In short, it does not seem prudent to allow the existence of some non-statutory powers to prevent or dictate the development of a doctrine for the review of statutory powers which, in any case, are much more numerous. I appreciate that the existence and reviewability of such powers present contentious questions about the scope of the administrative state and about the judicial role in overseeing it, but I see these questions as best answered with the sort of singular focus that I am unable to apply in this book.

In respect of executive or prerogative powers, it is simply difficult to comprehend why the same principles of judicial review should apply to them as to statutory powers, for anything other than reasons of convenience or historical happenstance. Statutory powers are delegated by statute, and – assuming that judicial review is legitimate – courts may police limits on the exercise of those statutory powers. But executive or prerogative powers are not delegated by statute. Rather, they are either delegated by a constitutional instrument, as in the United States,[6] or have developed as part of the constitutional firmament, as in the United Kingdom. Applying principles of judicial review developed in the context of statutory powers to the exercise of executive or prerogative powers may simply be inapt.[7]

I also do not address procedural fairness. The distinction between process and substance is not necessarily a sustainable one,[8] and may be particularly unstable where process is prescribed by statute,[9] but common law courts generally hold fast to the view that the development of principles of procedural fairness lies within the province of the judiciary: 'The courts have, in effect, devised a code of fair administrative procedure based on doctrines which are an essential part of any system of administrative justice.'[10] Even though the requirements of procedural

[6] Art. II, § 1 of the United States Constitution provides: 'The executive power shall be vested in a President of the United States of America.'

[7] But see below, Ch. 7.

[8] See e.g. David Dyzenhaus and Evan Fox-Decent, 'Rethinking the Process-Substance Distinction: *Baker* v. *Canada*' (2001) 51 UTLJ 193, 212; Laurence Tribe, 'The Puzzling Persistence of Process-Based Constitutional Theories' (1980) 89 Yale LJ 1063.

[9] David Dyzenhaus, 'The Politics of Deference: Judicial Review and Democracy' in Michael Taggart (ed.), *The Province of Administrative Law* (Oxford: Hart, 1997), p. 279, pp. 286–9.

[10] William Wade and Christopher Forsyth, *Administrative Law*, 10th edn (Oxford: Oxford University Press, 2009), p. 371.

fairness may vary according to context, common law courts have the final say as to whether they have been fulfilled or not:

> [W]hat the requirements of fairness demand when any body, domestic, administrative or judicial, has to make a decision which will affect the rights of individuals depends on the character of the decision-making body, the kind of decision it has to make and the statutory or other framework in which it operates. In particular, it is well-established that when a statute has conferred on any body the power to make decisions affecting individuals, the courts will not only require the procedure prescribed by the statute to be followed, *but will readily imply so much and no more to be introduced by way of additional procedural safeguards as will ensure the attainment of fairness.*[11]

In the United States, where procedural fairness is prescribed by constitutional requirements, a strikingly similar view has been taken: 'Once it is determined that due process applies, the question remains what process is due. It has been said so often by this Court and others as not to require citation of authority that due process is flexible and calls for such procedural protections as the particular situation demands.'[12] Accordingly, there is little scope for curial deference (at least as I shall define it below) and it seems prudent to exclude matters of procedural fairness from the present study.

As I have intimated, I also do not intend to develop a detailed theory of the administrative state. Accordingly, I use 'delegated decision-makers' to denote entities, legal or natural, to which power has been delegated by the legislature.[13] The term encompasses elected and non-elected members of the executive branch, executive-controlled administrators and independent administrators and their employees. Although it is cumbersome, it elides the difficult terminological and jurisprudential problem of whether delegated power should be classified as executive, administrative or something else entirely.[14] I use the term 'delegation' to refer to the legislature's granting of authority to administrative bodies, rather than to situations in which a delegate is invited to stand in the

[11] *Lloyd* v. *McMahon* [1987] AC 625 at 702–3, per Lord Bridge of Harwich. Emphasis added.

[12] *Morrissey* v. *Brewer* (1972) 408 US 471 at 481, per Burger CJ. See also *Mathews* v. *Eldridge* (1976) 424 US 319 at 334–5.

[13] See also *Canada (Citizenship and Immigration)* v. *Khosa* [2009] SCC 12; [2009] 1 SCR 339 at 386 per Rothstein J.

[14] See e.g. Peter Strauss, 'The Place of Agencies in Government: Separation of Powers and the Fourth Branch' (1984) 8 Colum LR 573.

shoes of the legislature, or those of an individual legislator. 'Delegation' is a more elegant term than the unwieldy 'granting of authority' and in any event captures the idea of the legislature granting to a delegate powers the delegate otherwise would not have. Occasionally, I retain the term 'agency' when quoting from the literature, to avoid square brackets interfering with the flow of text. Similarly, 'Congress' and 'Parliament' are sometimes retained in favour of 'legislature'; and I very occasionally follow the literature in using 'deference' or '*Chevron* deference' rather than 'curial deference'.

Overview of argument

In Chapter 1, I introduce different types of deference. Although this point has not been canvassed at great length in the literature, it seems to me that there are essentially two different types: epistemic deference and doctrinal deference. I provide examples of each, by reference to the three jurisdictions on which I focus. The doctrine of curial deference that I propose falls into the latter category.

In Chapters 2 and 3, I explain my reliance on legislative intent. I argue that there is a widely accepted constitutional principle, common to common law jurisdictions, that courts should give effect to legislative intent. I argue that, properly considered, this principle suggests that courts should (a) be deferential to administrative decision-makers and (b) accord administrative decision-makers a variable degree of deference. In the first instance, legislatures have delegated variable extents of power to administrators, which counsels not only judicial restraint, but variable amounts of judicial restraint. In the second instance, a proper consideration of the statutory provisions relevant to a particular case may reveal reasons for the delegation of power. I call these the 'practical justifications' for deference: expertise, complexity, democratic legitimacy and procedural legitimacy. These practical justifications are variable in nature and should be taken into account by reviewing courts, if an interpretation of the statutory language suggests that the practical justifications motivated the delegation of power. Even in situations where the statute does not seem to give much guidance to the reviewing court, judges can probe the limited statutory language to ascertain whether and to what extent a deferential approach is appropriate. The arguments based on the delegation of power and on practical justifications both suggest that reviewing courts should develop and implement a variable standard of review, in order to give effect to legislative intent.

In Chapter 4, I develop a variable standard of review. I analyse the concept of unreasonableness in the context of judicial review and elaborate on its internal reason and structure, thereby establishing its legitimacy. I am then able to formulate a conception of unreasonableness which can accommodate a variable standard of review. I argue that three standards are possible and desirable. These are: correctness, which allows a reviewing court to substitute its judgment for that of the administrative decision-maker; unreasonableness, which requires deference on the part of the reviewing court; and manifest unreasonableness, which requires a great deal of deference on the part of the reviewing court.

In Chapter 5, I contrast the conception of unreasonableness developed in Chapter 4 with the 'proportionality' test which has found judicial favour in many jurisdictions in recent decades. I sharply distinguish constitutional review from administrative review and argue that where fundamental rights have allegedly been infringed by state action, a standard of review of correctness should be applied by courts. However, I also note that deference does not slip entirely out of the picture: both doctrinal deference and, in particular, epistemic deference, can legitimately be accorded by courts in constitutional review.

In Chapters 6 and 7, I argue that the doctrine of curial deference developed in the previous chapters should have a wide scope. I suggest that the employment of complex concepts such as 'jurisdiction', 'error of law' and 'justiciability' as organising principles in judicial review may frustrate legislative intent. I urge instead that reviewing courts should undertake a general inquiry into unreasonableness or manifest unreasonableness whenever an exercise of delegated powers is impugned, except where a proper consideration of the relevant statutory provisions suggests that a standard of review of correctness is appropriate.

1

Defining deference

1.1 The meaning of deference

This chapter will serve as an introduction both to the concept of deference and the particular conception that I will be advancing over the course of this book. I will begin with a conceptual and linguistic analysis. I will then proceed to give examples of what I term epistemic deference and doctrinal deference. Finally, I will lay out and respond to what appear to me to be the major objections to doctrinal deference.

To forestall confusion, it is worth noting at this early point that my focus in this book will be on deference being paid by courts to other actors. I will not be addressing, for example, interesting questions about individuals' obligations to obey the law, which might be characterised as deference being paid by citizens to officials.[1]

1.1.1 Epistemic deference and doctrinal deference

Perhaps the most popular means of characterising deference is to associate it with the giving of weight. Brian Foley's approach is a good example: 'Reduced to its most basic form, the deference question concerns the *weight* which courts should attribute to the decisions of non-judicial institutions.'[2] The notion here is that deference involves the paying of respect to the decisions of others by means of according weight to those decisions.[3] I attach the label of *epistemic deference* to this notion.[4]

[1] See e.g. Philip Soper, *The Ethics of Deference: Learning from Law's Morals* (Cambridge: Cambridge University Press, 2002).

[2] Brian Foley, *Deference and the Presumption of Constitutionality* (Dublin: Institute of Public Administration, 2008), p. 256. Emphasis added.

[3] One could say that deference is given to the views of others. For present purposes, however, views will be equated with decisions, as it is through their decisions that delegated decision-makers express their views in legally relevant ways.

[4] See similarly T. R. S. Allan, 'Judicial Deference: Doctrine and Theory' (2011) 127 LQR 96, 102; Adrian Vermeule, 'Holmes on Emergencies' (2008) 61 Stan LR 163, 164. For

Focusing on epistemic deference, however, may cause one to overlook an equally important notion. Deference may also refer to the allocation of authority. Rather than simply paying respect to the decisions of another, one might allocate authority to another to make binding decisions. Such authority need not be absolute: its exercise might be subject to limitations of, to take a pertinent example, reasonableness. Decisions are binding, as long as they are, say, reasonable. I attach the label of *doctrinal deference* to this notion. The main focus of this book will be on doctrinal deference. Specifically, I aim to develop what I term a doctrine of curial deference which, I will argue, ought to be applied by reviewing courts whenever decisions of delegated decision-makers are challenged.

An example should shed some light on the distinction between epistemic deference and doctrinal deference. *Morse* v. *Frederick*[5] is a decision of the Supreme Court of the United States. In Juneau, Alaska, a group of high school students were allowed out during their school day to observe the Olympic Torch Relay en route to the Winter Games in Salt Lake City in 2002. During the Relay, one of the students unfurled a 14-foot banner, which declared: 'Bong Hits 4 Jesus'. On the basis that the reference to a bong – a device designed to facilitate the consumption of marijuana – violated the school's policy prohibiting public expression advocating the use of illegal drugs, the offending student was suspended from school for ten days. Subsequently, the student sued the school's principal for damages, on the basis that the former's right to freedom of expression – guaranteed by the First Amendment to the United States Constitution – had been violated.

In holding that the student's rights had not been violated, Roberts CJ relied on doctrinal deference and epistemic deference respectively. First, Roberts CJ affirmed that a school principal was entitled, consistent with the First Amendment, to punish speech which could be '*reasonably viewed* as promoting illegal drug use'.[6] This is an example of doctrinal deference: authority was allocated to the school principal to take punitive measures. However, that authority was not unbounded: any decision of the principal that speech could be construed as advocating illegal drug use would have to be reasonable. Assuming the reasonableness of the principal's view of this question, a court could not quash the measures

different uses of the term, see e.g. Scott Brewer, 'Scientific Expert Testimony and Intellectual Due Process' (1998) 107 Yale LJ 1535; Paul Horwitz, 'Four Facts of Deference' (2008) 83 Notre Dame LR 1061, 1086; Michael Moore, 'Four Reflections on Law and Morality' (2007) 48 William and Mary *LR* 1523, 1542.

5 (2007) 551 US 393. 6 *Ibid.*, p. 403. Emphasis added.

imposed. Secondly, Roberts CJ accorded weight to the principal's decision as to whether the banner actually could be construed as advocating illegal drug use. He quoted approvingly from affidavits of the principal and, noting that the banner could be read either as an imperative command to take drugs or as a celebration of drug taking, concluded that 'it *was* reasonably viewed as promoting illegal drug use'.[7] Roberts CJ was able to reach this conclusion by according epistemic deference to the decision of the school's principal. In other words, the court's conclusion was not entirely independent; it depended in part on having given weight to the decision of another body.

1.1.2 'Curial deference'

On a point of nomenclature, I employ the term 'curial deference' in preference to 'judicial deference' and 'deference'. Although Lord Steyn has professed himself 'reluctant to enter into an argument about labels', fearing that it might 'fetter our substantive thinking',[8] and 'labels are less important than the underlying approach or philosophy and its consequences',[9] the point is worth pursuing because, I will suggest, the use of 'curial deference' actually clarifies the terms of the discussion.

The root of 'curial' is the Latin word *curia*, which is not, descriptively speaking, limited to courts of law. One might be misled by the development of the Court of the King's Bench, which evolved from the *Curia Regis*. However, the *Curia Regis*, although it acted as an appellate court in complex matters, was primarily a body of wise counsellors.[10] *Curia*, then, does not denote a court of law, but a court of expert advisors. Accordingly, 'curial deference' denotes the paying of respect on the basis of another's competence.

The term 'curial deference' is preferable to both 'deference' and 'judicial deference'. Standing alone, 'deference' arguably has inappropriate 'overtones of servility, or perhaps gracious concession'.[11] Employing the alternative 'curial deference', by adding an extra word, means that

[7] *Ibid.*, p. 409. Emphasis added.

[8] Lord Steyn, 'Deference: A Tangled Story' [2005] PL 346, 350.

[9] Hugh Corder, 'Without Deference, with Respect: A Response to Justice O'Regan' (2004) 121 SALJ 438, 441.

[10] See Max Radin, *Handbook of Anglo-American Legal History* (St Paul: West, 1936), pp. 46–7.

[11] *R (ProLife Alliance)* v. *British Broadcasting Corporation* [2003] UKHL 23; [2004] 1 AC 185 at 240, per Lord Hoffman.

'deference' is less likely to be understood as having connotations of subservience. Moreover, to rule the word 'deference' out completely would be to overlook a distinction between 'submissive deference' and 'deference as respect':[12]

> Deference as submission occurs when the court treats a decision or an aspect of it as nonjusticiable, and refuses to enter on a review of it because it considers it beyond its competence. Deference as respect occurs when the court gives some weight to a decision of a primary decision-maker for an articulated reason, as part of its overall review of the justifications for the decision.[13]

I employ 'curial deference' to denote something closer to the latter (though evidently also including doctrinal deference) than to the former. By contrast, the use of 'judicial deference' is apt to be doubly misleading. First, the term has connotations of individuals, be they judges or members of the legal profession, humbly doffing the cap to others, whereas the deferring where appropriate to the considered views of others seems to capture more accurately the notion of deference as respect. Secondly, employing the term 'judicial deference' might lead its users to place judicial competence at the centre of the discussion, a point to be proved, not merely asserted. For these reasons, I prefer the term curial deference, which encompasses both epistemic deference and doctrinal deference.

1.1.3 Spheres of authority

Murray Hunt has argued powerfully that the notion of spheres of authority, some of which are assigned to the political branches of government and others of which are assigned to the judicial branch, has exerted a malign influence on Commonwealth public law theory.[14] Although my preferred approach is not entirely immune from criticism on the ground that it might tend to create spheres of authority,[15] I agree with the thrust of Hunt's argument.[16]

[12] David Dyzenhaus, 'The Politics of Deference: Judicial Review and Democracy' in Michael Taggart (ed.), *The Province of Administrative Law* (Oxford: Hart, 1997), p. 279, p. 286.

[13] Murray Hunt, 'Sovereignty's Blight' in Nicholas Bamforth and Peter Leyland (eds.), *Public Law in a Multi-Layered Constitution* (Oxford: Hart, 2003), p. 337, pp. 346–7.

[14] *Ibid.* [15] I identify and rebut this criticism below 3.7.

[16] But see Sir John Laws' approving view of 'territoriality' in 'Concluding Comments: Judicial Review's Constitutional Home' in Christopher Forsyth *et al.* (eds.), *Effective*

In particular, insofar as the development of spheres of authority in the abstract precludes certain bodies from trespassing beyond strictly demarcated boundaries in the concrete, it assumes that which is to be proved. Establishing spheres of authority suggests that decisions ought to be assigned to them on an absolute rather than a relative basis. However, the question that needs to be answered is: how should authority be allocated in the administrative state? To attach oneself at the outset to the notion of spheres of authority would be to preclude a clear-headed analysis of the very question that is in issue. Whether epistemic deference and doctrinal deference are appropriate should be determined by careful analysis, not by definitional diktat.

Moreover, thinking in terms of spheres of authority has the potential to lapse into formalism, thereby preventing judicial consideration of the relevant issues:

> Formalism is formal in that it requires judges to operate with categories and distinctions that determine results without the judges having to deploy the substantive arguments that underpin the categories and distinctions. Since those categories and distinctions must take on a life of their own in order to operate in this detached way, they are capable of determining results that contradict the very arguments for these categories and distinctions.[17]

A good example is the old distinction between jurisdictional and non-jurisdictional error.[18] The very establishment of the distinction compelled reviewing courts to assign a decision to one sphere or the other. Jurisdictional errors were in the judicial domain. Non-jurisdictional errors were not. A reviewing court's conclusion as to the appropriate assignment of the decision would effectively end the matter; hence the hoary maxim that a delegated decision-maker could have a 'right to be wrong'.[19] Once the categorisation was completed, no further discussion as to the nuances of the individual case, or the relevant statutory provisions, would be necessary; and inasmuch as the choice of the reviewing court might in fact have been based upon such considerations, the categorisation would obscure more than it would reveal.[20] In a very real sense, the distinction between

Judicial Review: A Cornerstone of Good Governance (Oxford: Oxford University Press, 2010), p. 434.

17 David Dyzenhaus, 'Constituting the Rule of Law: Fundamental Values in Administrative Law' (2002) 27 Queen's LJ 445, 450.

18 See below 6.1.

19 See e.g. *R* v. *Nat Bell Liquors* [1922] 2 AC 128 at 151–2, per Lord Sumner.

20 See generally Jack Beatson, 'The Scope of Judicial Review for Error of Law' (1984) 4 OJLS 22.

jurisdictional and non-jurisdictional error is an example of doctrinal deference: it operates so as to allocate authority between reviewing courts and delegated decision-makers. However, by virtue of its development of spheres of authority, it allocates authority on an absolute, rather than a relative basis. Because it assumes that which is to be proved, it ought to be rejected, at least at this early stage.

1.2 Doctrinal deference in practice

Although epistemic deference falls well within my field of vision,[21] my focus in this study is primarily on doctrinal deference. Indeed, my primary purpose is to develop a doctrine of curial deference. In developing my argument, I will draw almost exclusively on material from three jurisdictions, Canada, the United States and England.[22] I will generally confine myself to analysing the decisions of the superior appellate body in each of the jurisdictions, but I will occasionally refer to lower court decisions; and where relevant material from other jurisdictions is available, I will rely on it. In my three chosen jurisdictions, curial deference has developed in comprehensive and varied ways, such that sufficient information has been generated to assist in answering the three questions I identified in the Introduction. Curial deference is well-developed in Canada and the United States, but much less so in England. Although the reasons that curial deference has not been as well-developed in England contribute to an interesting comparison, choosing more than one Anglo-Australasian jurisdiction for comparative purposes would be inappropriate, because '[t]he deference principle does not feature prominently in judicial review outside of North America'.[23]

My approach is not purely comparative. I will proceed in a thematic manner and I will not simply compare the approaches followed in each of the jurisdictions. My argument is theoretical in nature. I aim to develop a doctrine of curial deference rather than to adopt a doctrine that has been developed in any particular jurisdiction. My disagreements with Canadian, American and English judges will become apparent as I develop my doctrine of curial deference. In the real world, the general principles of judicial review might have developed in such a way as to render impossible the

[21] See especially Ch. 5.

[22] I use the term England rather than the more unwieldy term 'England and Wales'.

[23] Philip Joseph, *Constitutional and Administrative Law in New Zealand*, 3rd edn (Wellington: Thomson Brookers, 2007), p. 835.

adoption in its entirety of my doctrine of curial deference. Nevertheless, it may be possible that it can be partially adopted, a point to which I will return in the Conclusion. Although I do not directly urge the transplantation of legal concepts into unfamiliar bodies of law, the wise words of Otto Kahn-Freund are borne in mind: '[the] rules which organise constitutional, legislative, administrative or judicial institutions … are the ones most resistant to transplantation'.[24] For example, the relative independence and impartiality of English judges, compared to their politically appointed Canadian and American counterparts, may go some way towards explaining a seemingly greater willingness to intervene to correct errors of law.[25]

I have confined my study entirely to common law systems. The decision is partly due to restrictions of time, expertise, language and resources. More importantly, the idea that generalist courts should defer to specialist administrators sits uneasily with the dual systems of administrative law that are to be found in many civil law jurisdictions.[26] In dual systems, dedicated administrative courts, often staffed by expert technocrats rather than generalist judges, oversee the formulation and implementation of policy by delegated decision-makers. A doctrine of curial deference would be antithetical to the French model, in which a body of experts, the Conseil d'État, sits in ultimate judgment on the decisions of delegated decision-makers.[27] The French model, which avowedly excludes generalist judges from administrative review, 'forms the basis of many continental systems'.[28]

[24] 'On Uses and Misuses of Comparative Law' (1974) 37 MLR 1, 17. See also Michael Taggart, 'Globalisation and Administrative Law' in Grant Huscroft and Michael Taggart (eds.), *Inside and Outside Canadian Administrative Law: Essays in Honour of David Mullan* (Toronto: University of Toronto Press, 2006), p. 259, p. 274. But see Alan Watson, *Legal Transplants: An Approach to Comparative Law* (Edinburgh: Scottish Academic Press, 1974) and J. W. F. Allison, 'Transplantation and Cross-Fertilisation in European Public Law' in Jack Beatson and Takis Tridimas (eds.), *New Directions in European Public Law* (Oxford: Hart, 1998), p. 169; Sujit Choudry, 'Migration in Comparative Constitutional Law' in Sujit Choudry (ed.), *The Migration of Constitutional Ideas* (Cambridge: Cambridge University Press, 2006), p. 1.

[25] See Michael Tolley, 'Judicial Review of Agency Interpretation of Statutes: Deference Doctrines in Comparative Perspective' (2003) 31 *Policy Studies Journal* 421, 434–7. See also Robert Dolehide , 'A Comparative "Hard Look" at *Chevron*: What the United Kingdom and Australia Reveal about American Administrative Law' (2010) 88 Tex LR 1381.

[26] Mary Ann Glendon, Michael Wallace and Christopher Osakwe, *Comparative Legal Traditions: Text, Materials and Cases*, 2nd edn (St Paul: West, 1994), p. 118.

[27] See Neville Brown and John Bell, *French Administrative Law*, 5th edn (Oxford: Oxford University Press, 1998), pp. 62–88, and pp. 126–74.

[28] *Ibid.*, p. 3.

That is not to suggest that my argument is irrelevant to systems in which many decisions are channelled through general appeals tribunals rather than into the courts.[29] First, final decisions of these bodies are generally subject to judicial review.[30] The doctrine of curial deference that I will develop can be applied to decisions of the tribunals by reviewing courts. Secondly, those tribunals themselves may apply a doctrine of curial deference to the decisions that are appealed to them. For instance, the Upper Tribunal created in England by the Tribunals, Courts and Enforcement Act 2007, has the power to grant the traditional public law remedies, but 'must apply the principles that the High Court would apply in deciding whether to grant that relief on an application for judicial review'.[31]

The fact that the legal systems in Canada and the United States are federal does not present any great difficulties, even though I also study the unitary English system (assuming that the issue of devolution is not relevant). The Supreme Court of Canada occupies a different institutional position to the House of Lords/United Kingdom Supreme Court, which occupies a different institutional position to the Supreme Court of the United States. However, the differences are, for present purposes, relatively minor. The Supreme Court of the United States has jurisdiction only over federal delegated decision-makers established by Congress and not, as a general rule, over delegated decision-makers established by state governments. Similarly, the House of Lords/United Kingdom Supreme Court has jurisdiction over delegated decision-makers established by Parliament. The Supreme Court of Canada does have jurisdiction over delegated decision-makers established under provincial law, but the jurisdiction arises because judicial review is 'constitutionally guaranteed in cases where it is alleged that a person exercising delegated power under a statute has exceeded the limits of that power'.[32] Thus, although the legal and institutional structures in the United States, Canada and England are quite different, the problem of allocating decision-making authority between reviewing courts and delegated decision-makers is a common one.[33]

[29] See generally, Peter Cane, *Administrative Tribunals and Adjudication* (Oxford: Hart, 2009).

[30] For an illuminating recent discussion, see *R (Cart)* v. *The Upper Tribunal* [2011] UKSC 28; [2011] 3 WLR 107.

[31] Tribunals, Courts and Enforcement Act 2007, s. 15(4).

[32] Patrick Monahan, *Constitutional Law*, 3rd edn (Toronto: Irwin, 2006), p. 139.

[33] See Paul Craig, 'Judicial Review and Questions of Law: A Comparative Perspective' in Susan Rose-Ackerman and Peter Lindseth (eds.), *Comparative Administrative Law* (New York: Edward Elgar, 2010), p. 449.

1.2.1 Canada

Over the course of nearly thirty years, the Supreme Court of Canada developed a sophisticated doctrine of 'curial deference'[34] to govern judicial review of delegated decision-makers. In the *New Brunswick Liquor* case,[35] Dickson J announced a change of course from the Canadian courts' previously interventionist tack.[36] In the instant case, because of the generous delegation of statutory authority, protected by a privative clause, to the labour relations tribunal whose decision was challenged; the need for the 'sensitivity and unique expertise' of the tribunal in balancing the purposes of the legislation; and the fact that the determination being reviewed fell squarely within the tribunal's jurisdiction, 'not only would the Board not be required to be "correct" in its interpretation, but one would think that the Board was entitled to err and any such error would be protected from review by the privative clause'.[37] Instead, a successful application for judicial review could be made out only where the Board's interpretation of the law was 'patently unreasonable'.[38]

In subsequent decisions, the court developed a 'pragmatic and functional analysis'[39] that became the overarching framework governing judicial review of delegated decision-makers in Canada.[40] By the time of its decision in *Pushpanathan* v. *Canada (Citizenship and*

[34] *Bell Canada* v. *Canada (Canadian Radio-Television and Telecommunications Commission)* [1989] 1 SCR 1722 at 1743–7, per Gonthier J.

[35] *Canadian Union of Public Employees, Local 963* v. *New Brunswick Liquor Corporation* [1979] 2 SCR 227.

[36] See *Metropolitan Life Insurance* v. *International Union of Operating Engineers, Local 796* [1970] SCR 425; *Bell* v. *Ontario (Human Rights Commission)* [1971] SCR 756. Views expressed at the time were not always critical. See e.g. Peter Hogg, 'The Supreme Court of Canada and Administrative Law, 1949–1971' (1973) 11 Osgoode Hall LJ 187; David Mullan, 'Jurisdictional Fact Doctrine in the Supreme Court of Canada: A Mitigating Plea' (1972) 10 Osgoode Hall LJ 440.

[37] *New Brunswick Liquor*, above n. 35, p. 236. [38] *Ibid.*, p. 237.

[39] *Union des employés de service, local 298* v. *Bibeault* [1988] 2 SCR 1048 at 1088, per Beetz J. It is now known as the 'standard of review analysis' (*Dunsmuir* v. *New Brunswick* [2008] SCC 9; [2008] 1 SCR 190 at 227, per Bastarache and LeBel JJ), but I prefer the older term here, as it is used in the majority of the judgments to which I refer. For an overview of the development of the approach, see Gabrielle Perrault, *Le Contrôle judiciaire des decisions de l'administration: de l'erreur juridictionnelle à la norme de contrôle* (Montreal: Wilson and Lafleur, 2002), pp. 66–85.

[40] *Dr Q* v. *College of Physicians and Surgeons of British Columbia* [2003] SCC 19; [2003] 1 SCR 226 at 235–8.

Immigration),[41] the court had refined the pragmatic and functional analysis to a four-factor inquiry into: first, whether a privative clause protected the decision, or conversely, a right of appeal was provided for; secondly, the expertise of the delegated decision-maker, relative to the court and relative to the question under review; thirdly, the purpose of the legislation as a whole and, in particular, the purpose of the statutory provision at issue; and fourthly, the nature of the question, whether closer to law and more suited to judicial resolution or closer to fact and more suited to resolution by the delegated decision-maker. No one factor was determinative: 'a highly technical or mechanistic approach is to be avoided; instead the interplay among the four factors determines the level of deference owed to the administrative decision itself'.[42]

Depending on the interplay of the four factors one of three standards of review was to apply: correctness, which would require the reviewing court to 'undertake its own reasoning process to arrive at the result it judges correct';[43] reasonableness *simpliciter*, which required the reviewing court to test the impugned decision to ascertain whether it could withstand a 'somewhat probing examination';[44] and patent unreasonableness, which required the reviewing court to affirm the decision unless it was 'so patently unreasonable that [it] cannot be rationally supported by the relevant legislation and demands intervention by the court upon review'.[45]

However, expressing disquiet about the difficulty that the complexity of the analysis created for litigators and judges, the court used the opportunity presented by *Dunsmuir* v. *New Brunswick*[46] to remove the patent unreasonableness standard of review and to refine the reasonableness *simpliciter* standard.[47] It also cast doubt on the appropriateness of the four-factor approach,[48] and has recently affirmed a categorical approach.[49] Pursuant to the categorical approach, a reviewing court's choice of the appropriate standard of review will depend on whether the

41 [1998] 1 SCR 982.
42 *Alberta Union of Provincial Employees* v. *Lethbridge Community College* [2004] SCC 28; [2004] 1 SCR 727 at 739, per Iacobucci J.
43 *Law Society of New Brunswick* v. *Ryan* [2003] SCC 20; [2003] 1 SCR 247 at 268–9, per Iacobucci J.
44 *Canada (Director of Investigation and Research)* v. *Southam* [1997] 1 SCR 748 at 776, per Iacobucci J.
45 *New Brunswick Liquor*, above n. 35, p. 237, per Dickson J.
46 *Dunsmuir*, above n. 39. 47 See below 4.4.3. 48 *Dunsmuir*, above n. 39.
49 *Smith* v. *Alliance Pipeline* [2011] SCC 7; [2011] 1 SCR 160.

impugned decision fits into one of a number of pre-set categories.[50] These categories were formulated by reference to the results of thirty years of application of the pragmatic and functional analysis. However, although the court has not expressly disavowed the four-factor analysis, its star seems to be very much on the wane. Moreover, categories have the capacity to take on lives of their own, mutating in fashions not necessarily suggested by their origins.[51]

1.2.2 United States

The conduct of judicial review of administrative action by the United States federal courts is regulated by the Administrative Procedure Act (APA), which gives the federal courts the power to review, inter alia, interpretations of law and exercises of discretion by delegated decision-makers. Developing a unified framework of review has been challenging, because '[t]he Supreme Court's decisions on the appropriate intensity of judicial review of administrative action do not fit any neat categorisation that reveals a single explanatory variable'.[52] Nonetheless, working from the text of the APA, a clear division can be observed as between judicial review of interpretations of law, governed by the *Chevron* doctrine, and judicial review of exercises of discretion, itself governed by two separate tests.

As for the latter, in the case of formal adjudications,[53] decisions must be supported by 'substantial evidence'[54] and in the case of informal adjudications, decisions must not be 'arbitrary, capricious [or] an

[50] *Ibid.*, p. 173: 'The standard of correctness governs: (1) a constitutional issue; (2) a question of "general law 'that is both of central importance to the legal system as a whole and outside the adjudicator's specialised area of expertise'"; (3) the drawing of jurisdictional lines between two or more competing specialised tribunals; and (4) a "true question of jurisdiction or *vires*". On the other hand, reasonableness is normally the governing standard where the question: (1) relates to the interpretation of the tribunal's enabling (or "home") statute or "statutes closely connected to its function, with which it will have particular familiarity"; (2) raises issues of fact, discretion or policy; or (3) involves inextricably intertwined legal and factual issues.' Internal citations omitted.

[51] See above, text accompanying n. 17.

[52] Jerry Mashaw, Richard Merrill and Peter Shane, *Administrative Law: The American Public Law System: Cases and Materials*, 5th edn (St Paul: Thomson West, 2003), p. 784. See generally William Eskridge and Lauren Baer, 'The Continuum of Deference: Supreme Court Treatment of Agency Statutory Interpretations from *Chevron* to *Hamdan*' (2008) 96 Geo LJ 1083. This despite the court's express recognition of 'the importance of maintaining a uniform approach to judicial review of administrative action'. *Dickinson* v. *Zurko* (1999) 527 US 150 at 154. See also *Mayo Foundation* v. *United States* (2011) 131 S Ct 704 at 713–14.

[53] The procedures for which are prescribed by §§ 556–7 of the APA.

[54] § 706(2)(E).

abuse of discretion'.[55] The latter has been interpreted as follows, in such a way as to resemble the English grounds of review for abuse of discretion:[56]

> Normally, an agency rule would be arbitrary and capricious if the agency has relied on factors which Congress has not intended it to consider, entirely failed to consider an important aspect of the problem, offered an explanation for its decision that runs counter to the evidence before the agency, or is so implausible that it could not be ascribed to a difference in view or the product of agency expertise.[57]

As for the former, the notion that curial deference should be accorded to interpretations of law was present in the United States even before the enactment of the APA in 1946.[58] In the *Chevron* case,[59] however, the Supreme Court of the United States announced a much more robust doctrine. The '*Chevron* doctrine' requires a two-step analysis to be undertaken by courts reviewing delegated decision-makers' interpretations of law. First, the reviewing court must ask whether the statutory provision at issue has a clear meaning. If so, it must apply the clear meaning of the provision, in order to give effect to congressional intent (*Chevron* step one). Secondly, however, if the statute is ambiguous (or vague) rather than clear, the reviewing court may quash or displace the delegated decision-maker's interpretation only if the interpretation is unreasonable (*Chevron* step two): 'arbitrary or capricious in substance, or manifestly contrary to the statute'.[60] *Chevron* 'dramatically expanded the circumstances in which courts [had to] defer to agency interpretations of statutes'.[61] The blunt rule of *Chevron*, however, has been modified by a recent series of decisions, which have added a '*Chevron* step zero' to the task of the reviewing court.[62] Where *Chevron* does not apply, interpretations of law are to be reviewed on the *Skidmore* standard.[63]

55 § 706(2)(A). 56 See below 1.2.3.
57 *Motor Vehicle Manufacturers Association* v. *State Farm Mutual Automobile Insurance* (1983) 463 US 29 at 43, per White J. See also *Citizens to Preserve Overton Park* v. *Volpe* (1971) 401 US 402 at 416.
58 See generally *Final Report of the Attorney General's Committee on Administrative Procedure* (Washington DC: United States Government Printing Office, 1941), pp. 87–92.
59 *Chevron USA* v. *Natural Resources Defence Council* (1984) 467 US 837.
60 *United States* v. *Mead* (2001) 533 US 218 at 227.
61 Thomas Merrill and Kristin Hickman, '*Chevron's* Domain' (2001) 89 Geo LJ 833.
62 Cass Sunstein, '*Chevron* Step Zero' (2006) 92 Va LR 187.
63 See e.g. *Gonzales* v. *Oregon* (2006) 546 US 243.

1.2.3 *England*

Although the language of deference has come to be used in England almost exclusively in respect of cases arising under the Human Rights Act 1998, I am concerned primarily with curial deference in respect of decisions that do not infringe fundamental rights.[64] As to questions of law, curial deference in England is almost non-existent.[65] Indeed, Roskill LJ's words in *Congreve* v. *Home Office*[66] would preclude the application of a doctrine of curial deference: '[legislative intent] at any rate in the majority of cases, is to be ascertained only from the relevant legislation, be it statute or delegated legislation. *How the Home Office interpreted or sought to administer that legislation is irrelevant*'.[67]

Nonetheless, curial deference can be perceived in judicial review of exercises of discretion, which is governed by *Wednesbury* unreasonableness. *Wednesbury* unreasonableness has typically had two distinct senses. In its broad sense, it refers to the traditional grounds of judicial review: a delegated decision-maker shall not, for example, fetter its discretion, act in bad faith or take into account irrelevant considerations. In its narrow sense, it refers to a particular ground of review, which itself is one of the traditional grounds of judicial review. In other words, as well as not having the power to fetter its discretion, and so on, a delegated decision-maker does not have the power to take a decision that is unreasonable.

For reasons explained below,[68] I am more interested in the narrow sense of *Wednesbury* unreasonableness,[69] which entitles a reviewing court

64 But see below Ch. 5.

65 The English courts generally follow what I shall describe in Ch. 6 as the 'broad approach' to judicial review of questions of law. There are some limited exceptions. See *Re Racal Communications* [1981] AC 374 at 383–4; *R* v. *Hull University Visitor, ex p. Page* [1993] AC 682 at 693–5. *R* v. *Monopolies and Mergers Commission, ex p. South Yorkshire Transport* [1993] 1 WLR 23, may also be authority for a limited exception, but its extent is very much a matter of uncertainty. See e.g. Paul Craig, *Administrative Law*, 6th edn (London: Sweet and Maxwell, 2008), pp. 467–70; Paul Daly, 'Deference on Questions of Law' (2011) 74 MLR 694.

66 [1976] QB 629. 67 *Ibid.*, p. 658. Emphasis added.

68 See below 6.3. To summarise that argument, I contend that the link between legislative intent and the grounds of review is obscure; that the distinction between interpretations of law and exercises of discretion is not tenable; and that the grounds of review are insufficiently deferential in theory (oddly, epistemic deference rather than doctrinal deference is employed by reviewing courts anxious not to step into the shoes of delegated decision-makers).

69 See Carol Harlow and Richard Rawlings, *Law and Administration*, 3rd edn (Cambridge: Cambridge University Press, 2009), pp. 42–4.

to intervene only if a delegated decision-maker took a 'decision that no reasonable body could have come to'.[70] *Wednesbury's* apparently exacting standard of review may, however, be ratcheted up or down: 'the courts, while broadly adhering to the monolithic language of *Wednesbury*, have to a considerable extent in recent years adopted variable standards of review'.[71] Where important interests have been affected by a decision, a court will give 'anxious scrutiny'[72] to the reasons provided in support of the decision: 'There is … what may be called a sliding scale of review; the graver the impact of the decision in question upon the individual affected by it, the more substantial the justification that will be required.'[73] The heightened standard of review employed in such cases is known as 'sub-*Wednesbury*' review.[74] At the other end of the spectrum, where complex questions which lie beyond the courts' areas of expertise and legitimacy fall to be decided, a 'super-*Wednesbury*' standard of review applies.[75] Hence the statement of Lord Bridge of Harwich in the *Hammersmith and Fulham* case that a Secretary of State's decision pertaining to the allocation of central government funding to local authorities

[70] *Associated Provincial Picture Houses* v. *Wednesbury Corporation* [1948] 1 KB 223 at 230, per Lord Greene MR. Attempts have been made to reduce the evidently tautological nature of the standard: see e.g. *Council of Civil Service Unions* v. *Minister for the Civil Service* [1985] AC 374 at 410, per Lord Diplock; *R* v. *Chief Constable of Sussex, ex p. International Trader's Ferry* [1998] UKHL 40; [1999] 2 AC 418 at 452, per Lord Cooke of Thorndon.

[71] Sir John Laws, '*Wednesbury*' in Christopher Forsyth and Ivan Hare (eds.), *The Golden Metwand and Crooked Cord: Essays on Public Law in Honour of Sir William Wade* (Oxford: Hart, 1998), p. 185, p. 187.

[72] *R* v. *Secretary of State for the Home Department, ex p. Bugdaycay* [1987] AC 514 at 531, per Lord Bridge of Harwich.

[73] *R (Mahmood)* v. *Secretary of State for the Home Department* [2000] EWCA Civ 315; [2001] 1 WLR 840 at 849, per Laws LJ. The *locus classicus* is *R* v. *Ministry of Defence, ex p. Smith* [1996] QB 517 at 554, per Sir Thomas Bingham MR.

[74] Mark Elliott, 'The Human Rights Act 1998 and the Standard of Substantive Review' (2001) 60 CLJ 301, 313–14.

[75] The existence of a super-*Wednesbury* standard has been doubted, by Lord Irvine of Lairg, 'Judges and Decision-Makers: The Theory and Practice of *Wednesbury* Review' [1996] PL 59, 66–7. See also *R (Javed)* v. *Home Secretary* [2001] EWCA Civ 789; [2002] QB 129 at 152. However, the standard has been adopted by the courts. See *Nottinghamshire County Council* v. *Secretary of State for the Environment* [1986] AC 240 at 250, per Lord Scarman, subsequently considered by Lord Bridge of Harwich to be 'an accurate formulation of an important restriction on the scope of judicial review'. The effect, Lord Bridge held, was to rule out unreasonableness challenges on grounds short of bad faith or improper motive. *R* v. *Secretary of State for the Environment, ex p. Hammersmith and Fulham London Borough Council* [1991] 1 AC 521 at 596. See also below 3.4.1.

could be reviewed, but only for error of law, bad faith, improper purposes or manifest absurdity and not for *Wednesbury* unreasonableness in the narrow sense.[76] The very flexibility of *Wednesbury* has led to the suggestion that it 'is now in terminal decline'.[77] However, notwithstanding such doubts, the '*coup de grâce* has not yet fallen'[78] and it remains good law: the Court of Appeal was quite clear that any 'burial rites' would have to be performed by the House of Lords or the Supreme Court[79] and the pipes have yet to begin to play.

1.3 Epistemic deference in practice

Chapters 2, 3 and 4 are devoted to the development of a doctrine of curial deference. I will treat of the concept of epistemic deference briefly in Chapter 4, but it will not be until Chapter 5 that the utility of the concept is fully explained. Nevertheless, having considered doctrinal deference, it may be helpful to now give some examples of epistemic deference, and a practical illustration.

I mentioned above that where *Chevron* deference is not applied to delegated decision-makers' interpretations of law in the United States, *Skidmore* deference may be appropriate. On this approach, described in the eponymous decision by Jackson J, the 'weight' to be given to a delegated decision-maker's interpretation of law will 'depend upon the thoroughness evident in its consideration, the validity of its reasoning, its consistency with earlier and later pronouncements, and all those factors which give it power to persuade'.[80] In a similar vein is the 'deference as respect' advocated by David Dyzenhaus:

76 *Hammersmith and Fulham*, above n. 75. See also *R* v. *Director of Public Prosecutions, ex p. Kebilene* [2000] 2 AC 326 at 371 (Lord Steyn) at 376 (Lord Hope of Craighead) at 394 (Lord Hobhouse of Woodborough).

77 William Wade and Christopher Forsyth, *Administrative Law*, 9th edn (Oxford: Oxford University Press, 2004), p. 371.

78 William Wade and Christopher Forsyth , *Administrative Law*, 10th edn (Oxford: Oxford University Press, 2009), p. 314.

79 *R (Association of British Civilian Internees: Far East Region)* v. *Secretary of State for the Defence Department* [2003] EWCA Civ 473; [2003] QB 1397 at 1413.

80 *Skidmore* v. *Swift and Co.* (1944) 323 US 134 at 140. I am not the only commentator to have associated *Skidmore* with epistemic deference. See e.g. Patrick Brennan, 'Delivering the Goods: Herein of *Mead*, Delegations and Authority' [2009] Mich St LR 307, 330; Elizabeth Magill and Adrian Vermeule, 'Allocating Power within Agencies' (2011) 120 Yale LJ 1032, 1047.

> When the statute is one that sets up a regulatory regime and a tribunal to decide disputes that may arise out of the regime, this interpretative approach requires judges to take the tribunal's decision seriously. More precisely, they have to take the tribunal's reasoning seriously because what they are primarily concerned to do is to find the reasons that best justify any decision, whether legislative, administrative or judicial. And, if the court has before it not only a statute to interpret, but also a tribunal's interpretation of that statute, then the tribunal's interpretation makes a difference to the structure of the interpretative context.[81]

There is some debate about the utility of such epistemic deference. As Scalia J stridently put it in dissent in *United States* v. *Mead Corporation*, 'Justice Jackson's eloquence notwithstanding, the rule of *Skidmore* deference is an empty truism and a trifling statement of the obvious: a judge should take into account the well-considered views of expert observers'.[82] Jacob Gersen and Adrian Vermeule have commented that the list of factors to which courts are directed to have attention pursuant to *Skidmore* are 'just helpful pointers to the best interpretation'.[83] Tom Hickman has gone further, suggesting that a 'circularity' infects the *Skidmore* approach, for a court 'cannot know whether the reasons supplied at the time are worthy of respect until it has first determined what reasons are sufficient to justify the decision'.[84]

Responding to the accusation of circularity permits a demonstration of the utility of epistemic deference. To an extent, Hickman's criticism is well placed. Were judges to give weight to delegated decision-makers' reasons on the basis of those reasons' weightiness, they would certainly be reasoning in circles. *Skidmore* deference, with its emphasis on validity, thoroughness and consistency, at least legitimates if not mandates such circular reasoning. However, where epistemic deference is accorded for external reasons, no circularity is present. A delegated decision-maker's 'power to persuade',[85] as Jackson J put it, may arise from, say, its expertise, or the variety of viewpoints it canvassed before reaching its decision. As Hickman acknowledges, where 'it is experience, knowledge and expertise that are the touchstones for deference, and not reasons', no circularity is present.[86] And because Dyzenhaus urges that 'deference as respect' should be accorded on the basis that the existence of a delegated

[81] Dyzenhaus, 'Politics of Deference', above n. 12, p. 303.
[82] (2001) 533 US 218 at 250.
[83] '*Chevron* as a Voting Rule' (2007) 116 Yale LJ 676, 691.
[84] *Public Law after the Human Rights Act* (Oxford: Hart, 2010), p. 151.
[85] *Skidmore*, above n. 80, at p. 140. [86] Hickman, *Public Law*, above n. 84, p. 153.

decision-maker's decision changes the interpretative landscape, no circularity is present there either. A decision's existence is distinct from its quality.

A good example of epistemic deference in action comes from the Supreme Court of the United States: *Federal Express* v. *Holowecki*.[87] The controversy at bar related to the interpretation of the term 'charge alleging unlawful discrimination'.[88] The company sought to have a case against it struck out on the basis that a statutory prerequisite was not satisfied: a charge was not filed sixty days before the lawsuit. The Equal Employment Opportunity Commission (EEOC) took a more generous view of the statutory provisions. It took the view that filling out an 'Intake Questionnaire' and sending it to the agency amounted to a 'charge alleging unlawful discrimination'. In the EEOC's view, receipt of the paperwork constituted the filing of a charge, and the sixty-day rule had been complied with. Perhaps understandably, the company disagreed, feeling that it would be unable to respond adequately to such allegations without the benefit of the full notice period, for the EEOC did not have a universal practice of giving notification when questionnaires had been filled out.

Applying *Skidmore* deference,[89] a majority of the Supreme Court of the United States adopted the view of the EEOC. In particular, Kennedy J noted, '[t]he EEOC … has drawn our attention to the need to define charge in a way that allows the agency to fulfil its distinct statutory functions of enforcing antidiscrimination laws and disseminating information about those laws to the public'.[90] Compared to the position advocated by the company, that held by the EEOC was 'a reasonable alternative that is consistent with the statutory framework'.[91] Kennedy J acknowledged that adopting the EEOC's position was not inevitable, but in the circumstances, held that it was appropriate to defer to the EEOC, on the basis of its experience and expertise:

> Reasonable arguments can be made that the agency should adopt a standard giving more guidance to filers, making it clear that the request to act must be stated in quite explicit terms. A rule of that sort might yield more consistent results. This, however, is a matter for the agency to decide in light of its experience and expertise in protecting the rights of

[87] (2008) 552 US 389. [88] Age Discrimination in Employment Act 1967, § 626(d).

[89] This was an alternative basis for the court's decision, but was fully argued before the court and fully reasoned by Kennedy J.

[90] *Federal Express*, above n. 87, at p. 400. [91] *Ibid.*, p. 402.

> those who are covered by the Act ... Where ambiguities in statutory analysis and application are presented, the agency may choose among reasonable alternatives.[92]

In other words, in the first place, epistemic deference will be given to the delegated decision-maker's assessment of the weight of the various interests at stake and, secondly, epistemic deference will be given to the choice by the delegated decision-maker amongst reasonable alternative interpretations of the statute.[93] Here, the court was first deferential to the EEOC's assessment of the weight of the relevant interests: those of employees who feel they have been discriminated against but desire not to formalise their complaint too early in the process for fear of provoking retaliatory action, as against those of employers, who have an interest in being put on notice of allegations against them. But secondly and critically, the according of epistemic deference by the reviewing court tipped the balance in favour of the delegated decision-maker's interpretation. Had the reviewing court undertaken a *de novo* inquiry into the meaning of the term at issue, it might have preferred a different interpretation of the statutory provision, striking a different balance between the interests at stake. Moreover, epistemic deference was accorded on the basis of the delegated decision-maker's 'experience and expertise'. It was, therefore, not necessary for Kennedy J to engage in any bootstrapping in order to defer to the reasons given by the delegated decision-maker. Contrary, then, to Scalia J's extrajudicial assertion that the concept is 'mealy-mouthed ... [and] not necessarily meaning anything more than considering ... views with attentiveness and profound respect, before we reject them',[94] epistemic deference is valuable.

1.4 Is deference possible?

Having introduced a number of variable standards of review, it is convenient to address some challenges to curial deference, because my defence against the challenges will lead into my argument for curial deference. These challenges, I should note, are to doctrinal deference, rather than to epistemic deference.

[92] *Ibid.*, p. 403. [93] See also Hickman, *Public Law*, above n. 84, pp. 130–7.
[94] 'Judicial Deference to Administrative Interpretations of Law' [1989] Duke LJ 511, 514.

1.4.1 *Judicial capacities*

A preliminary objection, to variable standards of review rather than doctrinal deference per se, is based on the cognitive limitations of judges: the only distinction judges can cope with is one between *de novo* and deferential review. Anything more complex than a binary choice would be too complex: 'More fine-grained standards of deference ... are difficult to express; cognitive capacities are typically inadequate to sustain a fine-grained *schema* of deference standards.'[95] Leaving aside for the moment the difficulty of developing variable standards of review,[96] the objection is unconvincing. In the first place, the decision to defer or not will inevitably be binary in nature: 'when one is speaking of deferring to the judgment of another decision-maker, the notion that there are degrees of deference is absurd. There are degrees of *respect* for the decision-maker, perhaps – but the court either defers, or it does not.'[97] Moreover, there is a distinction between the selection of the appropriate standard of review and its application. Selection may be difficult, but can be performed by reference to a set of external factors. Application of the standard may also be difficult, but it will be the application of a particular standard: it is not the case that judges have to apply multiple standards simultaneously. A distinct issue will have a distinct standard of review. In addition, even if it is the case that doctrines of curial deference give judges such difficulty that the doctrines operate inconsistently or even erratically in practice, the same could probably be said of almost any legal doctrine.

1.4.2 *Illogicality*

A more interesting challenge has been made by Luc Tremblay: any doctrine of curial deference that suggests that delegated decision-makers have a 'right to be wrong' is illogical.[98] For Tremblay, who takes an avowedly Dworkinian tack,[99] a multitude of ills and logical

95 Gersen and Vermeule, '*Chevron* as a Voting Rule', above n. 83, pp. 686–7. See also Stephen Breyer, 'Judicial Review of Questions of Law and Policy' (1986) 38 Admin LR 363, 379.

96 See below Ch. 4.

97 *Metropolitan Life Insurance* v. *Glenn* (2008) 554 US 105 at 130, n. 2, per Scalia J, dissenting. Emphasis original.

98 'La Norme de retenue judiciaire et les "erreurs de droit" en droit administratif: une erreur de droit? Au delà du fondationalisme et du scepticism' (1996) 56 Revue du Barreau 141, *passim*.

99 See below 6.2.2.1.

inconsistencies follow from judicial willingness to implement doctrinal deference. But for present purposes, his objection is as follows. Where a delegated decision-maker is required to do X, doctrinal deference will, in principle, require courts to respect a delegated decision-maker's right to *not* do X, as long as the decision to not do X is, say, reasonable. However, it seems at least incongruous that a delegated decision-maker could simultaneously have a right to do X and a right not to do X; and it seems, in particular, illogical that a legislature could simultaneously require a delegated decision-maker to do X and not to do X. The decision may be, say, reasonable – rendering judicial intervention inappropriate – but wrong, hence the alleged illogicality.

I would suggest, however, that there is no logical inconsistency here. It is entirely possible for an individual to have conflicting rights or duties.[100] It would be more accurate to say that the delegated decision-maker has been given a *power* to decide between alternatives, a power exercisable where, in the view of the delegated decision-maker, the criteria for its exercise have compellingly been made out. If the terminology of power rather than that of conflicting rights or duties is preferred, the weakness of the claim of illogicality is exposed. Tremblay rightly chafes at the suggestion of a 'right to be wrong', with its underlying notions that delegated decision-makers should feel entitled to make decisions that are disrespectful of individuals[101] and that there are spheres of absolute authority.[102] However, I submit that his is, ultimately, not a compelling challenge.

1.4.3 *Emptiness and perniciousness*

T. R. S. Allan has made a strong challenge to any argument that there ought to be a doctrine of curial deference. In his view, '[f]ree-standing principles of judicial deference – detached from analysis of specific legal duties and constitutional rights – reproduce the dubious distinctions characteristic of general doctrines of justiciability'.[103] As 'general rules cannot exclude the moral judgment that their application to particular

[100] Matthew Kramer, 'Rights without Trimmings' in Matthew Kramer, Nigel Simmonds and Hillel Steiner (eds.), *A Debate Over Rights* (Oxford: Oxford University Press, 2000), p. 7, pp. 17–20.

[101] See below 4.3.3. [102] See above 1.1.3.

[103] 'Common Law Reason and the Limits of Judicial Deference' in David Dyzenhaus (ed.), *The Unity of Public Law* (Oxford: Hart, 2004), p. 289, p. 295.

cases inevitably requires',[104] any doctrine of curial deference is inevitably 'empty'.[105] Allan does not use this term in a pejorative sense – something perhaps overlooked by his critics. For Allan, a doctrine of curial deference is inevitably empty because while it must appear to be external to a judicial decision, its operation is in fact inextricably tied to – and indistinguishable from – the substance of each individual case.

Rather, according to Allan, the appropriate degree of curial deference 'is determined by the court's assessment of the balance of public and private interests in the light of the reasons presented to it, informed by the evidence adduced in their support'.[106] Adherence to the principles of equality and due process, which are integral to the rule of law, compels a searching judicial inquiry whenever the exercise of state power is called into question: 'There must be adequate investigation of the circumstances of particular cases, so that all coercive action against specific individuals is truly justified by a defensible view of the public good.'[107] Automatic submission to the executive would be 'an abdication of the judicial role and a failure to protect legal rights',[108] but if a doctrine of curial deference even interferes with the required searching judicial inquiry, it tends towards automatic submission and is therefore necessarily 'pernicious':[109]

> The critical point is that the legal merits cannot be distinguished from constitutional and institutional factors in the manner that any doctrine of deference assumes. The proper limits of judicial intervention are set by the scope of legislative or executive discretion arising on correct analysis; and the nature and scope of the pertinent questions of law are determined, in large part, by the context, in which matters of fact and policy must be accorded their due. The requisite degree of deference is extended, therefore, by giving proper attention to the character and content of the legal questions arising in all the circumstances of the particular case. A failure to accord proper deference is simply a failure of legal analysis in which matters of law are insufficiently distinguished from, or adapted to, the relevant questions of fact and political judgment. When the relevant questions of law are correctly framed and answered, there remain no *further*, independent questions of institutional competence or legitimacy to be considered.[110]

[104] 'Human Rights and Judicial Review: A Critique of "Due Deference"' (2006) 65 CLJ 671, 673.

[105] *Ibid.*, p. 675. [106] Allan, 'The Limits of Judicial Deference', above n. 103, p. 299.

[107] *Constitutional Justice: A Liberal Theory of the Rule of Law* (Oxford: Oxford University Press, 2001), p. 125.

[108] Allan, 'Critique of "Due Deference"', above n. 104, p. 680. [109] *Ibid.*, p. 675.

[110] Allan, 'Doctrine and Theory', above n. 4, p. 105. Emphasis original.

I will respond to the claim of perniciousness in Chapters 2 and 3. In order to defeat Allan's claim of emptiness, I need to demonstrate that a doctrine of curial deference is capable of precluding a court from reaching particular conclusions, on the assumption that the preclusion of particular conclusions demonstrates that a doctrine can have effect independently of the context of a particular case.[111] By preclusion, I mean something that compels a judge to declare lawful a decision he or she would consider unlawful if not restrained by a doctrine of curial deference: 'Deference, to be meaningful, imports agency displacement of what might have been the judicial view *res nova* – in short, administrative displacement of judicial judgment.'[112] Preclusion will occur where the standard of review varies on account of factors external to the intrinsic quality of the decision.

It will be helpful to begin my response to Allan's claim of emptiness by using an example that demonstrates the force of his claim. In *International Transport Roth* v. *Secretary of State for the Home Department*,[113] Laws LJ identified what he described as 'principles of deference',[114] to be applied in the adjudication of claims that rights under the European Convention on Human Rights (the Convention) had been breached. First, 'greater deference is to be paid to an Act of Parliament than to a decision of the executive or subordinate measure'.[115] Secondly, there is 'more scope for deference "where the Convention itself requires a balance to be struck, much less so where the right is stated in terms which are unqualified"'.[116] Thirdly:

> greater deference will be due to the democratic powers where the subject-matter in hand is peculiarly within their constitutional responsibility, and less when it lies more particularly within the constitutional responsibility of the courts. The first duty of government is the defence of the realm … The first duty of the courts is the maintenance of the rule of law.[117]

Finally:

> greater or lesser deference will be due according to whether the subject-matter lies more readily within the actual or potential expertise of the

111 Allan appears to lay this down as the standard against which his claim is to be tested. 'Critique of "Due Deference"', above n. 104, pp. 674–5. His comment at p. 674 is instructive: '[judicial] conclusions … will (or should) be determined by the *substance* of the issues arising, rather than any set of principles operating independently'. Emphasis original.

112 Henry Monaghan, '*Marbury* and the Administrative State' (1983) 83 Colum LR 1, 5.

113 [2002] EWCA Civ 158; [2003] QB 728. 114 *Ibid.*, p. 774. 115 *Ibid.*, p. 765.

116 *Ibid.*, p. 766. Internal citation omitted. 117 *Ibid.*, p. 766.

> democratic powers or the courts. Thus, quite aside from defence, government decisions in the area of macro-economic policy will be relatively remote from judicial control.[118]

Similarly, Aileen Kavanagh has suggested that:

> the degree of deference in any particular case will be dependent on the overall context as determined by a number of different factors, such as the expertise of the primary decision-maker, the policy context in which the decision was reached, whether the court would be more or less likely to reach the right decision, which Convention right is involved and the extent of the alleged breach, and so on.[119]

Allan's criticism of Laws LJ is that the principles of curial deference the latter identified and purported to rely upon in *Roth* are essentially superfluous. The allegation is that the principles are taken into account in balancing the courts' role as guarantor of the rule of law and of human rights against Parliament's role as expositor of the wishes of the majority of the people. In Allan's view, the correct result would be reached by a judicial inquiry into the relationship between these constitutional principles. The *Roth* case concerned legislation which imposed penalties and placed a heavy onus of proof on trucking companies whose vehicles had been used by illegal immigrants to breach border security. In the final analysis, for Allan, the decision in *Roth* depended on a balancing of the responsibility of the courts to ensure fair criminal procedures against the power of Parliament to prescribe certain limits on fair criminal procedures, not on the invocation and application of the four principles. Crucially, Laws LJ's principles did not themselves preclude a particular judicial conclusion, or indeed operate independently of the substance of the case.[120]

As the House of Lords subsequently observed, it is difficult to perceive how giving weight to Laws LJ's four principles, or those adumbrated by Kavanagh, would be distinct from 'the ordinary judicial task of weighing up the competing considerations on each side and according appropriate weight to the judgment of a person with responsibility for a given

[118] *Ibid.*, p. 767.

[119] 'Deference or Defiance? The Limits of the Judicial Role in Constitutional Adjudication' in Grant Huscroft (ed.), *Expounding the Constitution: Essays in Constitutional Theory* (Cambridge: Cambridge University Press, 2008), p. 184, p. 203. See also Hunt, 'Sovereignty's Blight', above n. 13, pp. 353–4.

[120] Allan, 'Critique of "Due Deference"', above n. 104, p. 674.

subject-matter and access to special sources of knowledge and advice'.[121] To fail to consider the reasoned opinions of the legislature and executive, communicated through counsel, would surely be an abdication of the judicial function and a breach of procedural fairness. Hence Allan's claim that Laws LJ's four principles are superfluous and empty is correct, according to Allan's terms of engagement.[122] Epistemic deference is empty in the sense that the assignment of mere weight to the views of delegated decision-makers is insufficient to pass what I view as Allan's preclusion test.[123]

However, Allan's claim of emptiness cannot be sustained when levelled against the 'pragmatic and functional analysis' developed by the Supreme Court of Canada. The analysis requires[124] a reviewing court to increase or decrease the standard of review according to the outcome of a four-factor analysis which will indicate a higher or lower standard of review. Although the standard of review itself does not compel a particular judicial conclusion, it does preclude particular judicial conclusions. Unless the standard of review is correctness, even though a decision is wrong (in the court's view), a reviewing court is not permitted to correct it: a decision may be incorrect, but not unreasonable *simpliciter*. Likewise, a decision may be unreasonable *simpliciter*, but not patently unreasonable, and could not be quashed if the standard were patent unreasonableness. The preclusion of particular judicial conclusions demonstrates that the Canadian doctrine is not empty.[125]

[121] *Huang* v. *Secretary of State for the Home Department* [2007] UKHL 11; [2007] 2 AC 167 at 185, per Lord Bingham of Cornhill.

[122] For a full consideration of the role of epistemic deference in fundamental rights adjudication, see below 5.1.4.

[123] It does not follow that epistemic deference is worthless, as Allan himself has recently observed, drawing an analogy between it and the doctrine of precedent: 'If those who defend a doctrine of deference in public law envisage only something as loose as the "doctrine" of precedent, in which existing decisions limit and colour the canvas on which the court must paint in resolving a case correctly according to law, there would be nothing one could make objection to.' Allan, 'Doctrine and Theory', above n. 4, p. 116.

[124] Neither the abolition of the patent unreasonableness standard nor the demise of the pragmatic and functional analysis (both outlined above 1.2.1) affect my argument. My purpose is to demonstrate that doctrines of curial deference may preclude particular judicial conclusions. Using an old doctrine is perfectly justifiable for that purpose.

[125] The application of the pragmatic and functional analysis in a given case is not entirely independent of the decision under review. One cannot apply the expertise factor, which addresses the court's expertise relative to that of the delegated decision-maker in respect of the impugned decision, without taking some account of the decision. However, to take notice of the type of decision does not require the taking of a position, or indeed the

The *Chevron* doctrine developed by the Supreme Court of the United States also precludes particular judicial conclusions. As soon as a reviewing court holds that a statutory provision is ambiguous, it may not correct a decision that is, in its view, wrong; it may only correct a decision that is unreasonable. But if a reviewing court holds that the statutory provision is clear at step one of the *Chevron* analysis, it must apply the clear meaning, regardless of how well-reasoned the delegated decision-maker's interpretation, or how elaborate or inclusive the decision-making process leading to the interpretation. Because the type of decision, quality of the decision-making process and the identity of the decision-maker and all other factors save for the statutory language are irrelevant for the purposes of *Chevron* step one, the *Chevron* doctrine compels one of two scenarios, entirely independently of the intrinsic quality of the decision being reviewed. Leaving aside the inevitable problems in interpreting statutory language, it is impossible to defend a position that *Chevron* is empty.

One can usefully contrast *Chevron* deference with *Skidmore* deference.[126] *Skidmore* is analogous to Laws LJ's four principles in that it does not preclude particular judicial conclusions. While valuable, it is empty in the Allanite sense. But more robust doctrines of curial deference need not be empty in the same sense, as this brief consideration of the North American deference doctrines demonstrates.[127] To describe *Skidmore*, or deference as respect, as empty is simply to note that they are not examples of doctrinal deference.

1.4.4 *The value of doctrine in judicial review*

In a recent article,[128] which is something of a 'response to critics', Allan has linked his objection to doctrinal deference to his more general objection to the value of doctrinal analysis in public law:[129]

development of any view whatsoever, on the intrinsic quality of the decision. The choice of the appropriate standard of review is distinct from its application.

126 *Skidmore*, above n. 80, at p. 140.

127 It is possible that other rules and doctrines, such as the presumption of constitutionality, mentioned below 5.3, which have been developed because of and by reference to the principles adumbrated by Laws LJ and Kavanagh, would also defeat Allan's claim of emptiness. For example, a court obliged to apply a presumption of constitutionality when reviewing a statute for consistency with constitutional provisions would be precluded to some extent from reaching particular conclusions, by virtue of its obligation to presume that the impugned statute is constitutional.

128 Allan, 'Doctrine and Theory', above n. 4.

129 See generally, T. R. S. Allan, 'Doctrine and Theory in Administrative Law: An Elusive Quest for the Limits of Jurisdiction' [2003] PL 429.

> Matters relevant to deference are *internal* to ordinary legal analysis, just as application of the ordinary standards of review is itself dependent on close engagement with an almost infinite variety of circumstance, in which legal principle must accommodate specific demands of governance. Even such well-established grounds as error of law, improper purposes and irrelevant considerations express the *conclusions* of an analysis that depends, in each case, on a complex appraisal of interlocking matters of legal principle, factual assessment and policy choice: they articulate a distinction between review and appeal that varies in its nature and degree according to all the circumstances.[130]

Allan can perhaps be understood as advancing two separate claims, one descriptive, the other normative: first, that judges, when engaged in public law adjudication, *are in fact* working from constitutional principles; secondly, that judges, when engaged in public law adjudication, *should be* working from constitutional principles: 'legal form gives way, *as it should*, to political or constitutional substance'.[131] It does bear noting that Allan does not see *all* doctrine as evil; rather, he suggests that certain doctrines are hollow vessels, guided and filled by 'all the circumstances' of the individual case to which they are ostensibly applied. Nonetheless, given that the principles of public law have been described by some other observers as having 'no more substance at the core than a seedless grape',[132] it is worth addressing the broadest version of the sceptical view.

As a factual matter, judges clearly rely on doctrine to aid their adjudication in public law cases. Counsel present arguments in doctrinal terms and judges present conclusions in doctrinal terms. That on the surface judicial review operates in this way is not conclusive, however. Reliance on doctrine may mask the true nature of public law adjudication. In a similar spirit, Margit Cohn has outlined a series of reasons why judges might be tempted to rely on doctrine, or as she describes it, formula:

[130] Allan, 'Doctrine and Theory', above n. 4, p. 116. Emphasis original.

[131] Allan, 'Elusive Quest', above n. 129, p. 440. Emphasis added. It follows that Allan's difficulty with Paul Craig's assertion that '[t]he principle that … courts will substitute judgment for errors of law is based on normative assumptions about the relationship between courts and administrative bodies' would be that the application of the 'normative assumptions', and not the 'principle', is what dictates the outcome of a particular case. 'Legislative Intent and Legislative Supremacy: A Response to Professor Allan' (2004) 24 OJLS 585, 594. For Allan, the development of a general doctrine that courts should correct errors of law is otiose.

[132] Ernest Gellhorn and Glen Robinson, 'Perspectives on Administrative Law' (1975) 75 Colum LR 771, 780.

> Reliance on a formula carries a … distancing effect. Judges who rely on established and seemingly objective tests find shelter from accusations of politicisation, which are likely to arise whenever the case before them is politically laden … [T]he more politically-laden the issue, the greater the utility of formalisation. And the more detailed and elaborate the formula, the greater its distancing potential: a complex, highly-structured formula requires judges to jump through several hoops, which serve as a signal of judicial commitment to the application of complex, professional, even clinical processes that have nothing much to do with the political.[133]

The suggestion that doctrine might allow judges to take 'shelter' is striking and is also redolent of sceptical claims about the nature of public law adjudication. It is difficult for an outside observer to know whether judges in public law cases reach their conclusions by applying doctrine or by reasoning from constitutional principles. Proving the utility of public law doctrine empirically may be impossible, for it would require a window into the heart and soul of judges to observe what is truly motivating their decisions. Finding and opening such a window is beyond the scope of the present project. However, I think that the prevalence of doctrinal arguments in public law adjudication must have some effect on the judicial function. Stanley Fish has argued, in a manner similar to sceptics of doctrine in public law, that judicial invocations of doctrine are *ex post facto* rationalisations of positions arrived at independently of doctrine: 'the act of construction for which [the judge] says there is no room is one he is continually performing'.[134] But Fish goes on to suggest that these positions are arrived at *by virtue* of the process of argument before the judge: 'the legal process is always the same, an open, *though bounded*, forum where forensic battles are contingently and temporarily won; therefore, preferred outcomes are to be achieved not by changing the game, but by playing it more effectively'.[135] Whichever arguments are judged more 'persuasive' will win the day – but the nature of the forum imposes boundaries as to the arguments that are acceptable.[136] Moving to the public law setting, I would extrapolate that the reliance by counsel on doctrine influences the positions ultimately arrived at by the judge. What is ultimately viewed as persuasive

[133] Margit Cohn, 'Form, Formula and Constitutional Ethos: The Political Question/Justiciability Doctrine in Three Common Law Systems' (2011) 59 American Journal of Comparative Law (forthcoming).

[134] 'The Law Wishes to Have a Formal Existence' in *There's No Such Thing as Free Speech: And It's a Good Thing, Too* (Cary: Oxford University Press, 1994), p. 141, p. 145.

[135] *Ibid.*, p. 178. Emphasis added. [136] *Ibid.*, p. 155.

by the judge will be, in large part, a product of the arguments set forth by counsel. Doctrine's utility, then, lies in its capacity to frame the issues before the court. At the very least, continued reliance on doctrine creates a prima facie case in favour of its importance.

One might also ultimately reject the sceptical position as a matter of faith. One might simply believe that doctrine plays a critical or decisive role in public law adjudication. If that is the case, which I suspect it is for most practitioners and even most academics, then a focus on doctrinal deference is not problematic. But even if one adopts a sceptical position, there remains the prima facie case for my focus on doctrinal deference.

I do not necessarily reject Allan's normative claim. Certainly, judicial decisions should be held up to the light emanating from constitutional principles. The extent to which judicial decisions conform to the substantive values underlying a legal system ought to be a source of fruitful debate. Similarly, the extent to which doctrine conforms to substantive values may also be a source of debate.[137] Where doctrine seems to impede judges from reaching decisions that are in accordance with substantive values, strong arguments can be made that the doctrine should be jettisoned or reformed. Given doctrine's propensity to 'under-enforce' constitutional norms, such arguments are characteristic of public law discourse.[138] Indeed, such arguments, and the creative destruction that they engender, are the lifeblood of the law. One can acknowledge 'that neither judicial doctrine nor the legally authoritative texts of legislation or the constitution prescribe a complete and self-contained system of rules, answering all the problems that they will be used to solve',[139] but at the same time view doctrinal analysis as a valuable means of giving guidance to judges as to how to fulfil the substantive values underlying their legal system.

The prospect, moreover, of judges reasoning explicitly and exclusively from constitutional principles, is a troubling one. Judicial reliance on constitutional principles to the exclusion of doctrine carries with it the possibility of inconsistency and uncertainty. Troubling images of uneven

137 See Paul Craig, 'The Common Law, Shared Power and Judicial Review' (2004) 24 OJLS 237, 245.

138 Lawrence Sager, 'Fair Measure: The Legal Status of Under-enforced Constitutional Norms' (1978) 91 Harv LR 1212. See also Laurence Solum, 'The Interpretation-Construction Distinction' (2010) 27 *Constitutional Commentary* 95.

139 John Evans and Trevor Knight, 'Cory on Administrative Law' in Patrick Monahan and Sandra Forbes (eds.), *Peter Cory at the Supreme Court of Canada: 1989–1999* (Winnipeg: Canadian Legal History Project, 2001), p. 71, p. 72.

chancellors' feet and of unruly horses accompany any argument that judges should reason directly from constitutional principles. One must also be aware, however, of the risk that empty principles, which obscure more than they reveal, might be labelled as doctrine. Those of us who advocate a doctrinal approach in public law should be cautious to ensure that our proposed doctrines are sufficiently hard-edged to function as useful tools in the hands of judges and practitioners toiling at the judicial review coalface. Perhaps, then, the strongest case for the value of an overarching doctrinal approach has been put by Michael Taggart: 'unless we commit to that sort of mapping project the law will continue to be rather chaotic, unprincipled, and result-orientated'.[140] It is in that spirit that I proceed.

[140] Michael Taggart, 'Proportionality, Deference, *Wednesbury*' [2008] NZLR 423, 453. See similarly Yves-Marie Morissette, 'Rétrospective et prospective sur le contentieux administratif' (2008–2009) 39 RDUS 1, 42, expressing his fear of 'une floraison chaotique de normes contradictoires'; and Laws LJ, in *Nadarajah* v. *Secretary of State for the Home Department* [2005] EWCA Civ 1363 at [67], suggesting that '[l]egal principle lies between the overarching rubric of abuse of power and the concrete imperatives of a rule-book'.

2

The delegation argument

2.1 Declared constitutional principle: giving effect to legislative intent

Legislatures rarely if ever indicate what the general principles of judicial review ought to be:

> Although Congress has broad power to decide what kind of judicial review should apply to what kind of administrative decision, Congress so rarely discloses (or, perhaps, even has) a view on this subject as to make a search for legislative intent chimerical and a conclusion regarding that intent fraudulent in the mine run of cases.[1]

Even where principles are specified, room for interpretation remains. In the United States, the Administrative Procedure Act directs reviewing courts to determine 'all relevant questions of law'.[2] But the phrase 'all relevant questions of law' is not further defined and is instead left open to judicial interpretation. Section 18.1 of Canada's Federal Courts Act also seems to lay out a scheme of general principles of judicial review, but as the Supreme Court of Canada recently commented:

> Resort to the general law of judicial review is all the more essential in the case of a provision like section 18.1 of the Federal Courts Act which … is not limited to particular issues before a particular adjudicative tribunal but covers the full galaxy of federal decision-makers. Section 18.1 must retain the flexibility to deal with an immense variety of circumstances.[3]

The problem lies in determining how courts are to develop the general principles of judicial review if the legislature has not spoken clearly and

[1] David Barron and Elena Kagan, '*Chevron's* Non-delegation Doctrine' [2001] *Supreme Court Review* 201, 203. See similarly *Air New Zealand* v. *Wellington International Airport* [2009] 2 NZLR 713 at 744, per Baragwanath J, dissenting, but not on this point; Paul Craig, 'The Common Law, Shared Power and Judicial Review' (2004) 24 OJLS 237, 239.

[2] 5 USC § 706.

[3] *Canada (Citizenship and Immigration)* v. *Khosa* [2009] SCC 12; [2009] 1 SCR 339 at 365, per Binnie J.

comprehensively. Some means of allocating decision-making authority as between courts and delegated decision-makers must be identified. In Chapters 2 and 3, I will develop an argument that a doctrine of curial deference with a variable standard of review (which I will develop in Chapter 4) is necessary to 'cover the full galaxy' of delegated decision-makers. Clearly, although any such provision would be open to judicial interpretation, if the legislature directed that a variable standard of review should be applied, courts would be required to develop and implement a variable standard of review. I will argue that even in the absence of explicit legislative directions to apply a variable standard of review, a variable standard of review may nonetheless be required, based on a proper consideration of the relevant statutory provisions. The process of interpretation of a statute may indicate that the legislature intended to delegate power for particular reasons; because the extent of the delegation of power and at least some of the reasons for the delegation of power will be ascertainable from the statute, reviewing courts should take them into account in developing the general principles of judicial review. In sum, a doctrine of curial deference is both necessary and justified and would not be necessarily pernicious. The basic question animating my discussion in Chapters 2 and 3 is: why should courts defer to delegated decision-makers? To put the question another way: why should courts in the common law world adopt a secondary, reviewing, posture relative to delegated decision-makers? Although this seems like a straightforward question, answering it comprehensively has some interesting implications. My contention in this chapter will be that a widely accepted constitutional principle justifies curial deference and requires courts to develop a variable standard of review.

Although the existence of doubters ought to be noted, several commentators have tried to develop doctrines of curial deference based on factors similar to those I rely upon in Chapters 2 and 3.[4] For Lord Irvine of Lairg, the factors are 'a constitutional imperative', a 'lack of judicial expertise' and a 'democratic imperative';[5] for Jeffrey Jowell, 'constitutional competence' and 'institutional competence';[6] for Murray Hunt,

[4] For very similar factors, albeit without detailed explanation, see Bradley Lipton, 'Accountability, Deference, and the *Skidmore* Doctrine' (2010) 119 Yale LJ 2096, 2120–2.

[5] 'Judges and Decision-makers: The Theory and Practice of *Wednesbury* Review' [1996] PL 59, 60–1.

[6] 'Of Vires and Vacuums: The Constitutional Context of Judicial Review' [1999] PL 448, 451–2.

legislative choice and relative institutional competence;[7] for David Dyzenhaus, 'a formal reason' and a 'substantive rationale' for curial deference.[8] Perhaps because their arguments seem intuitively strong these commentators have not developed the constitutional basis for, or the contours of, a doctrine of curial deference in great detail. However, I hope to place curial deference on a firmer footing. My search will not be satisfied by a theory or doctrine that relies on a background theory, acceptance of which would necessarily depend on one's own political or philosophical beliefs.[9] I believe that an argument that is not tied explicitly to a background theory will prove less controversial, more enduring and more likely to win broad acceptance.[10]

I thus begin by identifying a principle which would generally be accepted as common to most legal systems. I adopt John Allison's definition of declared constitutional principle as 'a standard that is to be observed consistently as a requirement of justice or general political morality that has been authoritatively declared to establish, organise or rule governmental bodies'.[11] I am adapting the definition as well as adopting it. In particular I am not seeking a specific authoritative declaration; rather, something that is accepted by the legal community as having been authoritatively declared.[12] The declared constitutional principle upon which I wish to rely is that *courts must give effect to legislative intent*. The requirement that judges must give effect to legislative intent, as long as the legislature acts within constitutional

[7] 'Against Bifurcation' in David Dyzenhaus, Murray Hunt and Grant Huscroft (eds.), *A Simple Common Lawyer: Essays in Honour of Michael Taggart* (Oxford: Hart, 2009), p. 99, p. 112.

[8] 'The Politics of Deference: Judicial Review and Democracy' in Michael Taggart (ed.), *The Province of Administrative Law* (Oxford: Hart, 1997), p. 279, p. 290.

[9] But see Paul Craig, *Public Law and Democracy in the United Kingdom and the United States of America* (Oxford: Clarendon, 1990), p. 3.

[10] My argument might also win over sceptics who believe that questions of institutional and constitutional competence are entirely distinct. See e.g. Sir John Laws, 'Concluding Comments: Judicial Review's Constitutional Home' in Christopher Forsyth *et al.* (eds.), *Effective Judicial Review: A Cornerstone of Good Governance* (Oxford: Oxford University Press, 2010), p. 434, p. 440.

[11] *The English Historical Constitution* (Cambridge: Cambridge University Press, 2007), p. 76.

[12] I do not mean to tread into deep jurisprudential waters by invoking the acceptance of the wider legal community. The principle I am searching for is one that is so widely accepted as to be beyond serious debate or discussion.

boundaries,[13] is a declared constitutional principle in all common law legal systems.

In this and the next chapter I will identify the two key arguments based on the declared constitutional principle that courts must give effect to legislative intent: a delegation argument (Chapter 2) and an argument based on practical justifications for curial deference (Chapter 3). I will also develop these arguments. In addition, I will demonstrate that the delegation argument and the argument based on practical justifications are interrelated. My development implies that variable delegations of power to delegated decision-makers and the variable nature of the practical justifications for curial deference require a nuanced response from reviewing courts, in the form of a variable standard of review.

References to legislative intent are peppered throughout my argument, so I should explain my use of the term. The best means of explanation is to respond to two mutually exclusive arguments that might be levelled against invocations of legislative intent. One argument is that it is incoherent to ascribe intentions to a multi-member legislative body: 'A legislature certainly has no intention whatever in connection with words which some two or three men drafted, which a considerable number rejected, and in regard to which many of the approving majority might have had, and often demonstrably did have, different ideas and beliefs.'[14] The second is that the relevant search should be for the intentions of individual legislators, not that of the body as a whole. These intentions may be base. A cynical view of legislators is that they function as 'constituent service agents whose *raison d'être* is to recover for their constituencies as much … largesse as possible'.[15] Delegations of

13 Those constitutional boundaries may be the subject of much heated disagreement, but I do not enter that argument here. Compare e.g. Jeffrey Goldsworthy, *The Sovereignty of Parliament: History and Philosophy* (Oxford: Clarendon, 1999) with T. R. S. Allan, *Constitutional Justice: A Liberal Theory of the Rule of Law* (Oxford: Oxford University Press, 2001). Delegation itself may be subject to some constitutional constraints (see e.g. Gerard Hogan and David Morgan, *Administrative Law in Ireland*, 4th edn (Dublin: Thomson Reuters, 2010), pp. 12–20), but a generally permissive judicial attitude prevails: 'At the same time that we recognize the fundamentality of the rule of law and the courts' duty to protect it in our constitutional structure, we must acknowledge … that state powers exist and may be delegated to subordinate bodies.' Louis LeBel, 'Some Properly Deferential Thoughts on Deference' (2008) 21 CJALP 1, 4.

14 Max Radin, 'Statutory Interpretation' (1930) 43 Harv LR 863, 870.

15 Steven Calabresi, 'Some Normative Arguments for the Unitary Executive' (1995) 48 Ark LR 23, 36.

power may be made in order to appease powerful economic interests, or to avoid taking a decision on a contentious matter.[16] If legislators have cynical motives for delegating, significant doubt must be cast on any theory that seeks to give effect to legislative intent.

To respond to the first argument, it is commonsensical to describe a multi-member body as having a collective intention:

> Despite occasional suggestions that collective intentions are mythical entities that cannot really exist, it is obvious that they can. We can see them in action when we watch team sports, and hear them when we listen to orchestras. If legislation were never the product of collective intentions within legislatures, it would be a quite mysterious phenomenon.[17]

Moreover, it is certainly not the case that legal significance cannot be ascribed to collective intention: 'when judges disagree over the question whether the ordinary meanings of statutory language or the broader intentions of the legislature should be deemed decisive, they are hardly disagreeing about the wider question whether the legislature's enactments lay down authoritative standards'.[18] Difficulties in ascertaining legislative intent do not justify an abdication of the judicial duty to ascertain legislative intent. If it is accepted that courts must give effect to legislative intent, such complaints about difficulty necessarily morph into admonitions to try harder. In particular, as my response to the second argument will make clear, legal effect is given to the formal output of the legislative process, which is the expression of collective intention: 'The intention being communicated and given performative effect in the act of legislation is just the intention conventionally associated with the language of the enactment.'[19] Legislative intent, then, functions as shorthand, in place of

[16] Peter Aranson, Ernest Gellhorn and Glen Robinson, 'A Theory of Legislative Delegation' (1982–1983) 68 Cornell LR 1. For a comprehensive critique, see Stephen Croley, *Regulation and Public Interests: The Possibility of Good Regulatory Government* (Princeton: Princeton University Press, 2008). The even bleaker suggestion that the outcome of legislative processes is essentially random and thus incoherent has, however, been thoroughly debunked. See Daniel Farber and Philip Frickey, 'Legislative Intent and Public Choice' (1988) 74 Va LR 423, 425–37.

[17] Goldsworthy, *Parliamentary Sovereignty*, above n. 13, p. 251. Internal citation omitted. See similarly Stephen Breyer, 'On Uses of Legislative History' (1992) 65 So Cal LR 845, 864–6.

[18] Matthew Kramer, *In Defence of Legal Positivism: Law without Trimmings* (Oxford: Oxford University Press, 1999), p. 143.

[19] Jeremy Waldron, *The Dignity of Legislation* (Cambridge: Cambridge University Press, 1999), p. 26.

more cumbersome means of describing the relevant collective intention as manifested in a particular form.

To respond to the second argument, the suggestion that weight ought to be given to the intentions of individual legislators does not survive a probing critique performed by Ronald Dworkin.[20] Dworkin directed his argument against the contention 'that statutes should be read … according to what the legislators who actually adopted them intended'.[21] The contention, Dworkin argued, was incoherent for several reasons. First, leaving aside the considerable practical difficulties in actually ascertaining intentions, an intentionalist must decide whose intentions count. All members of the legislature? Just those who voted in favour? Just those who were in pivotal committee positions? Do the intentions of those casting decisive votes at various stages attract greater weight? What about the individuals, citizens, lobbyists and professional staff who participated in the drafting process? What about those outside the drafting process who sought to influence it? Secondly, having chosen the relevant group, how are their intentions to be combined? Will the intentions of a majority of them suffice, or a plurality, or a representative of the group, perhaps the hypothetical median legislator? Here, the intentionalist would have to rely 'on his own political judgment'.[22] Thirdly, in the unlikely event that these formidable hurdles are scaled, the intentionalist 'must confront the most difficult issue. [A person's] mental life is complex: which of her beliefs, attitudes, or other mental states constitutes her "intention"?'[23] Hopes and expectations about the effect of the legislation at issue may 'come apart',[24] making it necessary to choose between them. Dworkin went on to suggest that hopes may be cynical or venal and expectations ill-informed – an independent argument against reliance on actual intentions[25] – but it would be a brave intentionalist who would seek to combat Dworkin's three objections.[26] In the end, for Dworkin, any judicial interpretation of legislation must proceed in the

[20] Ronald Dworkin, *Law's Empire* (Cambridge, MA: Harvard University Press, 1986) pp. 313–37. See also Craig, 'Shared Power', above n. 1, pp. 239–40. For a recent attempt to overcome these difficulties, see James Macpherson, 'Legislative Intentionalism and Proxy Agency' (2010) 29 *Law and Philosophy* 1.

[21] Dworkin, *Law's Empire*, above n. 20, p. 314.

[22] *Ibid.*, p. 321. Any political judgment is apt to be controversial and would have to be defended in its own terms.

[23] *Ibid.*, p. 321. [24] *Ibid.*, p. 322.

[25] That avenue of attack is not open to me, because I am arguing that cynical or venal intentions are irrelevant.

[26] See also Cynthia Farina, 'Statutory Interpretation and the Balance of Power in the Administrative State' (1989) 89 Colum LR 452, 467–76.

manner of constructive interpretation suggested by his theory of law as integrity. However, Dworkin should not be taken as intimating that collective intention is something as impossible to reconstruct as actual intentions: 'Constructive interpretation can be directed to the record of institutions and practices as well as individuals, and [the judge] has no reason not to attribute convictions directly to the legislature itself.'[27]

Even though Jeremy Waldron has built further on Dworkin's attack on the idea of ascribing intentions to legislatures, he has offered a strong defence of reliance on what I have termed legislative intent:[28]

> Why not simply say that the act of a legislature is an artificial resultant of the acts of individual legislators, structured and related to one another through certain procedures ...? Why not say that while each of the latter actions – the individual actions – is of course the product of an intention, the resultant action – the act of the legislature itself – need not be?[29]

For Waldron, the authority of legislation results from the characteristics of the 'impersonal or mechanical' legislative process,[30] which help to achieve desirable outcomes, not from the intentions of any individual legislators, or indeed an intention ascribed to the legislature as a whole. Thus, we should:

> abandon all talk of legislative intentions apart from the intentionality that is part and parcel of the linguistic meaning ... of the legislative text itself. Beyond the meanings embodied conventionally in the text of the statute, there is no state or condition corresponding to 'the intention of the legislature' to which anything else – such as what particular individuals or groups of legislators said, wrote, or did – could possibly provide a clue ... There is simply no fact of the matter concerning a legislature's intentions apart from the formal specification of the act it has performed.[31]

[27] Dworkin, *Law's Empire*, above n. 20, p. 336.

[28] A deeper philosophical debate in which Waldron is participating is not strictly relevant for present purposes. Compare Andrei Marmor, *Interpretation and Legal Theory*, 2nd edn (Oxford: Oxford University Press, 2005). Marmor argues that as a matter of theory legislators' intentions may be important. However, the circumstances in which the intentions will be important are quite limited. Marmor also pitches his argument at the theoretical level, so he does not respond directly to the difficulties identified by Dworkin. Finally, Marmor's argument that legislators' intentions are relevant in limited circumstances depends on a more general jurisprudential argument about the obligation to obey the law which is beyond the scope of this book. I simply prefer Waldron's rival account of the authoritativeness of the formal acts of legislatures.

[29] *Law and Disagreement* (Oxford: Oxford University Press, 1999), p. 128.

[30] *Ibid.*, p. 138.

[31] *Ibid.*, p. 142. These formally specified acts may have authority, Waldron argues, for utilitarian, Condorcetian or deliberative reasons, but no one individual legislator's intentions are relevant to these reasons to ascribe authority to legislative acts.

Accordingly, when I use the term legislative intent, it is the 'formal specification of the act' to which I refer, not to the literal intentions of legislators. It follows that the possibly base motives of legislators are not relevant: 'We are not concerned with anything subjective. We do not delve into the mind of legislators or their draftsmen, or committee members.'[32] What is relevant is the language of the statute.[33] As Lord Reid put it, courts seek 'the meaning of the words which Parliament used'.[34] Those who remain cynical should note how it is possible, even in respect of statutes which are enacted under the influence of those with base motives, to adduce neutral reasons for enactment. Giving effect to these 'public-regarding' reasons would forestall any remaining objection that reliance on legislative intent could cause courts to give effect to the base motives of legislators.[35]

Whether legislative intent is to be found in the written words of the statute, the overall statutory structure, the level of 'fit' with previous decisions and the legal system as a whole, or in the legislative debates is irrelevant for present purposes. If members of different schools of statutory interpretation would reach different conclusions applying my doctrine of curial deference, that merely indicates that my doctrine is neutral as between schools of statutory interpretation. My argument is the sort of first-order theoretical argument that does not aim 'to cut between the alternative interpretative approaches that are available to judges at the mundane level of statutory interpretation',[36] although it does render unnecessary reliance on detailed background assumptions, presumptions and principles.[37]

[32] Felix Frankfurter, 'Some Reflections on the Reading of Statutes' (1947) 47 Colum LR 527, 539.

[33] Which may be informed by relevant legislative history: 'Legal convention [in the United States] stipulates … that statements made in a committee report accompanying an ordinary congressional bill are in effect enacted, as a kind of official group intention, along with the bill itself.' Ronald Dworkin, *A Matter of Principle* (Cambridge, MA: Harvard University Press, 1985), p. 42.

[34] *Black Clawson International* v. *Papierwerke Waldhof-Aschaffenberg AG* [1975] AC 591 at 613.

[35] Jonathan Macey, 'Promoting Public-regarding Legislation through Statutory Interpretation: An Interest Group Model' (1986) 86 Colum LR 223, 250–6.

[36] Adrian Vermeule, *Judging under Uncertainty: An Institutional Theory of Legal Interpretation* (Cambridge, MA: Harvard University Press, 2006), p. 42.

[37] Compare T. R. S. Allan, 'Legislative Supremacy and Legislative Intention: Interpretation, Meaning, and Authority' (2004) 63 CLJ 685, 690; 'Constitutional Dialogue and the Justification of Judicial Review' (2003) 23 OJLS 563, 566.

2.2 Alternative principles

As I have indicated, my overall argument will contain two interrelated subordinate arguments based on the judicial obligation to give effect to legislative intent: a delegation argument and an argument based on practical justifications for curial deference. In this chapter, I develop the delegation argument and in the next chapter, I will develop the practical justifications argument. But in developing the delegation argument, I will explore the American literature, because alternative declared constitutional principles for doctrines of curial deference have been advanced there. A large oak of literature has grown from *Chevron's* small acorn.[38] Most importantly for present purposes, *Chevron* has prompted arguments in its favour and against it, some of which attempt to justify *Chevron* by reference to declared constitutional principle.[39] Discussion of their shortcomings will pave the way for the introduction of my delegation argument.

2.2.1 Separation of powers

An institutional separation of powers classically involves a division of government into three branches: a legislature, an executive and a judiciary. However, the tripartite division tells us little or nothing about the functions that are properly assigned to each branch: for example, that there is a legislature tells us nothing about the legislative power save, presumably, that the legislature may make laws. The appropriate functions to be exercised by each branch of government are, if not inevitably contested, at least reliant on 'thin political assumptions'[40] about the appropriate nature of government and allocation and exercise of official powers. Separating powers is an important safeguard against abuses of power, but the separation of powers has been accused of being 'infected with so much imprecision and inconsistency that it may be counted little more than a jumbled portmanteau of arguments for policies which ought to be supported or rejected on other grounds'.[41] Accordingly, developing

[38] See generally Evan Criddle, '*Chevron's* Consensus' (2008) 88 BU LR 1271.

[39] For an overview, see Thomas Merrill and Kristin Hickman, '*Chevron's* Domain' (2001) 89 Geo LJ 833, 863–73. Space precludes a discussion of the 'adjudicative norm' justification, which has only been seriously proposed once, and has not been influential. See Maureen Callahan, 'Must Federal Courts Defer to Agency Interpretations of Statutes? A New Doctrinal Basis for *Chevron USA* v. *Natural Resources Defence Council*' [1991] Wisc LR 1275.

[40] Nick Barker, 'A Prelude to the Separation of Powers' (2001) 60 CLJ 59, 65.

[41] Geoffrey Marshall, *Constitutional Theory* (Oxford: Clarendon, 1971), p. 124.

general principles of judicial review from the separation of powers is a difficult task. However, I will explore four lines of reasoning which might lead to the conclusion that the separation of powers can compel the adoption of a doctrine of curial deference. Each line of reasoning will be rejected in turn, but they are not to be dismissed out of hand: each contains a seed of truth which will flourish under different conditions.

2.2.1.1 Checks and balances

The first line of reasoning might be called 'checks and balances', because it derives from an understanding of the separation of powers as a system of checks and balances: 'courts should see themselves not as supervisors of agencies, but more as a check or bulwark against abuses of agency power'.[42] However, the checks-and-balances line of reasoning does not indicate the extent to which courts should assume interpretive power. All it suggests is that there ought to be a judicial function which ought to encompass a power of judicial review – too bland a suggestion to assist in a search for a declared constitutional principle. A basic assumption is that a power of judicial review of delegated decision-makers exists and is legitimate. The question is not the existence of the power, but its extent.

2.2.1.2 Curial deference as discipline

The second line of reasoning might be called 'curial deference as discipline': '*Chevron* ... places the burden on Congress to legislate with greater precision if it wants to temper the agencies' new power.'[43] Delegations of power are typically phrased in broad terms, although individual legal systems differ as to the level of vagueness they permit.[44] Proponents of the curial-deference-as-discipline line of reasoning submit that a doctrine of curial deference requires legislatures to legislate more clearly if they wish to retain their pre-eminence in the lawmaking structure of the state, for if they do not speak to a particular point, they cede power to a delegated decision-maker or a court. The curial deference as discipline line of reasoning, however, has two defects. First, it has dubious origins, tending to be promoted by those who lament the rise of delegation and wish to roll back the apparatus of the modern

42 Kenneth Starr, 'Judicial Review in the post-*Chevron* Era' (1988) 3 Yale J on Reg 283, 300–1.

43 *Ibid.*, p. 311. See also Douglas Kmiec, 'Judicial Deference to Executive Agencies and the Decline of the Nondelegation Doctrine' (1988) 2 Admin LJ 269, 281–2.

44 For example, in the United States, Congress must 'lay down by legislative act an intelligible principle' of delegated decision-making. *JW Hampton Jr* v. *United States* (1928) 276 US 394 at 409, per Taft CJ.

administrative state: 'Although presented as an argument against vague delegations, the argument is really an argument against all legislation.'[45] Its dubious origins lead to a suspicion of vague delegations of power and in turn to dubious premises, one of which is that legislators will react to a doctrine of curial deference by legislating with greater specificity. But legislators may prefer to delegate power for several reasons[46] and no empirical evidence to the contrary has been produced.[47] Secondly, the contention that a doctrine of curial deference would promote legislative supremacy is of suspect validity. Curial deference tends to contract judicial review in some areas, thereby reducing the power of reviewing courts to ensure that some delegated decision-makers stay within the boundaries set for them by legislatures. It may be the case that a doctrine of curial deference could promote legislative supremacy by permitting a form of dialogue between courts and legislatures, in which the latter have the final say, but such a suggestion would be purely speculative.

2.2.1.3 Automatic deference

The third line of reasoning, which might be called 'automatic deference', holds that because a legislature has delegated power in a vague manner, the courts must give effect to any decisions of the delegated decision-maker.[48] Following this approach the legislature has given an express command which courts are obliged to follow. A court's role is to give effect to legislative intent which, if the delegation is at a certain level of vagueness, requires it to uphold all decisions taken by the delegated decision-maker, possibly because the delegated decision-maker is more politically accountable, by virtue of its location in the executive branch. However, the automatic deference argument does not withstand scrutiny. It is particularly weak in the concrete: in most legal systems courts are assigned significant decision-making authority, an assignment that can be overridden only by express legislative or constitutional provision, not merely a vague delegation.

The automatic deference argument also fails to survive in the abstract. The mere existence of a vague delegation tells us very little about the legislature's intention as to how that power should be allocated, and it

[45] Jerry Mashaw, *Greed, Chaos and Governance: Using Public Choice to Improve Public Law* (New Haven: Yale University Press, 1997), p. 143.

[46] See below Ch. 3.

[47] Mashaw, *Greed, Chaos and Governance*, above n. 45, pp. 142–8.

[48] There are hints of this reasoning in Tom Zwart, 'Deference Owed under the Separation of Powers' in John Morison, Kieran McEvoy and Gordon Anthony (eds.), *Judges, Transition and Human Rights* (Oxford: Oxford University Press, 2007), p. 73, pp. 87–8.

certainly cannot tell us that the power should be allocated exclusively to a delegated decision-maker.[49] Standing alone, vagueness is not a declaration that a delegated decision-maker's interpretation should be preferred to that of a court:

> All the constitutional structure suggests is that Congress has control over the allocation of authority to resolve statutory ambiguity. But if that is so, the appeal to constitutional norms is a strategy of infinite regress, as the failure of Congress to exercise its power forces the court to look to constitutional principles, which then merely point back to Congress.[50]

If the line of reasoning were reformulated slightly, such that delegated decision-makers are given lawmaking power *only* (i.e. a direct delegation of power held by the legislature), it seems stronger. However, quite apart from any constitutional concerns, the reformulation would have to rest on a distinction between lawmaking and law interpretation, and a reviewing court would still have to intervene if the delegated decision-maker overstepped the boundaries of its authority by engaging in law interpreting rather than lawmaking. Judicial review would not be automatically excluded.

2.2.1.4 Curial deference as enhancing the legislative power

The fourth line of reasoning might be called 'curial deference as enhancing the legislative power'. While the contention that a legislature will be *compelled* by a doctrine of curial deference to speak clearly in its statutes is unsustainable, a doctrine of curial deference might yet *enhance* the legislative power. A doctrine of curial deference, being a judicial mould into which provisions of legislation could be poured in any particular case, could give guidance to the legislature as to how it might by statute further its objective to insulate a body from, or expose it to, judicial scrutiny. If the doctrine were cast as a presumption or interpretive principle, or as a set of presumptions or interpretive principles, it would be capable of statutory

[49] A related argument is that courts should refrain from interfering with the policy-making function of the political branches of government. See Merrill and Hickman, '*Chevron's* Domain', above n. 39, p. 865; Richard Pierce, '*Chevron* and its Aftermath: Judicial Review of Agency Interpretations of Statutory Provisions' (1988) 41 Vand LR 301. As a general rule, the argument goes, judges will try to refrain from engaging the merits of particular policy decisions; but the general rule relates more to best practice in adjudication rather than anything as substantial as the declared constitutional principle being sought here. If pressed any further, an argument based on an unworkable distinction between 'law' and 'policy' is entirely unconvincing. See Thomas Sargentich, 'The Critique of Active Judicial Review of Administrative Agencies: A Re-evaluation' (1997) 49 Admin LR 599, 625–9.

[50] Barron and Kagan, '*Chevron's* Non-delegation Doctrine', above n. 1, p. 222.

override or amendment by express legislative language; or the courts could make it clear that particular presumptions or principles would be invoked depending on the language used in the relevant statutory provisions. The vesting of the final say in the legislature would further the separation of powers by giving added force to the legislative power.

Although intuitively attractive, the suggestion that curial deference would enhance the legislative power is not compelled by the separation of powers. While it would enhance the legislative power and, possibly, delegated decision-makers' power, it would erode judicial power to some extent. An erosion of judicial power is troublesome because '[t]he basic case for judicial review depends on the proposition that foxes should not guard henhouses'.[51] The separation of powers, *standing alone*, may not 'play favourites' between the political and judicial branches. If an erosion of judicial power is to take place, a justification must be sought somewhere other than the separation of powers *tout court*. Thus, while there is a great deal of truth and force in the suggestion that a doctrine of curial deference might enhance the legislative power, it ultimately falls short of the status of a declared constitutional principle.

2.2.2 *Implied delegation*

The reasoning in *Chevron* itself seemed to rest on implied delegation: 'Sometimes the legislative delegation to an agency on a particular question is implicit rather than explicit.'[52] The logic appeared to be that the creation of an agency, when combined with the use of vague statutory language – a 'gap left open by Congress' – functioned as an implied delegation of decision-making power to the agency, which was more politically accountable than the reviewing court and better able to solve complex problems.[53] The implied delegation approach is not spurious. The existence of a delegated decision-maker legitimately gives rise to at least some presumption that the legislature intended to delegate decision-making power to it.[54] However, implied delegation, I will argue, is not a declared constitutional principle.

51 Cass Sunstein, *After the Rights Revolution: Re-conceiving the Regulatory State* (Cambridge, MA: Harvard University Press, 1990), p. 143.

52 *Chevron USA* v. *Natural Resources Defence Council* (1984) 467 US 837 at 844, per Stevens J.

53 *Ibid.*, p. 866.

54 It is not clear, however, why the presence of vague statutory language should be considered a prerequisite to the operation of a doctrine of curial deference. See e.g.

Although it requires any doctrine of curial deference to be tied in some way to legislative intent, the implied delegation approach does not of itself require a particular doctrine of curial deference. It does not automatically follow from the logic of *Chevron* that a blanket rule like that employed by the Supreme Court of the United States will always be appropriate.[55] The court could have introduced a more nuanced doctrine and indeed it has recently shifted in the direction of greater nuance.[56] In fact, the existence of a vague statutory term could just as easily have been taken as an implicit delegation of authority to the *courts*, perhaps on the assumption that they are best placed to answer questions of law and have traditionally been vested with the power to do so.[57] What matters is the background assumption and the background theory underpinning it. As long as it is consistent with the background assumption, implied delegation could be used to justify the imputation of an extensive set of intentions to the legislature. Implied delegation is putty in the hands of courts and commentators: one can pour virtually anything one wants into a doctrine of curial deference by using the implied delegation logic. Any imputation would have to be consistent with a background theory, but no other limit could be placed on the imputation of intentions. Indeed, the importance of the background theory – in *Chevron*, ostensibly political accountability and complexity – undermines the reliance on implied delegation, for the background theory is what is doing most of the work.

A judge following the implied delegation approach could equally well hold that powers were delegated with an implicit condition that they were to be exercised reasonably and fairly. Such was the orthodox

Jack Beerman, 'End the Failed *Chevron* Experiment Now: How *Chevron* Has Failed and Why It Can and Should Be Overruled' (2010) 42 Conn LR 779, 810. The formulation of the statutory provision at issue might have been unintentional or even accidental; it would be incongruous to base a doctrine of such importance on such shaky foundations. Indeed, 'even adherents to [the *Chevron*] theory … acknowledge that the evidence of such enacting congressional intent is "weak" and even "fictional"'. Einer Elhauge, 'Preference-estimating Statutory Default Rules' (2002) 102 Colum LR 2027, 2132. Internal citations omitted.

55 See e.g. Stephen Breyer, 'Judicial Review of Questions of Law and Policy' (1986) 38 Admin LR 363, 370–2.

56 See Daniel Gifford, 'The Emerging Outlines of a Revised *Chevron* Doctrine: Congressional Intent, Judicial Judgment, and Administrative Autonomy' (2007) 59 Admin LR 783; and below 2.3.2.

57 See e.g. Farina, 'Statutory Interpretation', above n. 26; Jonathan Molot, 'Re-examining *Marbury* in the Administrative State: A Structural and Institutional Defence of Judicial Power over Statutory Interpretation' (2002) Nw U LR 1239.

justification of the development of grounds of review of administrative action in England. Of course, the justification was a fiction. The existence of many of these grounds of review:

> cannot be derived from the simple requirement that public bodies must be kept to the limits of their authority given by Parliament. Neither deductive logic nor the canons of ordinary language, which are the basic tools of statutory construction, can attribute them to that ideal, since although their application may be qualified by the words of any particular statute, in principle their roots have grown from another seed altogether. In some formulations, it is true, they have purportedly been justified by the attribution of an intention to the legislature that statutory decision-makers should act reasonably and fairly; but this is largely fictitious ... [The principles] are, categorically, judicial creations. They owe neither their existence nor their acceptance to the will of the legislature. They have nothing to do with the intention of Parliament, save as a fig-leaf to cover their true origins.[58]

If judicial review were fictional, judges would be free to craft their own contributions to the judicial review canon.[59] Quite a degree of authority, then, would be granted to judges if the implied delegation approach were followed.

An alternative English argument is that authority has been delegated implicitly to the judiciary. A legislative imprimatur could be taken as licensing judges to create principles of judicial review or, as they have come to be known, 'principles of good administration':[60]

> since the legislature took no steps to overturn the extension and development of judicial review by the judges, it may reasonably be taken to have accepted the creativity of the judicial role. The consequence is that the legislature may reasonably be taken to have given tacit approval to the development by the judiciary of the principles of judicial review, subject, crucially, to the recognition of legislative supremacy.[61]

[58] Sir John Laws, 'Law and Democracy' [1995] PL 72, 78–9.

[59] Ronald Krotoszynski, 'Why Deference? Implied Delegations, Agency Expertise, and the Misplaced Legacy of *Skidmore*' (2002) 54 Admin LR 735, 751.

[60] Denis Galligan, 'Judicial Review and the Textbook Writers' (1982) 2 OJLS 257, 261.

[61] Christopher Forsyth, 'Of Fig Leaves and Fairytales: The *Ultra Vires* Doctrine, Sovereignty of Parliament and Judicial Review' (1996) 55 CLJ 122, 135. In its most refined form, the argument is that Parliament must be taken to legislate in accordance with the rule of law, which thereby permits reviewing courts to impose limitations on the exercise of delegated powers. Mark Elliott, *The Constitutional Foundations of Judicial Review* (Oxford: Hart, 2001).

Regrettably, however, a justification of this sort could 'be wheeled out to justify the present embodiment of judicial doctrine, whatsoever it might be, as determined by the courts on the basis of common law principle'.[62] Such a breathtakingly wide implied delegation of authority to judges must call into question the reliance on implication to build judicial review doctrine. Virtually nothing would be ruled out by such an approach. The difference from *Chevron* is that the implied delegation is to the judiciary, but once it is accepted that the legislature can be taken to have delegated authority implicitly, virtually any intention at all can be imputed to it. The purported declared constitutional principle of implied delegation does not of itself allow a reviewing court to decide between holding that decision-making power has been delegated to delegated decision-makers, or alternatively that any delegation of authority to delegated decision-makers is accompanied by implied conditions. It does not give concrete guidance as to the appropriate relationship between reviewing courts and delegated decision-makers.

Even in Canada, where judges claim to be navigating the twists and turns of judicial review by the light of the 'polar star' of legislative intent,[63] reliance on the imputation of intentions to the legislature has revealed additional avenues. Consider again the four stages in the pragmatic and functional analysis. The first stage, where the presence or absence of a privative clause or a right of appeal is the factor to be taken into account, is certainly a clear indicator of legislative intent. I will argue in the next chapter that expertise, the factor at the second stage, can be linked to legislative intent. But as to the third and fourth stages it cannot plausibly be deduced from statutory language, at least in most cases, that the legislature intended the prescribed factors to be taken into account. Whether a decision (stage four) should be delegated to a delegated decision-maker does not depend on whether the decision is relatively legal or relatively factual. It might be perfectly plausible that the legislature would intend to delegate a legal question to a delegated decision-maker, or a factual question to a court. If the nature of the question is to be said to be related to legislative intent, it is necessary to make an assumption that the legislature intends legal questions to be answered

62 Paul Craig, 'Legislative Intent and Legislative Supremacy: A Reply to Professor Allan' (2004) 24 OJLS 585, 587.

63 *Canadian Union of Public Employees* v. *Ontario (Minister for Labour)* [2003] SCC 29; [2003] 1 SCR 539 at 610, per Binnie J.

by courts.[64] Similarly, whether a decision (stage three) should be delegated to a delegated decision-maker does not depend on the purpose of the particular provision. If the purpose of a delegation is to determine rights and entitlements, it might be appropriate for a delegated decision-maker to take the decision, even though determining rights and entitlements is traditionally within the province of the judiciary. Conversely, it might be thought appropriate for courts to determine some matters of policy (perhaps relating to sentencing, or parole). Again, a background assumption, to be imputed to the legislature, is necessary. But if these background assumptions are permissible, surely other background assumptions can be introduced as well. It becomes difficult to perceive whether the courts are navigating by the polar star of legislative intent, or some other source of light. Indeed, a proliferation of light sources may blind judges to their obligation to give effect to legislative intent.

A defender of the implied delegation justification might protest that the resulting doctrine, be it *Chevron*, some variant thereon or an entirely different approach, reflects a genuine legislative desire to delegate power to delegated decision-makers. But any such argument would have to rest on the actual intentions of legislators, the uncovering of which is a hazardous operation.[65] Otherwise, implied delegation simply employs legislative intent as a vehicle for policy preferences which should be supported on other grounds. It will generally be possible to develop a theory against which potential background assumptions can be judged: courts could 'fill in legislative silence about judicial review by making policy judgments based on institutional attributes, with [the legislature] then free to overrule these conclusions'.[66] Acknowledging that possibility, however, suggests that implied delegation does not, standing alone, give significant guidance as to the appropriate relationship between courts and delegated decision-makers. If the purported declared constitutional principle of implied delegation inevitably requires a background political theory, that theory will almost certainly be contestable and as such could not be considered as authoritative. Implied delegation cannot provide a declared constitutional principle in support of a doctrine of curial deference. Ultimately, with the inherent malleability of the implied delegation justification in mind, one might query whether it is appropriate that a great deal of authority should be entrusted to

[64] James Landis, 'Administrative Policies and the Courts' (1938) 47 Yale LJ 519, 532.
[65] See above 2.1.
[66] Barron and Kagan, '*Chevron's* Non-delegation Doctrine', above n. 1, p. 223.

delegated decision-makers by implication: 'the concept of an implied delegation of interpretative authority is difficult to characterise as a congressional command'.[67] A more convincing justification for a doctrine of curial deference seems necessary.

2.3 Curial deference and the delegation of power

2.3.1 The basic requirement of judicial restraint

I wish to argue that curial deference follows from the judicial obligation to give effect to legislative intent. My doctrine of curial deference relies on a proper consideration of the relevant statutory provisions and requires the ordinary use of the tools of statutory interpretation.

The first subordinate argument of my overall argument, the delegation argument, assumes that a legislature is capable of delegating wide powers to delegated decision-makers. It is generally true in modern legal systems that wide delegations of power are permissible: 'The Lockean principle that the grant of legislative power is one "only to make laws, and not to make legislators" has fallen before the inexorable momentum of the administrative state.'[68] Indeed, it would be:

> debilitatingly naïve to suppose that modern governments can accomplish the kinds of tasks we want them to fulfil without relying on a vertical division of labour between legislatures making laws and administrative agencies implementing them and in doing so exercising fundamentally important discretionary authority in further settling social ends.[69]

Because it is permissible to allocate decision-making power to delegated decision-makers, within constitutional limits, an important step in the argument is to note that the legislature could have delegated decision-making power to the courts but has not done so. Such a delegation could be accomplished in two ways. The legislature could vest decision-making

[67] Thomas Merrill, 'Judicial Deference to Executive Precedent' (1992) 101 Yale LJ 969, 1032. Contrast Merrill and Hickman, who suggest in '*Chevron's* Domain', above n. 39, p. 870 that the logic of implied delegation is that '[d]eference is mandatory because Congress has commanded it'.

[68] Henry Monaghan, '*Marbury* and the Administrative State' (1983) 83 Colum LR 1, 25. Internal citation omitted.

[69] Henry Richardson, *Democratic Autonomy: Public Reasoning about the Ends of Policy* (Oxford: Oxford University Press, 2002), p. 222. But see Gary Lawson, 'The Rise and Rise of the Administrative State' (1994) 107 Harv LR 1231: 'The post-New Deal administrative state is unconstitutional, and its validation by the legal system amounts to nothing less than a bloodless constitutional revolution.'

power in the courts directly. For example, it is commonly provided that the revocation or suspension of drivers' licences shall be a matter for local courts. Alternatively, an appeal could be created to allow a court to adjudicate a matter *de novo*, perhaps where a regulatory body has undertaken a complex investigation and imposed sanctions on an individual or a corporate entity. However, where no specific delegation of power has been made in respect of the courts, the judicial role is reduced accordingly.

The basic requirement of judicial restraint rests on significant judicial authority. In the *Wednesbury* case,[70] Lord Greene MR noted how a reviewing court, 'whenever it is alleged that the local authority have contravened the law, must not substitute itself for that authority',[71] because '[t]he effect of the legislation is not to set up the court as an arbiter of the correctness of one view over another'.[72] The House of Lords has also recognised that a reviewing court ought to be restrained on the basis that power was 'entrusted to the officers identified, and to no one else', including the courts.[73] In *Dunsmuir* v. *New Brunswick*,[74] a member of the Supreme Court of Canada eloquently elaborated the basic requirement of judicial restraint:

> When the applicant for judicial review challenges the substantive *outcome* of an administrative action, the judge is invited to cross the line into second-guessing matters that lie within the function of the administrator. This is controversial because it is not immediately obvious why a judge's view of the reasonableness of an administrative policy or the exercise of an administrative discretion should be preferred to that of the administrator to whom Parliament or a legislature has allocated the decision, unless there is a full statutory right of appeal to the courts, or it is otherwise indicated in the conferring legislation that a 'correctness' standard is intended.[75]

Conversely, if no delegation of power at all has been made in respect of a delegated decision-maker, then no curial deference is required. For example, the Supreme Court of the United States has refused to accord *Chevron* deference to delegated decision-makers' interpretations of

[70] *Associated Provincial Picture Houses* v. *Wednesbury Corporation* [1948] 1 KB 223.

[71] *Ibid.*, p. 228. [72] *Ibid.* at pp. 230–1.

[73] *R (Corner House Research and Campaign Against Arms Trade)* v. *Director of the Serious Fraud Office* [2008] UKHL 60; [2009] AC 756 at 841, per Lord Bingham of Cornhill.

[74] [2008] SCC 9; [2008] 1 SCR 190.

[75] *Ibid.*, p. 252, per Binnie J. Emphasis original. See similarly Harry Arthurs, 'Rethinking Administrative Law: A Slightly Dicey Business' (1979) 17 Osgoode Hall LJ 1, 18.

general statutes because there is no 'congressional delegation of administrative authority' to interpret general statutes.[76] *Chevron* deference is accorded only to the interpretation of statutes that the delegated decision-maker is 'charged with administering'.[77] In short, a delegation of power to a delegated decision-maker functions as a directive to courts to follow a restrained approach.

2.3.2 *Variable delegations of power*

The next step in my delegation argument is to note the bewildering array of statutory powers – and the variance between them – delegated to different delegated decision-makers. Consider the variety of statutory provisions which may govern the relationship between the legislature, the executive and delegated decision-makers. Some delegated decision-makers may not be subject to policy directions from the government; many others may be. There may also be differences in the mechanisms for accountability depending on the delegated decision-maker in question: usually, the chief executive officer must appear before legislative committees when summoned; however, on occasion, there may be a prohibition on expressing a view on the merits and demerits of government policy. Under such statutory structures, different types of delegated decision-maker also make different types of decision, pursuant to different procedures: consultation with interested parties may be required before a decision is taken; general rules or standards may have to be prescribed before individualised decisions are taken; procedural formalities may attend the decision-making process; or it may be possible to proceed with or without consultation, with or without prescribing general rules or standards, and with or without formal procedures. Moreover, some delegated decision-makers have extensive powers over a narrow area, others have extensive powers over an extensive area and still others have narrow powers over a narrow area or an extensive area.

My simple claim is that because the legislature has delegated variable degrees of power to delegated decision-makers, courts must also follow a variable approach in order to give effect to legislative intent. A uniform approach to judicial review would be inapposite in an era of many and varied delegated decision-makers with many and varied powers. If the same standard of review were to be applied, then the decision to delegate varying degrees of power would be undermined. It seems plain that in a very general

76 *Adams Fruit Company* v. *Barrett* (1990) 494 US 638 at 649, per Marshall J.
77 *Metropolitan Stevedore* v. *Rambo* (1997) 521 US 121 at 137, n. 9, per Souter J.

sense a decision, or series of decisions, was made to delegate varying levels of power to different delegated decision-makers. There are:

> [so] many different types of circumstances, including different statutes, different types of application, different substantive regulatory or administrative problems, and different legal postures in which cases arrive … [that] a blanket rule, applicable to all agency interpretations of law, such as 'always defer to the agency when the statute is silent', would be seriously overbroad, counterproductive and sometimes senseless.[78]

It would be contrary to legislative intent to apply the same standard of review across the board. A plausible inference from the variance in statutory schemes is that a legislature would intend that different types of decision would be treated with varying degrees of curial deference by a reviewing court:

> legislatures have delegated numerous powers in myriad ways, and have made various choices about how this delegated power should be supervised. There is no reason why the courts should wilfully disregard these complexities in order to make their supervisory role easier. Having access to multiple standards of review … allows courts to deal with these complexities in a sophisticated and, arguably, a more effective and practical way.[79]

I do not claim that delegations of power can be measured with precision, but I do claim that delegations of power can be measured in a rough sense. The variability of legislative delegations of power has, in such a rough sense, been recognised by the highest courts in Canada and the United States. Mindful of their obligation to give effect to legislative intent, these courts have considered the development of a variable standard of review a requirement of the modern administrative state, as I will discuss now.

2.3.2.1 The variable standard of review in Canada

The pragmatic and functional analysis developed and employed by the Supreme Court of Canada courts is holistic. It 'demands a … nuanced analysis based on consideration of a number of factors … whenever a court reviews the decision of an administrative body'.[80] Nevertheless,

[78] Breyer, 'Law and Policy', above n. 55, p. 373.

[79] Frank Iacobucci, 'Articulating a Rational Standard of Review Doctrine: A Tribute to John Willis' (2002) 27 Queen's LJ 859, 872–3. See also *Canadian Union of Public Employees*, above n. 63 at pp. 555–6.

[80] *Dr Q* v. *College of Physicians and Surgeons of New Brunswick* [2003] SCC 19; [2003] 1 SCR 226 at 237–8, per McLachlin CJ.

legislative intent has been described as the 'central inquiry'[81] of the pragmatic and functional analysis and it has been said that 'determining the applicable standard of review is accomplished by establishing legislative intent'.[82] In his seminal judgment in *Bibeault*, Beetz J was happy to jettison the language of jurisdiction for the pragmatic and functional analysis because the latter would provide a better signpost to legislative intent by 'focus[ing] the Court's inquiry directly on the intent of the legislator rather than on interpretation of an isolated provision'.[83] The only question to be asked by a reviewing court was: 'Did the legislator intend the question to be within the jurisdiction conferred on the [delegated decision-maker]?'[84] Clearly, despite the difficulties with its approach identified in 2.2.2, the Supreme Court of Canada has appreciated the importance of its obligation to give effect to legislative intent.

The overarching pragmatic and functional analysis was developed in response to some extent to the varying degrees of power delegated to delegated decision-makers. As Lamer CJ put it, 'the standard of review will vary from body to body, *based on the legislation establishing the board or tribunal*, the expertise of that body and the nature of the question'.[85] The 'various situations' that might arise were addressed by the development of a variable standard of review.[86] Iacobucci J was central to the development of the overarching framework.[87] Hints of the theoretical basis of his position can be found in his judgment in *Pezim*: he identified 'various standards of review with respect to *the myriad of administrative agencies* that exist in our country'[88] and also noted how, '[h]aving regard to the large number of factors relevant in determining the applicable standard of review, the courts have developed a *spectrum* that ranges from the standard of reasonableness to that of correctness'.[89] The variability of the standard of review is most clearly seen in how '[s]ome provisions within the same Act may require greater

81 *Pushpanathan* v. *Canada (Minister of Citizenship and Immigration)* [1998] 1 SCR 982 at 1004, per Bastarache J.

82 *Dunsmuir*, above n. 74, p. 213, per Bastarache and LeBel JJ.

83 *Union des employés de service, local 298* v. *Bibeault* [1988] 2 SCR 1048 at 1089, per Beetz J.

84 *Ibid.*, p. 1087, per Beetz J.

85 *Canada (Attorney General)* v. *Mossop* [1993] 1 SCR 554 at 606. Emphasis added.

86 *Dunsmuir*, above n. 74 at pp. 210 and 216–17, per Bastarache and LeBel JJ.

87 See Lorne Sossin and Colleen Flood, 'The Contextual Turn: Iacobucci's Legacy and the Standard of Review in Administrative Law' (2007) 57 UTLJ 581.

88 *Pezim* v. *British Columbia (Superintendent of Brokers)* [1994] 2 SCR 557 at 589. Emphasis added.

89 *Ibid.*, p. 590. Emphasis added.

curial deference than others'.[90] Reviewing courts have been, further, enjoined to 'be careful not to subsume distinct questions into one broad standard of review';[91] in other words, different standards of review may apply to different decisions taken by the same delegated decision-maker. The abolition of the patent unreasonableness standard of review in *Dunsmuir* because the doctrine as it had developed was unworkable does not alter the fact that the Supreme Court of Canada has sought to give effect to legislative intent by developing a variable standard of review, motivated to some extent by the variability of the relevant statutory provisions.

2.3.2.2 The variable standard of review in the United States

Recent developments in the United States tell a similar tale. An initial encroachment was made into '*Chevron's* domain'[92] by *Christensen* v. *Harris County*.[93] Here, a policy adopted by Harris County clearly conflicted with the federal Department of Labour's guidance as to the implementation of a statute. The guidance was contained in an opinion letter issued to the County, which the County ignored. Subsequently, the Department sued, claiming that its interpretation of the statute was entitled to *Chevron* deference. Thomas J held that *Chevron* was inapplicable: 'Interpretations such as those in opinion letters – like interpretations contained in policy statements, agency manuals, and enforcement guidelines, *all of which lack the force of law* – do not warrant *Chevron*-style deference.'[94] The interpretation was thus entitled only to *Skidmore* deference and was not persuasive in the instant case. Thomas J's brief, and rather gnomic,[95] justification drew excited support from Breyer J: 'where one has *doubt that Congress actually intended* to delegate … I believe that *Skidmore* [deference] nonetheless retains legal vitality'.[96]

The link between *Skidmore* and legislative intent became of great importance when a further encroachment onto territory previously under *Chevron's* sole occupation occurred in *United States* v. *Mead*

[90] *Pushpanathan*, above n. 81, p. 1005, per Bastarache J.

[91] *Lévis (City)* v. *Fraternité des policiers de Lévis* [2007] SCC 14; [2007] 1 SCR 591 at 608, per Bastarache J.

[92] Merrill and Hickman, '*Chevron's* Domain', above n. 39. [93] (2000) 529 US 576.

[94] *Ibid.*, p. 587. Emphasis added.

[95] See Thomas Merrill and Kathryn Watts, 'Agency Rules with the Force of Law: The Original Convention' (2002) 116 Harv LR 467 for an extended discussion of the meaning of the phrase 'force of law'.

[96] *Harris County*, above n. 93, p. 597. Emphasis added.

Corporation.[97] *Mead* introduced a '*Chevron* step zero':[98] a reviewing court must, before proceeding to step one of the *Chevron* analysis, determine whether *Chevron* deference applies. Here, the reason for encroachment was more clearly identified. Under the Secretary of the Treasury's power to issue rules and regulations concerning the importation of merchandise, offices of the Customs Service were given the ability to issue ruling letters, which stated the Service's official position on tariff classifications, binding on all concerned in a 'particular transaction … until modified or revoked'.[99] Only those on whom the letters were binding were entitled to notice of any modification or revocation. Most of the letters, which did not go through a process of notice and comment, were rather short on detail; only those issued by headquarters tended even to adumbrate any background rationale. A massive volume of ruling letters, some 10,000 to 15,000 annually from forty-six offices, poured forth from the Service. Against this backdrop, the Mead Corporation challenged a reclassification by seeking judicial review of the interpretation of law in the relevant ruling letter.

Not only did Souter J take the view that *Chevron* was inapplicable in the instant case, but also indicated that there were many other areas in which the *Chevron* doctrine would be inapplicable:

> [An inescapable] feature is the great variety of ways in which the laws invest the Government's administrative arms with discretion, and with procedures for exercising it, in giving meaning to acts of Congress. Implementation of a statute may occur in formal adjudication or the choice to defend against judicial challenge; it may occur in a central board or office or in dozens of enforcement agencies dotted across the country; its institutional law-making may be confined to the resolution of minute detail or extend to legislative rule-making on matters intentionally left by Congress to be worked out at the agency level … Although we all accept the position that the judiciary should defer to at least some of this multifarious administrative action, we have to decide how to take account of the great range of its variety … *if … it is simply implausible that Congress intended such a broad range of statutory authority to produce only two varieties of administrative action, demanding either Chevron deference or none at all, then the breadth of the spectrum of possible agency action must be taken into account.*[100]

In the instant case, the terms of the congressional delegation of power did not indicate that *Chevron* deference should be accorded. Instead, *Skidmore* deference was accorded. But of greatest interest for present

[97] (2001) 533 US 218.
[98] Cass Sunstein, '*Chevron* Step Zero' (2006) 92 Va LR 187.
[99] 19 CFR § 177.9(a).
[100] *Mead*, above n. 97, p. 236. Emphasis added.

purposes is the recognition by the court that the variety of delegated decision-makers, decision-making procedures and decisions requires a doctrine of curial deference with variable standards of review. Courts mindful of their obligation to give effect to legislative intent should respond to the varying delegations of power made by the legislature by varying the degree of curial deference afforded from case to case. In Souter J's pithy phrase, a reviewing court must, at the instance of the legislature, 'tailor deference to variety'.[101] A variable standard of review allows the variable degrees of power delegated by legislatures to fit the general principles of judicial review.

2.3.3 Ascertaining the extent of delegations of power

My delegation argument contains two subordinate arguments. First, because of the existence of a delegation of power to a delegated decision-maker, courts should adopt a secondary, reviewing stance relative to the delegated decision-maker. Secondly, because of the existence of variable delegations of power, courts should follow an approach which is capable of varying from case to case. My delegation argument operates on two levels: in general and in individual cases. If powers of varying extent have been delegated to delegated decision-makers, courts should develop and follow a variable approach in general to judicial review. The variable approach is then applied in individual cases. My delegation argument requires courts to pay close attention to the relevant statutory provisions. Cleaving to statutory language provides the link to legislative intent missing from the argument from the separation of powers for curial deference as enhancing the legislative power. Any erosion of judicial power is justified by reference to the declared constitutional principle that courts must give effect to legislative intent.[102]

2.3.3.1 The mechanics of the delegation argument

I do not claim that the extent of delegations of power can be precisely measured. However, an interpretive exercise can be undertaken by a reviewing court, in general and in individual cases (although the focus here is on the latter). The extent of the power delegated in any particular

[101] *Ibid.*, p. 236.

[102] To the extent that exercises of non-statutory powers depend on some written instrument which delegates power to a decision-maker, the doctrine of curial deference I am developing can be applied in the review of non-statutory powers (assuming that review is legitimate). I am content to flag but not press the point, for the reasons mentioned in the Introduction.

case can be determined by reference to four factors. First, the variety of the powers delegated: how many powers have been vested in the delegated decision-maker, and are they general or specific?[103] Secondly, the nature of the powers delegated: are they potentially intrusive and coercive, or do they relate more to the internal procedures of the delegated decision-maker? Thirdly, the field of jurisdiction: is it narrow or broad? Fourthly, autonomy: is the delegated decision-maker free of external controls, requirements to consult with other delegated decision-makers, and does it seem free to set the limits of its own jurisdiction?[104] When I refer to the extent of the power delegated, I am referring to the outcome of the interpretive exercise.

These considerations have been influential. As L'Heureux-Dubé J explained in her dissent in *Canada (Attorney-General)* v. *Mossop*:[105]

> it can be presumed that the legislature intended that more deference would be shown to bodies with broad powers than to bodies with highly circumscribed powers. Where a broader jurisdiction is given, it may be appropriate to conclude that more rather than less deference should be given. Similarly, where a board is given a clearly specified and defined jurisdiction, even if over a narrow subject-matter, great deference may be given to decisions that fall within that area.[106]

Similarly, as Stratas JA recently put it, dissenting, but not on this point: 'Parliament might constrain a tribunal by setting out a tightly-worded definition of a key statutory phrase, enumerating factors that the tribunal

[103] But see *Mayo Foundation* v. *United States* (2011) 131 S Ct 704 at 713–14, where the Supreme Court of the United States rejected the utility of such a distinction. In *Chevron*, above n. 52 at pp. 843–4, a distinction was made between 'explicit' and 'implicit' delegations of authority. Stevens J suggested that regulations adopted under an explicit delegation would be 'given controlling weight unless they are arbitrary, capricious, or manifestly contrary to the statute'. However, in respect of decisions made under an implicit delegation it was said merely that 'a court may not substitute its own construction of a statutory provision for a reasonable interpretation made by the administrator of an agency'. On its face the distinction suggests that greater deference should be granted where delegations of power are made explicitly. However, the factors I identify in the text urge a more nuanced judicial inquiry than reliance upon a distinction between explicit and implicit delegations. Moreover, assuming that the concern underlying the distinction made in *Chevron* is to give greater weight where the extent of a delegation is greater, my approach will better reflect legislative intent than an approach based on a formal distinction between 'explicit' and 'implicit'.

[104] Traditional means of sheltering delegated decision-makers from review, such as providing that a power shall be exercised 'if in the opinion of X it is necessary to do', and providing that decisions are to be 'final and conclusive' would be relevant here. I discuss privative clauses below 2.3.3.2.

[105] *Mossop*, above n. 85. [106] *Ibid.*, p. 596.

must consider, or prescribing a particular test to be followed.'[107] La Forest J's analysis for the Supreme Court of Canada of the statutory scheme in *Canadian Association of Industrial, Mechanical and Allied Workers* v. *Paccar of Canada*[108] is instructive. Here, a general purposes and objects clause in the relevant Labour Code defined the function of the Board as being 'to develop effective industrial relations in the interest of achieving or maintaining good working conditions and the well being of the public'.[109] Further sections gave the Board 'exclusive jurisdiction' to hear and determine applications or complaints made under the legislation and broad powers to answer any relevant questions, prevented the ordinary courts from hearing these matters and provided that decisions of the Board would be 'final and conclusive'.[110] In sum, the legislation gave the Board 'the exclusive jurisdiction to determine the extent of its jurisdiction under the Act, to determine any fact necessary to establish its jurisdiction, and to determine in what manner it shall exercise its jurisdiction'.[111] A significant extent of power had been delegated to the Board and accordingly, its decisions could only be quashed for patent unreasonableness.

Some other Canadian examples may be helpful. In *Dayco (Canada)* v. *National Automobile, Aerospace and Agricultural Implement Workers Union of Canada*,[112] La Forest J distinguished between the strong protection of a labour board's decision and the comparatively weaker protection of a labour arbitrator's decision in determining that the arbitrator should be subject to a relatively more intrusive standard of review: 'the decisions of the board are *shielded by a strong privative clause* ... In contrast, the arbitrator's role is confined to the resolution of grievances under a collective agreement.'[113] In *Canadian Broadcasting Corporation* v. *Canada (Labour Relations Tribunal)*[114] Iacobucci J noted how a 'broad privative clause is combined with wide powers in the Board to deal with questions put before it',[115] again indicating that because of the significant extent of the delegation of power, a high degree of curial deference should be shown.[116]

[107] *Kane* v. *Canada (Attorney General)* [2011] FCA 19, 328 DLR (4th) 193 at 233.
[108] [1989] 2 SCR 983. [109] Labour Code, RSBC 1979, c. 212, s. 27.
[110] *Ibid.*, ss. 33 and 34(2). [111] *Paccar*, above n. 108, p. 1003. [112] [1993] 2 SCR 230.
[113] *Ibid.*, p. 266. [114] [1995] 1 SCR 157. [115] *Ibid.*, p. 184.
[116] A change in the wording of a statute, to increase or reduce the power delegated, may also be relevant. See e.g. *Ivanhoe* v. *United Food and Commercial Workers, Local 500* [2001] SCC 47; [2001] 2 SCR 565 at 593.

A good example of a delegation of power of a significant extent, where the variety and nature of powers, field of jurisdiction and autonomy were all extensive is *Royal Oak Mines* v. *Canada (Labour Relations Board)*:[117]

> In examining the legislation itself it is apparent that Parliament has clearly given the Canada Labour Relations Board a wide remedial role. The wording … does not place precise limits on the Board's jurisdiction. In fact, the Board may order anything that is 'equitable' for a party to do or refrain from doing in order to fulfil the objectives of the Code. In my view, this was done to give the Board the flexibility necessary to address the ever changing circumstances that present themselves in the wide variety of disputes which come before it in the sensitive field of labour relations … By providing that the Board may fashion equitable remedies Parliament has given a clear indication that the Board has been entrusted with wide remedial powers. Furthermore, a broad privative clause … provides that, not only are the Board's *decisions* final, but so too are its *orders*.[118]

A focus on the extent of the power delegated can also be discerned in an important American case, *Gonzales* v. *Oregon*.[119] The federal Attorney-General had attempted, by issuing an interpretive rule interpreting a regulation issued under the Controlled Substances Act, to criminalise assisted suicide. The purported criminalisation was accomplished by defining 'legitimate medical purpose' accordingly,[120] pursuant to the Attorney-General's statutory powers to control the dispensing of controlled substances and register or de-register physicians. The Supreme Court of the United States was in the first instance exercised by the manner in which the Attorney-General had sought to achieve his goal: the original regulation largely repeated the wording of the Controlled Substances Act. A cynic might have suggested that the regulation was promulgated solely to allow the Attorney-General to interpret it – in a manner congenial to the present federal executive – and thereby qualify for curial deference, a concern which appeared to animate the court.[121]

[117] [1996] 1 SCR 369. [118] *Ibid.* at pp. 402–4, per Cory J. Emphasis original.

[119] (2006) 546 US 243. See similarly *Pharmaceutical Research and Manufacturers of America* v. *Thompson* (2004) 362 F 3d 817 at 821–2.

[120] 21 USC § 830(b)(3)(A)(ii); 21 CFR § 1306.04(a).

[121] The rule announced in *Auer* v. *Robbins* (1997) 519 US 452 accords substantial deference to agencies when they interpret their own regulations. Kennedy J rejected its applicability in *Oregon* because 'the underlying regulation does little more than restate the terms of the statute itself'. *Oregon*, above n. 119, p. 257. See generally John Manning, 'Constitutional Structure and Judicial Deference to Agency Interpretations of Agency

Kennedy J refused to accord *Chevron* deference to the interpretive rule because the Attorney-General had not surmounted the *Mead* threshold. The legislature had not delegated significant powers to the Attorney-General: 'The Controlled Substances Act gives the attorney general limited powers, to be exercised in specific ways.'[122] In particular, the power to control the dispensing of controlled substances was exercisable only after public notice and comment and an evaluation of the proposed exercise by the Secretary of Health and Human Services; the power to register or de-register physicians was circumscribed by five factors, none of which was considered in the interpretive rule. These were the only powers delegated to the Attorney-General by the statute: 'Congress did not delegate to the attorney general authority to carry out or effect all provisions of the Controlled Substances Act.'[123] In short, the statute gave no indication of a congressional intent to delegate a power to exercise medical judgement to the Attorney-General, who was a legal, not a medical, expert: 'the authority claimed by the attorney general is both beyond his expertise and *incongruous with the statutory purposes and design*'.[124] In particular, the creation of a criminal offence by the Attorney-General was not contemplated by the statute: 'The *idea that Congress gave* the attorney general *such broad and unusual authority* through an implicit delegation in the Controlled Substances Act's registration provision is not sustainable.'[125]

In effect, on a proper consideration of the relevant statutory provisions, the extent of the Attorney-General's powers were not such as to warrant a conclusion that significant authority had been delegated to him by the Controlled Substances Act: the powers delegated to him by the statute were narrow, they were not particularly intrusive, they were exercisable over a narrow field of jurisdiction and they could only be exercised after consultation with other officials. Thus, *Skidmore* deference, rather than *Chevron* deference, was accorded and the Attorney-General's interpretation of the regulation was held not to be persuasive.[126]

Thus, delegation of power = *f* {Variety of the Powers + Nature of the Powers + Field of Jurisdiction + Autonomy} and the extent of delegations of power can be visualised as running along a spectrum:

Rules' (1996) 96 Colum LR 612. I would treat departure by an agency from its own regulations as an *indicium* of unreasonableness. See generally below Ch. 4.

122 *Oregon*, above n. 119, p. 259. 123 *Ibid.*, p. 259.

124 *Ibid.*, p. 267. Emphasis added. 125 *Ibid.*, p. 267. 126 *Ibid.* at pp. 269–75.

Oregon *Dayco* (Labour arbitrator contrast) *Royal Oak Mines*

→

Delegation of Power

Delegations of power will not be infinite. For example, no matter how much power has been delegated to a delegated decision-maker, it will not have the power to definitively interpret the provisions of general statutes (such as freedom of information legislation).[127] However, the extent of the power delegated would be relevant to determining whether a delegated decision-maker has the authority to regulate a field which is not far from its home regulatory territory. On most occasions, the relevant question for the reviewing court will be straightforward: did the delegated decision-maker legitimately exercise a power or render an interpretation of law? Here, the extent of the power delegated in respect of the particular statutory provision, and related statutory provisions, will be relevant. In individual cases, the task for the reviewing court will be to determine the extent of the delegation of power in respect of the impugned decision.

2.3.3.2 Legislative intent and privative clauses

It might be argued that in order to truly give effect to legislative intent, a reviewing court would have to give full effect to a statutory provision that purports to exclude judicial oversight. This is not necessarily so. The problem with privative clauses, so called because they deprive a reviewing court of jurisdiction, is that they create tension within a statute. On the one hand are provisions that prescribe limits to statutory powers; on the other hand is a privative clause which purports to render these limits unenforceable by reviewing courts. Privative clauses are, as a result, incoherent, as the much-maligned Lord Hewart observed in the context of a 'conclusive evidence' provision:

> In passing such a clause Parliament, it may be thought, was really stultifying itself, because, having inserted express provisions in the Act for the protection of persons liable to have their property taken without their consent, and having enacted that the council in making ... an order must have regard to these provisions, it then, by means of this 'conclusive

[127] See e.g. *Adams Fruit Company*, above n. 76, p. 649. Of course, the delegated decision-maker may interpret such legislation in the course of its duties, but its interpretation may be displaced by a reviewing court.

> evidence clause' rendered such provisions nugatory, and, so far as victims are concerned, a mockery.[128]

Moreover, privative clauses are just one means of indicating legislative intent in respect of a particular delegated decision-maker. If the judicial task in individual cases is to construe the extent of a delegation of power in respect of the impugned decision, other factors are necessarily relevant. Indeed, there is no uniform formula even for privative clauses: 'Although their preclusive effect may be less obvious than that of the true privative clause, other forms of clauses purporting to restrict review may also have privative effect.'[129] Statutory language that fits into the category of privative clauses can be 'discovered' by a reviewing court. But if it is accurate to say that privative clauses are a matter of degree, it seems to prove the point that legislative intent in general can have the same effect as a privative clause,[130] because privative clauses are merely a particular way of manifesting legislative intent: 'legislative choice … is factored in by the court taking notice of specific *indicia* of legislative intention such as the presence or otherwise of [a privative] clause, or the conferral of a discretionary power in broad, unstructured terms'.[131] Moreover, if privative clauses are inserted in statutes as a matter of course – as is the case in Quebec – a holistic approach is preferable; it seems likely to better capture legislative intent than would relying solely on the possibly formalistic inclusion of a privative clause.[132]

128 *The New Despotism* (London: Benn, 1929), p. 72. The same logic applies even where, as in the United States, the enactment of privative clauses is permitted by a general statute. See below 7.1.4. The fact that they are provided for by a general statute does not make the individual statute in which they are placed any less incoherent.

129 *United Brotherhood of Carpenters and Joiners of America, Local 579* v. *Bradco Construction* [1993] 2 SCR 316 at 333, per Sopinka J. See also *Pasiechnyk* v. *Saskatchewan (Workers' Compensation Board)* [1997] 2 SCR 890 at 905.

130 See William Wade, *Constitutional Fundamentals*, rev. edn (London: Stevens, 1989), p. 85: 'Direct attacks on the jurisdiction of the courts … are relatively rare. A much commoner phenomenon is the indirect attack, which is made by granting power in such wide and subjective terms that there appears to be nothing left for the court to judge.' Compare *Khosa*, above n. 3, p. 388, per Rothstein J, concurring: '[it is only with the enactment of privative clauses that the legislature evidences] intent to oust, or at the very least restrict, the court's review role'.

131 Hunt, 'Against Bifurcation', above n. 7, p. 113.

132 See Gabrielle Perrault, *Le Contrôle judiciaire des decisions de l'administration: de l'erreur juridictionnelle à la norme de contrôle* (Montreal: Wilson and Lafleur, 2002), p. 75.

Thus it is entirely legitimate that in the sophisticated analysis previously favoured by the Supreme Court of Canada, privative clauses are taken as indications of legislative intent, 'a legislative signal to judges',[133] but are not treated as determinative of legislative intent. As one commentator has put it, 'the full privative clause has become a symbol in its own right rather than something to be taken literally, no longer semantic but semiotic'.[134] Treating privative clauses as indications, rather than as determinative, of legislative intent avoids doing violence to the rule of law by immunising decisions from judicial oversight – 'judges appreciate ... that to exempt any public authority from judicial control is to give it dictatorial power ...'[135] – and more importantly, resolves the tension created by the presence of a privative clause in a statute. In addition, treating privative clauses as indications of legislative intent, rather than effectively ignoring them after the fashion of the English courts,[136] respects the declared constitutional principle that courts should give effect to legislative intent. It might also be noted that the outright exclusion of judicial review may give rise to constitutional problems. Even in England, where Parliament remains sovereign, judges have suggested, albeit extrajudicially[137] and in *obiter*[138] that a clause depriving reviewing courts of jurisdiction might be void and of no effect. Exclusions of judicial review are so offensive to the rule of law that they may simply be outside the scope of even the broadest legislative power.[139]

133 David Dyzenhaus, 'Disobeying Parliament? Privative Clauses and the Rule of Law' in Richard Bauman and Tsvi Kahana (eds.), *The Least Examined Branch: The Role of Legislatures in the Constitutional State* (Cambridge: Cambridge University Press, 2006), p. 499, p. 513.

134 Robert Leckey, 'Territoriality in Canadian Administrative Law' (2004) 24 UTLJ 327, 344. It follows, as Leckey mischievously suggests, that 'provided that all parties agreed, a letter P or an image of a fish inserted into an enabling statute could signal deference in identical fashion'. But the agreement of 'all parties' is singularly unlikely to be forthcoming unless the relevant statutory provisions really do indicate a legislative intent to delegate power.

135 Wade, *Constitutional Fundamentals*, above n. 130, p. 82.

136 Aptly described as '[une] rouerie intellectuelle' by Yves-Marie Morissette, 'Rétrospective et prospective sur le contentieux administratif' (2008–2009) 39 RDUS 1, 11.

137 See e.g. Laws, 'Law and Democracy', above n. 58.

138 See *R (Jackson)* v. *Attorney General* [2005] UKHL 56; [2006] 1 AC 262 at 303–4 (Lord Steyn) at 318 (Baroness Hale); *Axa General Insurance* v. *Scottish Ministers* [2011] Scot CS CSIH 31, [89].

139 See also Douglas Edlin, 'A Constitutional Right to Judicial Review: Access to Courts and Ouster Clauses in England and the United States' (2009) 57 *American Journal of Comparative Law* 67, 73–80.

2.3.3.3 Statutory appeals

If no privative clause is present in the statute, but rather, an appeal has been provided for from a delegated decision-maker to a court (or another body applying judicial review principles), a doctrine of curial deference will be of assistance in determining the correct approach to follow. The fact that an appeal has been provided for – whether just on questions of law or on all questions – reduces the extent of the power delegated to the delegated decision-maker relative to the reviewing court: delegations of power have been made in respect of both. However, 'even where there is no privative clause and where there is a statutory right of appeal, the concept of the specialisation of duties requires that deference be shown to decisions of specialised tribunals on matters which fall squarely within the tribunal's expertise'.[140] One may complain that no practical considerations should be able to 'displace a statute's unambiguous wording'[141] or that according curial deference in the face of an appeal clause 'would be to pay lip service to the fact that the legislature has consciously decided to grant an unsuccessful party a right of appeal, rather than insulating its decisions from judicial review by means of the privative clause'.[142] But why delegate power at all, one might ask rhetorically, if a court will apply a standard of review of correctness to its exercise? Where the practical justifications for curial deference discussed in Chapter 3 are relevant, a full appeal in which a court considers the matter *de novo* may not be appropriate.[143]

2.4 Conclusion

The discussion in the last section provides a backdrop against which to judge David Dyzenhaus's suggestion that reliance on legislative intent may frustrate the development of a doctrine of curial deference: a reviewing court cognisant of its obligation to give effect to legislative intent will find itself faced simultaneously with a privative clause or other manifestation of legislative intent requiring it to follow a restrained approach, and other legal limits in the statute. Giving full effect to one or the other manifestation of

[140] *Pezim* v. *British Columbia (Superintendent of Brokers)* [1994] 2 SCR 557 at 591, per Iacobucci J.

[141] *Keddy* v. *New Brunswick (Workplace Health, Safety and Compensation Commission)* 2002 NBCA 24; 212 DLR (4th) 84 at 99, per Robertson JA.

[142] *Ibid.*, p. 109.

[143] See e.g. *Rehman* v. *Secretary of State for the Home Department* [2001] UKHL 47; [2003] 1 AC 153.

legislative intent would be unpalatable. Either judicial review would be ousted entirely, or no curial deference would be accorded: 'Since it presumes that there will be a fact of the matter as to legislative intent which judges are uniquely equipped to discover, its consequence is that, absent other factors, judges owe no deference to administrative determinations of the law.'[144] According to Dyzenhaus, another resultant risk is an illusory curial deference, accorded only in cases where a reviewing court takes the view that two or more answers can be reasonably accommodated by the statute. To accord curial deference where multiple answers are possible would not amount to curial deference in any meaningful sense. The question of the allocation of decision-making authority as between delegated decision-makers and reviewing courts would be answered cursorily: courts shall enforce the terms of the statute, by upholding a delegated decision-maker's interpretation of law only where the statute itself permits more than one reasonable interpretation.

However, the search for legislative intent that I am advocating is not a quest for some pre-existing fact 'which judges are uniquely equipped to discover'.[145] If such a narrowly positivistic view were taken, then curial deference might, indeed, not be accorded, and reliance on legislative intent would prevent the emergence of a doctrine of curial deference. But as my treatment of privative clauses suggests, I do not take the view that they are canonical expressions of legislative intent to which effect must be given. Rather, a holistic approach, which requires a proper consideration of the relevant statutory provisions, is necessary to ascertain the extent of the delegation of power. A blunt rule like *Chevron* seems to fly in the face of the declared constitutional principle that courts must give effect to legislative intent. Those who are not proponents of curial deference should recognise the force of the delegation argument: the array of delegated decision-makers and decision-making procedures in the modern administrative state requires judges who are mindful of their obligation to give effect to legislative intent to develop a doctrine of curial deference with variable standards of review.

[144] Dyzenhaus, 'Politics of Deference', above n. 8, p. 303. [145] *Ibid.*, p. 303.

3

The practical justifications for curial deference

In this chapter, I will explain and develop my argument based on practical justifications for curial deference.

3.1 Legislative intent and the practical justifications for curial deference

There will be reasons for the delegation of power to a delegated decision-maker: 'Presumably if Parliament entrusts a certain matter to a tribunal and not (initially at least) to the courts, it is because the tribunal enjoys some advantage that judges do not.'[1] I suggest that a reason or reasons for delegation can often be ascertained from the statute. Apart from demonstrating the extent of the power delegated,[2] a proper consideration of the relevant statutory provisions will indicate what level of expertise was thought to be a necessary characteristic of the delegated decision-maker, the complexity of the problem the legislature sought to solve by delegating, the democratic legitimacy required of the delegated decision-maker and the procedural legitimacy contemplated by the legislature. As a result, an abstract, background theory is unnecessary: a proper consideration of the relevant statutory provisions will indicate the appropriate standard of review. Reliance on background understandings, which I will detail in this chapter, is necessary, but I will not rely on any background assumptions as to what the legislature might have intended.[3]

1 *Canada (Director of Investigation and Research* v. *Southam* [1997] 1 SCR 748 at 776, per Iacobucci J.

2 See Ch. 2.

3 Not every aspect of these practical justifications for curial deference will be spelled out in the relevant statutory provisions: reliance on some background understandings will be necessary. In the case of complexity, for example, some background understanding of complexity (what it might mean for a problem to be complex) will be necessary. By tracing the contours of the practical justifications in this chapter, I hope to provide the necessary background understandings.

Just as a variable standard of review would be necessary if the legislature directed courts to develop and implement one, reference to the reasons why delegation took place would also be necessary if the legislature directed it. If reasons which explain the delegation of power can plausibly be inferred from a proper consideration of the relevant statutory provisions, then it can be argued that they influenced the legislative decision to delegate power to a body other than a court, and are thus factors that a reviewing court ought to consider. Such reasons for delegation are indicators of legislative intent. I call these the *practical justifications for curial deference.*[4]

The practical justifications for curial deference have five characteristics. First, they are reasons for the delegation of power, because they suggest that a delegated decision-maker will render better decisions than the legislature. Secondly, they are reasons for the delegation of power to a body other than a court, because they suggest that a delegated decision-maker will render better decisions than a court. Thirdly, they are ascertainable from a proper consideration of the relevant statutory provisions. These three characteristics, in particular the third, suggest that courts should take the practical justifications for curial deference into account. Fourthly, the practical justifications vary according to context: depending on the circumstances, delegated decision-makers might not render better decisions than courts or legislatures. The weight of the practical justifications in respect of different delegated decision-makers will vary. As with variable delegations of power, the variability of the practical justifications for curial deference suggests a variable degree of judicial restraint and, accordingly, a variable standard of review. Fifthly, however, the practical justifications are imperfect. Indeed, they have inherent flaws which would create significant difficulties for any attempt to build a doctrine of curial deference solely on the foundations of the practical justifications. But these inherent flaws would be reduced in importance if the practical justifications were taken into account by courts only where a proper consideration of the relevant statutory provisions indicates that they should do so.

[4] I should note, to forestall confusion, that there is no necessary link between the strength of the practical justifications and the extent of the power delegated. For example, a legislature might delegate power to an extremely expert body, but the breadth and depth of the powers may be limited. A central bank determining monetary policy is often in this position. Conversely, powers of significant breadth and depth might be delegated to a body which is not particularly expert. Refugee tribunals are often, arguably, in this position. Delegations of power and the practical justifications are linked, but they are not joined at the hip.

Consistent with their obligation to give effect to legislative intent, if, by reference to the relevant statutory provisions, it can plausibly be inferred that the practical justifications influenced the decision to delegate power, courts ought to look to the practical justifications in determining the appropriate degree of curial deference to accord to delegated decision-makers. It follows from my reliance upon legislative intent that only those practical justifications that can be ascertained by reference to the statute are relevant. Accordingly, reviewing courts are not required to 'engage in legislative mind reading' or to 'recover actual legislative reasons for … delegation'.[5] Their task in this context is to ascertain by reference to the statute, and the statute alone, what plausibly can be taken to have influenced the legislative decision to delegate power. It will thus be necessary to outline why the practical justifications might have influenced the legislative decision to delegate power to a body other than a court, to assist in clarifying what reviewing courts ought to be looking for in a statute and why they ought to be doing so. But it is only where a proper consideration of the relevant statutory provisions indicates that the practical justifications – individually or collectively – influenced the decision to delegate power that reviewing courts ought to take them into account. The argument based on practical justifications thus complements the argument based on delegation of power, because the extent of the delegation of power and the practical justifications can only be ascertained by means of a proper consideration of the relevant statutory provisions. Both arguments are based on the declared constitutional principle that courts must give effect to legislative intent.

In this chapter, I will consider the important features of each of the practical justifications, before noting how they might be linked to legislative intent. On occasion, my argument might lead to unpalatable conclusions. From different perspectives, my doctrine of curial deference might seem to accord importance to factors that are illegitimate or unimportant. However, these factors will only be relevant because of their relationship to legislative intent. Any unpalatable conclusions result from unpalatable legislative choices, and the appropriate remedy is the amendment of the offending statutory provisions.

3.2 Expertise

Relative to courts, delegated decision-makers generally have much greater expertise regarding the subject matter of the questions delegated

[5] Lisa Schultz Bressman, '*Chevron's* Mistake' (2009) 58 Duke LJ 549, 576.

to them. Although it may now be received wisdom that delegated decision-makers always have greater expertise relative to courts, expertise varies according to context. William Eskridge and Lauren Baer are too quick to assert that 'no one seriously disputes the New Deal-era adage that agencies are usually better informed than courts along several dimensions'.[6] Nevertheless, they have identified the important characteristics of expertise in much the same way I will do:

> [Delegated decision-makers] understand the subject-matter of their statutory scheme and the regulated industry with greater depth, have better access to experts … who provide specialised information in response to targeted inquiries, and have the kind of practical wisdom that comes from dealing with legal issues arising day-to-day under the statute (or perhaps triggered by the agency's own proposals and experiments).[7]

In short, expertise is a powerful practical justification for curial deference.

3.2.1 *Relevance of Expertise*

Expertise has positive and negative aspects. The positive aspect is that in resolving what often are complex problems, the relevant expertise is held by technocrats, not by legislatures or judges:

> the art of regulating an industry requires knowledge of the details of its operation, ability to shift requirements as the condition of the industry may dictate, the pursuit of energetic measures upon the appearance of an emergency, and the power through enforcement to realise conclusions as to policy.[8]

In particular areas, expertise may be indispensable. Risk regulation is a good example.[9] A number of key decisions of the Supreme Court of Canada highlight the relevance of expertise to deciding the appropriate degree of curial deference to accord to a delegated decision-maker. In

[6] William Eskridge and Lauren Baer, 'The Continuum of Deference: Supreme Court Treatment of Agency Statutory Interpretations from *Chevron* to *Hamdan*' (2008) 96 Geo LJ 1083, 1173.

[7] *Ibid.*, p. 1173.

[8] James Landis, *The Administrative Process* (New Haven: Yale University Press, 1938), pp. 23–4. The benefits of lay viewpoints in terms of expanding the range of perspectives available to the delegated decision-maker should not be gainsaid. See Peter Cane, *Administrative Tribunals and Adjudication* (Oxford: Hart, 2009), p. 92.

[9] See e.g. Stephen Breyer, *Breaking the Vicious Circle: Toward Effective Risk Regulation* (Cambridge, MA: Harvard University Press, 1993), pp. 42–3.

Canada (Attorney General) v. *Public Service Alliance of Canada*,[10] Cory J justified according curial deference to the decisions of the Public Service Staff Relations Board partly on the basis that it was an expert body:

> recognition must be given to the fact that the Board is composed of experts who are representative of both labour and management. They are aware of the intricacy of labour relations and the delicate balance that must be preserved between the parties for the benefit of society. These experts will often have earned by their merit the confidence of the parties.[11]

However, expertise also has a negative aspect, from which are drawn arguments emphasising the shortcomings of the judicial process relative to the decision-making processes of delegated decision-makers.[12] Technocratic administrators will often be more adept than legislatures, which have neither the time nor the ability to pass detailed legislation. They will also be more adept than generalist judges, at least when technical problems fall to be resolved. As Jerry Mashaw has asked, rhetorically:

> Why should anyone believe that particular issues raised in episodic litigation between parties having peculiar litigating interests should provide the judiciary with sufficient information for it to understand the administrative, political, social, economic, or scientific reality of a congressional-administrative programme, much less provide an opportunity to take effective action to mould that reality in desirable forms?[13]

Generally, I focus on the positive aspect of expertise. Legislatures can employ two means to ensure that expertise is brought to bear by the recipients of delegations of power.

[10] [1993] 1 SCR 941.

[11] *Ibid.*, p. 962. See also *Reference re Public Service Employee Relations Act (Alberta)* [1987] 1 SCR 313 at 416–17; *Canadian Broadcasting Corporation* v. *Canada (Labour Relations Tribunal)* [1995] 1 SCR 157 at 179–80; *Royal Oak Mines* v. *Canada (Labour Relations Board)* [1996] 1 SCR 369 at 403–4.

[12] See e.g. J. A. G. Griffith, 'The Common Law and the Political Constitution' (2001) 117 LQR 42, 65; Harry Street, *Justice in the Welfare State*, 2nd edn (London: Stevens, 1975), pp. 3–10.

[13] *Bureaucratic Justice: Managing Social Security Disability Claims* (New Haven: Yale University Press, 1983), p. 8. See *Heckler* v. *Chaney* (1985) 470 US 821 at 831–2; *Pension Benefit Guaranty Corporation* v. *LTV Corporation* (1990) 496 US 633 at 651–2; *International Longshoremen's and Warehousemen's Union, Ship and Dock Foremen, Local 514* v. *Prince Rupert Grain* [1996] 2 SCR 432 at 453. For both positive and negative aspects of expertise, see *National Corn Growers* v. *Canada (Import Tribunal)* [1990] 2 SCR 1324 at 1336 and *National Federation of Federal Employees, Local 1309* v. *Department of Interior* (1999) 526 US 86 at 95. See also Allan Hutchinson, 'Mice under a Chair: Democracy, Courts and the Administrative State' (1990) 40 UTLJ 374, 375.

3.2.1.1 Appointment of expert delegated decision-makers

The most straightforward means of ensuring expert delegated decision-making is to appoint expert delegated decision-makers. Qualifications can be required by statute, or legislation can provide for appointments to be made by or on the recommendation of a body composed of experts. The Canadian *Southam* case[14] provides a good example:

> the [Competition] Tribunal's expertise lies in economics and in commerce. The Tribunal comprises not more than four judicial members, all of whom are judges of the Federal Court – Trial Division, and not more than eight lay members, who are appointed on the advice of a council of persons learned in 'economics, industry, commerce or public affairs' … The preponderance of lay members reflects the judgment of Parliament that, for purposes of administering the Competition Act, economic or commercial expertise is more desirable and important than legal acumen. The particular dispute in this case concerns the definition of the relevant product market – a matter that falls squarely within the area of the Tribunal's economic or commercial expertise.[15]

The situation is subtly different in respect of members of the executive branch, who will often not personally possess any expertise relevant to their portfolios. Where power has been delegated to a minister, it has in effect been delegated not to the minister but to the government department headed by the minister:

> To treat the minister in his decision-making capacity as someone separate and distinct from the department of government of which he is the political head and for whose actions he alone in constitutional theory is accountable to Parliament is to ignore not only practical realities but also Parliament's intention. Ministers come and go; departments, though their names may change from time to time, remain. Discretion in making administrative decisions is conferred upon a minister not as an individual but as the holder of an office in which he will have available to him in arriving at his decision the collective knowledge, experience and expertise of all those who serve the Crown in the department of which, for the time being, he is the political head. The collective knowledge, technical as well as factual, of the civil servants in the department and their collective expertise is to be treated as the minister's own knowledge, his own expertise.[16]

The necessary background understanding is limited. It treats delegations to a minister as delegations to the department headed by the minister. This is perfectly reasonable; indeed, delegations of power to ministers

[14] *Southam*, above n. 1. [15] *Ibid.* at pp. 773–4.
[16] *Bushell* v. *Secretary of State for the Environment* [1981] AC 75 at 95, per Lord Diplock.

would not be understandable in the absence of the limited background understanding.

3.2.1.2 Accrual of expertise

It may, however, be even more important that delegated decision-makers accrue expertise over time: 'specialised knowledge' can be 'of an empirical character, developed by experience, rather than by formal training'.[17] Repeated exposure 'day in and day out' to a particular area and the legal, factual and policy issues that most often arise there,[18] should help delegated decision-makers to become more familiar with the subject matter of their decisions:[19] 'Being permanent appointments, members ... acquire experience in the questions they consider over the course of their appointments. Depending on the nature of the question at issue, members ... acquire experience and expertise that courts do not.'[20] A multifaceted expertise can be developed over time by communication with experts, a process which is easier for delegated decision-makers who have experience of particular subject matters:

> Bureaucracies develop expertise in administration, but also in the underlying subject-matter. They normally understand that subject-matter at least well enough to communicate with substantive experts, to identify the better experts, and to determine which insights of the underlying discipline can be transformed into workable administrative practices, and to what extent.[21]

Accrued expertise was relevant in *R* v. *Chief Constable of Sussex, ex p. International Trader's Ferry*.[22] Here, in deciding what policing resources to allocate to quell disruptive protests, the respondent Chief Constable was obliged to balance competing interests. The House of Lords emphasised that, in the review of such a balancing exercise, courts should be

[17] Max Weber, *The Theory of Social and Economic Organisation*, tr. A. M. Henderson and Talcott Parsons (New York: Oxford University Press, 1947), p. 335.

[18] *Mattel* v. *3894207 Canada* [2006] SCC 22; [2006] 1 SCR 772 at 794, per Binnie J.

[19] Anthony Downs, *Inside Bureaucracy* (Boston: Little Brown, 1967) pp. 18–20.

[20] *Canada (Deputy Minister for National Revenue)* v. *Mattel Canada* [2001] SCC 36; [2001] 2 SCR 100 at 116, per Major J.

[21] Breyer, *Risk Regulation*, above n. 9, p. 62. Compare Stephen Breyer, 'Judicial Review of Questions of Law and Policy' (1986) 38 Admin LR 363, 388: 'Industry information is often "suspect", insofar as industry's economic interests are at stake. Consumer groups may be as "suspect" or biased, though perhaps in a different direction. Independent experts may not have sufficiently detailed information or may have gotten it from industry.'

[22] [1999] 2 AC 418.

deferential because of the accrued expertise, some of it vicarious, of the Chief Constable: 'He knows through his officers the local situation, the availability of officers and his financial resources [and] the other demands on the police in the area at different times.'[23]

Following similar logic, a disciplinary committee composed of judges was held by the Supreme Court of Canada to have expertise relative to a reviewing court in assessing whether judicial conduct complained of would be such as to undermine public confidence in the judiciary, even though its case load was not heavy: 'the fact that the Council is engaged in this special and unique role gives it some degree of specialty not enjoyed by ordinary courts of review who have never, historically, been involved in such matters'.[24] Where delegated decision-makers are not appointed permanently, or act only on an ad hoc basis, they will be relatively less expert: 'members of [specialised] tribunals, on whatever basis they were appointed, are likely to gain more expertise … than would members of a tribunal that had jurisdiction to review various types of decision'.[25] Indeed, if reviewing courts accrue a great deal of expertise themselves in a particular area, they will not be at as great a disadvantage. One might also observe that the greater the breadth of the powers delegated to a decision-maker, the lesser the degree of specialisation and expertise in a particular area.[26]

3.2.2 *Legislative intent and expertise*

It is important, as I explained above, to link the practical justifications for curial deference to legislative intent. Only by analysing statutes closely will it be possible to plausibly infer that the legislature intended to delegate power on the basis of expertise. The terms of appointment of delegated decision-makers will be contained in the parent statute, or constitutive instrument, and will indicate whether or not expertise was a basis for appointment and whether 'it was intended by the legislature that the Board be composed of adjudicators having expertise and

23 *Ibid.*, p. 430, per Lord Slynn of Hadley.

24 *Moreau-Bérubé* v. *New Brunswick (Judicial Council)* [2002] SCC 11; [2002] 1 SCR 249 at 281, per Arbour J. See also *Starson* v. *Swayze* [2003] SCC 32; [2003] 1 SCR 722 at 764.

25 Cane, *Administrative Tribunals*, above n. 8, p. 93. See also H. Wade MacLauchlan, 'Administrative Interpretations of Law: How Much Formalism Can We Reasonably Bear?' (1986) 36 UTLJ 343, 378–9.

26 Cane, *Administrative Tribunals*, above n. 8, p. 115.

an acute understanding of human rights issues'.[27] In terms of ascertaining whether the legislature intended for the delegated decision-maker to accrue expertise over time, the relevant statutory provisions will again be instructive: if a delegated decision-maker is delegated the authority to investigate, formulate policy, develop rules and standards and enforce its rules and standards, it can plausibly be inferred that the legislature intended for the delegated decision-maker to accrue expertise in the course of carrying out its functions.

A link was made between the development of expertise over time and legislative intent by Cory J in *International Longshoremen's and Warehousemen's Union, Ship and Dock Foremen, Local 514* v. *Prince Rupert Grain*:[28]

> *Through their constant work* in this sensitive area, labour boards develop the special experience, skill and understanding needed to resolve the complex problems of labour relations. *There were very sound reasons for the establishment of labour boards and the protection of their decisions by broad privative clauses. Parliament and provincial legislatures have clearly indicated that decisions of these boards on matters within their jurisdiction should be final and binding.*[29]

The first highlighted section indicates the possibility of acquiring expertise in a particular area by virtue of continually rendering decisions in the area. The second highlighted section links legislative recognition of the expertise of delegated decision-makers to the decision of legislators to enact statutory provisions protecting delegated decision-makers from intrusive judicial review.[30] The link between legislative intent and the statutory delegations is perhaps expressed too strongly. It need not be the case that legislatures actually intended to delegate power for a specific reason. It is only necessary that a proper consideration of the relevant statutory provisions should indicate that expertise was a reason for the delegation of power to a body other than a court. Iacobucci J followed the

[27] *Gould* v. *Yukon Order of Pioneers* [1996] 1 SCR 571 at 633, per L'Heureux-Dubé J. See similarly *Canadian Union of Public Employees, Local 963* v. *New Brunswick Liquor Corporation* [1979] 2 SCR 227 at 235–6; *Toronto Board of Education* v. *Ontario Secondary School Teachers' Federation, District 15 (Toronto)* [1997] 1 SCR 487 at 505; *Ivanhoe* v. *United Food and Commercial Workers, Local 500* [2001] SCC 47; [2001] 2 SCR 565 at 590–1; *Association des courtiers et des agents immobiliers du Québec* v. *Proprio Direct* [2008] SCC 32; [2008] 2 SCR 195 at 206.

[28] *Prince Rupert Grain*, above n. 13. [29] *Ibid.* at pp. 446–7. Emphasis added.

[30] See similarly *Southam*, above n. 1 at 772.

right approach in *Canada (Director of Investigation and Research)* v. *Southam*:[31]

> Because an appellate court is likely to encounter difficulties in understanding the economic and commercial ramifications of the [Competition] Tribunal's decisions and consequently to be less able to secure the fulfilment of the purpose of the Competition Act than is the Tribunal, the *natural inference* is that the purpose of the Act is better served by appellate deference to the Tribunal's decisions.[32]

Gonthier J certainly went too far in *Macdonell* v. *Quebec (Commission d'accès à l'information)*.[33] He held that the Commission had 'relative expertise in respect of protecting privacy and promoting access to information held by a public body. That expertise is apparent from the powers conferred on the Commissioner to achieve the objectives of the Act, and from [other statutory provisions].'[34] But to provide the necessary link between legislative intent and expertise, a proper consideration of the relevant statutory provisions would have to indicate that the legislature actually created an expert body, or a body that would develop expertise over time. Here, the expertise of the delegated decision-maker might have been a motivation for delegating powers to the delegated decision-maker, but this could not be inferred from the mere existence of the delegated powers.[35]

[31] *Ibid.*, p. 772. [32] *Ibid.*, p. 773. Emphasis added.

[33] [2002] SCC 71; [2002] 3 SCR 661. [34] *Ibid.*, p. 670.

[35] Of course, it is possible that a legislature will care nothing for expertise. During a controversy about whether the Ontario Minister for Labour was required to appoint arbitrators from a list drawn up in consultation with an expert advisory body in accordance with past practice, the Ontario legislature passed a statute contained the following provision:

> (4) In appointing a replacement arbitrator, the Minister may appoint a person who, (a) has no previous experience as an arbitrator; (b) has not previously been or is not recognised as a person mutually acceptable to both trade unions and employers; (c) is not a member of a class of persons which has been or is recognised as comprising individuals who are mutually acceptable to both trade unions and employers.
>
> (5) In appointing a replacement arbitrator, the Minister may depart from any past practice concerning the appointment of arbitrators or chairs of arbitration boards, whether established before or after this Act comes into force, without notice to or consultation with any employers or trade unions.

Back to School Act (Toronto and Windsor) 2001, SO 2001, c. 1.

3.2.3 Expertise and context

It should not be forgotten, however, that 'expertise must be understood as a relative, not an absolute concept'.[36] It varies according to context. Crucially, the delegated decision-maker's expertise relative to that of the reviewing court will vary and ascertaining the expertise of the delegated decision-maker relative to that of the reviewing court will be of critical importance in identifying the appropriate degree of curial deference. Generally, a reviewing court will be at a disadvantage when a delegated decision-maker has rendered a decision within the delegated decision-maker's area of expertise, but will not be at a disadvantage where the decision lies closer to the competence of the reviewing court. Put simply, where a relatively general, relatively legal question is at issue, a reviewing court will have relatively more expertise to bring to bear; where a question intimately related to the jurisdiction of the delegated decision-maker is at issue, a reviewing court will have relatively less expertise to bring to bear: 'For as an interpretive question becomes more technical, the expertise of the agency charged with a statute's administration becomes greater and deferring to its construction ... becomes more appropriate.'[37]

Expertise varies according to context in two other important ways. First, delegated decision-makers can be more or less expert. It follows from what was said previously about appointment and accrual of expertise that a new delegated decision-maker, not composed of experts, will not be as expert as an established delegated decision-maker composed of experts.[38] Abella J inferred a legislative intent to delegate power to one agency rather than another from relative expertise in *Council of Canadians with Disabilities* v. *VIA Rail Canada*:[39]

> That is precisely why Parliament charged the [Canadian Transportation] Agency with the public responsibility for assessing barriers, not the Canadian Human Rights Commission. The Agency uniquely has the specialised expertise to balance the requirements of those with disabilities with the practical realities – financial, structural and logistic – of a federal transportation system.[40]

36 *Pushpanathan* v. *Canada (Minister of Citizenship and Immigration)* [1998] 1 SCR 982 at 1007, per Bastarache J.

37 *Pittston Coal Group* v. *Sebben* (1988) 488 US 105 at 150, per Stevens J, dissenting but not on this point. See also Abner Mikva, 'How Should the Courts Treat Administrative Agencies?' (1986) 36 Am U LR 1, 7–9.

38 See below 3.2.4.2. 39 [2007] SCC 15; [2007] 1 SCR 650. 40 *Ibid.*, p. 705.

Secondly, delegated decision-makers' expertise may vary even within their jurisdiction. For example, the members of a tribunal may not have as much expertise in respect of questions of civil procedure as they do to other, technical, scientific questions. Expertise must be considered in light of the decision being reviewed: 'though the Commissioner [of Patents] does possess considerable expertise in the areas of science, medicine and engineering, this expertise must be considered in the context of the problem under review'.[41]

Expertise may, indeed, be more relevant in some areas of delegated decision-making than others: it may be more important in the application of highly technical competition law concepts by a competition tribunal than in the application of impressionistic standards of professional conduct by a disciplinary tribunal. As a result, decisions according, or refusing to accord, curial deference on the basis of expertise will often be contestable. Expertise did not count in favour of the Immigration and Refugee Board in *Pushpanathan* v. *Canada (Citizenship and Immigration)*[42] in its determination whether the applicant's act of drug trafficking fell within the definition of 'acts contrary to the purposes and principles of the United Nations' contained in the Refugee Convention:

> the Board's expertise in matters relating to human rights is far less developed than that of human rights tribunals. The expertise of the Board is in accurately evaluating whether the criteria for refugee status have been met and, in particular, assessing the nature of the risk of persecution faced by the applicant if returned to his or her country of origin … Only 10 percent of the members of the Board are required to be lawyers … and there is no requirement that there be a lawyer on every panel. While this may not be a liability for the purposes of assessing the risk of persecution of an applicant if returned to his or her country of nationality, it renders unthinkable reposing the broad definition of a basic human rights guarantee exclusively in the hands of the Board. Nor is there any indication that the Board's experience with previous factual determinations of risk of persecution gives it any added insight into the meaning or desirable future development of the provision in question here … Here, the legal principle is easily separable from the undisputed facts of the case and would undoubtedly have a wide precedential value.[43]

41 *Harvard College* v. *Canada (Commissioner of Patents)* [2002] SCC 76; [2002] 4 SCR 45 at 120, per Bastarache J.

42 *Pushpanthan*, above n. 36.

43 *Ibid.* at pp. 1017–18, per Bastarache J. See similarly *Toronto (City)* v. *Canadian Union of Public Employees, Local 79* [2003] SCC 63; [2003] 3 SCR 77 at 91–2.

In *Canada (Attorney General)* v. *Mossop*,[44] the question arose whether a human rights tribunal should be accorded curial deference in its interpretation of a statute (not, let it be noted, a constitutional instrument). Although La Forest J recognised the valuable work done by the Human Rights Commission in educating, informing and advising the public, government and courts on human rights issues, he held that no analogy could be drawn to bodies such as labour arbitrators. A human rights tribunal would have no expertise on 'general questions of law', which are 'ultimately matters within the province of the judiciary, and involve concepts of statutory interpretation and general legal reasoning which the courts must be supposed competent to perform'.[45] But in point of fact, a Human Rights Commission engaged in a constant process of public debate and dialogue should develop considerable expertise on the likely effects of certain interpretations of law. Other reasons for reluctance to accord curial deference to such a body might be proposed, but it seems wrong to assail it on the ground that it lacks expertise relative to a court. L'Heureux-Dubé J was thus right to argue in dissent that '[i]n the exercise of its powers and functions, the Commission would inevitably accumulate expertise and specialised understanding of human rights issues as well as a body of governing jurisprudence'.[46]

But the presence of a provision which seems like a general question of law will not necessarily require curial deference to be accorded, as Abella J made clear in *Council of Canadians with Disabilities* v. *VIA Rail Canada*:[47] 'By attributing a jurisdiction-limiting label, such as "statutory interpretation" or "human rights", to what is in reality a function assigned and properly exercised under the enabling legislation, a tribunal's expertise is made to defer to a court's generalism rather than the other way around.'[48] Even on what seem to be general questions of law, expertise may favour the delegated decision-maker, rather than the reviewing court.

3.2.4 *Problems*

3.2.4.1 Shortcomings in expertise

Despite the foregoing paean to expertise, the limitations of expertise – and experts – ought to be appreciated. The application of expertise by

[44] [1993] 1 SCR 554. [45] *Ibid.*, p. 585. [46] *Ibid.*, p. 609.
[47] *Council of Canadians with Disabilities*, above n. 39. [48] *Ibid.*, p. 690.

experts cannot resolve all issues.[49] Experts, 'however adroit, are merely human[,] bear the burden of human limitations'[50] and have the same foibles as the rest of us, sometimes an even greater number due to their arrogance[51] and self-interest.[52] 'Bounded rationality'[53] and cognitive defects such as information and reputational cascades,[54] the availability heuristic[55] and hindsight-choice bias[56] afflict experts just as much as they afflict other individuals (including judges). Delegated decision-makers are also subject to the dangers of agency capture,[57]

[49] See generally Martin Shapiro, *Who Guards the Guardians? Judicial Control of Administration* (Athens: University of Georgia Press, 1988), pp. 140–4. See also Danielle Pinard, 'La Promesse brisé de *Oakes*' in Luc Tremblay and Grégoire Webber (eds.), *La Limitation des droits de la charte: essais critiques sur l'arrêt* R. c. Oakes (Montreal: Les Éditions Thémis, 2009), p. 131, p. 135: 'Les juristes ont parfois une vision naïve des sciences sociales, espèrent y retrouver des réponses précises alors que l'avancée de ces sciences ne fait que révéler l'étendue d'un abîme infini d'ignorance.'

[50] Clayton Gillette and James Krier, 'Risk, Courts and Agencies' (1990) 138 U Pa LR 1027, 1090.

[51] Jeffrey Rachlinksi and Cynthia Farina, 'Cognitive Psychology and Optimal Government Design' (2002) 87 Cornell LR 549, 579: '[Experts] are apt to be overconfident in their decision-making. Experts fail to look beyond the factors that their training and experience predispose them to consider; they tend not to test thoroughly their assumptions. Experts are right more often than lay persons, but not as often as they think.'

[52] Downs, *Inside Bureaucracy*, above n. 19. In the particular context of risk assessment in the sphere of national security, David Feldman has offered an important perspective. 'Human Rights, Terrorism and Risk: The Roles of Politicians and Judges' [2006] PL 364, 379.

[53] Herbert Simon, *Administrative Behaviour: A Study of Decision-making Processes in Administrative Organisation*, 4th edn (New York: Free Press, 1997), pp. 93–7. Humans are limited in their decision-making by cognitive and physical limitations, personal values which may diverge from those of the organisation and the absence of full knowledge and information.

[54] Sushil Bikhchandani, David Hirshleifer and Ivo Welch, 'Learning from the Behaviour of Others: Conformity, Fads, and Informational Cascades' (1998) 12(3) *Journal of Economic Perspectives* 151. Humans follow the decisions of others rather than trusting the (sometimes limited) information that is immediately available.

[55] Amos Tversky and Daniel Kahneman, 'Availability: A Heuristic for Judging Frequency and Probability' (1973) 5 *Cognitive Psychology* 207. Humans estimate the likelihood of future events based on the salience of past events rather than the probability of the events recurring.

[56] Kip Viscusi and Richard Zeckhauser, 'Recollection Bias and the Combat of Terrorism' (2005) 34 *Journal of Legal Studies* 27. Once events have occurred, humans tend to think that the events were more likely *ex ante* than was actually the case.

[57] Marver Bernstein, *Regulating Business by Independent Commission* (Princeton: Princeton University Press, 1955), pp. 157–60. A phenomenon whereby government entities come to favour the interests of entities in a regulated industry, often for the innocent reason that their success is equated with ensuring success in the regulated industry.

groupthink,[58] regulatory 'arteriosclerosis',[59] group polarisation[60] and various structural defects.[61]

Admittedly, clever institutional design can mitigate the effects of bounded rationality and cognitive biases:

> Experts have two opportunities for developing such decision-making competence that are typically unavailable to lay decision-makers: experience and training. By repeatedly making the same types of decisions, experts encounter the same problems and often (although not always) obtain useful feedback on their mistakes. Experience accompanied by feedback allows experts to identify situations in which they are using inappropriate heuristics or are trapped by misleading *schema* ... Even without feedback, experienced decision-makers acquire the ability to see commonalities across problems and to recognise new relationships between the characteristics of a problem and a sensible choice.[62]

Nevertheless, even though judges and courts also suffer from cognitive defects, and often lack expertise relative to expert delegated decision-makers, the prevalence of bounded rationality and cognitive defects in delegated decision-makers' decision-making processes, may yet allow judges to perform a valuable checking role.

Many of these problems were noticed by Harold Laski in the early 1930s. In a colourful essay, Laski suggested that the expert: 'sacrifices the insight of common sense to intensity of experience',[63] 'dislikes the appearance of novel views',[64] 'too often ... fails to see his results in their

[58] Irving Janis, *Groupthink: Psychological Studies of Policy Decisions and Fiascos*, 2nd edn (Boston: Houghton Mifflin, 1982), p. 9: 'a mode of thinking that people engage in when they are deeply involved in a cohesive in-group, when the members' strivings for unanimity override their motivation to realistically appraise alternative courses of action'.

[59] Louis Jaffe, *Judicial Control of Administrative Action* (Boston: Little Brown, 1965), p. 12: 'When the evil which gives rise to a reform has been partially alleviated, the initial dynamism [of the delegated decision-maker] may be dispersed.'

[60] Serge Moscovici and Marisa Zavalloni, 'The Group as a Polariser of Attitudes' (1969) 12(2) *Journal of Personality and Social Psychology* 125; Cass Sunstein, 'Group Judgments, Statistical Means, Deliberation and Information Markets' (2005) 80 NYU LR 962. A phenomenon whereby group judgments become more extreme than the judgments of individuals in a group if the individuals' initial judgments all tilted in a similar direction.

[61] Downs, *Inside Bureaucracy*, above n. 19.

[62] Rachlinksi and Farina, 'Cognitive Psychology' above n. 51, p. 559. They also emphasise the benefits of accountability to outside bodies. *Ibid.*, p. 588.

[63] 'The Limitations of the Expert' (1931) 162 *Harper's Monthly Magazine* 101. See also Martin Shapiro, 'Administrative Law Unbounded: Reflections on Government and Governance' (2001) 8 Indiana Journal of Global Legal Studies 369, 373–4.

[64] Laski, 'Limitations', above n. 63, p. 5.

proper perspective',[65] has a 'caste-spirit'[66] and 'simply by reason of his immersion in a routine tends to lack flexibility of mind once he approaches the margins of his special theme'.[67] As a result:

> He is incapable of rapid adaptation to novel situations. He unduly discounts experience which does not tally with his own. He is hostile to views which are not set out in terms he has been accustomed to handle ... Specialism seems to breed a horror of unwonted experiment, a weakness in achieving adaptability, both of which make the expert of dubious value when he is in supreme command of a situation.[68]

More damagingly, the expert 'rarely understands the plain man'[69] and only 'remains expert upon the condition that he does not seek to coordinate his specialism with the total sum of human knowledge'.[70] Some of Laski's criticisms are hyperbolic, and he should not be taken as disparaging the importance of expertise rather than the veneration of experts.[71] Traces of hyperbole should not be allowed to obscure his key point, which is that experts should be 'on tap, not on top'.[72] Expertise cannot solve all problems.[73]

Accordingly, permitting expertise to be the sole rationale for the delegation of power, or for curial deference, would give rise to difficulties. Hence the value of my reliance on legislative intent. Where a proper consideration of the relevant statutory provisions suggests that the practical justifications influenced the legislature's decision to delegate power to the delegated decision-maker in question, in preference to a court, the reviewing court should take expertise into account in determining the appropriate degree of curial deference. Courts should remain alive to the possible shortcomings of expertise, but where a proper consideration of the relevant statutory provisions indicates that they

65 *Ibid.*, p. 6.

66 *Ibid.*, p. 6. That is, '[t]here is ... no expert group which does not tend to deny that truth may possibly be found outside the boundary of its private Pyrenees'.

67 *Ibid.*, p. 6. 68 *Ibid.*, pp. 6–7. 69 *Ibid.*, p. 7. 70 *Ibid.* p. 8.

71 He argues that his advice may not be heeded because the expert 'is accustomed to a veneration not very different from that of the priest in primitive societies'. *Ibid.*, p. 14.

72 Bernstein, *Regulating Business*, above n. 57, p. 120. See similarly Henry Richardson, *Democratic Autonomy: Public Reasoning about the Ends of Policy* (Oxford: Oxford University Press, 2002), p. 225.

73 See also Brian Foley, *Deference and the Presumption of Constitutionality* (Dublin: Institute of Public Administration, 2008), pp. 264–7; Louis Jaffe, 'The Illusion of Ideal Administration' (1973) 86 Harv LR 1183; Jerry Mashaw, *Due Process in the Administrative State* (New Haven: Yale University Press, 1985), p. 18; Cass Sunstein, 'Factions, Self-Interest and the Administrative Procedure Act: Four Lessons Since 1946' (1986) 72 Va LR 271, 281.

should do so, they can be comfortable in giving weight to expertise (subject to the reservations I express in the next subsection).

3.2.4.2 Difficulties in ascertaining expertise

In *Pushpanathan* v. *Canada (Citizenship and Immigration)*,[74] Bastarache J held that evaluating the expertise of a delegated decision-maker requires a court to take three steps: 'the court must characterise the expertise of the tribunal in question; it must consider its own expertise relative to that of the tribunal; and it must identify the nature of the specific issue before the administrative decision-maker relative to this expertise'.[75] A close analysis of the characteristics of the delegated decision-maker will be necessary. A reviewing court must examine 'the board whose decision is impugned, including whether it possesses a developed jurisprudence, how its members are selected, how they participate in decision-making, and experience or context which gives them special advantages or insights'.[76]

Ascertaining expertise will not always be straightforward, but the question of actual expertise 'cannot be avoided indefinitely'.[77] Rothstein J's recent argument that '[t]he legislatures that create administrative decision-makers are better able to consider the relative qualifications, specialisation and day-to-day workings of tribunals, boards and other decision-makers which they themselves have constituted'[78] carries some force, but a court which appreciates the relationship between expertise and legislative intent will have regard only to the relevant statutory provisions and need not engage in a free-ranging inquiry into the expertise of the delegated decision-maker. The inquiry I am advocating requires a reviewing court to consider whether the 'relative qualifications, specialisation and day-to-day workings' of delegated decision-makers are provided for in the statute. If they are provided for, then curial deference may be accorded on the basis of the delegated decision-maker's expertise. No detailed parsing of 'the *curricula vitarum* of the deciding members of the tribunal under review' is necessary.[79]

[74] *Pushpanathan*, above n. 36. [75] *Ibid.*, p. 1007.

[76] *Canadian Broadcasting Corporation*, above n. 11, p. 210, per McLachlin J.

[77] MacLauchlan, 'Formalism', above n. 25, p. 380.

[78] *Canada (Citizenship and Immigration)* v. *Khosa* [2009] SCC 12; [2009] 1 SCR 339 at 396–7.

[79] David Mullan, 'Establishing the Standard of Review: The Struggle for Complexity?' (2004) 17 CJALP 59, 71. See also Ann Chaplin, 'Who is Best Suited to Decide? The Recent Trend in Standards of Judicial Review' (1994) 26 Ottawa LR 321, 354–5; Julius Grey, 'Standards of Judicial Review: Is it Time to Change our Analysis?' (2004) 45 Cahiers de Droit 541, 546–51.

A possible difficulty is whether the expertise of the delegated decision-maker was actually applied to the decision under review.[80] Sometimes, presumably, expertise will not have been exercised: 'the assumption that expertness is relevant can, if mechanically invoked, become ludicrous'.[81] Similarly, doubt might be cast on a delegated decision-maker's purported accrual of expertise, or the efficacy of its internal controls and training programmes; or the suggestion may be made that certain decisions are beyond the reach even of the expertise of the would-be experts.[82] After all, '[i]t is one thing to accept the need to defer to an opinion which can be seen to be the product of reasoned consideration based on policy; it is quite another thing to be required to accept, without question, an opinion for which no reason of policy is advanced'.[83] But as Lorne Sossin has suggested, recognising this difficulty creates a dilemma: on the one hand, whether expertise was utilised in a particular case 'sheds little light on legislative intent', but on the other hand, a failure to consider whether expertise was utilised in a particular case risks inviting a 'very rigid and formalistic analysis'.[84]

The best response to the dilemma is to say that where expertise is not present, or not used, curial deference is not appropriate: the legislature has presumably delegated power on the understanding that expertise will be applied, not just because the delegated decision-maker is, or will become, expert. Although it might, strictly speaking, be necessary to conduct probing examinations of delegated decision-makers in order to ensure that expertise was actually applied, the time and cost of such examinations is unlikely to be justified by the few cases in which it is necessary to conduct them to ascertain that expertise was not actually applied.[85] A sense of how probing, and costly, such examinations would

80 See *Smith* v. *Alliance Pipeline* [2011] SCC 7, [2011] 1 SCR 160 at 197–8, per Deschamps J, concurring.

81 Jaffe, *Judicial Control of Administrative Action*, above n. 59, p. 577.

82 See e.g. Geneviève Cartier, 'Le Principe de précaution et la déférence judiciaire en droit administratif' (2002) 43 Cahiers de Droit 79.

83 *Wilson* v. *First County Trust* [2001] EWCA Civ 633; [2001] 3 WLR 42 at 56.

84 'Empty Ritual, Mechanical Exercise or the Discipline of Difference? Revisiting the Standard of Review in Administrative Law' (2003) 27 Advocates' Quarterly 478, 493. Cf. H. Wade MacLauchlan, 'Transforming Administrative Law: The Didactic Role of the Supreme Court of Canada' (2001) 80 Can BR 281, 290–4.

85 Robert Chesney, 'National Security Fact Deference' (2009) 95 *Va LR* 1361, 1419 has suggested, in the context of national security, that the delegated decision-maker be required to furnish a statement attesting to its application of expertise. A requirement of such a statement seems superfluous in light of the approached I urge in the text. Moreover, a requirement would be at risk if introduced of being fulfilled in a formulaic

be can be gained by reference to the range of sources cited in section 3.2.4.1 above in respect of shortcomings in expertise. For the most part, reviewing courts should readily be able to ascertain from the record whether expertise was applied or not. Opposing counsel will doubtless have an incentive to uncover, through discovery if necessary, and point out to the court instances in which expertise has not actually been applied. Lawyers might, indeed, legitimately rely on some of the shortcomings outlined above.

A more troubling objection might be based on the risk that delegated decision-makers will be appointed on the basis of something other than their expertise: perhaps for reasons of political patronage.[86] I have to concede that I am not able to offer a cure for this particular disease. Allowing courts to criticise the credentials of individuals appointed by the political branches – save perhaps in extreme cases, where the individuals appointed clearly do not meet the statutory criteria and litigation is initiated on that basis – would be extremely time-consuming, invite judicial value judgements and risk drawing judges into public controversy. That a process is time-consuming, involves judicial value judgements or could cause controversy does not dictate that the process should not be employed, but problems of political patronage would probably be better addressed by the political branches of government, rather than by the judiciary.

Finally, admitting that the length of time a delegated decision-maker has been rendering decisions in a particular area is relevant to ascertaining the appropriate degree of curial deference introduces an element of vagueness into the analysis. Although one might accept that a venerable, well-established delegated decision-maker is worthy of a significant degree of respect, could a reviewing court hold that a delegated decision-maker lacked expertise because it was newly created? In the case of a delegated decision-maker constituted by experts, the difficulty would not arise. But even in the case of a delegated decision-maker not constituted by experts, by the time the first decisions are rendered, the delegated decision-maker will have gained some exposure to the area. It may be impossible to identify a particular point in time at which a delegated decision-maker *became* expert. But similar indeterminacy exists in many

manner, for example, by a *pro forma* statement, which would not obviate the need for some investigation by the reviewing court of the delegated decision-maker's *bona fides*. Unless one is overwhelmingly confident about the *bona fides* of all delegated decision-makers, no such statement should obviate the need for some investigation.

86 See Jaffe, *Judicial Control of Administrative Action*, above n. 59, p. 25.

areas of the law.[87] Crucially, indeterminacy is not so pervasive here as to make it impossible to say that a particular delegated decision-maker has accrued, or not accrued, expertise. Even if the exact point at which a delegated decision-maker became expert by the accrual of expertise over time is indeterminate, it does not follow that expertise is indeterminate, because it will be possible to identify whether or not delegated decision-makers have or have not accrued expertise.

3.3 Complexity

Some areas of decision-making are so complex that they may be better suited to resolution by delegated decision-makers than by courts or legislature.[88] A mere description of the 'really responsive regulation'[89] which has recently been proposed ought to demonstrate how complex delegated decision-making can be:

> What 'really responsive regulation' sets out to do is to offer a framework for regulation which responds to firms' attitudinal settings, recognises the significance of the institutional environment (or 'regulatory character'), which develops an awareness of the differential nature of the logics of different regulatory tools and strategies, which is performance sensitive, and which responds to change.[90]

As the advocates of really responsive regulation dryly conclude, '[a]ll are fairly formidable tasks'.[91] Choosing between punishment and persuasion and correctly calibrating the number and level of available penalties and rewards are inherently complex tasks,[92] best undertaken by a body which works closely with the bodies regulated. In fact, it may only be possible for an expert delegated decision-maker to amass the relevant information and develop the close contacts necessary to effectively regulate a particular industry, or firm or group of firms within an industry.[93]

Generally speaking, it is the expertise of delegated decision-makers that gives them the advantage over courts and legislatures in respect of

[87] See generally Matthew Kramer, *Objectivity and the Rule of Law* (Cambridge: Cambridge University Press, 2007).

[88] See e.g. Bernstein, *Regulating Business*, above n. 57, p. 156.

[89] Robert Baldwin and Julia Black, 'Really Responsive Regulation' (2008) 71 MLR 59.

[90] *Ibid.*, pp. 75–6. [91] *Ibid.*, p. 76.

[92] Ian Ayres and John Braithwaite, *Responsive Regulation: Transcending the Deregulation Debate* (Oxford: Oxford University Press, 1992), p. 50.

[93] See also Cane, *Administrative Tribunals*, above n. 8, pp. 97–8.

decision-making in complex areas. The Canadian *Southam* case[94] again provides a good example:

> The particular dispute in this case concerns the definition of the relevant product market – a matter that falls squarely within the area of the Tribunal's economic or commercial expertise. Undeniably, the determination of cross-elasticity of demand, which is in theory the truest *indicium* of the dimensions of a product market, requires some economic or statistical skill. But even an assessment of indirect evidence of substitutability, such as evidence that two kinds of products are functionally interchangeable, needs a variety of discernment that has more to do with business experience than with legal training. Someone with experience in business will be better able to predict likely consumer behaviour than a judge will be. What is more, indirect evidence is useful only as a surrogate for cross-elasticity of demand, so that what is required in the end is an assessment of the *economic* significance of the evidence; and to this task an economist is almost by definition better suited than is a judge.[95]

But it may also be the case – especially where a problem is polycentric in nature – that the procedural flexibility of delegated decision-makers will make them better-placed to resolve complex problems. Where a problem is complex, the institutional shortcomings of courts will be keenly felt:

> Problems may flow from the fact that the courts are adversarial, participation of parties is limited, and the law of evidence may operate to constrain what is put before the court for consideration. Since the courts are not inquisitorial, they are largely dependent on the parties as to what is put before them by way of evidence and argument. The approach to evidence and argument has traditionally been conservative, with, for example, relatively little use of empirical evidence. The courts will often not have access to the breadth and depth of evidence, and spectrum of points of view, that are potentially available to the executive and legislature when they are involved in public decision-making. The executive and the legislature have the potential to listen to a wider range of people, and to bring a greater degree of direction and financial resource to the acquisition of thorough research and commentary that in many circumstances will allow better informed decision-making than can be provided by the courts.[96]

94 *Southam*, above n. 1

95 *Ibid.*, p. 774, per Iacobucci J. Emphasis original. See also *Pauley* v. *Bethenergy Mines* (1991) 501 US 680 at 697–8.

96 Bruce Harris, 'Judicial Review, Justiciability and the Prerogative of Mercy' (2003) 62 CLJ 631, 641. See also Roger Cramton, 'A Comment on Trial-Type Hearings in Nuclear Power Plant Siting' (1972) 58 Va LR 585, 589–90; Eric Posner and Adrian Vermeule,

By contrast, the procedural flexibility of delegated decision-makers can give them an advantage in addressing complex problems.[97]

It is an open question as to whether these limitations of the adjudicative process ought to be countered by reform,[98] but unless or until they are, they are relevant in determining the appropriate balance between courts and delegated decision-makers. Relative to legislatures the procedural flexibility of delegated decision-makers is also an advantage:

> [Apart from some limited matters] the full range of rule-making activity of federal administrative agencies represents work of a type which Congress could do if it had the time and deemed it wise to do it. Independently of the comparative advantages of administrative action, various inherent limitations upon its own functioning militate in these cases against action by Congress itself. The total time available is the most obvious. Time spent on details must be at the sacrifice of time spent on matters of broad public policy. Lack of specialised information is another; lack of a staff or a procedure adapted to acquiring it is a third. The complexity of the problems which have to be determined, even after basic policy has been settled, is the governing consideration … Even if Congress had the time and facilities to work out details, there would be constant danger of harmful rigidity if the result were crystallised in the form of a statute.[99]

It is clear, then, that complexity will often provide a good reason to delegate power to a body other than a court. Combined with expertise, the delegation of power becomes an attractive legislative means of resolving problems in an efficient manner. I turn now to address the two key contributors to complexity: polycentricity and uncertainty. My focus on these two should not be taken to exclude the importance of complexity *tout court*, where problems are highly technical, but in such situations the need to accord curial deference to expert delegated decision-makers will be very clear indeed. Polycentricity and uncertainty, one might say, are more complex.

Terror in the Balance: Security, Liberty and the Courts (Oxford: Oxford University Press, 2007), p. 31.

97 See e.g. Peter Hogg, 'The Jurisdictional Fact Doctrine in the Supreme Court of Canada: *Bell* v. *Ontario Human Rights Commission*' (1971) 9 Osgoode Hall LJ 204, 208.

98 See e.g. Abram Chayes, 'The Role of the Judge in Public Law Litigation' (1976) 89 Harv LR 1281; J. A. G. Griffith, 'Judicial Decision-making in Public Law' [1985] PL 564; J. W. F. Allison, *A Continental Distinction in the Common Law*, rev. edn (Oxford: Oxford University Press, 2000), p. 206.

99 *Final Report of the Attorney General's Committee on Administrative Procedure* (Washington DC: United States Government Printing Office, 1941) 14. See also *Smiley* v. *Citibank (South Dakota)* (1996) 517 US 735 at 740.

3.3.1 Polycentricity

Lon Fuller suggested that adjudication was inapt to resolve polycentric problems, which 'cannot be resolved independently and sequentially; they are, rather, interdependent and a choice from one set of alternatives has implications for preferences within other sets of alternatives. The decision-maker must take into account the whole network before she can reach a single decision.'[100] These often arise in administrative law: 'the solution of polycentric problems by adjudication has most often been attempted ... in the field of administrative law'.[101] From the point of view of judicial review of such decisions, the risk is that a court decision could pull a strand of a 'spider web' of interwoven policies, shifting tensions from one part of the web to another and, *in extremis*, possibly causing it to unravel:[102] '[Fuller's] analysis ... is also relevant to the adjudicative court or tribunal which must resolve the disputes subject to its jurisdiction. It shows that an adjudicator, informed only by the litigating parties, is ill-equipped to determine the complex repercussions of a proposed decision.'[103] Note that it is not the number of interests involved that make a question polycentric, but the fact that they interlock.

A good example of polycentricity and the possible dangers of judicial intervention where a careful balance has been struck by a delegated decision-maker can be found in White J's dissent from the majority of the Supreme Court of the United States in *Sullivan* v. *Zebley*:[104]

> The Social Security Administration processes over 100,000 child-disability claims a year. The agency has a finite amount of funds with which to work. By requiring ... unspecified individualised determinations in cases where an applicant fails to satisfy the agency that he is otherwise disabled, the majority imposes costs on the agency that surely will detract from the pool of benefits available to the unfortunate children that Congress has sought to protect through the Supplemental Security Income Programme.[105]

In the Canadian pragmatic and functional analysis, polycentricity has been treated as relevant to the inquiry into the purpose of the legislation as a whole and of the relevant statutory provision. Considerations of polycentricity may favour according a high degree of curial deference:

100 Anthony Ogus, *Regulation: Legal Form and Economic Theory* (Oxford: Clarendon, 1994), p. 117.
101 'The Forms and Limits of Adjudication' (1978) 92 Harv LR 353, 400.
102 *Ibid.*, p. 395. 103 Allison, *Continental Distinction*, above n. 98, p. 194.
104 (1990) 493 US 521. 105 *Ibid.*, p. 548.

> While judicial procedure is premised on a bi-polar opposition of parties, interests, and factual discovery, some problems require the consideration of numerous interests simultaneously, and the promulgation of solutions which concurrently balance benefits and costs for many different parties. Where an administrative structure more closely resembles this model, courts will exercise restraint.[106]

The problem of polycentricity is often exacerbated by problems of incommensurability: a delegated decision-maker may have to weigh up competing interests and values that are difficult to measure, let alone compare.[107] But polycentricity is not synonymous with complexity. Although polycentricity is an important aspect of complexity, 'something can be complex without being polycentric. Scientific questions arising in court can be enormously complex without being polycentric in any way.'[108]

Jeff King has recently argued that too much emphasis is placed on polycentricity: 'The law abounds with … examples of courts adjudicating polycentric issues.'[109] It is true to say the problems of polycentricity are not confined to the area of judicial review. However, because King's goal is different from mine,[110] he draws his examples from fields which are not relevant to my inquiry. In the law of tort and contract law, certainly, no delegated decision-maker is present to which curial deference can be accorded.[111] As to the law of human rights, I will argue below that curial deference is of less importance.[112] And as to the law of taxation, which is the main subject of King's recent article, I take the view that more, not less, curial deference should be accorded by reviewing courts to the decisions of the taxation authorities; I am one of those who 'may view the existence of polycentricity in tax cases as a reason for curtailing judicial activity in those cases too', rebuttal of whose arguments is

[106] *Pushpanathan*, above n. 36, p. 1009, per Bastarache J. See also *R (Corner House Research and Campaign Against Arms Trade)* v. *Director of the Serious Fraud Office* [2008] UKHL 60; [2009] AC 756 at 841, per Lord Bingham of Cornhill.

[107] But see Matthew Adler and Eric Posner, *New Foundations of Cost-Benefit Analysis* (Cambridge, MA: Harvard University Press, 2006).

[108] Jeff King, 'The Pervasiveness of Polycentricity' [2008] PL 101, 103.

[109] *Ibid.*, p. 111.

[110] He focuses on judicial review of resource allocation generally. See also 'The Justiciability of Resource Allocation' (2007) 70 MLR 197.

[111] See Cynthia Farina, 'Statutory Interpretation and the Balance of Power in the Administrative State' (1989) 89 Colum LR 452, 464. I leave aside the question of the liability of state bodies in tort and contract.

[112] See below Ch. 5.

'beyond the scope and interest of [King's] article'.[113] Moreover, here I simply wish to make the modest claim that courts are not the optimal forums for the resolution of polycentric problems, a consideration which may have influenced the legislative decision to delegate power to a body other than a court, a claim not squarely addressed by King.

It is also true that '[w]ithout a protractor to determine differences of degree, the court cannot be certain where to draw the line between disputes that vary in the significance of their polycentricity',[114] but as I have emphasised, the practical justifications for curial deference need not be measurable by a precise mathematical formula. That a court is capable only of estimating whether a problem is sufficiently complex to justify according curial deference need not prevent a court from evaluating the complexity of a problem in general terms.

3.3.2 *Uncertainty*

Another factor which contributes to complexity, particularly in the fields of national security and economic policy, is uncertainty.[115] Often in sensitive areas decision-makers must act without being certain of the likely consequences of their actions, because the set of variables which determines the future may not be fully known or understood. The lack of information about and the difficulty of assessing the probability of future actions of entities such as financial markets makes their regulation inherently complex. As Thomas Poole has commented, in the national security context: 'The twin issues of (exceptional) risk and limited (often secret) knowledge may be said to represent ... *conditions of uncertainty*, in which courts in terrorist cases must operate.'[116]

Uncertainty was treated as relevant by the House of Lords to calibrating the standard of review in *R* v. *Secretary of State for the Home Department, ex p. Launder*,[117] which concerned the reasonableness of the minister's decision to extradite the applicant to Hong Kong, which by the time of the trial was to have come under Chinese control. Lord Hope of Craighead held that the minister had to consider not only the

[113] King, 'Pervasiveness', above n. 108, p. 112.
[114] Allison, *Continental Distinction*, above n. 98, p. 195.
[115] Uncertainty and polycentricity are themselves related, in that uncertainty can contribute to polycentricity, and polycentricity can contribute to uncertainty.
[116] 'Courts and Conditions of Uncertainty in "Times of Crisis"' [2008] PL 234, 247. Emphasis original.
[117] [1997] 3 All ER 961.

'framework of law' put in place to govern the hand-over but also the 'hearts and minds' of the officials who would be in charge of the system after the hand-over. As a result, the decision required 'the exercise of judgment of a kind which lies beyond the expertise of the court'.[118]

In a similar vein is *Reid* v. *Secretary of State for Scotland*,[119] which was concerned with whether a psychopath (who had been convicted of murder) could lawfully be detained in a mental hospital, despite a change in general medical opinion about the treatability of his condition, or whether he would have to be discharged, entirely or subject to conditions. One of the questions for resolution was whether the applicant was benefiting from 'medical treatment'. The sheriff who was delegated the power to take this decision took the view that the applicant was getting some benefit. Prior to reaching his conclusion the sheriff had heard conflicting evidence from medical experts. The House of Lords was reluctant to interfere with the sheriff's conclusion: 'Where one only has an incomplete record of the evidence and the evidence is that of highly qualified experts dealing with the delicate matter of mental disorder, great caution ought to be taken in revisiting the substance of the decision which the sheriff reached.'[120]

Delegated decision-makers will generally have a better, although often imperfect, grasp of the problems created by uncertainty than will courts, because of their relative expertise and the procedural informality with which they can reach and revise decisions. This is not to say that courts may not play a valuable role, particularly in highlighting obvious flaws in methodology,[121] but it is to say that uncertainty counsels against close judicial scrutiny. Judicial oversight should not be prevented, let alone nullified, but judges have limitations relative to other decision-makers.

A practical problem relating to uncertainty is the availability of evidence. Obtaining evidence may be easier for a delegated decision-maker, operating under less judicialised procedures than a court.[122] In addition, an argument will often be made that evidence cannot be put before the court because of concerns that doing so might well compromise vital intelligence sources or reveal privileged information:[123]

[118] *Ibid.*, p. 979. [119] [1999] 2 AC 512. [120] *Ibid.*, p. 542, per Lord Clyde.

[121] See e.g. *Alton* v. *Secretary of State for the Home Department* [2008] EWCA Civ 443; [2008] 1 WLR 2341; *A* v. *Her Majesty's Treasury* [2008] EWCA Civ 1187; [2009] 3 WLR 25.

[122] Cane, *Administrative Tribunals*, above n. 8, pp. 97–8.

[123] Sometimes the problem will be that the evidence is simply inaccessible, perhaps because it is held by different departments. The approach I advocate in the text would be equally applicable to cases in which such a problem arises.

> If a court, in carrying out its reviewing role, does not have access to all the information on which the primary decision was based, this fact alone will lead it to pay more deference to the primary decision-maker, because it will be less confident that it could arrive at a better decision than the primary decision-maker.[124]

Indeed, in such cases:

> courts have no other choice but to be deferential … and to give the elected branches of government the benefit of any doubts they may have, either about the executive decision itself or the intelligence on which it is based … [I]t is very difficult for the courts to challenge executive decisions on a sure footing when they are not in possession of the information leading to the decision.[125]

If a reviewing court does not have the information, it simply cannot act upon it and must exclude it from its decision-making process. Whether a state of affairs in which a court may be restricted from considering all the evidence relevant to a case is desirable or not is a separate question. These difficulties, which may be mitigated by the development of a 'duty of candour',[126] will arise with or without a doctrine of curial deference, because it is very difficult to judge the bona fides of government agencies when they claim that evidence cannot be made available by reason of its sensitivity. Perhaps a national security court, *in camera* hearings, the use of special advocates or oversight by an independent commissioner could alleviate some of the difficulties raised by governmental reticence to release certain information. Indeed, such specialised bodies (perhaps including specialised courts) could amass such a great deal of knowledge and experience of their assigned areas as to reduce the degree of curial deference that ought to be accorded by them to delegated decision-makers.[127] But where the decisions of specialised bodies fall to be reviewed, restriction of judicial access to relevant information might plausibly be taken to suggest a legislative intent to reduce judicial oversight of the relevant delegated decision-makers. The conclusion that keeping information from a judicial forum increases the appropriate

124 Aileen Kavanagh, 'Judging the Judges under the Human Rights Act' [2009] PL 287, 301.

125 Aileen Kavanagh, 'Deference or Defiance? The Limits of the Judicial Role in Constitutional Adjudication' in Grant Huscroft (ed.), *Expounding the Constitution: Essays in Constitutional Theory* (Cambridge: Cambridge University Press, 2008), p. 184, p. 208. See similarly Adam Tomkins, 'The Role of the Courts in the Political Constitution' (2010) 60 UTLJ 1, 15.

126 See e.g. *Marshall* v. *Deputy Governor of Bermuda* [2010] UKPC 9 at [27–41].

127 See also Feldman, 'Human Rights', above n. 52, 380–2.

degree of curial deference may be unpalatable, but it seems to follow from the judicial obligation to give effect to legislative intent.

3.3.3 *Legislative intent*

Complex problems might not be apt for legislative or judicial resolution. The more complex a particular problem is, the more pronounced the difficulties of achieving legislative clarity and consensus will be, the more willing the legislature will probably be to have a delegated decision-maker resolve the problem and the less willing the legislature will probably be to delegate the resolution of the problem to a court. Whether or not a problem is complex will be evident from the statute, although by reference to a background understanding of complexity. But it is not simply the delegation of the power to resolve a complex problem that will suggest that complexity influenced the legislative decision to delegate. Only where a statute delegates the resolution of a complex problem to an expert delegated decision-maker, or provides for procedural flexibility and responsiveness over time to the resolution of a technical, uncertain or polycentric problem, can it plausibly be inferred that complexity influenced the decision to delegate power to a body other than a court.

Recognition of complexity can thus sometimes be inferred from the legislature's decision to vest specialised powers and authority in a delegated decision-maker:

> The *legislator has clearly opted for a flexible, proactive mechanism* which provides optimum protection for the public and facilitation of the use of legal means and regulated pressure tactics to resolve disputes. The effectiveness of this system depends upon the Council's power to make decisions and orders which are sensitive to the circumstances involved and reflective of the mechanisms established in the Code.[128]

As Stevens J commented in *Massachusetts* v. *Environmental Protection Agency*:[129]

> While the Congresses that drafted [the legislation] might not have appreciated the possibility that burning fossil fuels could lead to global warming, they did understand that without regulatory flexibility, changing circumstances and scientific developments would soon render the [legislation]

[128] *Canadian Union of Public Employees, Local 301* v. *Montreal (City)* [1997] 1 SCR 793 at 823, per L'Heureux-Dubé J. Emphasis added.

[129] (2007) 549 US 497.

> obsolete. *The broad language of [the statute] reflects an intentional effort to confer the flexibility necessary to forestall such obsolescence.*[130]

In *Ivanhoe* v. *United Food and Commercial Workers, Local 500*,[131] Arbour J thought:

> [It is] clear that the purpose of the [Labour] Code is to establish a scheme that will 'promote collective bargaining as a better means of guaranteeing industrial peace and of establishing equitable relations between employer and employees'. The *legislature believed that to attain that objective*, a specialised tribunal that would allow for the speedy and final resolution of disputes was needed.[132]

Expertise was also relevant here, but the identification of a link between complexity and legislative intent seems clear.

Reviewing the reasonableness of the minister's decision in *R* v. *Secretary of State for the Home Department, ex p. Launder*[133] required the House of Lords to assess a complex decision: 'whether it is unjust or oppressive to order the respondent's return to Hong Kong must in the end depend on whether [China] can be trusted in implementation of its treaty obligations to respect his fundamental human rights, allow him a fair trial and leave it to the courts, if he is convicted, to determine the appropriate punishment'.[134] In commenting on the difficult nature of the decision taken by the minister, Lord Hope of Craighead identified the link between legislative intent and complexity:

> [The] decision has had to be taken amidst an atmosphere of mistrust and suspicion which a court is in no position to penetrate. The visible part is the framework of law … That part can be explained and analysed. The invisible part is about the hearts and minds of those who will be responsible for the administration of justice in Hong Kong after the hand-over. This is not capable of analysis. It depends, in the end, on the exercise of judgment of a kind which lies beyond the expertise of the court. *That, no doubt, is why the decision whether or not to grant the warrant has been entrusted to the Secretary of State by Parliament.*[135]

Critically, the decision was held to have been delegated to the minister *because* of the expertise of the minister and the complexity of the decision.[136]

[130] *Ibid.*, p. 532. Emphasis added. [131] *Ivanhoe*, above n. 27.
[132] *Ibid.*, p. 591. Emphasis added. Internal citation omitted.
[133] *Launder*, above n. 117. [134] *Ibid.*, p. 979. [135] *Ibid.*, p. 979. Emphasis added.
[136] An undertone of democratic legitimacy (see below 3.4) may also be perceived: it may be more acceptable for a minister than for a judge to take a decision of this nature, something of which the legislature is likely to be aware.

The close relationship between expertise and complexity, and indeed legislative intent, is neatly encapsulated in the following passage from an opinion authored for the Supreme Court of the United States by Breyer J: 'the statute's complexity, the vast number of claims that it engenders, and *the consequent need for agency expertise and administrative experience* lead us to read the statute as delegating to the agency considerable authority to fill in, through interpretation, matters of detail related to its administration'.[137] As McLachlin CJ put it in *Dr Q* v. *College of Physicians and Surgeons of British Columbia*:[138]

> Reviewing courts should also consider the breadth, specialisation, and technical or scientific nature of the issues that the legislation asks the administrative tribunal to consider. In this respect, the principles animating the factors of relative expertise and legislative purpose tend to overlap. A legislative purpose that deviates substantially from the normal role of the courts suggests that the legislature intended to leave the issue to the discretion of the administrative decision-maker and, therefore, militates in favour of greater deference.[139]

However, legislative intent is a double-edged sword. A proper consideration of the relevant statutory provisions may suggest that complexity is not relevant.[140]

3.3.4 Complexity and context

Complexity varies according to context: first, the types of questions addressed by different delegated decision-makers can be more or less complex; secondly, the types of questions addressed by a particular delegated decision-maker can be more or less complex; and, thirdly, as seen in the preceding subsections, delegated decision-makers may more often address complex issues than courts and legislature.

First, a government minister setting national security threat levels is wrestling with a more complex problem than a competition tribunal trying to decide what sort of order to make to remedy anti-competitive behaviour in a geographically limited area because, for the minister, the

137 *Barnhart* v. *Walton* (2002) 535 US 212 at 225. Emphasis added. See also *EI du Pont de Nemours* v. *Train* (1975) 430 US 112 at 135, n. 25, citing *American Meat Institute* v. *Environmental Protection Agency* (1975) 526 F 2d 442 at 450, n. 16.

138 [2003] SCC 19; [2003] 1 SCR 226.

139 *Ibid.* at pp. 240–1.

140 See e.g. *Harvard College*, above n. 41 at pp. 120–1, per Bastarache J.

optimal response requires developing a view of the likelihood of the occurrence of a range of future events, and the balancing of many different factors, some or all of which may be unknown or unknowable. Secondly, a competition tribunal could be faced with a complex question about the cross-elasticity of demand for a particular product, or a relatively more straightforward question about the observed effects of competition on competitors in a marketplace.

In any event, only where complexity is an aspect of the legislative intent to delegate power can it legitimately be considered a practical justification for curial deference. Although complexity is often a strong reason for judicial restraint, its importance should not be overemphasised. Not every invocation of national security, or economic policy, should lead to curial deference being accorded. Following my approach, complexity cannot be ritually invoked to justify according a high degree of curial deference. Complexity did not counsel, for example, that curial deference should be accorded by the Supreme Court of Canada to the Immigration and Refugee Board's determination whether an individual's act of drug trafficking was an act 'contrary to the purposes and principles of the United Nations': 'The context in which the adjudicative function takes place is not a "polycentric" one of give-and-take between different groups, but rather the vindication of a set of relatively static human rights, and ensuring that those who fall within the prescribed categories are protected.'[141]

It is surely correct to suggest that the importance of complexity can be overstated: 'Judges and lawyers are not troubled by complexity as such; they revel in it. Though much of law is about coping with complexity, about simplifying overly complex law, you cannot simplify intelligently if you cannot master complexity.'[142] Only where a link to legislative intent can plausibly be inferred from a proper consideration of the relevant statutory provisions should such invocations be of any effect: they only have merit where power has been exercised by an expert delegated decision-maker who has been vested with procedural flexibility and responsiveness by the legislature. Indeed, complexity is only one of the practical justifications for curial deference and the others must also be factored into the equation in determining the appropriate degree of curial deference to accord.

[141] *Pushpanathan*, above n. 36 at pp. 1018–19, per Bastarache J.

[142] Richard Posner, 'Legal Scholarship Today' (2002) 115 Harv LR 1314, 1322.

3.4 Democratic legitimacy

3.4.1 The paradigm cases of democratically legitimate delegated decision-makers

An advantage that some delegated decision-makers have relative to courts is democratic legitimacy. A delegated decision-maker who has been elected may render decisions that are more legitimate than those rendered by an unelected judge: 'the decision of a member of the government answerable to [the legislature], and who is himself a member of that body, on a matter properly his to decide, is emphatically entitled to deference in a democratic state'.[143] It seems plausible to infer that where decision-making power has been delegated to a member of the executive branch of government, rather than to a court, the delegation was made on the basis that the resulting decisions would be more likely to be legitimate:[144] 'In a democracy the greater claim to legitimacy by an elected politician compared to an unelected judge is simply a modern fact of life.'[145]

But on reflection, democratic legitimacy is less compelling as a practical justification for curial deference. To begin with, unlike the practical justifications of expertise, complexity and procedural legitimacy, it is not clear that the delegated decision-maker has an advantage, or 'edge',[146] relative to the legislature. The legislature is at least as democratically legitimate as any delegated decision-maker: 'Congress is directly elected by the people; agencies are at most indirectly accountable to the electorate through the President.'[147] In addition, if democratic legitimacy is

143 *Meadows* v. *Minister for Justice, Equality and Law Reform* [2010] IESC 3; [2010] 2 IR 701 at [200], per Hardiman J, dissenting.

144 Note that my paradigmatically democratically legitimate decision-maker is elected, rather than accountable to the legislature. As I discuss below, 3.4.4, accountability is too vague a notion to be of utility.

145 Murray Hunt, 'Against Bifurcation' in David Dyzenhaus, Murray Hunt and Grant Huscroft (eds.), *A Simple Common Lawyer: Essays in Honour of Michael Taggart* (Oxford: Hart, 2009), p. 99, p. 109.

146 Michael Herz, 'Deference Running Riot: Separating Interpretation and Lawmaking under *Chevron*' (1992) 6 Admin LJ 187, 189.

147 Thomas Merrill, 'Judicial Deference to Executive Precedent' (1992) 101 *Yale LJ* 969, 979. See also *R (Bancoult)* v. *Secretary of State for Foreign and Commonwealth Affairs (No. 2)* [2008] UKHL 61; [2009] AC 453 at 482, per Lord Hoffman: 'The principle of the sovereignty of Parliament as it has been developed by the courts over the past 350 years, is founded upon the unique authority Parliament derives from its representative character.'

claimed on the basis that an elected official has supervisory power over the delegated decision-maker, a strong claim to democratic legitimacy is difficult to establish.[148] Moreover, legislatures insistent on delegating power to take advantage of the democratic legitimacy of a delegated decision-maker could look to design populist or community-based institutions,[149] instead of empowering members of the political elite. Finally, unlike the practical justifications of expertise and complexity, the democratic legitimacy of a delegated decision-maker does not necessarily suggest that the delegated decision-maker is more likely than some other body to reach the best decision: 'In the modern state, the only "offices" for which no technical qualifications are required are those of ministers and presidents.'[150] Martin Shapiro has expressed the point in colourful terms:

> Imagine our outrage if, at the end of a court trial, the president of the United States called up the judge and told her how he wanted the case to come out. Let us suppose an agency has held a rule-making proceeding that involved hundreds of hours of testimony and thousands of pages of written submissions. It has listened at length to every interested group and heard the rebuttal of each group to the testimony of every other. It has compiled a thousand-page-long rule-making record. It has then composed a statement showing that it has acted synoptically to consider every significant issue and arrive at the best possible decision. Those who have been watching and participating in such a process are going to be equally outraged if, just before the agency publishes its final rule, the president calls to tell the agency what rule it should adopt.[151]

These sentiments were echoed by Binnie J in *Dunsmuir* v. *New Brunswick*:[152] 'Administrative decision-makers generally command respect more for their expertise than for their prominence in the administrative food chain.'[153] These factors may explain why democratic legitimacy is invoked much less often by courts determining the appropriate degree of curial deference to accord than are expertise and complexity.

[148] See below 3.4.4.

[149] See e.g. Gerald Frug, 'Administrative Democracy' (1990) 40 UTLJ 559, 567–73; Michael Dorf and Charles Sabel, 'A Constitution of Democratic Experimentalism' (1998) 98 Colum LR 267.

[150] Weber, *Theory*, above n. 17, p. 335.

[151] Shapiro, *Guardians*, above n. 49, p. 112. Shapiro's point is directed towards the effect of the judicialisation of administrative procedure, but it holds for present purposes.

[152] [2008] SCC 9; [2008] 1 SCR 190.

[153] *Ibid.*, p. 255.

Nevertheless, democratic legitimacy is of some utility: it suggests a reason for legislative decisions to delegate powers to delegated decision-makers who have been elected. This would explain why Binnie J suggested in *Mount Sinai Hospital Centre* v. *Quebec (Minister of Health and Social Services)*[154] that the 'highest standard of deference' was presumptively appropriate when reviewing exercises of discretion by ministers.[155]

In two House of Lords decisions regarding local government financing, democratic legitimacy bore on the question of the appropriate standard of review: first in *Nottinghamshire County Council* v. *Secretary of State for the Environment*[156] and subsequently in *R* v. *Secretary of State for the Environment, ex p. Hammersmith and Fulham London Borough Council.*[157] Common to both cases was a procedure which required the minister's decision as to certain matters of local government finance to be approved by resolution of the House of Commons before taking effect. In the *Nottinghamshire* case, the allegation of the applicant local authorities was that expenditure guidance issued by the minister was 'so disproportionately disadvantageous [to the applicants] when compared with its effect upon others' as to be 'a perversely unreasonable exercise of the power conferred by the statute'.[158] Lord Scarman adduced reasons for scrutinising the minister's decision less closely than would ordinarily be the case:

> We are in the field of public financial administration and we are being asked to review the exercise by the [minister] of an administrative discretion which inevitably requires a political judgment on his part and which cannot lead to action by him against a local authority unless that action is first approved by the House of Commons.[159]

Two factors emerge from the quoted passage as relevant to the setting of the appropriate standard of review: the 'political judgment' required of the delegated decision-maker and the fact that any decision before becoming effective must be 'approved by the House of Commons'. In addition, Lord Scarman noted how the present case raised 'in acute form the constitutional problem of the separation of powers' because 'Parliament has enacted that an executive power is not to be exercised save with the consent and approval of one of its Houses'.[160] As a result, Lord Scarman applied a lower standard of review than would have been normal.[161]

154 [2001] SCC 41; [2001] 2 SCR 281. 155 *Ibid.*, p. 316. 156 [1986] AC 240.
157 [1991] 1 AC 521. 158 *Nottinghamshire*, above n. 156, p. 246. 159 *Ibid.*, p. 247.
160 *Ibid.*, p. 250. 161 See above 1.2.3.

In the *Hammersmith and Fulham* case, the lower standard of review was again applied. However, Lord Bridge of Harwich did not place the same emphasis on the fact that the House of Commons had passed a resolution:

> The formulation and the implementation of national economic policy are matters depending essentially on political judgment. The decisions which shape them are for politicians to take and it is in the political forum of the House of Commons that they are properly to be debated and approved or disapproved on their merits.[162]

It was not the formal approval of the House of Commons which reduced the standard of review. Rather, it was the substantive discussion by the House of Commons of economic policy which did so. In other words, the principle would be capable of applying to the review of decisions not formally approved by the House of Commons. The key variable in Lord Bridge's formulation is the policy-laden, political nature of the decision under review, which suggests that such decisions ought to be taken by democratically legitimate decision-makers.[163]

The democratic legitimacy of elected local bodies has also received judicial recognition. Although he accepted in *Nanaimo (City)* v. *Rascal Trucking*[164] that a standard of review of correctness applied to decisions as to the jurisdiction of local authorities, Major J held that *intra vires* decisions would attract significant curial deference:

> Municipal councillors are elected by the constituents they represent and as such are more conversant with the exigencies of their community than are the courts. The fact that municipal councils are elected representatives of their community, and accountable to their constituents, is relevant in scrutinising *intra vires* decisions. The reality that municipalities often balance complex and divergent interests in arriving at decisions in the public interest is of similar importance. In short, these considerations warrant that the *intra vires* decisions of municipalities be reviewed upon a deferential standard.[165]

Democratic legitimacy's strong lure can be perceived in *R* v. *Chief Constable of Sussex, ex p. International Trader's Ferry*.[166] For Lord

162 *Hammersmith and Fulham*, above n. 157, p. 597.
163 See also *Axa General Insurance* v. *Scottish Ministers* [2011] Scot CS CSIH 31 at [87].
164 [2000] SCC 13; [2000] 1 SCR 342.
165 *Ibid.*, p. 357. See similarly *Chamberlain* v. *Surrey School District No. 36* [2002] SCC 86; [2002] 4 SCR 710 at 726.
166 *International Trader's Ferry*, above n. 22.

Hoffman, the fact that the Chief Constable was implementing the policing plan of a local police authority was important:

> He was not merely entitled but statutorily obliged, in the allocation of the resources under his command, to have regard to the fact that the police authority, mainly appointed by the democratically-elected institutions of local government, wished priority to be given to the objectives stated in the plan.[167]

Even mere appointment by local officials might be said to enhance democratic legitimacy, on Lord Hoffman's view. To regard appointment as a source of democratic legitimacy, however, would be to stretch the argument a little too much. The same logic would have to apply to individuals appointed by members of a national government, an argument that seems unrealistic because such individuals are scarcely appointed on the basis of their being keenly attuned to popular sentiment. Nonetheless, the strong attraction of democratic legitimacy is clear from the quoted passage.

3.4.2 Legislative intent and democratic legitimacy

As with expertise and the other practical justifications, it is necessary in order to accord curial deference to ascertain, from a proper consideration of the relevant statutory provisions, a link between the decision to delegate power and the democratic legitimacy of the delegated decision-maker. The characteristics that make ministers democratically legitimate will not be apparent from the statute. However, it is plausible that the legislature appreciates that its ministerial delegates are democratically legitimate delegated decision-makers. Indeed, not to impute such knowledge would be bizarre. Thus, in *Canadian Union of Public Employees* v. *Ontario (Minister for Labour)*,[168] Bastarache J posited a link between democratic legitimacy and legislative intent: 'empowering the minister, as opposed to an apolitical figure such as the Chief Justice of the province, *suggests a legislative intent* that political accountability also play a role'.[169] It is important to emphasise that Bastarache J relied on a background understanding – that an elected official will be more democratically legitimate than an unelected official – rather than a background assumption as to legislative intent.

167 *Ibid.*, p. 443. 168 [2003] SCC 29; [2003] 1 SCR 539.
169 *Ibid.*, p. 559. Emphasis added.

Ministers are not the only type of democratically legitimate delegated decision-maker. An excellent example of how local bodies can be democratically legitimate is provided by *R* v. *Gloucestershire County Council, ex p. Barry*.[170] The question for resolution by the House of Lords here was whether a local authority's resources could be relevant to the assessment of whether provision was 'necessary in order to meet the needs' of a person to whom s. 2(1) of the Chronically Sick and Disabled Persons Act 1970 applied. Their Lordships agreed that the question was one of degree and that the answer could vary from local authority to local authority.[171] The question would be answered by local authority organs. In his dissenting speech, Lord Lloyd of Berwick made an explicit link between legislative intent and democratic legitimacy:

> Who then decides what are the contemporary standards against which the social worker assesses the individual's needs? Again the answer seems straightforward. The standard is that set by the social services committee of the local authority in question. *No doubt this was one of the reasons why social services committees were set up in the first place* by section 2 of the Local Authority Social Services Act 1970, so as to represent the views of ordinary members of the public.[172]

These committees had been established by the legislature in an attempt to represent the views of people living in the local authority area. They would have had greater expertise than courts in ascertaining the needs of individuals in local communities and also greater democratic legitimacy, in that they were to function as the voice of the local community: 'in every case, simple or complex, the need of the individual will be assessed against the standards of civilised society as we know them in the United Kingdom, or, in the more homely phraseology of the law, by the standards of the man on the Clapham omnibus'.[173] As Lord Lloyd recognised, the legislature's decision to delegate power to a democratically legitimate delegated decision-maker justified a measure of curial deference.

3.4.3 *Democratic legitimacy in context*

Democratic legitimacy varies according to context. Delegated decision-makers can be more or less democratically legitimate, relative to one another, relative to the different types of decision that they render, and relative to reviewing courts. For example, a minister will be more

[170] [1997] AC 584. [171] See below 6.2.2.2. [172] *Barry*, above n. 170, p. 598.
[173] *Ibid.*, p. 598.

democratically legitimate than lower-ranking officials in the department.[174] In addition, certain questions may require more of a political judgement than others. Democratic legitimacy will be more relevant in sensitive cases requiring political judgement than in less sensitive cases:

> The more purely political (in a broad or narrow sense) a question is, the more appropriate it will be for political resolution and the less likely it is to be an appropriate matter for judicial decision. The smaller, therefore, will be the potential role of the court. It is the function of political and not judicial bodies to resolve political questions. Conversely, the greater the legal content of any issue, the greater the potential role of the court ...[175]

In *Chevron*, the contrast in relative democratic legitimacy between the judiciary and delegated decision-makers was emphasised by the Supreme Court of the United States:

> Judges are not experts in the field, and are not part of either political branch of the Government ... While agencies are not directly accountable to the people, the Chief Executive is, and it is entirely appropriate for this political branch of the Government to make such policy choices ... [F]ederal judges – *who have no constituency* – have a duty to respect legitimate policy choices made by those who do. The responsibilities for assessing the wisdom of such policy choices and resolving the struggle between competing views of the public interest are not judicial ones.[176]

David Barron and Elena Kagan have argued that curial deference should be entirely contingent on the identity of the delegated decision-maker. Only where 'the official Congress named in the relevant delegation [has] personally assumed responsibility for the decision prior to issuance' should curial deference be accorded,[177] because this approach would 'promote the values of accountable and disciplined decision-making'.[178] A high-ranking official is more likely to be publicly known and responsible to 'political institutions and public constituencies';[179] the 'tendency

[174] See e.g. *Baker* v. *Canada (Citizenship and Immigration)* [1999] 2 SCR 817; *Mount Sinai Hospital Centre*, above n. 154; *Canadian Union of Public Employees*, above n. 168, p. 611.

[175] *A* v. *Secretary of State for the Home Department* [2004] UKHL 56; [2005] 2 AC 68 at 102, per Lord Bingham of Cornhill.

[176] *Chevron USA* v. *Natural Resources Defence Council* (1984) 467 US 837 at 865–6, per Stevens J. Emphasis added. See similarly Laurence Silberman, '*Chevron* – the Intersection of Law and Policy' (1990) 58 Geo Wash LR 821, 822. I will argue in the next subsection, however, that the notion of accountability relied upon by the Supreme Court of the United States is not a practical justification for curial deference.

[177] '*Chevron's* Non-delegation Doctrine' [2001] Supreme Court Review 201, 235.

[178] *Ibid.*, p. 241. [179] *Ibid.*, p. 243.

of agencies to diffuse and cloak responsibility' would be countered;[180] and the 'prospect of high-level review' would occasion 'scrupulous consideration of proposed agency action within the bureaucracy'[181] and 'promote the integration of diverse agency actions into a coordinated stream of policy aimed at achieving set objectives'.[182]

Barron and Kagan's proposal is at once too harsh – on low-level delegated decision-makers, who are presumed without any evidence to be of inferior calibre to their commanding officers – and too generous – to high-level delegated decision-makers, who are presumed to be able to generate rational policy agendas, despite the evidence that they may not always be capable of doing so.[183] More generally, as Richard Mulgan has observed, whether a single individual or many individuals ought to be made accountable 'depends on the context and circumstances, such as the type of issue and the level of public interest, as well as the particular institutional structure'.[184] A 'plurality of accountability points'[185] may make it easier for a delegated decision-maker to be held publicly accountable, concealing or obfuscating information may become more difficult and the likelihood of there being individuals within the organisation willing and able to release information may increase. But it may also encourage buck-passing and avoidance of accountability. By contrast, '[s]ingle accountability'[186] reduces the possibility of buck-passing, but also 'allows for much tighter control of information and makes it easier for those in power to frustrate public accountability'.[187] At the very least, contrary to Barron and Kagan's confident assertions, 'the question whether accountability obligations should be concentrated in a single leader or dispersed among several spokespeople and different groups of officials does not admit of a clear or easy answer'.[188]

3.4.4 *Outside the paradigm: statutory and non-statutory control*

A difficulty is presented by delegated decision-makers who, though themselves not elected, are controlled to some extent by elected officials. In certain instances, the executive, or legislative, branch will exercise authority over delegated decision-makers:

180 *Ibid.*, p. 243. 181 *Ibid.*, p. 244. 182 *Ibid.*, p. 245. 183 See above 3.2.4.1.

184 *Holding Power to Account: Accountability in Modern Democracies* (Basingstoke: Palgrave Macmillan, 2003), p. 196.

185 *Ibid.*, p. 195. 186 *Ibid.*, p. 196. 187 *Ibid.*, p. 196. 188 *Ibid.*, p. 210.

> the fact that the members of administrative agencies are not directly accountable to the people through electoral or political processes hardly means that they are freed from constraints that such accountability imposes. To a very significant degree agencies are subject to influence, supervision, and sometimes control by those who have been elected by the people – that is, the President and the Congress – and bear a relationship of accountability to them.[189]

A good example is the executive branch of the United States government. Officers of the United States are not themselves directly elected, but appointed by the president who, by virtue of his position as head of the executive branch, may exercise authority over them. Some scholars have contended that because the president serves a national electoral constituency and can exercise control over the administrative process, delegations of power are justified on the basis of the president's democratic legitimacy.[190] However, as a matter of constitutional law, the extent of the president's authority is unclear. The president has a general power of removal, but limitations may legitimately be placed by Congress on the presidential power to remove executive branch officials as long as the limitations do not unduly fetter the president's exercise of the executive power.[191] But it is not clear whether the president can veto or nullify the acts of members of the executive branch, or act in the place of members of the executive branch.[192] Moreover, it is not clear, if these powers do

[189] James Freedman, *Crisis and Legitimacy: The Administrative Process and American Government* (Cambridge: Cambridge University Press, 1978), p. 128. See also Steven Calabresi, 'Some Normative Arguments for the Unitary Executive' (1995) 48 Ark LR 23, 50–5. Calabresi details three means by which the legislature might exercise influence over the process of administration (Calabresi's argument concerns the executive, but his points have wider relevance): holding oversight hearings, making budget allocations and extracting commitments as to future action from prospective appointees.

[190] See Jerry Mashaw, *Greed, Chaos and Governance: Using Public Choice to Improve Public Law* (New Haven: Yale University Press, 1997), pp. 152–6. Compare Farina, 'Statutory Interpretation', above n. 111, pp. 511–26. See also Matthew Stephenson, 'Optimal Political Control of the Bureaucracy' (2008) 107 Mich LR 53. Stephenson argues that it will not necessarily be the case that the president will represent the views of the median member of the national electoral constituency.

[191] See *Morrison* v. *Olson* (1988) 487 US 654 at 691, per Rehnquist CJ, where the Supreme Court of the United States held that the legislature could impose limits on the president's control over executive branch officers as long as the restrictions did not 'impede the President's ability to perform his constitutional duty' (a formulation which leaves many questions, beyond the scope of this argument, unanswered).

[192] I draw these possible means of exercising authority over the executive branch from Steven Calabresi and Kevin Rhodes, 'The Structural Constitution: Unitary Executive, Plural Judiciary' (1992) 105 Harv LR 1153, 1166.

exist, whether Congress can limit the president's exercise of them.[193] These constitutional questions provide a backdrop to the administrative law problem I am considering here.

One of two background presumptions must be operating.[194] If the background presumption is that the president does not have the authority to veto or nullify acts of members of the executive branch or to act in their place,[195] then no difficulty arises: democratic legitimacy simply does not function as a practical justification for curial deference, because the notion of accountability in such situations is extremely vague, as discussed below. However, if the background presumption is that the president has *some* authority, democratic legitimacy may function as a practical justification for curial deference. But if – and only if – this background presumption is operative, the president's authority may be foreclosed by statute.[196] And if the focus is on the statute, then the relevant inquiry would be into the extent of the power delegated to the delegated decision-maker. When delegated decision-makers located in the executive branch are insulated by statute from presidential control, or control by other external actors, a focus on the extent of the power delegated will indicate that increased powers have been delegated, which suggests a higher degree of curial deference. For example, a legislature can explicitly exclude the possibility of requiring cost–benefit analyses to be conducted or other means of non-statutory control by the executive.[197] Responsiveness to elected officials, then, is largely a function of statute. Whether or not the statute bars the executive from influencing the exercise of power by the delegated decision-maker is a matter of the extent of the power delegated to the delegated decision-maker.

As with non-statutory controls exercised by the executive, it appears superficially as if the legislature, by imposing requirements that a

[193] Elena Kagan, 'Presidential Administration' (2001) 114 Harv LR 2245, 2322. I would be sympathetic to an argument that cabinet-level officials can claim democratic legitimacy by virtue of their very close relationship with the president. Accordingly, even though the extent of the president's powers over them is uncertain, cabinet-level officials are excluded from the reservations I express in the text.

[194] Any presumption here arises from the correct interpretation of the relevant constitutional provisions and not from any assumptions as to legislative intent.

[195] This appears to be the conventional position. See Peter Strauss, 'The Place of Agencies in Government: Separation of Powers and the Fourth Branch' (1984) 84 Colum LR 573, 649–50.

[196] Kagan, 'Presidential Administration', above n. 193, p. 2326.

[197] Sidney Shapiro and Robert Glicksman, *Risk Regulation at Risk: Restoring a Pragmatic Approach* (Stanford: Stanford University Press, 2003), pp. 31–40.

delegated decision-maker must appear before legislative committees to give an account of its actions, increases the democratic legitimacy of the delegated decision-maker while at the same time decreasing the scope of its powers:[198]

> those members of Congress with a particular interest in a programme usually have enormous influence. They have the appropriations process, investigative powers, reauthorisation powers, confirmation hearings, and extensive links to the media – not to mention the power of constant harassment.[199]

At least, it is arguable that a delegated decision-maker who is required to regularly report to or appear before and answer to legislative committees might have less freedom of action than a delegated decision-maker who is not required to do so. Certainly, it is arguable that the legislature has manifested an intention to give a delegated decision-maker less power where it makes the delegated decision-maker subject to ongoing reporting and accounting requirements.

But this relationship is exceedingly complex. Legislators and delegated decision-makers:

> trade speculatively and on credit; they are continually repaying past favours and building up a stock of credits useful for obtaining additional favours sometime in the future. Bureaucrats allocate expenditures both in gratitude for past support and in hopes of future congressional support; and congressmen support agencies both because they owe them for past allocations and because they desire future allocations.[200]

Delegated decision-makers are accountable to legislators in the sense that legislators may at some point in the future make adverse decisions about delegated decision-makers' budgets. The same applies to the possibility of removal in respect of executive branch officials. But the media and public – to name but two entities – may influence how politicians view delegated decision-makers, and how delegated

198 Needless to say, '[s]trict lines of authority are *particularly* elusive when Congress and the President both exert a measure of control over an agency'. *Federal Communications Commission* v. *Fox Television Stations* (2009) 129 S Ct 1800 at 1825, per Stevens J, dissenting. Emphasis added. See also Jack Beerman, 'End the Failed *Chevron* Experiment Now: How *Chevron* Has Failed and Why it Can and Should Be Overruled' (2010) 42 Conn LR 779, 803–5.

199 R. Shep Melnick, 'Administrative Law and Bureaucratic Rationality' (1992) 44 Admin LR 245, 254. Compare Farina, 'Statutory Interpretation', above n. 111, pp. 502–11.

200 R. Douglas Arnold, *Congress and the Bureaucracy* (New Haven: Yale University Press, 1979), p. 36.

decision-makers view politicians; indeed, they may influence how delegated decision-makers view their own tasks. Accountability, in this sense, is too vague to be useful: freedom of action can be curtailed by a relationship with any number of constituencies and constituents, public and private.[201] Requiring a reviewing court to accurately measure any increases in democratic legitimacy resulting from this sort of informal control seems unrealistic. This is *a fortiori* in the Westminster system, where the accountability of ministers to Parliament 'now deserves the status of a legal fiction'.[202] And even if it were possible to measure democratic legitimacy resulting from accountability, it is implausible to categorise it as a reason for the delegation of power, because the legislature itself will be subject to the same accountability mechanisms as the delegated decision-makers it empowers.

The analysis should instead be conducted in terms of the extent of the power delegated to the delegated decision-maker by the relevant statutory provisions. What matters is the formal structure that allows delegated decision-makers to avoid, or exposes them to, external pressures. Formal structures relate to the extent of delegations of power. In short, outside the paradigm case of democratic legitimacy, which involves the direct delegation of power to an elected delegated decision-maker, democratic legitimacy is too vague to be of relevance in formulating a doctrine of curial deference.

3.4.5 *Independence and curial deference*

In his dissenting opinion in *Federal Communications Commission* v. *Fox Television Stations*[203] Breyer J suggested that the decisions of independent agencies should be more closely scrutinised by courts because such

[201] See generally Jerry Mashaw, 'Accountability and Institutional Design: Some Thoughts on the Grammar of Governance'; Edward Rubin, 'The Myth of Non-Bureaucratic Accountability and the Anti-Administrative Impulse'; and Colin Scott, 'Spontaneous Accountability' in Michael Dowdle (ed.), *Public Accountability: Designs, Dilemmas and Experiences* (Cambridge: Cambridge University Press, 2006), pp. 115, 52, 174; Bradley Lipton, 'Accountability, Deference, and the *Skidmore* Doctrine' (2010) 119 Yale LJ 2096, 2101–20; and Mulgan, *Accountability*, above n. 184.

[202] David Feldman, 'Public Law Values and the House of Lords' (1990) 106 LQR 246, 254. See generally Mike Radford, 'Mitigating the Democratic Deficit? Judicial Review and Ministerial Accountability' in Peter Leyland and Terry Woods (eds.), *Administrative Law Facing the Future: Old Constraints and New Horizons* (London: Blackstone, 1997), p. 35; Bruce Stone, 'Administrative Accountability in the "Westminster" Democracies: Towards a New Conceptual Framework' (1995) 8 *Governance* 505.

[203] *Fox*, above n. 198.

agencies are immune from political oversight: 'that agency's comparative freedom from ballot-box control makes it all the more important that courts review its decision-making to assure compliance with applicable provisions of the law'.[204]

However, while rhetorically attractive, Breyer J's claim that independent agencies should be subject to a greater intensity of judicial review to make up for a lower intensity of political oversight cannot be sustained. Breyer J does not call attention to the converse proposition: that increased political oversight should lead to a reduction in the intensity of judicial review. The neglect of the converse proposition is important, because the source of Breyer J's claim is unclear. The source may be the rule of law – at least, one could plausibly argue that the rule of law requires increased intensity of judicial review to make up for a reduction in political oversight. But the rule of law is unlikely to look kindly on the converse proposition: the intensity of judicial review can hardly be decreased on the basis of a *potential*, as opposed to an actual, political remedy.

Another potential claim, that the diminished democratic legitimacy of independent agencies, compared to executive agencies, would justify a lower degree of curial deference,[205] is foreclosed by my analysis in 3.4.4. Any claim of this nature must ultimately be resolved by reference to legislative intent, but legislative intent is also an unlikely source of support for Breyer J's view.[206] *Ex hypothesi*, the legislature has not expressed a view on the appropriate intensity of judicial review. If the legislature wished to enact Breyer J's rhetorically attractive view (with or without its converse proposition) it could do so. In the silence, it is at least equally plausible that the legislature intended to have *less* oversight by the judiciary. Indeed, it might be more plausible. *Ex hypothesi*, a decision to delegate a significant extent of power to the independent delegated decision-maker can be discerned, which counsels relatively less intense judicial review, certainly not more.

204 *Ibid.*, p. 1830. In the United States, an independent agency is one the heads of which cannot be removed by the president otherwise than for cause.

205 See Randolph May, 'Defining Deference Down: Independent Agencies and *Chevron* Deference' (2006) 58 Admin LR 429, 442–51 and, commenting on the *Fox* case, 'Defining Deference Down, Again: Independent Agencies, *Chevron* Deference, and *Fox*' (2010) 62 Admin LR 433.

206 Moreover, as Scalia J pointed out in response, the text of the Administrative Procedure Act 'makes no distinction between independent and other agencies'. *Fox*, above n. 198, p. 1817.

In conclusion, in some cases, democratic legitimacy might be a reason to delegate power to a body other than a court, or even to a representative body other than a central legislature. Particularly in the latter instance, democratic legitimacy is a practical justification for curial deference. It explains why the legislature would delegate power and why the delegated decision-maker is more likely to reach a better decision than the reviewing court or the legislature. But beyond these confines, democratic legitimacy is not relevant.

3.5 Procedural legitimacy

Broadly speaking, I use the term 'procedural legitimacy' to describe participation by interested parties in the decision-making process of a delegated decision-maker.[207] A legislature could itself hold extensive hearings on a particular issue, but its time and resources are limited. As a result, it is plausible that a legislature would delegate decision-making power on the basis that a delegated decision-maker would be better able to provide a forum for interested parties to contribute their views. It is also plausible that the delegation of power would be to a body other than a court. Judicial time and resources are also limited, and subject to the shortcomings of the adversarial process, which would prevent many interested parties from participating in the process of decision-making. Even in respect of decisions affecting one individual, or a small number of individuals, the more relaxed procedural rules that delegated decision-makers are often free to employ may make participation more effective.[208]

3.5.1 Contributors to procedural legitimacy

I see four ways, which I will explain in this subsection, in which participation might contribute to procedural legitimacy. First, participation could lead to more accurate delegated decision-making by exposing

[207] I prefer the term 'procedural legitimacy' to 'participation' because it is not just the mere fact of participation that is important: the type and quality of the participation are also important. Ultimately, the goal of permitting or requiring participation must be to improve the quality of a decision in some way. Referring to legitimacy seems a good way of capturing what I mean.

[208] See e.g. Geneviève Cartier, 'La Discrétion administrative: une occasion de dialogue entre citoyens et tribunaux?' in Stephen Coughlan and Dawn Russell (eds.), *Citizenship and Citizen Participation in the Administration of Justice* (Montreal: Les Éditions Thémis, 2001), p. 233.

delegated decision-makers to a greater variety of views and sources of information. Secondly, it could allow delegated decision-makers to aggregate the preferences of individuals. Thirdly, it could lead to deliberation about the appropriate means of achieving certain policy goals. Fourthly, participation could be viewed as valuable per se. Each may be relevant whenever legislation permits or requires participation in delegated decision-making.

Although various theorists have at various times attempted to develop theories of procedural legitimacy based on one or more of the four contributors, difficulties attend each of the four. The difficulties present serious problems for theorists attempting to develop theories of judicial review (or of administration, more generally) based solely on procedural legitimacy. However, I am not attempting to develop a stand-alone theory based on procedural legitimacy. Accordingly, although I note the difficulties with each of the four contributors to procedural legitimacy that I have identified, I do not attempt to gainsay them. I simply claim that these four contributors to procedural legitimacy could motivate legislatures to delegate power to bodies other than courts. Indeed, the approach outlined here has the potential to integrate procedural legitimacy into judicial review without making an unsustainable claim that procedural legitimacy should be the key value, or organising principle, of judicial review. Following my approach, procedural legitimacy would be integrated into judicial review doctrine because as a practical justification for curial deference it must on a proper consideration of the relevant statutory provisions be taken into account by a reviewing court in determining the appropriate degree of curial deference. Moreover, where the legislature has permitted or required participation, the difficulties attendant upon participation have less relevance: participation is to be taken into account because of the judicial obligation to give effect to legislative intent, not because of participation's intrinsic benefits, minus its intrinsic costs, as determined on a case-by-case basis.

3.5.1.1 Improving decision-making

Participation could improve the accuracy of delegated decision-making: 'Public consultation has long been seen as a tool for improving regulation by allowing those parties who are affected by regulation to input into regulatory processes their expertise, perspectives and ideas for alternative actions.'[209] Participants can 'bring to the attention of ministers and

[209] Robert Baldwin, 'Is Better Regulation Smarter Regulation?' [2008] PL 485, 493.

civil servants options and information of which they would not otherwise be aware'.[210] Thus, in *American Hospital Association* v. *National Labour Relations Board*,[211] Stevens J commented that:

> Given the extensive notice and comment rule-making conducted by the Board, its careful analysis of the comments that it received, and its well-reasoned justification for the new rule, we would not be troubled even if there were inconsistencies between the current rule and prior … pronouncements.[212]

In that case, participation gave all interested parties the opportunity to comment on and develop arguments against the inconsistencies. More generally, participation 'can serve as a safety valve allowing interested persons and groups to express their views before policies are announced and implemented' and 'can ease the enforcement of administrative programmes relying upon public cooperation'.[213] Participation may also increase accuracy in an egalitarian sense: 'as the number of participants (access points) in an administrative process is expanded at the various levels of delegated decision-making, the amount of monopoly rents powerful interest groups may be able to extract will decrease'.[214] An increased number of participants might give a delegated decision-making process a 'self-corrective quality' by ensuring that delegated decision-makers are not misled by one-sided presentations of relevant information.[215] Finally, participation might improve delegated decision-making in a very general sense because it would:

> help each party to grasp the normative basis on which things are being done. That understanding is a necessary step towards developing genuine confidence in the decision-process; it is also a condition of the true growth of citizenship and in turn of civic virtue. Quite apart from the

[210] Wyn Grant, *Pressure Groups and British Politics* (Basingstoke: Macmillan, 2000), p. 219. Or, to put it more colourfully, '[w]hile there are many officials who may believe that consultation is a good democratic thing, uppermost in their minds is the desire to avoid embarrassment, or, to use a popular phrase, … "things going pear-shaped"'. Edward Page, *Governing by Numbers: Delegated Legislation and Everyday Policy-making* (Oxford: Hart, 2001), p. 144. See also Jenny Steele, 'Participation and Deliberation in Environmental Law: A Problem Solving Approach' (2001) 21 OJLS 415, 437–8.

[211] (1991) 499 US 606. [212] *Ibid.*, p. 618.

[213] Ernest Gellhorn, 'Public Participation in Administrative Proceedings' (1972) 81 Yale LJ 359, 361.

[214] Jim Rossi, 'Participation Run Amok: The Costs of Mass Participation for Deliberative Agency Decision-making' (1997) 92 Nw U LR 173, 213.

[215] Edward Rubin, 'Getting Beyond Democracy' (2000–2001) 149 U Pa LR 711, 780.

> effects participation might have on the individual person, it may also help to improve the process, not just in the sense of contributing to better outcomes, but in raising the quality of decision-making in a general way. Participation not only helps to open up the process but also prepares the way for the giving of reasons to explain and justify how the decision has been made. A decision-maker who has to respond to the evidence and arguments advanced may, as a result, be more measured and reflective in his judgment.[216]

Despite these many potential benefits, participation may in fact hinder delegated decision-making, as I discuss below.[217]

3.5.1.2 Aggregating interests

Adherents to the pluralist conception of politics[218] argue that the common good consists of the aggregated interests of the citizenry, as individuals or as represented by groups:

> Under the pluralist view, politics mediates the struggle among self-interested groups for scarce social resources. Only nominally deliberative, politics is a process of conflict and compromise among various social interests. Under the pluralist conception, people come to the political process with pre-selected interests that they seek to promote through political conflict and compromise. Preferences are not shaped through governance, but enter into the process as exogenous variables ... The common good amounts to an aggregation of individual preferences.[219]

Indeed, from a pluralist's perspective, participation may enhance democracy: 'Pressure groups permit citizens to express their views on complex issues which affect their lives' more often than voting in elections, and 'democracy finds it difficult ... to take account of the intensity of opinion on a particular issue', a problem which might be ameliorated by widespread participation.[220] Participation in the process of delegated

216 Denis Galligan, *Due Process and Fair Procedures: A Study of Administrative Procedures* (Oxford: Hart, 1996), p. 157.

217 See below 3.5.4.

218 Pluralism can be political (see e.g. Arthur Bentley, *The Process of Government: A Study of Social Pressures* (Bloomington: Principia, 1908); David Truman, *The Governmental Process: Political Interests and Public Opinion* (Westport: Greenwood, 1951)) as well as economic (see e.g. George Stigler, 'The Theory of Economic Regulation' (1971) 2 *Bell Journal of Economics and Management* 3). See generally Paul Craig, *Public Law and Democracy in the United States and the United Kingdom* (Oxford: Clarendon, 1990), pp. 80–136.

219 Cass Sunstein, 'Interest Groups in American Public Law' (1985) 38 Stan LR 29, 32–3.

220 Grant, *Pressure Groups*, above n. 210, pp. 35–6.

decision-making, then, may be seen as giving effect to individual preferences to a greater extent than would be possible in the legislative process.

Nonetheless, serious difficulties lie in the way of accepting that the aggregation of interests is the sole legitimate means of reaching decisions. The inherent problem with pluralism is that:

> It rests on a view of society as a market place of competing interests and yet offers no normative basis for choosing amongst them. The result is that either the more powerful interests prevail or the decision-maker appeals to some external principle. The former offers an unsatisfactory basis for ordering society, while to adopt the latter by relying on an external standard would be to introduce a view of the common good which goes beyond competing interests and so undermines the model itself.[221]

Nonetheless, it is only necessary here to raise the possibility that legislatures might wish to use participation as a means of aggregating interests on a particular issue. Unable, or unwilling, to do so themselves, legislatures might wish to require delegated decision-makers to measure the number and magnitude of affected interests, in order to reach the optimal decision from a pluralist perspective. Because it enhances accuracy and accords legitimacy from the perspective of a leading theory of political philosophy, aggregation of interests is a good reason to require participation in delegated decision-making and, more importantly, a good reason to delegate power in the first place. It is also a good reason not to delegate to a court: the aggregation of interests would be at odds with the traditional role of the common law judge as an impartial arbiter reaching a decision that is correct in law and independent of the interests of the parties, rather than as a facilitator brokering a compromise between competing interests.

3.5.1.3 Deliberation

Deliberative democracy and republicanism have been major themes in political and legal philosophy in recent decades. For ease of exposition, I shall treat the two under one head, 'deliberation'.[222] As applied to

221 Galligan, *Due Process*, above n. 216, p. 469. See similarly Robert Reich, 'Public Administration and Public Deliberation: An Interpretive Essay' (1985) 94 Yale LJ 1617, 1637. See also Roger Cramton, 'The Why, Where and How of Broadened Public Participation in the Administrative Process' (1972) 60 Geo LJ 525, 527–30.

222 See Mark Seidenfeld, 'A Syncopated *Chevron*: Emphasising Reasoned Decision-making in Reviewing Agency Interpretation of Statutes' (1994) 73 Tex LR 83, 125, n. 224.

administrative law, deliberation aims to counter some of the potentially negative effects of pluralism. Because 'under pluralistic democracy, the state may actually end up pursuing values that the political community, after deliberation, would universally consider repugnant',[223] proponents of deliberation argue that the interests of individuals, or of groups representing individuals, should be starting points in a process of dialogue between members of a political community in the pursuit of policies that implement the common good. Through the process of deliberation, those interests can be continually revised, so that individuals' perceptions of their own interests may change,[224] leading to the pursuit of the common good, around which a consensus ultimately forms:

> public deliberation allows people to discover latent *public* values that they have in common with others, and in the process to create new public values. Together, citizens begin to define targets of voluntary action, to identify what they value most about the community, and to uncover goals and commitments that transcend their narrower self-interests. Not incidentally, along the way they achieve a deeper understanding of one another, and refine their political identity.[225]

Another evil of pluralism that deliberation aims to counter is that of domination by wealthy groups; it 'attempts to overcome [pluralism's] systematic bias by requiring the state to justify its decisions in terms other than the promotion of interests of politically influential factions'.[226]

Several theorists have discussed the potential for deliberation in the context of administrative law.[227] Delegated decision-makers can permit deliberation to take place:

223 Mark Seidenfeld, 'A Civic Republican Justification for the Administrative State' (1992) 105 Harv LR 1511, 1533.

224 Sunstein, 'Interest Groups', above n. 219, p. 31.

225 Reich, 'Administration and Deliberation', above n. 221, pp. 1636–7. Emphasis original. See also Seidenfeld, 'Syncopated *Chevron*', above n. 222, p. 126; Select Committee on Public Administration, *Sixth Report: Innovations in Citizen Participation in Government* (2001), [50].

226 Seidenfeld, 'Civic Republicanism', above n. 223, p. 1536. Other aspects of deliberation, such as the suggestion made by civic republicans that decision-makers must justify their decisions in terms of the public good (see e.g. Shapiro, *Guardians*, above n. 49, p. 168) are not relevant here.

227 See e.g. Reich, 'Administration and Deliberation', above n. 221; Richardson, *Democratic Autonomy*, above n. 72; Seidenfeld, 'Civic Republicanism', above n. 223; Steele, 'Participation and Deliberation', above n. 210; Sunstein, 'Interest Groups', above n. 219.

> In addition to administrative agencies' place in government, their internal structure also encourages deliberative decision-making aimed at furthering public rather than private values. At the core of almost every agency is a professional staff, chosen for its knowledge rather than for its political views or affiliations. The staff forms the base of a pyramid that has the ultimate decision-makers, who are generally political appointees, at the apex. Although these appointees generate the agency's policy agenda, they depend on the bureaucrats below to evaluate the various alternatives for implementing broad policies. Career staff members derive their power primarily from their professional training and their relationships with interest group representatives who frequently control important information – in other words, from job-specific expertise. This expertise allows bureaucrats to exert significant influence on public policy even when their role is merely advisory. Although career staff rarely initiate consideration of general policies, the debate over policy alternatives often starts at lower levels and travels up the pyramid. This process has the potential to focus the debate on a professional understanding of the public interest rather than on accommodation of private interests.[228]

Hence the argument of the Supreme Court of the United States that a higher degree of curial deference should be accorded where 'fairness and deliberation' have been fostered by the delegated decision-maker's decision-making process.[229]

As with the other contributors to procedural legitimacy, difficulties attend deliberation. In particular, it is not clear that the lofty ambitions of the proponents of deliberation can be realised. Indeed, one might ask, rhetorically, whether men could be trusted to put aside their powerful personal and economic interests in order to help to achieve the common good. Neither men nor delegated decision-makers are angels. Although judicial oversight might assist in ensuring that deliberation takes place effectively,[230] it may not be sufficient to overcome the potentially selfish interests of participants or delegated decision-makers. Even if interests are not selfish, it may be the case that participants simply have irreconcilable differences about fundamental issues. The differences could run so deep that prolonged discussion would be 'more likely to deepen and congeal disagreement than to overcome it'.[231] Moreover, requirements

[228] Seidenfeld, 'Civic Republicanism', above n. 223, p. 1554.

[229] *United States* v. *Mead Corporation* (2001) 533 US 218 at 230, per Souter J.

[230] See Sunstein, 'Factions', above n. 73, pp. 284–7; 'Interest Groups', above n. 219, pp. 74–5.

[231] Richard Posner, *Law, Pragmatism and Democracy* (Cambridge, MA: Harvard University Press, 2003), p. 139.

of deliberation that seem unimpeachable in theory could prove to be time-consuming, costly and unmanageable in practice.[232]

A tension may exist between participation and deliberation.[233] The greater the number of participants, the less opportunity there will be for deliberation, unless the process is to continue endlessly. If everybody is to be heard, less time will be available for everybody to reflect. It will not always be possible to handpick participants either, perhaps creating a situation in which less sophisticated participants make arguments less convincingly than more sophisticated participants; to the extent that participants are not competent, deliberation will be less effective. In addition, deliberation, to be effective, requires co-operation, but ideal speech scenarios rarely present themselves in real life. It is possible that participants will not participate in good faith; or at least, it is possible that they might participate with one or both eyes trained solely on achieving the best outcome from their point of view. The greater the number of participants in the process, the greater the likelihood that an attempt to act otherwise than in good faith will go unnoticed. Indeed, '[r]ather than promoting dialogue and movement toward consensus, additional information may have the effect of increasing the divergence between participants' preferences and interests, or further entrenching pre-existing preferences and interests, as participants are encouraged to join pre-defined factions'.[234]

3.5.1.4 Participation per se

In a follow-up to their original work on deliberative democracy,[235] Amy Gutmann and Denis Thompson claimed that public participation has a non-instrumental value:

> if we were to regard deliberation as only instrumental, we would fail to recognise the moral significance of the political fact that the decisions of government bind people other than the decision-makers themselves. Political officials cannot rightly decide an issue simply by claiming that they know that their preferred policies are right for their fellow citizens. They need to seek the views of those citizens who have to live with the results of their policies. When binding decisions are routinely made

[232] See below 3.5.4.

[233] Note, 'Civic Republican Administrative Theory: Bureaucrats as Deliberative Democrats' (1994) 107 Harv LR 1401.

[234] Rossi, 'Amok' above n. 214, p. 227. Compare Steele, 'Participation and Deliberation', above n. 210, pp. 428–9.

[235] *Democracy and Disagreement* (Cambridge, MA: Harvard University Press, 1996).

> without deliberation, the government not only conveys disrespect for citizens, but also exposes its lack of adequate justification for imposing the decision on them.[236]

However, although ultimately advocating powerfully for increased participation in delegated decision-making, Denis Galligan has disparaged the notion that participation in a decision-making process can have value independent of its ability to further other ends. His argument is that participation is a purposive activity whose 'primary purpose is to shape outcomes' and that the purpose of achieving any other value must also be established:[237] 'Whether participation has value [per se] depends on a particular vision of society, and visions rest finally on faith, not proof. Many do not share that vision. Some argue that participation has little value in itself, and even that too much participation has harmful consequences.'[238]

But my claim is a modest one: that the legislature may have decided to provide for participation on the basis that it intuitively seems like a good thing.[239] Unlike the targets of Galligan's critique, I am not attempting to build a system of procedural fairness from the ground up with the value of participation per se as the keystone. The simple point is that members of a legislature may take the view that participation is inherently valuable. In Galligan's terms, it can be argued that legislators may sometimes be men of faith, rather than men of reason, with a particular vision of how administration ought to be conducted. Although the accuracy of the final decision will not be improved, participation may have independent value and if the legislature has provided for participation, it is plausible that it was influenced in part by its view of the inherent value of participation.[240]

236 *Why Deliberative Democracy?* (Princeton: Princeton University Press, 2004), pp. 22–3.

237 Galligan, *Due Process*, above n. 216, p. 136.

238 *Ibid.*, p. 156. See also Robert Baldwin, *Rules and Government* (Oxford: Clarendon, 1995), p. 44.

239 For a stronger statement, see T. R. S. Allan, 'Procedural Fairness and the Duty of Respect' (1998) 18 OJLS 497, 509: 'The interpretation of law as a moral claim to the citizen's allegiance rests on a view of the law's subjects as morally responsible and autonomous persons entitled to respect. The fairness of the law-making [and law-applying] procedures is an essential element in that claim to allegiance.' See also *AF* v. *Secretary of State for the Home Department* [2009] UKHL 28, (2009) 26 BHRC 738.

240 A variation on the theme of participation and deliberation is the model of collaborative decision-making, proposed most forcefully by Jody Freeman, 'Collaborative Governance in the Administrative State' (1997) 45 UCLA LR 1. See also Philip Harter, 'Negotiating Regulations: A Cure for Malaise' (1982) 71 Geo LJ 1; Henry Richardson, 'Administrative Policy: Rule of Law or Bureaucracy?' in David Dyzenhaus (ed.), *Recrafting the Rule of Law:*

3.5.2 *Legislative intent and procedural legitimacy*

As with the other practical justifications, it is important to relate procedural legitimacy to legislative intent. Sometimes the link will be obvious, as an English parliamentary organ has noted: 'Increasingly, participation is a legal requirement.'[241] An excellent example of judicial recognition that legislatures may delegate power in order to increase the procedural legitimacy of decisions is the decision of the House of Lords in *In re Harvey*.[242] The challenge here concerned a decision by an education authority to close a number of schools due to falling pupil numbers. The decision was to close three of the six schools in Paisley. Geographic considerations were taken into account in the decision, such that one school would continue to serve the residents of a particular part of the town. In effect, the two schools in each of the three areas were to be amalgamated. A challenge was mounted to the reasonableness of the decision taken to amalgamate the schools in one of the areas.

At particular issue was a statutory provision which required the education authority to give effect, so far as possible, to 'the general principle that … pupils are to be educated in accordance with the wishes of their parents'.[243] In order to give effect to the principle, an 'area review group was set up with a widely representative membership, including some parents, and it carried out a wide consultation exercise including meetings with over 3,000 parents in the area'.[244] Pursuant to another legislative provision, consultative documents were also issued and representations received. The fact that these representations were taken into account went a 'long way towards indicating' that regard was had to the general principle.[245] The consultation procedure was not simply seen by the court as fulfilling the objectives of the legislation, but also assisted in establishing the reasonableness of the decision: the decision was 'fully capable of standing on its own feet' partly because it 'was the *subject of a consultative document and report* separate from the other two proposed closures, and was separately resolved upon'.[246]

A question was raised in *Canadian Association of Industrial, Mechanical and Allied Workers* v. *Paccar of Canada*[247] by L'Heureux-Dubé J as to the

The Limits of the Legal Order (Oxford: Hart, 1999), p. 309, pp. 325–7. But see William Funk, 'Bargaining Toward the New Millennium: Regulatory Negotiation and the Subversion of the Public Interest' (1997) 46 Duke LJ 1351, 1374–87; Galligan, *Due Process*, above n. 216, p. 481.

241 Select Committee on Public Administration, above n. 225, [36].

242 *The Times*, 30 June 1989. 243 Education (Scotland) Act 1980, s. 28(1).

244 *Harvey*, above n. 242. 245 *Ibid.* 246 *Ibid.* Emphasis added. 247 [1989] 2 SCR 983.

appropriateness of the British Columbia Labour Relations Board introducing a change in industrial relations law by means of an individual decision rather than a consultative process. The accuracy of the decision-making process may have suffered: 'The Board did not benefit from the input other parties may have had to offer in this respect had another route been chosen to formulate its policy. In that fashion the spectrum of the consequences of the proposed policy may not have been fully brought to the Board's attention.'[248] Moreover, the relevant statutory provisions:

> *indicate a legislative intent favouring broad participation* by the members of the labour relations community in proceedings involving issues of widespread interest. While policy issues may be present in some form in private adjudications, and while the Board is empowered ... to make declaratory opinions in certain cases, some policy issues necessarily involve the use of the mechanisms provided for ... I would only add that in a case like the present one, where a previous policy orientation is reversed, where the area concerned involves a void in the enabling statute, and where the question raised is of crucial importance to employers, unions and individual employees at large, the matter may more properly have been dealt with in a policy-making hearing.[249]

In *United States* v. *Mead Corporation*,[250] a link was made by the Supreme Court of the United States between procedural legitimacy and legislative intent: 'It is fair to assume generally that Congress *contemplates* administrative action with the effect of law *when it provides for* a relatively formal administrative procedure tending to foster the fairness and deliberation that should underlie a pronouncement of such force.'[251] The dictum in *Mead* is far-reaching. It appears to impose a requirement that participation lead to a deliberative process, rather than a requirement of participation *tout court*. It does not seem appropriate for a court to impose a further requirement that a participatory delegated decision-making process should be deliberative. There are several reasons that the legislature might delegate power to take advantage of delegated decision-makers' ability to broaden participation, and it would ill-behove a court to second-guess such legislative choices.

3.5.3 *Procedural legitimacy in context*

As with the other practical justifications, procedural legitimacy will vary according to context. Some of the reasons for this will be explored at

[248] *Ibid.* at pp. 1044–5.
[249] *Ibid.*, p. 1046. Emphasis added. See also *Council of Canadians with Disabilities*, above n. 39, p. 707.
[250] *Mead*, above n. 229. [251] *Ibid.*, p. 230, per Souter J. Emphasis added.

length in the next subsection, so here I will simply indicate briefly how procedural legitimacy might vary, in that it may be achieved to a greater or lesser extent. Considering the ways in which procedural legitimacy may be reduced is illustrative. A process may be defective in gathering information, by leaving out important parties, or ignoring apparently relevant inputs; the aggregation of interests may similarly be imperfect due to the exclusion of important parties or relevant inputs; deliberation may be hampered by the inclusion of too many, or too few, parties, the imposition of time limits hindering full discussion or ineffective leadership, preventing full and frank discussion; and the value of participation per se may be reduced by not allowing affected parties to state their claims as fully as they might like. That establishing when procedures are defective might lead reviewing courts into deep waters is a problem addressed below. In addition, a court might be just as capable, in some instances, of providing the same procedural legitimacy as a delegated decision-maker, particularly in the case of classic bi-polar disputes, which traditional judicial adjudicative procedures would be well capable of resolving. Whether procedural legitimacy is a plausible reason for the delegation of power to a body other than a court will depend on context.

3.5.4 *Difficulties with procedural legitimacy*

As noted, difficulties attend each of the four contributors to procedural legitimacy mentioned above. Some have already been mentioned and others are detailed in this subsection. The primary purpose of this subsection is to elucidate some general concerns about participation in the delegated decision-making process.

3.5.4.1 Practicality

It is possible that there could be too much of a good thing. If too many participants are involved in the delegated decision-making process, too much information may be placed before the delegated decision-maker. If too much information is received, processed, assessed and analysed, it is possible that bad, irrelevant information will crowd out good, relevant information. It may become more difficult to sift the bad, irrelevant information from the good, relevant information.[252]

[252] Rossi, 'Amok', above n. 214, p. 216. See also J. J. Richardson and A. G. Jordan, *Governing under Pressure: The Policy Process in a Post-Parliamentary Democracy* (Oxford: Martin Robertson, 1979), pp. 53–5.

A related problem was identified by Breyer J in his 1992 Holmes Lectures: 'efforts to explain risks to the public at open meetings, may not suffice to alleviate risk regulation problems'.[253] Due to the various factors that hamper individuals' assessments of risk, the result of participation may be 'no consensus, but increased confusion'.[254] To this one might add the risk of group polarisation: if the inputs to a decision-making procedure are tilted to one side, the views of the group as a whole will tend to become more extreme than the views initially held.[255] The observation applies, *mutatis mutandis*, to any complex area of delegated decision-making. In addition:

> [a] frequently noted complaint is that the indirect nature of rule-making tends to undermine problem solving and reward adversarialism. Because the agency is the focal point of informal rule-making, parties miss opportunities to engage constructively with each other in a sustained way. They often take extreme positions in notice and comment, preferring to posture in anticipation of litigation rather than focus on the regulatory problem posed by the agency. This encourages the agency to compromise or split the difference between competing positions, which can constrain the range of solutions to numeric limits or standards that fall somewhere between the poles represented by the parties.[256]

In short, identifying the optimal level of participation is very difficult. Too much participation and the accuracy of the delegated decision-making process in correctly identifying and aggregating the relevant interests, as well as the ability of delegated decision-makers to foster deliberation and the inherent value of participation, could be greatly reduced.

3.5.4.2 Ossifying the decision-making process

A closely related difficulty is that too much participation can impede the delegated decision-making process.[257] If all comments, or even all relevant comments, are to be received, processed, assessed and analysed, such that they are given due consideration in the delegated decision-making process, the process could slow to a snail's pace. The opportunity

[253] Breyer, *Risk Regulation*, above n. 9, p. 38.

[254] *Ibid.*, p. 39. See also Gillette and Krier, 'Risk', above n. 50, p. 1105; Maria Lee and Carolyn Abbot, 'The Usual Suspects? Public Participation under the Aarhus Convention' (2003) 66 MLR 80, 84.

[255] Sunstein, 'Group Judgments', above n. 60.

[256] Freeman, 'Collaborative Governance', above n. 240, pp. 11–12.

[257] But see Gellhorn, 'Public Participation', above n. 213, pp. 384–7.

cost of extra participation is especially relevant: the more time a delegated decision-maker spends listening to participants in a hearing, the less time there is remaining to listen to other participants, render decisions and develop expertise. It is probably for these reasons that the Supreme Court of the United States has limited the use of formal rule-making procedures to cases where a statute clearly indicates that formal rule-making must be employed,[258] and forbidden reviewing courts to require extra procedures in addition to those chosen by a delegated decision-maker which is proceeding informally.[259] Even then, however, participatory procedures can provide 'powerful political constituencies with ample opportunity to mobilise against individual rule-making initiatives' and slow down the delegated decision-making process.[260]

3.5.4.3 Delegated decision-maker's choice of procedures

Some tension may be present between a delegated decision-maker's power, typical though not inevitable, to choose the most appropriate means of implementing a statute, and the desire to increase participation. Delegated decision-makers are usually delegated significant authority to choose between case-by-case adjudication and general rule-making to develop their policies: 'even where an agency's enabling statute expressly requires it to hold a hearing, the agency may rely on its rule-making authority to determine issues that do not require case-by-case consideration'.[261] Indeed, the delegated decision-maker has latitude in deciding whether policy should be developed in a comprehensive or incremental manner.[262] Thus, when the Supreme Court of the United States held in *United States* v. *Mead Corporation*[263] that curial deference should be accorded where a delegated decision-making process fostered 'fairness and deliberation',[264] Scalia J protested in dissent that the

[258] *United States* v. *Florida East Coast Railway* (1973) 410 US 224.

[259] *Vermont Yankee Nuclear Power Corporation* v. *Natural Resources Defence Council* (1978) 435 US 519.

[260] Thomas McGarity, 'Some Thoughts on "Deossifying" the Rule-making Process' (1992) 41 Duke LJ 1385, 1397.

[261] *Heckler* v. *Campbell* (1983) 461 US 458 at 467, per Powell J. See also *Securities and Exchange Commission* v. *Chenery (No. 2)* (1947) 332 US 194 at 202; *Bushell*, above n. 16 at 96–7 (Lord Diplock), at 122–3 (Lord Lane).

[262] Colin Diver, 'Policy-making Paradigms in Administrative Law' (1981) 95 Harv LR 393, 433. Compare Simon, *Administrative Behaviour*, above n. 53 with Charles Lindblom, 'The Science of "Muddling Through"' (1959) 19 *Public Administration Review* 79; 'Still Muddling, Not Yet Through' (1979) 39 *Public Administration Review* 517.

[263] *Mead*, above n. 229. [264] *Ibid.*, p. 230.

long-accepted freedom of a delegated decision-maker to choose between adjudication and rule-making would be compromised by the majority's decision.[265]

3.5.4.4 Imperfect representation

Another difficulty relates to ascertaining who should participate in a delegated decision-making process: 'Unless the public participant can represent its interest adequately, intervention will not be maximally productive.'[266] One response is that any party that wishes to participate may do so. Where a delegated decision-maker is assembling a record based on written submissions, it may be feasible to allow participation by any interested member of the general public. However, where a trial-type hearing is envisaged and certain parties are to be accorded the right to legal representation, to lead evidence and to cross-examine witnesses, some mechanism will have to be developed to decide who ought to be accorded participatory rights. In a hearing over the siting of a nuclear power plant, for example, it might be clear that residents living in the area should be represented, but which individual or group would best represent them? A local activist who has spent years studying the problem? A residents' association that has retained counsel? What if there are several residents' associations? Would a national environmental organisation that has been active in many similar hearings be more effective on behalf of the residents? Deciding who ought to be accorded significant participatory rights, then, may be problematic.[267]

In addition, '[e]ven if they wished to embrace collaboration ... chronically understaffed public interest groups cannot afford to participate in multiple negotiations over multiple policy issues and at the same time continue to fight their traditional battles in courts and legislatures'.[268] Industry groups might not be hampered by similar resource constraints and louder, well-financed voices may well drown out quieter, less well-financed voices:[269] 'Power, like beauty or money, is not evenly

[265] *Ibid.* at pp. 243–5. [266] Gellhorn, 'Public Participation', above n. 213, p. 382.

[267] See generally Richard Stewart, 'The Reformation of American Administrative Law' (1975) 88 Harv LR 1667, 1760–90. In addition, an initial decision to accord participation rights to one group over another may affect the initially disfavoured group's ability to participate in future. See Reich, 'Administration and Deliberation', above n. 221, pp. 1626–7.

[268] Freeman, 'Collaborative Governance', above n. 240, p. 76.

[269] See Mashaw, *Due Process*, above n. 73, pp. 23–4.

distributed.'[270] Indeed, if groups perceive themselves to be excluded from delegated decision-making processes, increasing the number of participatory initiatives 'may actually re-inforce exclusion by providing a wider range of forums from which people can feel themselves shut out'.[271]

3.5.4.5 Assessing the quality of participation

Amy Gutmann and Denis Thompson have raised an interesting difficulty: 'To assess the justifiability of a procedure in particular instances, even a procedure as widely accepted as majority rule, we need to know what kind of discussion took place, who participated, what arguments they presented, and how each responded to the claims of others.'[272] While procedures can contribute to the legitimacy of decisions, the quality of the procedure in the individual case will also matter. Gutmann and Thompson's argument implies that the existence of a legitimating procedure can justify curial deference only if the procedure is properly employed. Following their logic, a court could not accord curial deference simply on the assertion that particular procedures were followed. Further evidence would have to be adduced as to how extensive the procedures were. Various dangers lie along this path. As I have already suggested, courts may not be in a position to judge the optimal level of participation: they may find it difficult to identify the persons or parties who should be permitted to participate, let alone to identify the extent of the required participation. One can say that procedures must be 'responsive to the dynamics of policy-making'[273] but in the present context, the admonition adds little value.

Nonetheless, without delving too deeply into specifics, a reviewing court should be able to differentiate between a procedure that enables differing viewpoints to be taken into account for the purposes of further discussion and one that does not; it might develop a spectrum, with paradigm cases at either end, to assist it in its endeavours, guided always by the delegated decision-maker's view of the appropriate limits of participation. As with expertise,[274] opposing counsel will have ample interest and opportunity to expose delegated decision-making which did not in fact engender participation or deliberation.

[270] Richardson and Jordan, *Governing under Pressure*, above n. 252, p. 187.
[271] Select Committee on Public Administration, above n. 225, [40].
[272] Guttman and Thomson, *Democracy and Disagreement*, above n. 235, p. 33.
[273] Galligan, *Due Process*, above n. 216, p. 481. [274] See above 3.2.4.

3.5.4.6 Participation not required by statute

A more general difficulty is presented by participation which occurs even though it has not been expressly permitted or required by statute. What of participation under the auspices of a government department, for example? What of an ad hoc consultation process conducted by a minister? The answer is that such participation cannot be seen as relevant to the doctrine of curial deference proposed here. Although as a free-standing practical justification for curial deference, the conducting of an ad hoc consultation would counsel according curial deference, the fact that it is not envisaged in the delegation of power counsels against according curial deference. Where procedures are long-standing or required by convention,[275] it might be reasonable to impute knowledge of the procedures to the legislature. But generally, if the legislature did not empower the delegated decision-maker to utilise and benefit from participatory procedures, the case for curial deference is accordingly weakened. The outcome is admittedly anomalous, in that the free-standing practical justification may be stronger than one based on legislative intent, but results from the judicial obligation to give effect to legislative intent. However, the outcome could be changed by the simple insertion in the relevant statute of a new provision allowing participatory delegated decision-making.

A related issue arises where participation is required for constitutional reasons. A constitutional right to procedural fairness, or natural justice, might require participation.[276] Where a statute is interpreted so as to require participation, it will be necessary to impute to the legislature the intention to require participation or deliberation. When courts interpret statutes to as to include procedural requirements, those interpretations are treated as binding expressions of legislative intent. Thus, where a procedure is required to ensure that a statute is not struck down as unconstitutional, the relevant statutory provisions have to be read as including a requirement of participation, and participation thereby becomes an aspect of legislative intent.

[275] In England, for example, much participation occurs in the absence of statutory authorisation. See e.g. Baldwin, *Rules and Government*, above n. 238, p. 75; Paul Craig, 'Perspectives on Process: Common Law, Statutory and Political' [2010] PL 275, 293–5; Galligan, *Due Process*, above n. 216, pp. 492–3.

[276] See e.g. *Yamataya* v. *Fisher* (1903) 189 US 86; *Wong Yang Sung* v. *McGrath* (1950) 339 US 33.

3.5.5 *Procedural legitimacy reassessed*

Linking procedural legitimacy to legislative intent actually strengthens it as a practical justification for curial deference. It is only where the legislature, despite the potential pitfalls, has taken the decision to require or permit participation that a reviewing court should defer on the basis of procedural legitimacy. A reviewing court will not be required to wander aimlessly in the foothills of political theory. For those who favour increased participation, proceeding along the lines suggested here may, because it accords primacy to legislative intent, be preferable to piecemeal, and possibly inapt, reform by courts: 'judicial review … is too clumsy a technique for the concocting of administrative experiments in participatory governance. In all likelihood, it will be too slow to respond initially, too uninformed to be apt, and too slow again to make changes or adjustments.'[277] Even if not mandated by statute, informal participatory procedures are likely to continue in operation, assuming that they have some or all of the benefits ascribed to them. But if they are not required by statute, the risks of building judicial review doctrine around participatory procedures are too great. It would be much more likely that procedural legitimacy would gain a central place in judicial review if legislatures and delegated decision-makers were able to experiment with different modes and forms of participation.

3.6 Free-standing practical justifications

In developing a doctrine according to which the standard of review for *Wednesbury* unreasonableness increases or decreases depending on the circumstances of a particular case, the English courts have not emphasised the importance of legislative intent. The English approach raises a question: why not treat the practical justifications as reasons for curial deference entirely independently of legislative intent?

At the super-*Wednesbury* end of the spectrum, in *Nottinghamshire County Council* v. *Secretary of State for the Environment*,[278] there was no reliance on legislative intent to bolster, let alone justify, the additional judicial restraint. Similarly, when Sir Thomas Bingham MR described the super-*Wednesbury* end of the spectrum in *R* v. *Ministry of Defence, ex p. Smith*,[279] no link with legislative intent was identified:

[277] Mashaw, *Due Process*, above n. 73, p. 263. [278] *Nottinghamshire*, above n. 156.
[279] [1996] QB 517.

> The greater the policy content of a decision, and the more remote the subject-matter of a decision from ordinary judicial experience, the more hesitant the court must necessarily be in holding a decision to be irrational. That is good law and, like most good law, common sense. Where decisions of a policy-laden, esoteric or security-based nature are in issue even greater caution than normal must be shown in applying the test, but the test itself is sufficiently flexible to cover all situations.[280]

At the other end of the spectrum, the heightened scrutiny afforded by the English courts to decisions infringing important rights or interests also has its origins elsewhere than in legislative intent. *Bugdaycay* v. *Secretary of State for the Home Department*[281] is the *locus classicus* of more intrusive review.[282] There, the respondent had decided to send a failed asylum seeker back to a third country, the decision having been made on the assumption that the third country would not send the asylum seeker back to his country of origin. Legislative intent was not referred to, let alone adduced as a justification for ratcheting up the intensity of judicial scrutiny.[283] In *Bugdaycay*, the House of Lords was more concerned with 'the examination of the decision-making process',[284] but the rule that decisions infringing important rights or interests should be subjected to more rigorous examination on judicial review escaped the confines of review of the decision-making process and travelled to the substantive review of exercises of discretion. In *Smith*,[285] the applicants challenged the legality of a blanket ban on service by homosexuals in the armed forces. Sir Thomas Bingham MR accepted that the intensity of judicial review should be increased *pro rata* to the interference with the applicant's fundamental rights and rejected the respondent's assertion that because matters of policy were in question the court should adopt a relatively restrained stance.[286] Again legislative intent was conspicuous by its absence.

But if no link between legislative intent and variable standards of review has been identified, from whence do the variable standards of review come? In Sir John Laws' grandiloquent phrasing, variable standards of review are located in:

> man's very nature as an autonomous rational being living in society … Public power may bear upon the values of individual autonomy in different ways and different contexts. A statute authorising the imprisonment

[280] *Ibid.*, p. 556. [281] [1987] AC 514. [282] See above 1.2.3.
[283] *Bugdaycay*, above n. 281, p. 531. [284] *Ibid.*, p. 537, per Lord Templeman.
[285] *Smith*, above n. 279. [286] *Ibid.*, p. 556.

> of immigrants awaiting removal is one thing. A statute regulating the use of handguns is another. Now, if the common law has no *choice* but to deliver Kant's [categorical] imperative in concrete form, it is bound also to take differential approaches to the uses of power devolved by such statutes.[287]

For Laws, the requirement of variable standards of review is located in the common law and not in statute; they are free-standing rather than tethered to legislative intent. This appears to reflect the reasoning of the English courts.[288] But the English approach is problematic for three reasons.

First, the approach is inconsistent with the foundations of curial deference in English law. If the reason relied upon by the courts to justify a deferential posture in the first place is legislative intent,[289] it seems to follow that the reason for a variably deferential posture must also be legislative intent. The failure to explain the variability of reasonableness review by reference to legislative intent sits uneasily with the underlying justification for judicial restraint.

Secondly, as I have sought to demonstrate, the practical justifications each contain flaws. Experts may not be as expert as they seem. Invocations of complexity may be routine and lacking in substance. Democratic legitimacy may not improve the quality of a decision. Procedural legitimacy requires participation in the delegated decision-making process, but identifying the appropriate type of participation is very difficult. If the practical justifications were treated as free-standing, courts would have to address these potential flaws on a case-by-case basis. Doing so would require the expenditure of judicial time and resources on matters that judges are not especially well equipped to adjudicate: has a delegated decision-maker been 'captured' by a regulated entity? Is a delegated decision-maker capable of resolving a polycentric problem? Does the fact that a minister has been elected make it more likely that a correct decision will be rendered on a question of public morality? Did a participatory process foster a sufficiently deliberative atmosphere? Quite apart from being time-consuming to answer and lying outside the normal field of judicial expertise, these questions

287 '*Wednesbury*' in Christopher Forsyth and Ivan Hare (eds.), *The Golden Metwand and Crooked Cord: Essays on Public Law in Honour of Sir William Wade* (Oxford: Hart, 1998), p. 185, p. 190. Emphasis original.

288 Although as far as I am aware no judge deciding a case has explicitly invoked Kant to justify varying the standard of review!

289 See above 2.3.1.

are provocative and liable to lead judges into controversial territory. By linking the practical justifications for curial deference with legislative intent, however, these questions do not have to be considered in great detail. Indeed, any consideration of these questions is justified:[290] the reason that expertise, complexity, democratic legitimacy and procedural legitimacy would be relevant to establishing the appropriate standard of review is that courts are obliged to consider them, by virtue of their obligation to give effect to legislative intent. Justifying the use of the practical justifications for curial deference would be significantly more difficult if they were detached from legislative intent.

Thirdly, if the practical justifications were not related to legislative intent, the set of practical justifications would be potentially infinite. Any practical justification for curial deference could be developed and could legitimately be given effect to (although it would face questions similar to those I posed of expertise, complexity, democratic legitimacy and procedural legitimacy). Flexibility would be greatly increased, but at the expense of certainty: litigants would not know which practical justifications would prove to be relevant. Judges, might, indeed, feel obliged to trawl through legislative history in order to find the real reasons for delegation, an operation which would be as hazardous as it would be difficult.[291] If the practical justifications are linked to legislative intent, the scope for judicial creativity is reduced, and legal certainty is increased. Although the process of determining the appropriate standard of review is a difficult one, it can take place within a relatively stable framework.

3.7 Conclusion

If the legislature were to direct that a variable standard of review is appropriate, courts would be required to develop and implement a variable standard of review. Where the legislative direction is not explicit but may be inferred from a proper consideration of the relevant statutory provisions, reviewing courts mindful of their obligation to give effect to legislative intent should develop and implement a variable standard of

[290] In addition, it explains why Ivan Hare is wrong to claim that 'mere expertise in an arcane field of law is not a justification for deference which sounds on the constitutional plane'. 'The Separation of Powers and Judicial Review for Error of Law' in Christopher Forsyth and Ivan Hare (eds.), *The Golden Metwand and Crooked Cord: Essays on Public Law in Honour of Sir William Wade* (Oxford: Hart, 1998), p. 113, p. 137.

[291] See above 2.1.

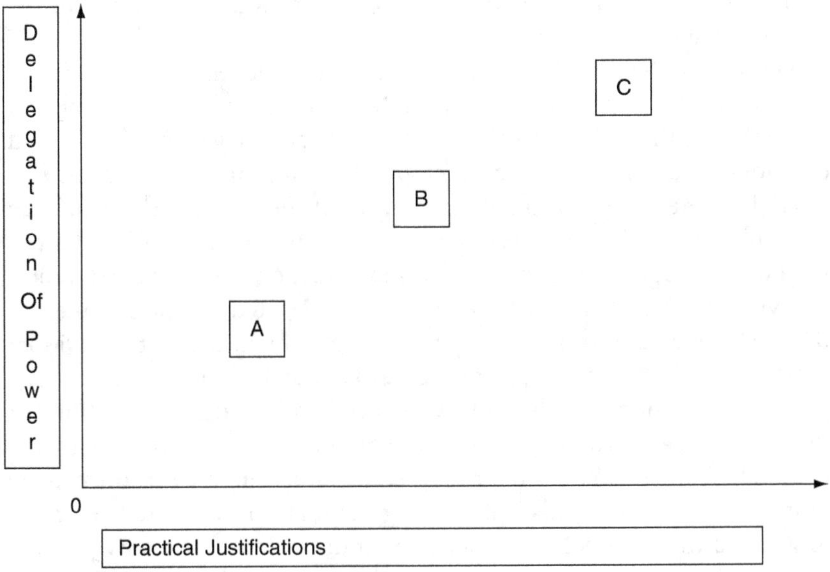

Figure 1: The visualisation described in section 3.7.

review. The fact that 'delegatory intent must sometimes be sought through inference and construction, rather than from direct manifestations of [legislative] will' does not create serious difficulties.[292]

As with the extent of delegations of power, the practical justifications for curial deference vary. Legislative intent, to which reviewing courts are obliged to give effect, can thus be visualised as depicted in Figure 1. Here, delegation of power = *f* {Variety of the Powers + Nature of the Powers + Field of Jurisdiction + Autonomy}. Practical justifications = *f* {Expertise + Complexity + Democratic Legitimacy + Procedural Legitimacy}. Legislative intent has to be determined in a rough sense. I do not contend that the delegation of power or the practical justifications can be precisely quantified. However, roughly speaking, a particular decision, made by a particular delegated decision-maker following a particular process can be mapped on the graph (as with points A, B and C). This should address judicial criticism that the process of determining how much curial deference to accord involves wading into a 'quagmire'.[293]

292 Robert Anthony, 'Which Agency Interpretations Should Bind Citizens and the Courts' (1990) 7 Yale J on Reg 1, 5.

293 *State of California Department of Social Services* v. *Thompson* (2003) 321 F 3d 835 at 848, per Berzon J.

I address the standard of review appropriate to different points on the graph in the next chapter.

The approach I am advocating operates on two levels, as I explained in Chapter 2:[294] the existence of varying delegations of power and practical justifications that vary according to context across a galaxy of delegated decision-makers requires the development of a framework such as this one. Then, the identification of the appropriate degree of curial deference to accord in a particular case depends on the interaction of the extent of the power delegated and the practical justifications for curial deference. A reviewing court can chart the place of a delegated decision-maker on the graph in an abstract sense. But the graph's main use is in individual cases, to identify the appropriate degree of curial deference in respect of a particular decision, which might vary 'even within different sections of the same Act, and with regard to different types of decisions taken by the tribunal in question'.[295] In principle, any impugned decision can be plotted on the graph. This is not to suggest that I have created 'a terrain to which different types of decisions are transported',[296] thereby reintroducing the dubious spatial distinctions I sought to exclude in Chapter 1.[297] Rather, the graph is an illustration of the possible outcomes of the unrelentingly substantive analysis which proper appreciation of the obligation to give effect to legislative intent requires reviewing courts to undertake.

294 See above 2.3.3.

295 *Pushpanathan*, above n. 36, p. 1019, per Bastarache J. See also *Macdonell*, above n. 33, p. 693.

296 Robert Leckey, 'Territoriality in Canadian Administrative Law' (2004) 24 UTLJ 327, 363.

297 See above 1.1.3.

4

Variable standards of review

I have argued that a doctrine of curial deference according to which varying degrees of curial deference ought to be accorded to delegated decision-makers by reviewing courts follows from the judicial obligation to give effect to legislative intent. I now attempt to develop a variable standard of review to complement the framework developed in Chapters 2 and 3, thereby completing my development of a doctrine of curial deference. In this chapter I will explain how the concept of unreasonableness can accommodate a variable standard of review. I will not claim that developing a variable standard of review within the concept of unreasonableness is the only available option.[1] Indeed, one could believe simply and straightforwardly that, having established that curial deference is appropriate, the according of epistemic deference is sufficient.[2] However, I take the view that a doctrinal approach is preferable, given its potential to induce a greater degree of rigour on the part of reviewing courts.[3] The attraction of employing unreasonableness to this end is its familiarity. Rationality review has aptly been described as a 'conventional safeguard'[4] and thereby provides a useful vehicle in which

[1] See similarly Luc Tremblay, 'La Norme de retenue judiciaire et les "erreurs de droit" en droit administratif: une erreur de droit? Au delà du fondationalisme et du scepticism' (1996) 56 *Revue du Barreau* 141. Tremblay suggests, correctly in my view, that the factors relied upon by the Supreme Court of Canada in its pragmatic and functional analysis did not require any particular combination of standards of review. Similarly, it cannot be said that the approach I will advocate in this chapter follows inexorably from the argument I laid out in Chs. 2 and 3.

[2] See e.g. David Dyzenhaus, 'The Politics of Deference: Judicial Review and Democracy' in Michael Taggart (ed.), *The Province of Administrative Law* (Oxford: Hart, 1997), p. 279; Murray Hunt, 'Sovereignty's Blight' in Nicholas Bamforth and Peter Leyland (eds.), *Public Law in a Multi-Layered Constitution* (Oxford: Hart, 2003), p. 337; Tremblay, 'Retenue Judiciaire', above n. 1, pp. 232–8.

[3] See similarly Gabrielle Perrault, *Le Contrôle judiciaire des decisions de l'administration: de l'erreur juridictionnelle à la norme de contrôle* (Montreal: Wilson and Lafleur, 2002), p. 86.

[4] *Air New Zealand* v. *Wellington International Airport* [2009] 2 NZLR 713 at 738, per Baragwanath J, dissenting, but not on this point.

a variable standard of review can journey through the vast expanse of administrative law.

4.1 Correctness and epistemic deference

Before beginning my analysis of unreasonableness, it will be convenient to describe the standard of review of correctness. A straightforward treatment would be to say that, where a standard of correctness applies, the court must resolve the issue at hand, taking a *de novo* view of the question and substituting its judgment for that of the delegated decision-maker. Superficially, this is the case. Where correctness is the standard of review, the final word is that of the reviewing courts; they 'retain a legitimate role as the ultimate authority on the interpretation of law'.[5] However, in determining what its final word ought to be, it may be necessary for reviewing courts to accord epistemic deference to delegated decision-makers. There are two ways in which epistemic deference might be appropriate. First, the fact that a delegated decision-maker has made a decision inexorably alters the interpretative landscape.[6] A reviewing court cannot proceed without taking into account the decision being reviewed, and the reasons underpinning it. To some extent, by virtue of the reviewing court's obligation to take relevant matters into account, weight must be accorded to the decision. Secondly, it will not always be the case, where a reviewing court concludes that a standard of review of correctness is appropriate, that the practical justifications for curial deference are entirely irrelevant. The delegated decision-maker may have some expertise, for example, which, while not enough to justify a deferential standard of review, should justify the according of some weight to its view. Epistemic deference in this context requires what Cora Hoexter has described as:

> a judicial willingness to appreciate the legitimate and constitutionally-ordained province of administrative agencies; to admit the expertise of those agencies in policy-laden or polycentric issues; to accord their interpretation of fact and law due respect; and to be sensitive in general to the interests legitimately pursued by administrative bodies and the practical and financial constraints under which they operate.[7]

[5] Dyzenhaus, 'Politics of Democracy', above n. 2, p. 303. [6] See above 1.3.

[7] 'The Future of Judicial Review in South African Administrative Law' (2000) 117 SALJ 484, 501–2.

The point has been well explained by a Canadian appellate judge:

> Almost all arguments about statutory interpretation in this Court, and indeed arguments about many other questions, consist of reasoned thinking supporting one view or the other. In the end, the judges tend not to say that one argument is correct and the other incorrect. They say that they adopt, accept, or prefer one argument to the other and give their opinions accordingly. So, in the end, it is possible to give one argument greater weight than another in deciding which to prefer. If an argument is made that deference on the interpretation of the statute should be given to those who are experts in its functioning, that does not mean that the standard of 'correctness' is being abandoned. What it means is that deference is being given through acceptance of one of the arguments, which, in turn, may decide the balance between the competing arguments, in relation to applying the standard of 'correctness'. In such a situation, neither of the competing arguments need be categorised as 'wrong', but only one of them is preferred. That one, but not the other one, then meets the standard of 'correctness'. And that argument may be supported by, among other points, a degree of deference to the opinion of the tribunal whose jurisdiction is in issue.[8]

Application of a standard of review of correctness then, is not an open invitation to judicial imperialism. Reviewing courts may have the final word, but its content will in part be a product of the pronouncements of the delegated decision-maker.

4.2 Unreasonableness and merits review

Review of the unreasonableness of an impugned decision inevitably involves a reviewing court in a consideration of the merits, or substance, of the impugned decision. However, the consideration of matters which go to the merits of a decision, or its substance, is not particularly problematic, because a consideration of the merits or substance is inevitable in any review for unreasonableness:

> Any adjudication upon the reasonableness of a decision must involve an evaluation of the merits. Reasonableness is not a quality that exists in isolation. When a court says that a decision under review is 'reasonable' or 'patently unreasonable' it is making a statement about the logical relationship between the grounds of the decision and premises thought

[8] *Northwood* v. *British Columbia (Forest Practices Board)* [2001] BCCA 141; 86 BCLR (3d) 215 at 229, per Lambert JA. See similarly *Van Unen* v. *British Columbia (Workers Compensation Board)* [2001] BCCA 262; 87 BCLR (3d) 277 at 285–6.

> by the court to be true. Without the reference point of an opinion (if not a conclusion) on the merits, such a relative statement cannot be made.[9]

A consideration of the merits is not the same as a decision on the merits.[10]

This is also true where correctness is the appropriate standard of review. If a standard of review of correctness is appropriate, it will be appropriate because the legislature has delegated the decision to the court. In most cases, in the absence of a direct delegation of authority to the court, or an appeal to the court from the original decision, correctness review of discretionary decisions will be unlikely. As LeBel J commented in *Montreal (City)* v. *Montreal Port Authority*:[11]

> [where] a discretion exists, exercising it can lead to the adoption of varying opinions and solutions depending on the application of the relevant legal principles to the facts of the case, and on reviewing a decision of this nature, the court must show deference to the administrative decision maker.[12]

In any event, even in reviewing for correctness a decision to exercise, or not to exercise, a discretionary power, a court would not have expansive powers. The fact that a reviewing court will be, broadly speaking, limited to affirming or quashing a delegated decision-maker's discretionary decision is important. As a result, it will not stand in the shoes of the delegated decision-maker.

[9] *Canadian Association of Industrial, Mechanical and Allied Workers, Local 14* v. *Paccar of Canada* [1989] 2 SCR 983 at 1018, per Sopinka J. I do not think a great deal turns on whether the standard of review is characterised as reasonableness or unreasonableness. However, characterising it as unreasonableness would indicate that the burden is on the applicant to demonstrate why the decision ought to be struck down, whereas characterising it as reasonableness indicates that the delegated decision-maker must positively satisfy a test of reasonableness. See e.g. Evan Fox-Decent, 'The Internal Morality of Administration: The Form and Structure of Reasonableness' in David Dyzenhaus (ed.), *The Unity of Public Law* (Oxford: Hart, 2004), p. 143; Lorne Sossin, 'An Intimate Approach to Fairness, Impartiality and Reasonableness in Administrative Law' (2002) 27 Queen's LJ 809, 827–30. Unreasonableness, then, is the term more in accordance with current practice. Moreover, the fact that unreasonableness has been identified as the appropriate standard of review, a process which takes account of many of the factors that would be relevant to satisfying a test of reasonableness, would appear to shift any burden to the applicant.

[10] See also David Feldman, 'Convention Rights and Substantive *Ultra Vires*' in Christopher Forsyth (ed.), *Judicial Review and the Constitution* (Oxford: Hart, 2000), p. 245, pp. 250, 257.

[11] [2010] SCC 14; [2010] 1 SCR 427.

[12] *Ibid.*, p. 446.

4.3 What is unreasonableness?[13]

One preliminary point is worth addressing. Sometimes, judges suggest that a decision is only unreasonable in situations where a delegated decision-maker has taken leave of its senses. An exemplar is the following passage from an Irish High Court decision, handed down by O'Sullivan J:

> the kind of error that produces invalidity is one which no rational or sane decision maker, no matter how misguided, could [make]. It is not sufficient that a decision maker goes wrong or even hopelessly or fundamentally wrong: he must have gone completely and inexplicably mad: taken leave of his senses and come to an absurd conclusion. It is only when this last situation arises or something akin to it that a court will review the decision for irrationality.[14]

However, as Paul Craig has observed, to take such language literally would mean placing 'an almost insurmountable hurdle' before an applicant for judicial review: 'it is very difficult, if not impossible, to come up with real-world cases in which such extreme irrationality has been present'.[15] Attention to the nuances of legislative intent suggests that such an imposing barrier should not *routinely* be placed in front of individuals who wish to challenge the decisions of delegated decision-makers. Perhaps the exacting standard described by O'Sullivan J should be part of a judge's judicial review toolkit, but principle suggests that it should not be the sole utensil found therein.

To describe a decision as unreasonable tells us nothing of *why* the decision is unreasonable: 'The incantation of the word "unreasonable" simply does not provide sufficient justification for judicial intervention. Intellectual honesty requires a further and better explanation as to *why*

[13] I use the term unreasonableness in preference to irrationality, which has been treated as synonymous with it (see e.g. *Council of Civil Service Unions* v. *Minister for the Civil Service* [1985] AC 374 at 410), because irrationality has pejorative connotations. See Paul Walker, 'What's Wrong with Irrationality?' [1995] PL 556, 569; William Wade and Christopher Forsyth, *Administrative Law*, 10th edn (Oxford: Oxford University Press, 2009), p. 296.

[14] *Aer Rianta* v. *Commissioner for Aviation Regulation*, unreported, High Court, 16 January 2003. See also Dean Knight, 'Mapping the Rainbow of Review: Recognising Variable Intensity' [2010] NZLR 393, 404; and e.g. *R* v. *Lord Chancellor, ex p. Maxwell* [1997] 1 LRC 469 at 474, per Henry LJ ('Decisions so unreasonable as to warrant interference jump off the page at you').

[15] 'Proportionality, Rationality and Review' [2010] NZLR 265, 274.

the act is unreasonable.'[16] Even if one were to say that a decision would be unreasonable if 'so outrageous in its defiance of logic or of accepted moral standards that no sensible person who had applied his mind to the question to be decided could have arrived at it',[17] it would still be necessary to ask *why* the decision defied logic or accepted moral standards:

> Rationality requires that decisions be made for reasons which are rational in terms of our understanding of the world. But of course rationality is an extremely complex notion; decisions can be more or less rational from different points of view, and indeed what constitutes a rational decision may itself depend upon the objects to be achieved and the means available.[18]

A New Zealand judge has stated the problem in a more positive manner: 'Ultimately, the Court must exercise a judgment in assessing the reasonableness or unreasonableness of the authority's action, and what is required is assistance in the way that judgment is to be exercised.'[19]

In this chapter, I aim to move beyond assertions that an unreasonable decision is one no reasonable decision-maker could make and bromides about reasonableness connoting a range of reasonable decisions. It is a sorry state of affairs that, more than twenty years after Dickson CJ commented that 'patent unreasonableness rests to a large extent on unarticulated and undeveloped values and lacks the same degree of structure and sophistication of analysis [as a proportionality test]',[20] the values and structure of unreasonableness remain unarticulated and undeveloped. I hope I can provide some assistance in this chapter.[21]

[16] Anthony Lester and Jeffrey Jowell, 'Beyond *Wednesbury*: Substantive Principles of Administrative Law' [1987] PL 368, 371. Emphasis original.

[17] *Council of Civil Service Unions*, above n. 13, p. 410, per Lord Diplock.

[18] Denis Galligan, *Discretionary Powers: A Legal Study of Official Discretion* (Oxford: Clarendon, 1986), p. 5. The same point applies to the sliding scale developed by the English courts in respect of judicial review for alleged breaches of legitimate expectations. See e.g. *R (Begbie)* v. *Department of Education and Employment* [1999] EWCA Civ 2100; [2000] 1 WLR 1115, 1129–31, per Laws LJ. Guidance in determining what constitutes *Wednesbury* unreasonableness, sub- and super-, remains necessary.

[19] *Waitakere City Council* v. *Lovelock* [1997] 2 NZLR 385 at 403, per Thomas J.

[20] *Slaight Communications* v. *Davidson* [1989] 1 SCR 1038 at 1049.

[21] My dataset for analysis comprised decisions rendered by the Supreme Court of Canada from 1979; by the Supreme Court of the United States from 1984 (*Chevron*) and 1960 (arbitrary and capricious); by the House of Lords from 1960 (*Wednesbury* unreasonableness); and by the English Court of Appeal from 1991 (anxious scrutiny). All that is needed here is a general overview of what makes a decision unreasonable; I am not, in other words, conducting a comprehensive study or survey of unreasonableness.

4.3.1 Indicia *of unreasonableness*

The case law is (almost) resolutely opaque. Mysterious references by reviewing courts to multiple factors, judgment and balancing are commonplace. Therefore it was necessary to examine the case law closely to ascertain what reviewing courts take into account in determining whether or not a decision is unreasonable. I have found that what I call '*indicia*' of unreasonableness[22] exist. These are factors which lead a court to consider that a decision is, or might be, unreasonable.

4.3.1.1 Illogicality

One *indicium* is illogicality: where the means chosen by a delegated decision-maker to achieve a particular aim are not apt to achieve the aim, the inaptness points towards the decision being unreasonable. An excellent example is *Zenner* v. *Prince Edward Island College of Optometrists.*[23] A requirement to fulfil several conditions was imposed on Z, who had fallen short of meeting his continuing professional development obligations, before he could resume the practice of optometry in Prince Edward Island. One of the conditions was that he complete an ethics course. However, the Supreme Court of Canada held it was unreasonable of the College to impose a requirement that Z sit an ethics exam because 'at the relevant time [no ethics course was] accredited or offered by the College or prescribed in the Regulations'.[24] A clearer illogicality than a purported imposition of the impossible is hard to imagine.[25]

4.3.1.2 Disproportionality

A second *indicium* is disproportionality: where the means employed to attain a given aim impose costs on an individual that are out of proportion to the wider benefit the delegated decision-maker hopes to achieve (or where another means of achieving the aim, which would not have imposed such costs on the individual, could have been employed).[26] The

[22] *Canada (Citizenship and Immigration)* v. *Khosa* [2009] SCC 12; [2009] 1 SCR 339 at 360, per Binnie J. See also David Mullan, 'Proportionality: A Proportionate Response to an Emerging Crisis in Canadian Judicial Review Law?' [2010] NZLR 233, 253. See also *ibid.*, p. 245, referring to 'badges of unreasonableness'.

[23] [2005] SCC 77; [2005] 3 SCR 645. [24] *Ibid.*, p. 661, per Major J.

[25] See also *Fawcett Properties* v. *Buckingham County Council* [1961] AC 636 at 674; *Allentown Mack and Sales* v. *National Labour Relations Board* (1998) 522 US 359; *United States* v. *Eurodif* (2009) 555 US 305.

[26] Note that I am using proportionality here in a narrower sense than its possible adoption as an independent ground of review. See below 5.2.2.

Conseil des services essentiels is an administrative tribunal established in Quebec to govern labour disputes pertaining to the provision of public services. In *Canadian Union of Public Employees, Local 301* v. *Montreal (City)*[27] an application had been made to the Conseil in anticipation of concerted action by city employees during the period of a holiday weekend. The Conseil granted an order preventing *all* city employees, regardless of their individual motives, from exercising the right, enshrined in a collectively bargained agreement, to refuse to work overtime. L'Heureux-Dubé J recognised the force of a submission that the order swept too broadly:

> The [Conseil's] order in this case might have been interpreted by the employer or employees as allowing the City to insist on overtime hours from all 'blue-collar' employees, at its behest, regardless of any potential reason for refusing, and for the entire period preceding the acquisition of the right to strike. This would involve a direct temporary suspension of a right in the collective agreement, even in the absence of participation in a concerted action, and may arguably not have withstood review even on the most deferent standard.[28]

However, the fact that the order was ultimately enforceable by contempt proceedings reduced the effect of the disproportionality: 'the principle that contempt of court is *strictissimi juris* would actually serve to ensure that the quasi-penal sanctions … will only target the union representatives and those employees who participated in the overtime ban'.[29] Thus the disproportionality was not fatal to the decision. Moreover, abrogating the individual rights was inevitable in the circumstances[30] and the decision was not tainted by any illogicality.[31]

4.3.1.3 Inconsistency with statute

A third *indicium* is inconsistency with statute. Various types of inconsistency may be alleged, each of which is an *indicium* of unreasonableness. I describe them in order of specificity. First, departure from the apparently

[27] [1997] 1 SCR 793. [28] *Ibid.*, p. 834. [29] *Ibid.*, p. 835. [30] *Ibid.*, p. 832.

[31] *Ibid.*, p. 833. See also *R* v. *Secretary of State for the Home Department, ex p. Brind* [1991] 1 AC 696; *Royal Oak Mines* v. *Canada (Labour Relations Board)* [1996] 1 SCR 369. See generally Fox-Decent, 'Internal Morality', above n. 9; Guy Regimbald, 'Correctness, Reasonableness and Proportionality: A New Standard of Judicial Review' (2005–2006) 31 Manitoba LJ 239; Lord Woolf, Jeffrey Jowell and Andrew Le Sueur, *De Smith's Judicial Review of Administrative Action*, 6th edn (London: Sweet and Maxwell, 2007), p. 585.

plain meaning of the statute is an *indicium* of unreasonableness.[32] Secondly, a statutory duty may be imposed by the relevant statute and failure to fulfil it is also an *indicium* of unreasonableness.[33] The third, fourth and fifth types of inconsistency refer to purpose, policy and value respectively. A purpose, policy or value may underpin a statute or statutory provision and inconsistency with the purpose, policy or value is an *indicium* of unreasonableness.[34] It is appropriate to consider such matters because of 'the importance of the scheme and purpose of an Act in construing the particular words used by the legislature to disclose its true intent'.[35] Courts 'must reject administrative constructions of the statute, whether reached by adjudication or by rulemaking, that are inconsistent with the statutory mandate or that frustrate the policy that Congress sought to implement'.[36]

[32] See especially *Whitman* v. *American Trucking Associations* (2001) 531 US 457 and see also *Federal Reserve System* v. *Dimension Financial* (1986) 474 US 361; *Rust* v. *Sullivan* (1991) 500 US 173; *Brown* v. *Gardner* (1994) 513 US 115; *Babbitt* v. *Sweet Home Chapter of Communities for a Great Oregon* (1995) 515 US 687; *Smiley* v. *Citibank (South Dakota)* (1996) 517 US 735; *Your Home Visiting Nurse Services* v. *Shalala* (1999) 525 US 449; *Macdonell* v. *Quebec (Commission d'accès à l'information)* [2002] SCC 71; [2002] 3 SCR 661; *Alberta Union of Public Employees* v. *Lethbridge Community College* [2004] SCC 28; [2004] 1 SCR 727; *Global Crossing Telecommunications* v. *Metrophones Telecommunications* (2007) 550 US 45; *Entergy* v. *Riverkeeper* (2009) 129 S Ct 1498.

[33] *R* v. *Chief Constable of Sussex, ex p. International Trader's Ferry* [1999] 2 AC 418; *Chamberlain* v. *Surrey School District No. 36* [2002] SCC 86; [2002] 4 SCR 710.

[34] 'Parliament must have conferred the discretion with the intention that it should be used to promote the policy and objects of the Act.' *Padfield* v. *Minister for Agriculture* [1968] AC 997 at 1030, per Lord Reid. For purposes cases, see *United Kingdom Association of Professional Engineers* v. *Conciliation and Arbitration Service* [1981] AC 424; *Japan Whaling Association* v. *American Cetacean Society* (1986) 478 US 221; *Devon County Council* v. *George* [1989] AC 573; *Pauley* v. *Bethenergy Mines* (1991) 501 US 680; *Arkansas* v. *Oklahoma* (1992) 503 US 91; *Edelman* v. *Lynchburg College* (2002) 535 US 106; *Barnhart* v. *Walton* (2002) 535 US 212; *Chevron USA* v. *Echazabal* (2002) 536 US 73. For policies cases, see *Lonrho* v. *Secretary of State for Trade and Industry* [1989] 2 All ER 609; *Pension Benefit Guaranty Corporation* v. *LTV Corporation* (1990) 496 US 633; *Lopez* v. *Davis* (2001) 531 US 230; *Yellow Transportation* v. *Michigan* (2002) 537 US 36; *Giguère* v. *Chambre des notaires du Québec* [2004] SCC 1; [2004] 1 SCR 3; *Lévis (City)* v. *Fraternité des policiers de Lévis* [2007] SCC 14; [2007] 1 SCR 591; *Montreal Port Authority*, above n. 11. For a values case, see *Baker* v. *Canada (Minister of Citizenship and Immigration)* [1999] 2 SCR 817 and see also Geneviève Cartier, 'The *Baker* Effect: A New Interface between the *Canadian Charter of Rights and Freedoms* and Administrative Law – the Case of Discretion' in David Dyzenhaus (ed.), *The Unity of Public Law* (Oxford: Hart, 2004), p. 61, pp. 74–9.

[35] *Canadian Union of Public Employees* v. *Ontario (Minister for Labour)* [2003] SCC 29; [2003] 1 SCR 539 at 589, per Binnie J.

[36] *Federal Election Commission* v. *Democratic Senatorial Campaign Committee* (1981) 454 US 27 at 32, per White J.

To speak of departures from statutory language as mere *indicia* of unreasonableness may seem unusual. Where the statutory language is clear, it may not be appropriate to permit deviation from it:

> Of course it can *always* be assumed that Congress would prefer *whatever* would preserve, in light of unforeseen eventualities, 'the legislature's overriding purpose'. We are not governed by legislators' 'overriding purposes', however, but by the laws that Congress enacts. If one of them is improvident or ill-conceived, it is not the province of this court to distort its fair meaning (or to sanction the executive's distortion) so that a *better* law will result. The immediate benefit achieved by such a practice in a particular case is far outweighed by the disruption of legal expectations in *all cases* – disruption of the *rule of law* – that government by *ex post facto* legislative psychoanalysis produces.[37]

But sometimes the apparently plain meaning of the statutory language will not actually be so plain, and a delegated decision-maker may legitimately decide to deviate from it to give better effect to the purposes of the statute. No psychoanalysis is necessary: it is precisely the delegated decision-maker's function to give effect to the statute's overriding purpose. A reviewing court may, nonetheless, use the apparently plain statutory language as a guide to assessing the unreasonableness of the delegated decision-maker's interpretation. If the language is stretched too far, the interpretation, and thus the decision relying on it, may be unreasonable.[38]

A straightforward example of how inconsistency with statutory language might be an *indicium* of unreasonableness is provided by *National*

[37] *Regions Hospital* v. *Shalala* (1998) 522 US 448 at 469, per Scalia J, dissenting. Emphasis original.

[38] Yves-Marie Morissette has suggested the metaphor of a bell curve to assist in understanding this phenomenon:

> il faut se représenter une courbe normale, *a bell curve* selon l'expression consacrée en anglais. À chaque extrémité de la courbe se trouvent les interprétations les moins plausibles, voire les plus invraisemblables, et qui mènent de part et d'autre à des résultats opposés; on peut les qualifier de manifestement déraisonnables. Au centre de la courbe se trouve une bande de largeur moyenne où des décideurs, selon qu'ils se placent à gauche ou à droite de la ligne imaginaire μ, peuvent, tout à fait raisonnablement, en venir à des conclusions différentes sur le sens (ou 'l'interpré tation') d'un texte et sur l'effet qu'il aura en l'espèce.

'Rétrospective et Prospective sur le Contentieux Administratif' (2008–2009) 39 RDUS 1, 22. See also Matthew Stephenson and Adrian Vermeule, '*Chevron* Has Only One Step' (2009) 95 Va LR 597.

Labour Relations Board v. *Kentucky River Community Care.*[39] The National Labour Relations Act excludes 'supervisors' from its coverage. What are supervisors, as distinct from employees, covered by the Act?:

> The term 'supervisor' means any individual having authority in the interest of the employer, to hire, transfer, suspend, lay off, recall, promote, discharge, assign, reward, or discipline other employees, or responsibly to direct them, or to adjust their grievances, or effectively recommend such action, if in connection with the foregoing the exercise of such authority is not of a merely routine or clerical nature, but requires the use of independent judgment.[40]

Here, the employer claimed that six registered nurses were supervisors within the definition and thus should be excluded from a bargaining unit comprised of its employees. However, the Board classified the sort of supervision a registered nurse engages in – supervising a nurse's aide in the administration of care – as a routine, non-management function which requires the exercise of ordinary professional or technical judgement. That is, the Board took the view that registered nurses do not use 'independent judgment', as required by the Act, in directing less-skilled employees to deliver services in accordance with standards specified by the employers.

Scalia J held that two aspects of the Board's interpretation were problematic. First, by focusing on a 'particular *kind* of judgment' – namely, ordinary professional or technical judgement – 'a startling categorical exclusion' had been inserted into a 'statutory text that does not suggest its existence'.[41] A focus on the *degree* of judgement required in a particular role would have been consistent with the text of the statute, but a focus on the *kind* of judgement was not. Moreover, the Board's interpretation would have 'startling' breadth: 'What supervisory judgment worth exercising … does not rest on "professional or technical skill or experience"?'[42] The Board's interpretation would have subsumed almost all supervisors in the employee category and was accordingly overbroad.

Secondly, the Board applied its interpretation of independent judgement only to those directing less-skilled employees (the 'responsibly to direct' component of the definition quoted above). But again, the interpretation ran into the text of the statute: '*Every* supervisory function listed by the Act is accompanied by the [independent judgement]

[39] (2001) 532 US 706. [40] 29 USC § 152(11).
[41] *Kentucky River*, above n. 39, p. 714. Emphasis original. [42] *Ibid.*, p. 715.

requirement.'[43] The Board interpreted independent judgement as qualifying only the 'responsibly to direct' function, but there was 'no apparent textual justification for this asymmetrical limitation, and the Board has offered none'.[44] Scalia J accepted that there was nothing wrong with the Board attempting to give effect to the legislative purpose 'to include professionals in the Act',[45] and construing the definition of supervisor slightly narrowly. However, 'the policy cannot be given effect through this statutory text'.[46] He suggested that the Board could achieve its aims in a manner compatible with the text of the statute, but emphasised that a decision to change its interpretation in response to the court's ruling was a matter for the Board.[47]

An example of inconsistency with the underlying policy of a statute is presented by *Giguère* v. *Chambre des notaires du Québec*.[48] Here, F was the notary to an elderly lady whose mental capacities were in decline. In one transaction, a valuable property was transferred to F for $1. G later became the lady's curator and in that capacity made various claims from the respondent's indemnity fund. Seeking reimbursement from F was not possible, because he had been declared bankrupt, and his professional insurance did not extend to fraudulent acts. The relevant statute provided that the indemnity fund should be used 'to re-imburse the sums of money or other securities used by a notary for purposes other than those for which they had been delivered to him in the practice of his profession'.[49] The respondent's Indemnity and Administrative Committees decided that this was a personal act, not a professional act, and that G could thus not be re-imbursed from the indemnity fund. The Supreme Court of Canada quashed the decision of the Administrative Committee. Inter alia, Gonthier J held that the purpose of the indemnity fund was to reimburse individuals when professional insurance did not apply and that the Committee had thus acted unreasonably: 'by characterising the transaction as personal, the two Committees took [the] fraud outside the scope of the fund, thus revoking the very protection the fund is intended to give'.[50]

[43] *Ibid.*, p. 715. Emphasis original. [44] *Ibid.*, p. 716. [45] *Ibid.*, p. 720.
[46] *Ibid.*, p. 720. [47] See similarly *American Trucking Associations*, above n. 32.
[48] *Giguère*, above n. 34.
[49] *Regulation respecting the indemnity fund of the Chambre des notaires du Québec*, RRQ 1981, c. N-2, r. 8, s. 2.01.
[50] *Giguère*, above n. 34, p. 22. See similarly *Fraternité des policiers de Lévis*, above n. 34 at pp. 630–5. See also *Lopez*, above n. 34 at pp. 242–3; *Yellow Transportation*, above n. 34 at pp. 46–8.

4.3.1.4 Unexplained changes in policy

A fourth *indicium* is differential treatment: where different decisions are reached in respect of similar factual situations, one or both of the decisions may be unreasonable.[51] Closely related to differential treatment is a fifth *indicium*: unacknowledged or unexplained changes in policy.[52] Although policy changes are legitimate in general (assuming the delegated decision-maker has the power to make policy changes), a change in policy is nonetheless an *indicium* of unreasonableness and legitimate only if explicable.[53] In *Federal Communications Commission* v. *Fox Television Stations*,[54] the Supreme Court of the United States considered the issue of changes in policy. Under statute, American television licensees are not permitted to broadcast material containing utterances which contain 'any obscene, indecent, or profane language'.[55] Certain aspects of the Commission's interpretation of the prohibition had evolved over the years. Previously, it had distinguished between literal and non-literal uses of expletives. A one-off expletive, if used *literally*, was always considered to run afoul of the prohibition. However, non-literal uses of expletives were punishable only if repeated. Thus a one-off, non-literal expletive was not punishable. However, the Commission decided to change its policy. It doubted the soundness of the distinction between literal and non-literal expletives, feared that categorical exemption of one-off non-literal expletives would lead to more widespread use of them and noted that technological advances made the 'bleeping out' of explicit language easier. Instead of the distinction between literal and non-literal expletives, it announced its intention to prefer a context-based inquiry into all uses of expletives to determine whether they fell within the prohibition.[56]

51 See *R (L (A Minor))* v. *Governors of J School* [2003] UKHL 9; [2003] 2 AC 633 and *R (O'Brien)* v. *Independent Assessor* [2007] UKHL 10; [2007] 2 AC 312. It is also possible for changes in policy to lead to findings of procedural unfairness. For a recent discussion, see *Tate and Lyle Sugars* v. *Secretary of State for Energy and Climate Change* [2011] EWCA Civ 664.

52 See also *Lumba* v. *Secretary of State for the Home Department* [2011] UKSC 12.

53 An applicant will first have to establish that there actually *was* a change of policy. For a failed attempt to do so, see *Coeur Alaska* v. *Southeast Alaska Conservation Council* (2009) 129 S Ct 2458 at 2474–7.

54 (2009) 129 S Ct 1800.

55 18 USC § 1464. See *Federal Communications Commission* v. *Pacifica Foundation* (1978) 438 US 726.

56 To take a relatively well-known example, when President Obama signed a momentous healthcare bill into law in 2010, the signing ceremony was covered live on television networks. Vice President Biden's comment to the president, that the signing of the bill

The court rejected the possibility of a heightened standard for review of changes in policy. Generally, Scalia J held, it would be necessary only for an agency to 'display awareness that it *is* changing position' without giving a detailed explanation of why it decided to change: 'it suffices that the new policy is permissible under the statute, that there are good reasons for it, and that the agency *believes* it to be better, which the conscious change of course adequately indicates'.[57] A more detailed justification would only be necessary where a previous policy was based on prior factual findings which had changed, or reliance interests had been created by the previous policy. Here, the Commission had 'forthrightly acknowledged' its change in policy.[58] This may have been enough to dispose of the case,[59] but Scalia J did go on to consider the substance of the new policy in some detail.[60] Indeed, it seems inevitable that a consideration of a new policy will involve some consideration of the delegated decision-maker's rationale for changing its position: it will in many cases be impossible to explain a particular decision without explaining the context in which it was reached, of which the previous decision will form a part. Breyer J, although dissenting as to the outcome, followed an approach which did not differ greatly from Scalia J's approach to the substance of the new policy:

> To explain a change requires more than setting forth reasons why the new policy is a good one. It also requires the agency to answer the question, 'Why did you change?' And a rational answer to this question typically requires a more complete explanation than would prove satisfactory were change itself not at issue. An (imaginary) administrator explaining why he chose a policy that requires driving on the right-side, rather than the left-side, of the road might say, 'Well, one side seemed as good as the other, so I flipped a coin'. But even assuming the rationality of that explanation for an *initial* choice, that explanation is not at all

was 'a big f*****g deal' was picked up by television microphones. Under the old standard, the vice president's comment, as a fleeting, non-literal expletive, would not have been punishable. But under the new standard, broadcasting the comment was potentially punishable.

57 *Fox*, above n. 54, p. 1811. Emphasis original.

58 *Ibid.*, p. 1812.

59 Kennedy J, although joining most of Scalia J's opinion, concurred to emphasise that the Commission was obliged to 'demonstrate that the new policy rests upon principles that are rational, neutral, and in accord with the agency's proper understanding of its authority'. *Ibid.*, p. 1823. It is probable that Scalia J's extended discussion of the substance of the policy, ostensibly a response to the reasoning of the Court of Appeals, was included in response to Kennedy J's concurrence.

60 *Ibid.* at pp. 1812–19.

> rational if offered to explain why the administrator *changed* driving practice, from right-side to left-side, 25 years later.[61]

The new policy does not have to be justified as better than the old policy. It has to be justified in its own terms; *some explanation* of the new policy relative to the old policy will inevitably be required, but it will not be necessary to explain why the new policy is *better* than the old policy. A wholly unexplained and unacknowledged change of policy will be unreasonable, but where an explanation can be made of the new policy, it should be upheld.[62]

These *indicia* of unreasonableness are sufficient for explanatory purposes. Others[63] are inconsistency with the traditional grounds of judicial review,[64] conflict with principles of interpretation,[65] conflict with judicial precedents,[66] conflict with international law[67] and uncertainty.[68] I do not claim that I have identified a full, closed set of *indicia* of unreasonableness: I have simply drawn these from the case law.[69]

4.3.1.5 Failure to establish indicia of unreasonableness

If an applicant fails to establish the presence of *indicia* of unreasonableness, an impugned decision cannot be struck down for unreasonableness. Decisions in which no *indicia* of unreasonableness could be established are

61 *Ibid.* at pp. 1830–1. Emphasis original. See also *American Hospital Association* v. *National Labour Relations Board* (1991) 499 US 606.

62 See generally Cass Sunstein, 'Is Tobacco a Drug? Administrative Agencies as Common Law Courts' (1998) 47 Duke LJ 1013, 1055–68. The doctrine of legitimate expectations may have particular applicability in these circumstances. What I say below about the variability of the standard of review would be applicable to cases where a reviewing court has to determine the validity of a delegated decision-maker's change of policy contrary to the legitimate expectations of an affected person or persons.

63 See also Lester and Jowell, 'Beyond *Wednesbury*', above n. 16.

64 *Dr Q* v. *College of Physicians and Surgeons of British Columbia* [2003] SCC 19; [2003] 1 SCR 226 at 237; *Canadian Union of Public Employees*, above n. 35.

65 *Moreau-Bérubé* v. *New Brunswick (Judicial Council)* [2002] SCC 11; [2002] 1 SCR 249; *National Association of Home Builders* v. *Defenders of Wildlife* (2007) 551 US 644 at 668–9.

66 *Safeway* v. *Retail, Wholesale and Department Store Union, Local 454* [1998] 1 SCR 1079; *Negusie* v. *Holder* (2009) 129 S Ct 1159.

67 *National Corn Growers* v. *Canada (Import Tribunal)* [1990] 2 SCR 1324; *Baker*, above n. 34; *R (Corner House Research and Campaign Against Arms Trade)* v. *Director of the Serious Fraud Office* [2008] UKHL 60; [2009] AC 756.

68 See e.g. *Barnhart*, above n. 34; *Verizon Communications* v. *Federal Communications Commission* (2002) 535 US 467 (though in neither of these cases was uncertainty established).

69 I return to this issue in the Conclusion.

illustrative.[70] They demonstrate that it will not avail an applicant to make a general claim that a decision was unreasonable. The applicant must be able to point to something that throws the reasonableness of the decision into doubt. For example, no *indicia* of unreasonableness were established in *R* v. *Investors Compensation Scheme, ex p. Bowden*.[71] The applicants had lost a significant amount of money in an investment and applied for compensation under a statutory scheme which reimbursed principals in situations where their losses would not be recoverable from their agent. The governing rules provided that 'fair compensation' would be granted.[72] However, the amount of compensation payable was reduced by £10,400. In a private law action against the operators of the investment scheme, the £10,400 would probably have been recoverable. The House of Lords held that the delegated decision-maker's view that reimbursing the applicants would have given them a double benefit (in that they had already had the use of the money) was not unreasonable. Even though the money may have been recoverable in a private law action, the delegated decision-maker was 'entitled to decide … that the inclusion of the £10,400 was not essential to provide fair compensation'.[73] None of the *indicia* of unreasonableness had been established.

4.3.1.6 Separateness of indicia of unreasonableness and standards of review

The *indicia* of unreasonableness are separate from the factors that determine the appropriate standard of review. For example, although the complex nature of the decision and the delegated decision-maker's expertise are relevant in determining the appropriate standard of review, they do not touch on the reasonableness of the decision per se. A decision will not be any more or less reasonable because it was rendered by an expert delegated decision-maker or because it required the exercise of judgement, although because of variations in the standard of review these factors will make it more or less likely that a decision will be struck down.

An example should suffice to make the point. In *R* v. *Secretary of State for the Home Department, ex p. Launder*,[74] the applicant challenged the minister's decision to extradite him to face trial on politically sensitive

[70] See *Lonrho*, above n. 34; *R (Mullen)* v. *Secretary of State for the Home Department* [2004] UKHL 18; [2005] 1 AC 1; *National Cable and Telecommunications Association* v. *Brand X Internet Services* (2005) 545 US 967.

[71] [1996] AC 261.

[72] Financial Services (Compensation of Investors) Rules 1990, r. 2.04.

[73] *Bowden*, above n. 71, p. 281, per Lord Lloyd of Berwick.

[74] [1997] 3 All ER 961.

charges of bribery in Hong Kong. Although the relevant decision and the challenge to it were made before the handing-over of Hong Kong to the Chinese government, it was clear that by the time of the trial, Hong Kong would no longer be under British control. Accordingly, the applicant feared that he might not receive a fair trial, possibly resulting in inhumane punishment, and on this basis challenged the decision to extradite.

There were factors which suggested that a lower standard of review would be appropriate,[75] but the presence of a fundamental right required the court to apply anxious scrutiny in its review of the decision.[76] The House of Lords took the view that two legitimate points of view could be held: one that China was, in view of previous actions, 'incapable of giving effect to the rule of law'; the other that China had 'good reason to make every effort in [Hong Kong] to preserve the existing criminal justice system, in recognition that it would not be appropriate to practise the socialist system and policies there'.[77] A failure of the rule of law in this or other cases would have serious repercussions for China, giving the Chinese an 'obvious interest'[78] in ensuring that the applicant received a fair trial. Thus a reasonable minister could be confident about the chances of the applicant receiving a fair trial.

Analytically, the right of the applicant to a fair trial and the policy-infused nature of the decision were factors to be taken into account in determining the standard of review, not in determining whether the decision was unreasonable per se. While the applicant demonstrated that a fundamental right was at stake, he could not identify any *indicium* of unreasonableness. Heightened scrutiny was of no assistance to him. Similarly, the minister's expertise in reaching a decision on a complex question did not affect the unreasonableness of the decision per se, although it counselled a deferential approach on the part of the reviewing court.

4.3.2 The burden of justification

But establishing the presence of *indicia* or an *indicium* of unreasonableness will not automatically justify a reviewing court in quashing the impugned decision. The delegated decision-maker may be able to explain how the decision is in fact justifiable, despite the presence of *indicia* of unreasonableness. The notion of, say, an explicable illogicality

[75] See above 3.3.2.
[76] *Bugdaycay* v. *Secretary of State for the Home Department* [1987] AC 514 at 531.
[77] *Launder*, above n. 74, p. 979. [78] *Ibid.*, p. 979.

may be slightly strange, but the underlying idea is that a slight dissonance between the means and the aim need not vitiate an entire decision, as long as the dissonance can be explained by the delegated decision-maker: 'In some circumstances a departure from strict logic may be permissible … without it being able to be said that the ensuing decision is unreasonable.'[79] It is only an unjustifiable aberration that will vitiate a decision. This is entirely sensible: administrative decision-making is not a perfect science. Similarly, differential treatment or inconsistency may be justifiable: 'A level of consistency that would be a virtue in adjudication, governed by law, may be a vice in administration, inhibiting action intended to further the public good.'[80] This too is entirely sensible: a foolish consistency is the hobgoblin of the mediocre mind.

A consideration of some of the case law will demonstrate that the presence of *indicia* of unreasonableness will not necessarily be fatal. Per se, an illogicality, disproportionality, or inconsistency (and so on) cannot destroy a decision. However, once *indicia* of unreasonableness are identified, an onus, which might be described as a burden of justification, is then placed on the delegated decision-maker to demonstrate that the decision is not unreasonable, but justifiable. It may seem jarring to think of a delegated decision-maker having to justify itself, but as Thomas Poole has observed, 'what else was "traditional" judicial review but a mechanism for demanding from government (certain kinds of) justification for (certain kinds of) impugned decisions?'[81] The burden is not placed on the delegated decision-maker in a literal sense, in the way that the burden of proof might be shifted during a criminal or civil trial. Instead, the question for the reviewing court will be whether sufficient justification exists in the record: 'Deference becomes an exercise of accepting justification, rather than of tolerating errors.'[82] Several English cases demonstrate how *indicia* of unreasonableness may be relied upon to attack a decision, but also how their presence may be explained in such a way as to render the decision justifiable.

A series of protests by animal rights groups resulted in major ferry companies refusing to carry livestock across the Channel from England to France and led to the litigation at issue in *R* v. *Chief Constable of*

[79] *Waitakere City Council*, above n. 19, p. 405, per Thomas J.

[80] T. R. S. Allan, 'Doctrine and Theory in Administrative Law: An Elusive Quest for the Limits of Jurisdiction' [2003] PL 429, 436.

[81] 'The Reformation of English Administrative Law' (2009) 68 CLJ 142, 147.

[82] Robert Leckey, 'Territoriality in Canadian Administrative Law' (2004) 24 UTLJ 327, 356.

Sussex, ex p. International Trader's Ferry.[83] The applicant organisation was formed by a group consisting mainly of farmers and hauliers who wished to continue transporting livestock. However, their operations were also plagued by protests which often included such an extent of illegal activity that the applicant organisation required significant police protection. Because providing full protection for each sailing would have required the presence of more than one-third of the members of his normally available force, the Chief Constable was only prepared to offer limited protection. A less satisfactory port was, as a result, used by the applicant organisation, which eventually went out of business. In seeking to have the decision to offer limited protection quashed as unreasonable, the applicant organisation alleged inter alia that the Chief Constable's actions were inconsistent with his statutory duty to uphold the law.

In upholding the Chief Constable's decision, the House of Lords focused on manpower and financial resources. First, it was 'not realistically possible' for the Chief Constable to detail more than one-third of his available officers to protecting the applicant organisation.[84] Indeed, there was evidence that the achievement of 'the objectives which had been given priority in the policing plan'[85] had suffered as a consequence of the increased number of officers detailed to police the port. Secondly, the money was simply not available and the various means of raising more were impractical. Thus, although an inconsistency had been established, in that the Chief Constable was not doing all he could to combat illegal activity, it was justified because of constraints on manpower and financial resources.[86]

A case in which the justification for differential treatment was also convincingly established in *Mayo Foundation* v. *United States*.[87] At issue was the application of a taxing statute to medical residents. Medical residency involves for the most part caring for patients, but also includes examinable educational components. The question at bar was whether medical residents fell within the general exemption from social insurance contributions for 'service performed in the employ of … a school, college, or university … if such service is performed by a student who is enrolled and regularly attending classes at such school, college, or

[83] *International Trader's Ferry*, above n. 33.

[84] *Ibid.*, p. 431, per Lord Slynn of Hadley. [85] *Ibid.*, p. 443, per Lord Hoffman.

[86] See also *Chamberlain*, above n. 33; *Continental Airlines* v. *Department of Transportation* (1988) 843 F 2d 1444 at 1452.

[87] (2011) 131 S Ct 704.

university'.[88] Previously, the Treasury Department – the delegated decision-maker charged with the application of the exemption – had interpreted the provision as exempting those employed by a school incidental to their course of study and conducted case-by-case analyses to determine whether the work satisfied this criterion. Following an adverse court decision relating to the application of the exemption to medical residents, the Department revised its interpretation to specifically exclude from the exemption any employee normally scheduled to work forty hours or more per week. In such cases, according to the Department, the work could not be considered incidental to a course of studies. Given that medical residents at the Mayo Clinic spend many more than forty hours a week caring for patients, they were not entitled to the exemption. To put the point neatly, those working forty hours or more weekly were to be treated differently from those not shouldering such a heavy workload.

Mayo claimed in the alternative that the categorical exclusion of its medical residents was unreasonable under *Chevron* step 2, on the basis that residents' employment is educational per se; they quite literally 'learn on the job'. However, the Supreme Court of the United States unanimously rejected this suggestion: 'Focusing on the hours an individual works and the hours he spends in studies is a perfectly sensible way [to] … distinguish between workers who study and students who work.'[89] Relying on such a categorical distinction would make the statutory provision more administrable. On its own, the reduction in cost would represent a rather weak attempt to discharge the burden of justification, for a similar argument could be run in respect of many decisions. Unsurprisingly, the court buttressed its position by reference to a second consideration, namely that the Department's interpretation cohered with the purpose of the statute:

> Although Mayo contends that medical residents have not yet begun their 'working lives' because they are not 'fully trained', the Department certainly did not act irrationally in concluding that these doctors – 'who work long hours, serve as highly skilled professionals, and typically share some or all of the terms of employment of career employees' – are the kind of workers that Congress intended to both contribute to and benefit from the Social Security system. The Department's rule takes into account the … concern that exempting residents … would deprive residents and their families of vital disability and survivorship benefits that Social Security provides.[90]

[88] 26 USC §3121(b)(10). [89] *Mayo Foundation*, above n. 87, p. 715.
[90] *Ibid*., p. 715. Internal citations omitted.

Accordingly, the burden of justification was discharged. The differential treatment was justified, and the Department's interpretation prevailed.[91]

4.3.3 Discharging the burden of justification

In the cases, two approaches have been taken to establishing how the burden of justification is to be discharged. The first looks at the cogency of the delegated decision-maker's reasons and reasoning. The second assesses whether there was sufficient evidence before the delegated decision-maker. In both cases, relevant material must support the attempt to discharge the burden of justification.[92] For example, as the United States Court of Appeals for the Federal Circuit put it, in respect of differential treatment, 'an agency action is [unreasonable] when the agency *offers insufficient reasons* for treating similar situations differently'.[93] As Iacobucci J put it, 'a court reviewing a decision [for unreasonableness] must look to see whether any reasons support it. The defect, if there is one, could presumably be in the evidentiary foundation itself or in the logical process by which conclusions are sought to be drawn from it.'[94] I should note that I do not address the question, which I adjudge to be a separate one best answered by experts in the law of evidence, of the standard of proof needed to convince a court that reasoning or evidence is cogent or sufficient. I am concerned with the standard of review, rather than the standard of proof, and therefore address the requirements for discharging the burden of justification, not the means of establishing those requirements to the satisfaction of the reviewing court.[95]

[91] In *Re Cartaway Resources* [2004] SCC 26; [2004] 1 SCR 672 at 700, Binnie J convincingly rejected a complaint about inconsistent treatment, holding that to make individual settlements binding on other cases would 'unduly fetter the … mandate' of the Ontario Securities Commission. See also *Nottinghamshire County Council* v. *Secretary of State for the Environment* [1986] AC 240; *Nationsbank of North Carolina* v. *Variable Annuity Life Insurance Company* (1995) 513 US 251.

[92] See further below 4.4.4.

[93] *Dongbu Steel* v. *United States* (2011) No. 2010–1271, slip opinion at 16.

[94] *Canada (Director of Investigation and Research)* v. *Southam* [1997] 1 SCR 748 at 776–7, per Iacobucci J.

[95] See further Paul Craig, *EU Administrative Law* (Oxford: Oxford University Press, 2006), pp. 465–70; Ennis McBride, 'Is the Civil "Higher Standard of Proof" a Coherent Concept?' (2009) 8 *Law, Probability and Risk* 323, 333–4.

4.3.3.1 Cogent reasons and reasoning

An example of reasons and reasoning being insufficient to justify the presence of an *indicium* of unreasonableness is *AT & T* v. *Iowa Utilities Board*.[96] At issue was the interpretation of the Telecommunications Act 1996, a deregulatory statute that aimed to open up competition in local telephone markets. Incumbent local telephone companies made various complaints about how the Federal Communications Commission had interpreted and implemented the Act. Inter alia, the statute required incumbents to provide new entrants to markets with access to network elements where access was 'necessary' and its absence 'would impair the ability' to provide services.[97] The Commission issued what was effectively a blanket rule requiring access.

Scalia J held that the rule was unreasonable: 'the Act requires the FCC to apply *some* limiting standard, rationally related to the goals of the Act, which it has simply failed to do'.[98] By assuming that '*any* increase in cost (or decrease in quality)' satisfied the requirements of necessity and impairment, the Commission had effectively excluded consideration of whether the entrant could provide the network element itself or lease it from an incumbent.[99] The difficulty with the Commission's reasoning was that its premises were flawed: 'In a world of perfect competition, in which all carriers are providing their service at marginal cost, the Commission's total equating of increased cost (or decreased quality) with "necessity" and "impairment" might be reasonable; *but it has not established the existence of such an ideal world*.'[100] The inconsistency with the statutory language was an *indicium* of unreasonableness and the justification contained a logical flaw. Thus the justification lacked sufficient cogency to be acceptable.

Where a delegated decision-maker has to pursue multiple statutory purposes, policies, duties or values, justifying a decision which contains an *indicium* of unreasonableness may be easier. A delegated decision-maker can argue that although its decision might have been unreasonable if viewed from the perspective of one statutory purpose or duty, it might be unimpeachably reasonable if viewed from different perspectives. *Committee for the Equal Treatment of Asbestos Minority Shareholders* v. *Ontario (Securities Commission)*[101] provides a good example. The litigation resulted from the desire of the government of

[96] (1999) 525 US 366. [97] 47 USC § 251(d)(2).
[98] *AT & T*, above n. 96, p. 388. Emphasis original. [99] *Ibid.*, p. 389. Emphasis original.
[100] *Ibid.*, p. 390. Emphasis added. [101] [2001] SCC 37; [2001] 2 SCR 132.

Quebec that the province should move from asbestos production into asbestos processing. It accomplished its objective by complex means, with the unfortunate result that share values in a company in which Quebec acquired a controlling interest plummeted. The applicant group, which represented the interests of minority shareholders, sought a remedy from the Ontario Securities Commission, but the Commission refused to exercise its public interest jurisdiction to remove trading privileges granted to Quebec. The Commission was to be guided in its actions by two key statutory purposes: 'to provide protection to investors from unfair, improper or fraudulent practices' and 'to foster fair and efficient capital markets and confidence in capital markets'.[102] The nub of the applicant group's submission was that the Commission ought to have exercised its jurisdiction because it found that Quebec had failed to comply with the spirit of the takeover laws: they alleged that an inconsistency with the policy underpinning the legislation vitiated the decision. Iacobucci J acknowledged the inconsistency but pointed out that the Commission had to take into account the wider effects of any remedial action:

> [It] was open to the [Commission] to give weight to the fact that there has been no abuse of investors or other misconduct by the province of Québec ... in the 13 years since the transaction at issue in this appeal. The [Commission] was also entitled to give weight to the fact that the removal of the province's exemptions is a very serious response that could have negative repercussions on other investors and the Ontario capital markets in general. Furthermore, the [Commission] did not find that there was no transactional connection with Ontario in this case, but that the transactional connection was insufficient to justify its intervening in the public interest ... It is true that the [Commission] placed significant emphasis on the transactional connection factor. However, it was entitled to do so in order to avoid using the open-ended nature of [its] powers as a means to police too broadly out-of-province transactions ... There are a myriad of overlapping regulatory jurisdictions governing securities transactions. [Under the legislation, one] of the fundamental principles that the [Commission] has to consider is that '[t]he integration of capital markets is supported and promoted by the sound and responsible harmonisation and coordination of securities regulation regimes'. A transaction that is contrary to the policy of the Ontario Securities Act may be acceptable under another regulatory regime. Thus, the [Commission's] insistence on a more clear and direct connection with Ontario in this case reflects a sound and responsible

[102] Ontario Securities Act, RSO 1990, c. S5, s. 1.1.

> approach to long-arm regulation and the potential for conflict amongst the different regulatory regimes that govern the capital markets in the global economy.[103]

In effect, then, the conflicting policy objectives of the Commission justified it in failing to give full effect to one policy objective.[104] It provided cogent reasons and reasoning to justify the presence of an *indicium* of unreasonableness and the decision was not unreasonable.

4.3.3.2 Sufficient evidence

An excellent example of an 'evidence' case is presented by *Bowen* v. *American Hospital Association*.[105] Section 504 of the Rehabilitation Act 1973 provided that handicapped individuals should not 'solely by reason of [their] handicap, be excluded from the participation in, be denied the benefits of, or be subjected to discrimination under any [federally funded] programme'.[106] Regulations promulgated thereunder required hospitals, inter alia, to post informational notices specifying that handicapped infants should not be excluded from treatment on the basis of their disability and to put in place procedures to 'prevent instances of unlawful medical neglect of handicapped infants'.[107]

Stevens J quashed the regulations because of the absence of evidence to support them. The Secretary of Health and Human Services' first reason in support of the regulations was that refusal to provide treatment solely by reason of handicap constituted discrimination. His second reason was that failure by hospitals to report suspected cases of medical neglect violated s. 504. But in the regulations the Secretary had noted that the requirement of parental consent to treatment could not be overridden. If that were so, treatment could only be denied on the basis of a handicap if parents withheld consent to treatment. But there was no evidence that treatment had been denied in cases where parental consent had not been withheld:

> Now that the Secretary has acknowledged that a hospital has no statutory treatment obligation in the absence of parental consent, it has become clear that the [regulations] *are not needed* to prevent hospitals from denying treatment to handicapped infants [because] the administrative record *contains no evidence* that hospitals have ever refused treatment authorised either by the infant's parents or by a court order.[108]

[103] *Asbestos Minority Shareholders*, above n. 101 at pp. 158–60.
[104] See similarly *Royal Oak Mines*, above n. 31. [105] (1986) 476 US 610.
[106] 29 USC § 794. [107] 45 CFR § 84.55.
[108] *Bowen*, above n. 105, p. 631. Emphasis added.

Moreover, the parental interest in drawing official attention to refusals of treatment would adequately further the purpose of s. 504. Critically, the supposed need for the regulations was based on cases where parental consent had been *refused*: 'they provide no support for [the Secretary's] claim that federal regulation is needed in order to forestall comparable cases in the future'.[109] Equally, the other cases relied on to support the procedural requirement imposed on hospitals failed 'to disclose any discrimination'.[110] In sum, Stevens J held, 'deference cannot fill the lack of an evidentiary foundation'.[111]

4.3.3.3 Both approaches

Both approaches can be perceived in *Champion* v. *Chief Constable of the Gwent Constabulary*.[112] A serving police constable was elected to serve as a parent governor of a local school and was subsequently appointed to the appointments subcommittee, which had responsibility for the interviewing of candidates for teaching positions and the making of recommendations on appointments for ratification by the board of governors. He was refused leave to serve on the committee on the ground that it was an 'activity ... likely to interfere with the impartial discharge of [the applicant's] duties or ... likely to give rise to the impression amongst members of the public that it may so interfere'[113] for two reasons.

The first reason arose from the fact that a police officer may, in the course of duty, learn sensitive information about a candidate for a particular position. Thus, the respondent had suggested, a disappointed applicant might allege publicly that the police officer had used the sensitive information in coming to a decision, which public allegations would damage the force's reputation for impartiality. Lord Griffiths was unimpressed: because '[a]n applicant for a teaching post must ... declare any criminal convictions ... it is at least most unlikely that the local police will have further confidential information that reflects badly on an applicant'.[114] The reasoning adduced to justify the presence of these *indicia* of unreasonableness was insufficiently cogent:

109 *Ibid.*, p. 632. 110 *Ibid.*, p. 635.

111 *Ibid.*, p. 643. See also *United States* v. *Riverside Bayview Homes* (1985) 474 US 121; *Bugdaycay*, above n. 76; *International Trader's Ferry*, above n. 33; *Alaska Department of Environmental Conservation* v. *Environmental Protection Agency* (2004) 540 US 461.

112 [1990] 1 All ER 116. 113 Police Regulations, SI 1979/1470, sch. 2, para. 1.

114 *Champion*, above n. 112, p. 119.

> Suspicion of theft or, even worse, child abuse were suggested in argument, but is it likely that a person under such suspicion would apply for a post and, if he fails to get it, that he will then spread abroad this suspicion as the reason for his failure to get the appointment, and that this, in turn, will lead to an impression among the public that the policeman on the appointments sub-committee cannot discharge his duties impartially? *You cannot make an event likely by adding one unlikely event to another unlikely event.*[115]

The second reason was that a police officer might become embroiled in public controversy as a result of a decision taken by an appointments subcommittee. However, the respondent could not point to a 'single instance of the appointment of a teacher causing public controversy'[116] in the school or his jurisdiction: 'there must be material on which the Chief Constable can reasonably apprehend such public controversy and, in the circumstances of this case, I *can find no material whatever* to support the view that the appointment of a teacher is likely to lead to public controversy'.[117] The absence of sufficient evidence to justify the illogicality and disproportionality vitiated the decision. In terms of the *indicia* of unreasonableness, three were relevant: illogicality, in that the means chosen would not achieve the aim of avoiding adverse publicity; inconsistency with the policy underpinning the regulations, which was to prevent police officers from engaging in partisan activities, not harmless, non-partisan activities; and disproportionality, in that the general social benefit of the decision was quite small compared to the detriment to the police officer and, perhaps, the local community.

Thus, both approaches can be relevant, sometimes in the same case. Cogent reasons and reasoning seem to be an ever-present requirement to discharge the burden of justification, but sufficient evidence may also be required: where the presence of the *indicium* of unreasonableness can only be explained by reference to evidence, or reliance on evidence is necessary to discharge the burden of justification, an evidential basis for discharging the burden will have to be demonstrated.

4.3.4 *The reason and structure of unreasonableness*

It seems, then, that a reviewing court's determination of whether or not a decision is unreasonable proceeds in the following manner. First, the applicant argues that one of the *indicia* of unreasonableness is present.

[115] *Ibid.*, p. 119. Emphasis added. [116] *Ibid.*, p. 119. [117] *Ibid.*, p. 120. Emphasis added.

The applicant will have to demonstrate the presence of an *indicium* of unreasonableness. It may be immediately evident, or it may have to be developed at some length by the applicant. On occasion, the applicant will fail to establish that any *indicium* of unreasonableness is present. On other occasions, *indicia* of unreasonableness will be established to be present. If so, the delegated decision-maker must explain how and why the decision is justifiable, despite the presence of *indicia* of unreasonableness. A consideration of the case law demonstrates how *indicia* of unreasonableness, although established to be present, are not necessarily fatal to the impugned decision. But once an *indicium* is identified, a burden of justification is then placed on the delegated decision-maker. Two means of discharging the burden emerge from the case law: cogent reasons and reasoning, or sufficient evidence, will be deemed adequate.[118]

Unreasonableness, when understood in this sense, does not require a judge to pronounce from on high a subjective view of whether or not a decision is unreasonable. Nevertheless:

> Since the precise way in which courts interfere with agency findings cannot be imprisoned within any form of words, new formulas attempting to rephrase the old are not likely to be more helpful than the old. There are no talismanic words that can avoid the process of judgment. The difficulty is that we cannot escape, in relation to this problem, the use of undefined defining terms.[119]

Nonetheless, following the approach that I have outlined, the considerations which may lead to a finding of unreasonableness, and the reasons for accepting or rejecting the delegated decision-maker's explanations, will be brought into the open, where they can be parsed by the wider legal community.

118 One question that I have deliberately left unanswered is the relationship between the reason and structure of unreasonableness and Art. 6 of the European Convention on Human Rights and Fundamental Freedoms. It is possible that Art. 6 might in certain contexts require a greater intensity of judicial review. See generally *R (Alconbury)* v. *Secretary of State for the Environment, Transport and the Regions* [2001] UKHL 23; [2003] 2 AC 295. But the case law in this area is still developing, and it would be beyond the scope of the general argument I am developing to examine how Art. 6 would interact with the delegation argument, the practical justifications for curial deference and, in particular, the reason and structure of unreasonableness that I have identified.

119 *Universal Camera Corporation* v. *National Labour Relations Board* (1951) 340 US 474 at 489, per Frankfurter J.

It is convenient to address at this point Yves-Marie Morissette's extra-judicial contention that one can only assert unreasonableness, not prove its presence: 'La conclusion qu'une interprétation est "déraisonnable", manifestement ou non, est par essence *assertorique*, c'est-à-dire que c'est une affaire d'opinion, aussi autorisée, éclairée et défendable puisse-t-elle être.'[120] The contention is partially valid. Even the presence of cogent reasons or reasoning or sufficient evidence does not lend itself to scientific proof. However, the reason and structure of unreasonableness that I have laid out provides a roadmap for judges charged with determining whether or not a particular decision is unreasonable. The existence of such a roadmap gives the lie to the contention that the determination of unreasonableness must be based solely on the brute fact of an assertion as to a decision's reasonableness or unreasonableness.[121]

Concretised, Morissette's contention supports the flawed doctrinal suggestion that a decision should be considered unreasonable only if a reviewing court unanimously or by super-majority considers the decision to be unreasonable.[122] Such despair should be counselled only after all other options have been exhausted, unless one believes that force of judicial numbers, rather than the force of argument, should determine cases.[123] Moreover, the 'voting rule' proposal offers no assistance to judges. It would require a judge to determine a decision's unreasonableness by reference to the judge's own view of whether the decision is unreasonable. But how could a judge determine a decision's unreasonableness without some external conception of unreasonableness? Indeed, by rejecting the importance of an external conception, the 'voting rule' proposal is circular. It would require a judge charged with determining the unreasonableness of a decision to ask herself whether she thinks that the decision is unreasonable; but the only benchmark for determining unreasonableness would be the judge's answer to that very question. Thus, the answer to the question 'Is the decision unreasonable?' is: 'That depends on what I consider to be unreasonable' – which leads only to

120 'Rétrospective et Prospective' above n. 38, pp. 27–8. Emphasis original.

121 One might suggest that the determination of whether a delegated decision-maker has discharged the burden of justification ultimately rests on an assertion. I think, however, that the determination of the presence or absence of cogency or sufficiency (or relevancy – a concept to be introduced below 4.4.4) need not rest on assertion, for cogency and sufficiency are standards which must be satisfied if the burden of justification is to be discharged. Assertion is not sufficient to satisfy such standards.

122 See e.g. Morisette, 'Rétrospective et Prospective', above n. 38, p. 29; Jacob Gersen and Adrian Vermeule, '*Chevron* as a Voting Rule' (2007) 116 Yale LJ 676.

123 See generally William Eskridge, 'No Frills Textualism' (2006) 119 Harv LR 2041.

another question: 'Do I think the decision is unreasonable?' The only way out of the circle is to develop, as I have, an external conception of unreasonableness.

4.3.5 *Underneath unreasonableness*

That the principles of judicial review of delegated decision-making are developed primarily by courts is now a truism. What is often less clear is the normative well from which judges are drawing inspiration. Unreasonableness, properly considered, incorporates a number of what Jowell and Lester termed 'substantive principles';[124] I have described these as *indicia* of unreasonableness. *Indicia* must themselves be drawn from some source. They are immanent in the case law but judges are drawing from a deeper normative well: they are exercising a 'judgment [that] will draw on a range of constitutional values'.[125] Perhaps they are influenced by the rule of law, particular conceptions of justice, or, less contentiously, by considerations of good administration: 'If the courts understand their role as ensuring that decisions are legally "reasonable" then what is understood as reasonable will depend upon prescriptions about good public administration.'[126]

Using the *indicia* of unreasonableness identified above as a reference point, one can perceive the influence of the principles of good administration and of the rule of law in influencing the development of judicial review. If the principles of good administration are conceived of as guidelines to the effective functioning of the machinery of the administrative state, illogicality and coherence with statutory purpose can be said to spring from that source. An illogical decision does not serve the furthering of the ends of the delegated decision-maker, and a decision that does not advance those ends would represent a poor use of the delegated decision-maker's powers and resources. However, some of the *indicia* of unreasonableness can more readily be perceived as springing from a deeper source: the rule of law. For example, differential treatment may be perfectly efficient and assist in good administration: many

124 'Beyond *Wednesbury*', above n. 16. See also Philip Bryden, 'Understanding the Standard of Review in Administrative Law' (2005) 54 UNBLJ 75, 92–9; Dean Knight, 'A Murky Methodology: Standards of Review in Administrative Law' (2008) 6 NZJPIL 117.

125 T. R. S. Allan, 'Constitutional Dialogue and the Justification of Judicial Review' (2003) 23 OJLS 563, 570.

126 Elizabeth Fisher, *Risk Regulation and Administrative Constitutionalism* (Oxford: Oxford University Press, 2007), p. 92.

exercises in administrative line-drawing will reduce costs and aid the achievement of delegated decision-makers' goals, at the expense of treating differently individuals who are similarly situated in every respect save for their position vis-à-vis the line drawn. With differential treatment, the concern is not inefficiency, but that failing to treat like cases alike is inequitable. The rule of law may, then, be said to represent a deeper reservoir of values. Not that *indicia* of unreasonableness need be attributed exclusively to one of these sources. Disproportionality, for example, could be said to find its source in both.

Flowing underneath the reason and structure of unreasonableness are these sources of inspiration. Notice that the doctrine of curial deference that I have developed does not take the principles of good administration or the rule of law as its starting point. However, the doctrine as I have developed it is *consistent* with both. Rather than using the sources as a foundation – which may prove flimsy if there is disagreement about their content or normative value – I have instead constructed a channel through which they can flow. Accordingly, my doctrine of curial deference is established upon strong foundations, but is located above ready sources of normative inspiration.

4.4 Workable standards of review

It is now necessary to begin developing a variable standard of review.[127] When I refer to variability in the standard of review, I refer exclusively to variability in the burden of justification. The *indicia* of unreasonableness have an all-or-nothing character: they are either present, or not present. A decision either contains an illogicality, or it does not; a policy has either been changed, or it has not; similarly situated people have either been treated differently, or they have not; and so on. Even if it is theoretically possible that the *indicia* would have to pass a certain threshold of egregiousness before they qualified as *indicia* of unreasonableness, or that more egregious *indicia* of unreasonableness would carry a heavier burden of justification, it would be inappropriate to permit variability. Levels of egregiousness would be difficult if not impossible to identify and apply: variations in magnitude do not provide a solid basis for a means of varying the standard of review.[128] I thus argue that variability is possible only in respect of the burden of justification.

[127] For a sketch of an alternative approach, see Knight, 'A Murky Methodology', above n. 124.
[128] See below 4.4.3.

It should be recalled that because of the distinction already identified between unreasonableness and correctness, at least two standards of review can be accommodated within my doctrine of curial deference, and to that extent the standard of review is variable. However, a binary choice between correctness and unreasonableness seems insufficient to cover the range of possible interactions between the extent of delegations of power and the practical justifications for curial deference. Indeed, without a third standard, two decisions very different in character could be treated in precisely the same way (in terms of the standard of review). Unless an infinite number of standards of review were prescribed, any doctrine of curial deference would tend to over-simplify matters, but reducing deference to a binary choice between correctness and unreasonableness seems simplistic.[129]

Unfortunately, there is little or no discussion in the cases of how the burden of justification might vary. In the vast majority of cases the reasoning or evidence of the delegated decision-maker is simply deemed sufficiently cogent or substantial to discharge the burden of justification. Accordingly, my exposition of a variable standard of review will be slightly abstract.

4.4.1 *A protean conception of unreasonableness*

A good starting point is provided by the conception of unreasonableness proposed by the Supreme Court of Canada in *Dunsmuir* v. *New Brunswick*:[130]

> A court conducting a review for reasonableness inquires into the qualities that make a decision reasonable, referring both to the process of articulating the reasons and to outcomes. In judicial review, reasonableness is concerned mostly with the existence of justification, transparency and intelligibility within the decision-making process. But it is also concerned with whether the decision falls within a range of possible, acceptable outcomes which are defensible in respect of the facts and law.[131]

This conception of unreasonableness maps the reason and structure of unreasonableness that I identified earlier in this chapter. In addition, as the closing sentence of the quotation indicates, it could be applied to judicial review of facts and of law, or to put it in the terminology that I have been

[129] See below 4.4.2. [130] [2008] SCC 9; [2008] 1 SCR 190.
[131] *Ibid.* at pp. 220–1, per Bastarache and LeBel JJ.

using: reasoning and evidence. It is evidently compatible with a focus on the cogency of reasons and reasoning and sufficiency of evidence.

Although it seems plausible that the range of 'outcomes' and extent of 'justification, transparency and intelligibility' could vary according to context, it is not clear from the quoted passage how the burden of justification might vary. However, the leading statement of the English anxious scrutiny standard does suggest how the burden of justification might vary within such a conception of unreasonableness. Anxious scrutiny requires a delegated decision-maker to have relatively more convincing reasons than those that would be required to discharge the burden of justification if *Wednesbury* were the appropriate standard of review:

> The court may not interfere with the exercise of an administrative discretion on substantive grounds save where the court is satisfied that the decision is unreasonable in the sense that it is beyond the range of responses open to a reasonable decision-maker. But in judging whether the decision-maker has exceeded this margin of appreciation the human rights context is important. The more substantial the interference with human rights, the more the court will require by way of justification before it is satisfied that the decision is reasonable ...[132]

If one reads the reference to human rights as a reference to the burden of justification, the anxious scrutiny standard as formulated here envisages a zone of reasonable decisions, which contracts when the anxious scrutiny standard applies. The converse proposition, that where discretion is greater, the zone of reasonable decisions is greater because the burden of justification is lesser, surely follows.[133] What is unreasonable will depend on the context, which may cause the burden of justification to increase or decrease. A conception of unreasonableness within which the burden of justification can increase or decrease is protean in nature and may be capable of application to a wide range of delegated decision-making.

4.4.2 *The case for a third standard of review*

4.4.2.1 The difficulty of stretching a protean conception of unreasonableness widely

Yet it is not clear precisely how the burden of justification would increase or decrease. My study of anxious scrutiny cases in the English Court of

[132] *R* v. *Ministry of Defence, ex p. Smith* [1996] QB 517 at 554, per Sir Thomas Bingham MR (adopting a submission on behalf of the applicant by David Pannick QC).

[133] Michel Bastarache, 'Modernising Judicial Review' (2009) 22 CJALP 227.

Appeal, and of the cases decided by the Supreme Court of Canada on the unreasonableness and patent unreasonableness standards of review did not disclose any difference in judicial reasoning between nominally more and less intrusive standards of review. Take for example *R (Mahmood)* v. *Secretary of State for the Home Department*,[134] in which Laws LJ applied anxious scrutiny to the review of a refusal to allow the applicant to remain in the United Kingdom. However, the substantive points addressed by Laws LJ in his application of anxious scrutiny were the effect of the decision on the applicant's family and the 'barrenness' of requiring the applicant to leave (given that he would satisfy the criteria for re-entry).[135] It is, with respect, impossible to see how these *indicia* of unreasonableness – which fit naturally the descriptions of disproportionality and illogicality offered above – could not have been raised if anxious scrutiny had not been applied. As Jeff King has suggested, '[h]eightened scrutiny does require more, but it is not at all clear just how much more. It is a mood in search of a standard.'[136] On reflection, the absence of a difference should not be surprising: although it is possible for reasons to be more or less cogent or for evidence to be more or less sufficient, it is difficult to describe a justification in terms of its greater or lesser cogency, because the burden is not quantitative in nature, but qualitative. What matters is not the number of reasons or amount of evidence that a delegated decision-maker can advance to justify a decision, but the inherent cogency of the reasons or sufficiency of the evidence advanced. A focus on cogency and sufficiency is invariably qualitative. Even with evidence, itself relatively less ethereal than reasoning, it is difficult to differentiate between burdens of justification, as the American experience with variable standards of review of evidential findings in administrative law demonstrates:

> The upshot in terms of judicial review is some practical difference in outcome depending upon which standard is used. The ['substantial evidence'] standard, as we have said, is somewhat less strict than the ['clearly erroneous'] standard. But the difference is a subtle one – so fine that (apart from the present case) we have failed to uncover a single instance in which a reviewing court conceded that use of one standard rather than the other would in fact have produced a different outcome.[137]

[134] [2000] EWCA Civ 315; [2001] 1 WLR 840. [135] *Ibid.*, p. 849.
[136] 'Proportionality: a Halfway House' [2010] NZLR 327, 360.
[137] *Dickinson* v. *Zurko* (1999) 527 US 150 at 162–3, per Breyer J.

The basic problem, in the present context, is that it is very difficult to explain how reasoning can be more or less cogent, or evidence can be more or less sufficient. A deeper problem may be lurking. Varying the necessary level of cogency or sufficiency might require the development of threshold levels of cogency or sufficiency.[138] It seems as though a reviewing court applying a protean conception of unreasonableness might have to identify a threshold in each particular case: reasoning or evidence would then have to reach a particular level of cogency or sufficiency in order to discharge the burden of justification. If so, the reviewing court would effectively be requiring that an explanation would have to be very cogent, or evidence very sufficient, to discharge the burden of justification. While describing something as 'more cogent' or 'more sufficient' is not tautological, describing something as 'very cogent' or 'very sufficient' does seem to be tautological. The tendency towards threshold levels is quite problematic.

Moreover, uncertainty about the appropriate means of discharging the burden of justification is very serious. The practical justifications for curial deference are, I have suggested, contextual in nature: delegated decision-makers may be more or less expert and democratically legitimate, problems may be more or less complex and delegated decision-making processes may be more or less procedurally legitimate. In determining the appropriate degree of curial deference to accord, each of the practical justifications should be taken into account (if a proper consideration of the relevant statutory provisions so indicates). Making an error as to the level to which each of the practical justifications is present may not carry severe consequences, especially if more than one of them is to be taken into account. In some cases, an error may result in the wrong standard of review being chosen. But even an error as to the appropriate standard of review would be less serious than an error as to whether or not the burden of justification has been discharged. The appropriate standard of review is determined by reference to the practical justifications for curial deference, but the outcome of a case is determined by whether or not the burden of justification has been discharged. An error as to whether or not the burden of justification has

[138] See also *Dunsmuir*, above n. 130 at pp. 255–7, where Binnie J suggested that 'degrees of deference' remain within the protean conception of unreasonableness. See further Ron Goltz, '"Patent Unreasonableness is Dead. And We Have Killed It". A Critique of the Supreme Court of Canada's Decision in *Dunsmuir*' (2008) 46 Alta LR 253; David Mullan, '*Dunsmuir* v. *New Brunswick*, Standard of Review and Procedural Fairness for Public Servants: Let's Try Again!' (2008) 21 CJALP 117, 133–6.

been discharged will have significant consequences; it would probably result in a case being wrongly decided. Thus a level of uncertainty which may be acceptable in respect of the practical justifications for curial deference would not be acceptable in respect of the burden of justification.

4.4.2.2 Arguments in favour of a third standard of review

Accordingly, caution ought to be exercised before requiring a protean conception of unreasonableness to cover too much ground. Instead, a burden of justification distinct from the cogency of reasons and reasoning and/or the sufficiency of evidence should be developed. Here, I will develop a third standard of review (which would join correctness and unreasonableness), with its own burden of justification.

Apart from the difficulties with a protean conception of unreasonableness with one burden of justification that I have identified, there are good reasons for developing a third standard of review. First, the existence of a third standard would indicate to reviewing courts that in certain situations they should intervene only *in extremis*. In the rare circumstances in which a delegation of power and the practical justifications for curial deference combine with great force, it would be incongruous to treat the resultant decision in the same manner as one where a delegation of power and the practical justifications were not present to the same extent. Accordingly, one of the values of the third standard in Canada was that 'at the high end "patent" unreasonableness (in the sense of manifestly indefensible) was not a bad description of the hurdle an applicant had to get over to have an administrative decision quashed on a ground of substance'.[139] The very presence of a third standard, then, could help to give effect to the values central to a doctrine of curial deference with variable standards of review. It could have psychological disciplining effects, in the same way that 'Lord Greene's definition of unreasonableness sought to *make the judges think twice* about interfering with the merits of official decisions'.[140]

Secondly, without a third standard, it would be possible that a decision to which a high degree of curial deference ought to be accorded may not in fact be accorded the appropriate high degree of curial deference.

[139] *Dunsmuir*, above n. 130, p. 257, per Binnie J.

[140] Lester and Jowell, 'Beyond *Wednesbury*', above n. 16, p. 372. Emphasis added. See also *Universal Camera Corporation*, above n. 119, p. 487; David Mullan, 'Establishing the Standard of Review: The Struggle for Complexity?' (2004) 17 CJALP 59, 93.

Reviewing courts could subtly relax the requirements of unreasonableness by reducing the burden of justification. This is an ever-present risk, but it would be heightened if all decisions were to be analysed by reference to a protean conception of unreasonableness: 'As an overarching, all-pervasive concept, unreasonableness review was and remains a threat to edge closer and closer to relatively unconstrained merits review.'[141] Developing a third standard would help to prevent slippage within a protean conception of unreasonableness by preventing a category of decisions from wrongly being accorded a lower degree of curial deference than is due. Thus, in *Law Society of New Brunswick* v. *Ryan*,[142] Iacobucci J rejected a suggestion that the standard of review of unreasonableness could 'float along a spectrum of deference such that it is sometimes quite close to correctness and sometimes quite close to patent unreasonableness'.[143] Unreasonableness was said by Iacobucci J to require 'deferential self-discipline' on the part of the reviewing court, but if the standard could float, 'courts could hold that decisions were unreasonable by adjusting the standard towards correctness'.[144] Conversely, if no third standard existed, reviewing courts might be too deferential. If they were to accept any justification for the presence of an *indicium* of unreasonableness, they could empty the protean conception of unreasonableness of its meaning. A third standard would help to maintain the integrity and consistency of unreasonableness.

Thirdly, a well-defined third standard would give the reviewing court a touchstone on either side when deciding, on application of the intermediate standard, whether a burden of justification has been discharged by cogent reasons and reasoning and sufficient evidence: it should not apply a correctness standard; but neither should it apply a highly deferential standard. Reviewing courts would be able to compare the burdens of justification and by quickly ascertaining whether the decision would come out differently, reflect on their application of the relevant burden to the decision under review. A similar exercise could be engaged in vis-à-vis the intermediate standard when applying the correctness standard, and vis-à-vis the intermediate standard when applying the highly deferential standard. Judicial awareness of the other standards would, again, help to maintain the integrity and consistency of unreasonableness.

[141] David Mullan, 'Proportionality: A Proportionate Response to an Emerging Crisis in Canadian Judicial Review Law?' [2010] NZLR 233, 262. See similarly Tom Hickman, 'Problems for Proportionality' [2010] NZLR 303, 317.

[142] [2003] SCC 20; [2003] 1 SCR 247. [143] *Ibid.*, p. 266. [144] *Ibid.*, p. 267.

Fourthly, the logic of an approach to deference based on legislative intent is that the universe of standards of review is infinite:

> If the appropriate degree of intensity of judicial scrutiny of administrative action depend[s] on such a broad range of context-sensitive, pragmatic and functional considerations, [is] it really feasible or appropriate to provide the courts with only three options? Could the subtleties of the differences between various review contexts be comprehended within three rather crude categories?[145]

Adding a third standard would go at least some way towards meeting the challenge of theoretical consistency.

Fifthly, attempting to stretch the protean conception of unreasonableness too widely risks duplication. To say simply that unreasonableness 'is a single standard that takes its colour from the context'[146] leaves unanswered the question of what constitutes 'context'. For reasons explained in the next subsection, the magnitude of the *indicia* of unreasonableness cannot be used to determine the context. Instead, those factors relevant to determining the context will presumably be the practical justifications for curial deference identified in Chapter 3.[147] As David Mullan has warned, 'deploying an appropriate intensity of review will often require returning to the … factors that dictated the outcome of the choice between correctness and unreasonableness review in the first place'.[148] But reliance on these factors would at least constitute unnecessary duplication. It would be wasteful and conceptually confusing to count them a second time if they have already been taken into account in formulating the standard of review. Moreover, it would result in inappropriate deference being accorded, if the factors were taken into account in determining unreasonableness to be the appropriate standard of review, and then taken further into account in determining that

145 Mullan, 'Struggle for Complexity', above n. 140, p. 88. See similarly Lorne Sossin and Colleen Flood, 'The Contextual Turn: Iacobucci's Legacy and the Standard of Review in Administrative Law' (2007) 57 UTLJ 581, 588; Perrault, *Le Contrôle judiciaire des decisions de l'administration*, above n. 3, pp. 85–6; Adrian Vermeule, *Judging under Uncertainty: An Institutional Theory of Legal Interpretation* (Cambridge, MA: Harvard University Press, 2006), p. 222.

146 *Canada (Citizenship and Immigration)* v. *Khosa*, above n. 22, p. 378, per Binnie J.

147 Relying on a wider set of practical justifications would be problematic. First, it would ignore the good reasons explained in Ch. 3 for relying on the practical justifications identified therein. Secondly, it would be possible for reviewing courts to draw on whatever practical justifications seemed relevant to the particular case, undermining certainty and predictability.

148 'Proportionate Response', above n. 141, p. 251. See also *Discount Brands* v. *Northcote Mainstreet* [2005] NZSC 17; [2005] 2 NZLR 597, 607, per Elias CJ.

a 'high degree' of unreasonableness would have to be demonstrated before the impugned decision could be struck down. Such double counting ought to be avoided. Accordingly, although the possibility that 'it all depends on context' is both a familiar and comforting one to the legal mind, it should be rejected.

The visualisation I offered at the end of Chapter 3 demonstrates the vast range of possible interactions between delegations of power and the practical justifications for curial deference. Ultimately, a protean conception of unreasonableness may simply be too vague to cover the whole field of delegated decision-making. If courts formulated ad hoc burdens of justification within a protean conception of unreasonableness based solely on the context of the particular case, the resulting doctrine would be so variable as to defy categorisation. A floating burden of justification would render a protean conception of unreasonableness 'incompatible with the idea of a meaningful standard'.[149] It would then, crucially, provide no guarantee that different delegated decision-makers were in fact being treated appropriately by reviewing courts. Instead, it would probably assist courts in applying a variable standard of review to think of the different standards as 'points occurring on a spectrum'.[150] Picking a number of fixed standards of review might be arbitrary, and even crude, but it would have the merit of certainty and of tending to give effect to legislative intent, albeit not perfectly.

4.4.3 *The difficulties of developing a third standard*

An extended attempt was made by the Supreme Court of Canada to formulate a meaningful distinction between unreasonableness and patent unreasonableness and its ultimate failure to do so provides a starting point for discussion. A distinction between unreasonableness and patent unreasonableness was developed and persisted with for several years. However, the distinction was subject to criticism. As a lower court judge in Canada put it:

> [In] attempting to follow the [Supreme] Court's distinctions between 'patently unreasonable', 'reasonable' and 'correct', one feels at times as though one is watching a juggler juggle three transparent objects. Depending on the way the light falls, sometimes one thinks one can see

149 *Ryan*, above n. 142, p. 268, per Iacobucci J.

150 *Canada (Deputy Minister for National Revenue)* v. *Mattel Canada* [2001] SCC 36; [2001] 2 SCR 100 at 114, per Major J. See similarly *Pezim* v. *British Columbia (Superintendent of Brokers)* [1994] 2 SCR 557 at 590–1.

> the objects. Other times one cannot and, indeed, wonders whether there are really three distinct objects at all.[151]

Subsequently, the distinction between unreasonableness and patent unreasonableness came under strong attack from LeBel J in his concurring reasons in *Toronto (City)* v. *Canadian Union of Public Employees, Local 79*.[152] In his view, there were 'significant practical problems inherent in distinguishing meaningfully between the two standards'.[153] Was the defining characteristic of a patently unreasonable decision – as opposed to an unreasonable decision – the magnitude or obviousness of the error(s)? Was it the importance of the error(s) to the impugned decision, or the ease with which error(s) could be discerned by a reviewing court? These questions had not been answered satisfactorily by the court.

As for magnitude, Wilson J had presciently expressed uncertainty about 'how helpful it is to substitute one adjectival phrase for another and define patent unreasonableness in terms of rational indefensibility. It seems to me that this simply injects one more opportunity for ambiguity into a test which is already fraught with ambiguity.'[154] In the end, a focus on verbal formulations had to prove unavailing, because to say that a decision is 'clearly irrational' rather than 'irrational' is 'surely a tautology':[155]

> There seems to me to be no qualitative basis on which to differentiate effectively between these various characterisations of a rationality analysis; how, for instance, would a decision that is not 'tenably supported' (and is thus 'merely' unreasonable) differ from a decision that is not 'rationally supported' (and is thus patently unreasonable)?[156]

[151] *Miller* v. *Workers' Compensation Commission (Newfoundland)* (1997) 154 Nfld and PEI R 52 at 57–8, per LD Barry J. See also Julius Grey, 'Standards of Judicial Review: Is it Time to Change our Analysis?' (2004) 45 *Cahiers de Droit* 541, 557–61; David Jones, 'Deciphering the Standard of Review' (2005) 29 Advocates' Quarterly 417, 454.

[152] [2003] SCC 63; [2003] 3 SCR 77. [153] *Ibid.*, p. 137.

[154] *Paccar*, above n. 9, p. 1022. See also Lord Denning MR's attempt to articulate, in the *Tameside* case, a distinction between a delegated decision-maker being 'very wrong' (and thus not unreasonable) and 'completely wrong' (and thus unreasonable). [1977] AC 1014 at 1026.

[155] David Mullan, 'Recent Developments in Standard of Review' in *Taking the Tribunal to Court: A Practical Guide for Administrative Law Practitioners* (Ontario: Canadian Bar Association, 2000), p. 25.

[156] *Toronto (City)*, above n. 152, p. 136, per LeBel J.

As Bastarache J put it, extrajudicially: 'Much like being somewhat pregnant, one cannot be somewhat unreasonable.'[157] These difficulties with a focus on magnitude of error apply with equal force to a focus on the magnitude of *indicia* of unreasonableness, or of the burden of justification.

As for obviousness, a focus on it would also be problematic. The suggestion would have to be that hidden, or hard-to-find, but very serious errors would not render a decision unreasonable. But, LeBel J argued, it would be offensive to the rule of law and possibly contrary to legislative intent to employ a system of administrative review which allowed admittedly unreasonable decisions to survive judicial scrutiny.[158] Similar difficulties would arise if patent unreasonableness were defined as a minimally searching form of judicial review, such that a reviewing court would not be able to act if a defect were latent (such that minimal review would not uncover it) but of a patently unreasonable magnitude. The use of a minimally searching form of judicial review would raise 'a more theoretical quandary: the difficulty of articulating why a defect that is obvious on the face of a decision should present more of an imperative for court intervention than a latent defect'.[159] Moreover, the difficulty of defining what is meant by the obviousness of a defect is considerable: is it obviousness 'in the sense of its transparency on the face of the decision', or obviousness 'in terms of the ease with which, once found, it can be identified as severe'?[160] In terms of transparency, it would make little sense to conceptualise a variable standard of review as requiring more or less judicial attention to be paid to the record. Surely judicial ethics and the requirements of procedural fairness would compel a judge to have regard to all relevant material; it would be faintly ludicrous to suggest that a highly deferential judge would read a brief fewer times, or less carefully, than a less deferential judge. In terms of severity, the difficulties of making distinctions based on magnitude recur. As already mentioned, these difficulties would apply equally to a focus on the obviousness of *indicia* of unreasonableness or the burden of justification.

[157] Bastarache, 'Modernising Judicial Review', above n. 133, p. 235. Of course, there are degrees of pregnancy: 'heavily pregnant' is a label in common usage, for example. But the existence of pregnancy, as opposed to its extent, is non-scalar. For discussion of the scalar/non-scalar distinction, see Matthew Kramer, *Objectivity and the Rule of Law* (Cambridge: Cambridge University Press, 2007), pp. 105–9 and *The Quality of Freedom* (Oxford: Oxford University Press, 2003), pp. 169–84.

[158] *Toronto (City)*, above n. 152 at pp. 143–4. See also Tremblay, 'Retenue judiciaire', above n. 1.

[159] *Toronto (City)*, above n. 152, p. 143. [160] *Ibid.*, p. 138.

Ultimately, because the unreasonableness and patent unreasonableness standards were 'united at their theoretical source' by the notion that a delegated decision-maker may make multiple acceptable decisions,[161] no meaningful distinction could ever be made between the standards of unreasonableness and patent unreasonableness.

4.4.4 *A third standard proposed*

I wish to propose a standard based on relevancy, to join the protean conception of unreasonableness introduced above: *a decision shall be upheld unless it is unsupported by relevant reasoning and evidence.*

My proposed standard is similar to and inspired by the Irish Supreme Court's gloss on *Wednesbury* unreasonableness: 'it is necessary that the applicant should establish to the satisfaction of the court that the decision-making authority had before it no *relevant material* which would support its decision'.[162] The New Zealand Court of Appeal applied a similar standard in *Discount Brands* v. *Westfield (New Zealand)*:[163] 'there must have been some material capable of supporting the decision'.[164] On appeal, a majority of the Supreme Court adjudged this standard to be inappropriate, but the comments of Keith J are instructive: 'the cases on which the Court of Appeal principally relies for its essentially deferential position … concern … substantive decisions taken by public bodies with relevant expertise, democratic accountability or both'.[165] One can infer from Keith J's comments that where a body did have such expertise or accountability, such deference might be appropriate.

The New Zealand case prompts two observations: first, that a standard similar to that which I propose has found favour beyond Irish shores; secondly, the very reason that the Supreme Court refused to apply the deferential standard was because the characteristics of the body being reviewed could not justify doing so. A standard based on relevancy would be highly deferential: the reasoning and evidence relied upon would not have to lack cogency or sufficiency before a decision could be struck down, but would have to lack relevancy.[166] In the vast

161 *Ibid.* p. 137, per LeBel J.
162 *O'Keeffe* v. *An Bord Pleanála* [1993] 1 IR 39 at 72, per Finlay CJ. Emphasis added.
163 [2004] 3 NZLR 619. 164 *Ibid.*, p. 633. 165 *Discount Brands*, above n. 148, p. 622.
166 I should also emphasise that the presence of relevant reasons and reasoning and evidence is a basic requirement. Where a standard of review of unreasonableness applies, such that cogent reasons and reasoning and sufficient evidence may be relied

majority of cases, some relevant reasoning or evidence can be marshalled from the record in support of a decision.[167] Quite severe in its application in many cases, the relevancy standard is nonetheless appropriate for use in the review of decisions to which a very high degree of curial deference ought to be accorded.

4.4.4.1 Justifying the third standard

My proposed standard is a workable one, which addresses the problems raised by the Canadian experience. First, although relevancy is not quantifiable, it is relatively more tangible than a burden of justification based on magnitude. A burden of justification based on relevancy would leave much less scope for a reviewing court to strike down decisions than a conception of unreasonableness based on cogency and sufficiency. Relevancy requires a reviewing court to ask a simple question of the decision under review: are the reasoning and evidence provided to discharge the burden of justification *relevant* to the decision reached by the delegated decision-maker? Evaluating cogency and sufficiency, by contrast, must involve a court in assessing whether the justification adequately explains the decision, which inevitably requires a more detailed and difficult inquiry. Secondly, assessing relevancy is a familiar judicial task. For example, evidence can only be introduced at trial if relevant; and there, relevancy is judged *in relation to a particular fact*, just as with the third standard I propose, where reasoning and evidence would have to be relevant *in relation to a particular decision*. Lawyers are trained to identify when facts and evidence are relevant; it would not be a great leap also to ask lawyers to identify relevant reasoning.

Thirdly, the introduction of a standard of relevancy would not lead to an abdication of the judicial function or the tolerance of irrational decisions.[168] Consider, from the point of view of my proposed third standard, the decision of the Supreme Court of the United States in *Massachusetts* v. *Environmental Protection Agency*.[169] Here, the EPA

upon to discharge the burden of justification, the underlying reasons and reasoning and evidence must be relevant.

167 See also Paul Daly, 'Deference and Redefining Reasonableness' (2007) 12 BR 216.

168 But see Jaime Arancibia, 'The Intensity of Judicial Review in the Commercial Context: Deference and Proportionality' in Christopher Forsyth *et al.* (eds.), *Effective Judicial Review: A Cornerstone of Good Governance* (Oxford: Oxford University Press, 2010), p. 287, p. 292.

169 (2007) 549 US 497.

denied a petition requesting it to initiate a rule-making in respect of greenhouse gases (GHGs) on the basis, first, that it had no statutory authority to regulate GHGs and, secondly, that it would not be prudent to regulate in any event because to do so would conflict with other measures being taken to reduce GHGs. The key provision required the EPA to prescribe 'standards applicable to the emission of any air pollutant from any class or classes of new motor vehicles or new motor vehicle engines, which in [its] judgment cause, or contribute to, air pollution which may reasonably be anticipated to endanger public health or welfare'.[170] Air pollutant was broadly defined to include 'any air pollution agent or combination of such agents, including any physical, chemical, biological, radioactive … substance or matter which is emitted into or otherwise enters the ambient air'.[171]

Having held that the EPA had authority to regulate GHGs, Stevens J also held that the EPA had failed to explain its position and had acted arbitrarily and capriciously:[172] the decision was alleged to be illogical and inconsistent with statutory language. Any judgement that the EPA exercised not to regulate had to be relevant to whether the air pollutant was one which threatens public health or welfare: 'The use of the word "judgment" is not a roving licence to ignore the statutory text.'[173] But here, the 'laundry list of reasons not to regulate' encompassed a desire not to interfere with voluntary executive branch programmes to reduce GHGs or the president's negotiations with developing nations to reduce GHGs, and a fear of an inefficient, piecemeal approach emerging: 'Although we have neither the expertise nor the authority to evaluate these policy judgments, it is evident they *have nothing to do with* whether greenhouse gas emissions contribute to climate change.'[174] And references to uncertainty in the science of climate change were also insufficient: 'If the scientific uncertainty is so profound that it precludes EPA from making a reasoned judgment as to whether [GHGs] contribute to global warming, EPA must say so … The statutory question is whether sufficient information exists to make an endangerment finding.'[175] Thus the absence of *relevant* reasoning and evidence in support of the EPA's position was fatal to it.

[170] 42 USC § 7521(a)(1). [171] 42 USC § 7602(g).

[172] In violation of 42 USC § 7607(d)(9)(A) rather than the analogous provision in the APA.

[173] *Massachusetts*, above n. 169, p. 533. [174] *Ibid.*, p. 533. Emphasis added.

[175] *Ibid.*, p. 534.

Indeed, the relevant material will have to be adduced in respect of the particular *indicium* of unreasonableness that has been identified by the applicant. The presence of relevant material that is capable, on the whole, of justifying the decision will not be sufficient. That this should further assuage the concerns of those sceptical about my proposed third standard of review is exemplified by the judgment of Finlay Geoghegan J in an Irish High Court case, *Dikilu* v. *Minister for Justice.*[176] Here, the applicants were two sisters from the Democratic Republic of the Congo whose asylum claims had been refused. Oddly, their sister (they were three in total) was granted asylum by the Refugee Appeals Tribunal. Their factual situations were virtually the same, though the sister whose claim was granted was more visibly involved in the MPR political party – involvement in which gave rise to the necessary well-founded fear of persecution. However, the other sisters also occupied positions in the party, although their involvement was not as visible. Finlay Geoghegan J held that the decision was unreasonable because there was no relevant material before the Tribunal to justify the conclusion that the unlucky sisters did not have the well-founded fear of persecution that their sister did. In other words, there was an *indicium* of unreasonableness – differential treatment – but there was no relevant material available to discharge the burden of justification. In particular there was no evidence that the positions occupied by the unlucky sisters were not significant, '*nor indeed any relevant material which would support what must be the implicit conclusion* that the [unlucky sisters'] positions … were not such that, in accordance with country of origin information or other information, would objectively support a well-founded fear of persecution whilst the position of their sister … did'.[177]

Thus, if my proposed third standard of review were applicable, the reviewing court would not have to assess the cogency of the reasoning and sufficiency of the evidence provided to discharge the burden of justification. However by requiring the presence of relevant reasoning and evidence, my proposed third standard of review would at least require that some explanation be forthcoming. Because of the requirement of relevancy, a spectre of irrational decisions being approved by reviewing courts does not haunt my proposed third standard. Moreover, the requirement to identify *indicia* of unreasonableness is unaffected: even when a court applies the proposed third standard, *indicia* of unreasonableness must first be established.

[176] [2003] IEHC 40. [177] *Ibid.*, p. 13.

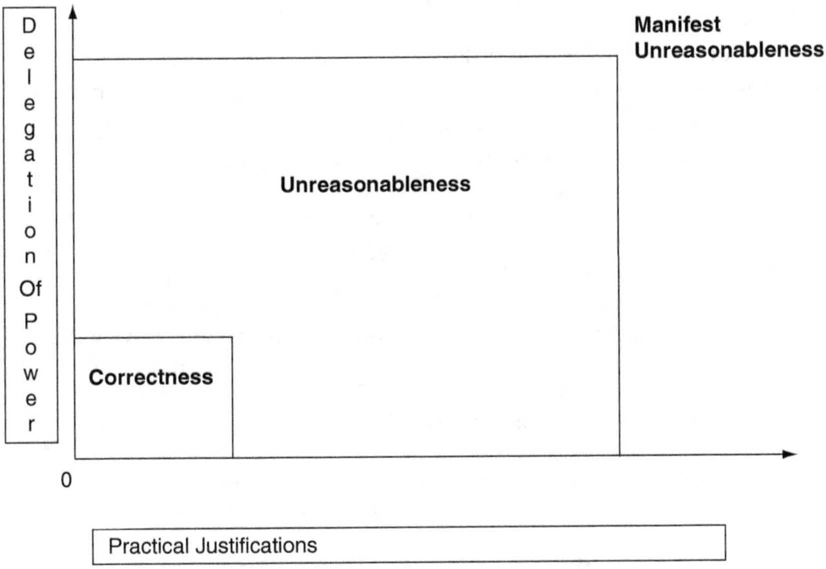

Figure 2: The visualisation described in section 4.4.4.2.

4.4.4.2 Labelling the third standard: manifest unreasonableness

The label for the third standard of review is not as important as the description of the burden of justification. A label of *manifest unreasonableness* could be affixed to the third standard of review that I have proposed.[178] Manifest unreasonableness shares with patent unreasonableness the virtue of signalling that decisions to which it applies should only be struck down in rare circumstances. Its label is also distinct from the patent unreasonableness label discarded by the Supreme Court of Canada and thus does not carry historical baggage. Using the word unreasonableness retains the close link between manifest unreasonableness and the protean conception of unreasonableness. The three standards of review – with manifest unreasonableness applying only where the delegation of power and practical justifications for curial deference combine with great force – can be visualised as depicted in Figure 2.

[178] See also Knight, 'Murky Methodology', above n. 124, pp. 146–50.

4.4.5 *Decision costs*

One objection to variable standards of review is that they impose burdensome costs on reviewing courts. Every minute spent determining the correct standard of review is a minute lost to some other controversy. Some of these costs are ultimately borne by litigants:

> The disposition of the case may well *turn* on the choice of standard of review. If litigants do take the plunge, they may find the court's attention focused not on their complaints, or the government's response, but on lengthy and arcane discussions of something they are told is the pragmatic and functional test. Every hour of a lawyer's preparation and court time devoted to unproductive 'lawyer's talk' poses a significant cost to the applicant. If the challenge is unsuccessful, the unhappy applicant may also face a substantial bill of costs from the successful government agency ... A small business denied a licence or a professional person who wants to challenge disciplinary action should be able to seek judicial review without betting the store or the house on the outcome.[179]

As a result of these 'pre-decision costs', the argument goes, reviewing courts should rely on simple rules in judicial review, such as the original two-step *Chevron* analysis.[180] Four responses are sufficient to dispose of the argument based on costs.

First, although consistency between theory and practice is costly, its costs result from choices made by the legislature:

> The complexity was created not by courts but by the legislatures, who wisely decided that not all administrative agencies would operate in the same way. It is a complexity that the courts must attempt to deal with and it would be irresponsible simply for judges to wish it away.[181]

Secondly, judicial review is inevitably a costly enterprise. There is no means of avoiding the complex assessment of the unreasonableness of impugned decisions. Even a simplified rule that all reasonable interpretations of ambiguous statutory provisions should be upheld, would nonetheless require a reviewing court to determine whether or not the

[179] *Dunsmuir*, above n. 130 at pp. 253–4, per Binnie J. Emphasis original. See also Deborah Lovett, 'That Enigmatic Curial Deference and the Continuing and Most Curious Search for Legislative Intent: What to Do, What to Do?' (2004) 17 CJALP 207.

[180] See e.g. Vermeule, *Judging under Uncertainty*, above n. 145, p. 220.

[181] Frank Iacobucci, 'Articulating a Rational Standard of Review Doctrine: A Tribute to John Willis' (2002) 27 Queen's LJ 859, 872.

interpretation of law is unreasonable. Necessarily, a reviewing court will have to examine the interpretation for *indicia* of unreasonableness and, if *indicia* are present, determine whether or not the decision is justifiable. Review for unreasonableness always requires a sensitive, context-based inquiry. Moreover, although a blanket rule, that if deference is to be accorded a standard of review of unreasonableness should be applied, might reduce costs to some extent, even a simplified rule would nonetheless impose costs: a reviewing court would have to expend resources on determining whether or not the rule ought to apply in the particular case. For example, if applying the original *Chevron* doctrine, a reviewing court would have to decide whether the impugned interpretation of law was clearly foreclosed by the relevant legislation, an inevitably costly inquiry. Because my doctrine of curial deference does not require ambiguity to trigger deference,[182] a case-by-case analysis of the relevant statutory provisions to ascertain whether or not they are ambiguous is rendered unnecessary. Indeed, as the Supreme Court of Canada has recognised, as time goes by, precedents will accrue and the appropriate standard of review can be determined by looking to previously decided cases rather than conducting the analysis afresh in every case.[183]

Thirdly, the introduction of a third standard of review may actually reduce costs. Where the third standard of review applies, instead of determining whether or not a justification is cogent, a reviewing court would need to determine only whether relevant reasoning or evidence supported the impugned decision. It is difficult, if not impossible, to determine *ex ante* whether the overall result will be to reduce costs. Costs may increase in that the determination of the appropriate standard of review would have to be made in all cases (unless it could be determined by reference to precedent), but the third standard of review would likely be applicable only in a limited number of cases. However, savings in the small number of cases in which the third standard of review applies may be sufficient to offset the increased costs incurred by a general requirement to determine the standard of review. It is simply impossible to say, but it would be inappropriate to sacrifice theoretical consistency on the altar of cost–benefit analysis where neither the costs nor the benefits are known.[184]

[182] See below 6.2.4.
[183] *Dunsmuir*, above n. 130 at pp. 223–5. See also *Brand X*, above n. 70.
[184] See also Eskridge, 'No Frills Textualism', above n. 123, p. 2051.

4.5 Conclusion

A requirement of reasonableness is not the only means of controlling delegated decision-makers. It is possible that legal control is not required at all and that alternative mechanisms of dispute resolution could be employed.[185] Because I assume that judicial review is available and legitimate,[186] however, I do not consider non-legal alternative means of control. It is also possible that some requirement other than unreasonableness could be employed.[187] However, in terms of implementing a variable standard of review, unreasonableness provides a useful tool. It is familiar to common law courts, which regularly hold delegated decision-makers to standards of unreasonableness, both in the exercise of discretion and in the interpretation of statutory provisions, and can accommodate a variable standard of review.

Moreover, as I have sought to demonstrate, unreasonableness is a legitimate concept. A 'culture of justification' is in fact hard-wired into unreasonableness: 'The basic principle is that all decisions backed by the public force that goes with invoking the authority of "the people" are legitimate only if they can be shown to be justifiable.'[188] As soon as an *indicium* of unreasonableness is identified, its presence must be justified by the delegated decision-maker. The absence of any *indicia* of unreasonableness would presumably have justificatory effect too, in that if nothing could be demonstrated to be wrong with the decision, the decision must be justifiable. Indeed, Murray

[185] Although even a prominent 'political constitutionalist' has recently accepted the legitimacy of judicial review to ensure that state action has a legitimate basis in law, and is based on evidence. Adam Tomkins, 'The Role of the Courts in the Political Constitution' (2010) 60 UTLJ 1. See also J. A. G. Griffith's equivocal support for limited judicial review in 'The Political Constitution' (1979) 42 MLR 1, 15.

[186] See Introduction.

[187] An alternative means of varying the standard of review would be to exclude or add grounds of review depending on the degree of curial deference to be accorded. This is one of the options presented by Knight, 'Mapping the Rainbow', above n. 14, pp. 429–31. However, I will argue below, 6.3.2, that grounds of review are an inappropriate means of control. In addition, deciding in a non-arbitrary manner precisely which grounds of review should be excluded would give rise to difficulties. Moreover, it would be decidedly strange, and possibly offensive to the rule of law, if a reviewing court could not quash a decision that, for example, was obviously or admittedly unreasonable, or relied on an obvious or admitted error of law.

[188] David Dyzenhaus, 'Law as Justification: Etienne Mureinik's Conception of Legal Culture' (1998) 14 SAJHR 11, 35. See also Sian Elias, 'Administrative Law for "Living People"' (2009) 68 CLJ 47, 62–6; Etienne Mureinik, 'Reconsidering Review: Participation and Accountability' [1993] Acta Juridica 35.

Hunt's fear that '[some] accounts of deference … do not give any role to the quality of the reasons relied upon to justify the decision' should, insofar as it is relevant in the present context, be assuaged.[189] Because the requirement of justification goes beyond a requirement of simply explaining and providing reasons for decisions and 'implies that the reasons supporting a decision must be "good" reasons, and this, in turn, requires norms or rules for determining what counts as a "good" reason',[190] unreasonableness need not be considered 'the antithesis of the rule of reason'.[191]

[189] Murray Hunt, 'Against Bifurcation' in David Dyzenhaus, Murray Hunt and Grant Huscroft (eds.), *A Simple Common Lawyer: Essays in Honour of Michael Taggart* (Oxford: Hart, 2009), p. 99, p. 114.

[190] David Dyzenhaus, Murray Hunt and Michael Taggart, 'The Principle of Legality in Administrative Law: Internationalisation as Constitutionalisation' (2001) 1 *Oxford University Commonwealth Law Journal* 5, 29.

[191] Michael Taggart, 'Re-inventing Administrative Law' in Nicholas Bamforth and Peter Leyland (eds.), *Public Law in a Multi-Layered Constitution* (Oxford: Hart, 2003), p. 311, p. 324.

5

Deference, proportionality and fundamental rights

Having spent Chapters 2, 3 and 4 developing a doctrine of curial deference, it is now necessary to turn to the appropriate scope of that doctrine. I will argue in this chapter that the doctrine of curial deference developed in the previous chapters should *not* be applied by reviewing courts in respect of decisions that are alleged to infringe fundamental rights. I will argue for a broad scope in Chapters 6 and 7.

I will begin this chapter by arguing in favour of a distinction between administrative review and constitutional review. I note, however, that there are significant affinities between the two. These affinities are a result of the according of epistemic deference and doctrinal deference in constitutional review. Although reference to the practical justifications for curial deference is not required as a matter of declared constitutional principle, I suggest that they can legitimately play a role in constitutional review. My intention is not to develop a theory of constitutional interpretation; rather I am concerned to highlight the affinities between administrative review and constitutional review.

I go on to discuss the proportionality test, prominent because of its popularity as a means of adjudicating on alleged infringements of fundamental rights, and contrast it with the standards of review developed in Chapter 4. I note that the proportionality test is a more intrusive form of review, which thus provides an appropriately high standard of protection for fundamental rights, but I also observe that its application may be leavened by the according of epistemic deference. I will then explain and reject, in the context of administrative review, the canon of constitutional avoidance developed by the Supreme Court of the United States, before, finally, addressing whether important interests short of fundamental rights should be taken into consideration in determining the appropriate standard of review.

I should note at the outset that by fundamental rights, I mean those rights which are granted the highest possible protection by a particular legal system. For example, in the United States, the fundamental rights are those recognised by the federal Constitution; in Canada, those recognised by the Charter of Rights and Freedoms (the Charter); and in the United Kingdom, those recognised by the Human Rights Act (which, in turn, are contained in the European Convention on Human Rights (the Convention)).[1] What I have to say about fundamental rights applies *mutatis mutandis* to other constitutional provisions and to procedural fairness, but the main controversy in recent times has concerned fundamental rights, so I have chosen to write in those terms. In addition, I am concerned here with individualised decisions alleged to infringe fundamental rights, and not with particular statutory provisions or legislative schemes that are alleged to be incompatible with fundamental rights.

5.1 Administrative review and constitutional review

In this section, I will advocate that courts should maintain a distinction between decisions that do not affect fundamental rights and decisions that affect fundamental rights; between administrative review and constitutional review.[2] In an extended argument for a 'culture of justification', David Dyzenhaus, Murray Hunt and Michael Taggart have urged that the distinction should be abolished. Rather, administrative decision-making should conform to a 'principle of legality', which would require 'a more or less intrusive standard of review ... depending on a variety of context-dependent factors ..., a duty on administrative decision-makers to give reasons for their decisions, and judges to defer to the extent that they find that the justification meets the applicable standard'.[3] If such a highly contextual approach were to be followed by reviewing courts, the standard of review would increase or decrease depending on the relative

[1] I appreciate that the Human Rights Act 1998 is a statute, which may lead one to wonder whether it can appropriately be grouped with the other instruments. I do not want to enter the debate over whether the Act has constitutional status. However, there are commonalities between the Act and constitutional provisions in other jurisdictions. Most importantly, all delegated decision-making must conform to the Act, as it must to constitutional bills of rights in jurisdictions which have constitutional bills of rights. Even the possibility of repeal is common to the Act and constitutional bills of rights. Whether or not the Act has constitutional status, therefore, it is legitimate for me to group it with constitutional provisions, rather than statutory provisions, for present purposes.

[2] I borrow the terms, with a slight modification, from Aileen Kavanagh, *Constitutional Review under the United Kingdom Human Rights Act* (Cambridge: Cambridge University Press, 2009), p. 5.

[3] David Dyzenhaus, Murray Hunt and Michael Taggart, 'The Principle of Legality in Administrative Law: Internationalisation and Constitutionalisation' (2001) 1 Oxford University Commonwealth Law Journal 5, 6. But note the narrower view taken subsequently by Taggart in 'Proportionality, Deference, *Wednesbury*' [2008] NZLR 423.

importance of the individual right or interest at stake, leaving no room for the distinction. Recent developments in Commonwealth common law theory, Dyzenhaus, Hunt and Taggart claimed:

> point towards adoption of a 'constitutional rights' methodology, and that provides the opportunity for constitutional and administrative law to be unified in name and approach under the banner of public law. Some may see this 'constitutionalisation' of administrative law as a bad thing, but the alternative is likely to be a bifurcated public law, with certain issues involving selected rights being determined one way, and other interests outside the charmed constitutional circle being determined another … The thought of an administrative law rump, isolated from the rights-based developments, is unappealing.[4]

If this approach were followed, review of fundamental rights would take place within the same framework as the review of any other decision made by a delegated decision-maker. I reject this approach.

I accept that:

> Administrative law is … particularly vulnerable to the permeation of human rights claims, since, like human rights law, it primarily constrains the exercise of public power, often in controversial areas of public policy, with a shared focus on the fairness of procedure and an emphasis on the effectiveness of remedies.[5]

However, I contend that the distinction is wholly tenable.

5.1.1 The analytical difference

An important analytical difference between administrative review and constitutional review can be identified, in legal systems which, as is typical, vest the protection of fundamental rights in courts.[6] It is uncontroversial to observe that the purpose of entrenching fundamental rights is to protect them from infringement by the state. Their protection is delegated to courts,

4 Dyzenhaus, Hunt and Taggart, 'The Principle of Legality in Administrative Law', above n. 3, p. 31. See similarly Murray Hunt, 'Against Bifurcation' in David Dyzenhaus, Murray Hunt and Grant Huscroft (eds.), *A Simple Common Lawyer: Essays in Honour of Michael Taggart* (Oxford: Hart, 2009), p. 99 and see also T. R. S. Allan, 'Deference, Defiance, and Doctrine: Defining the Limits of Judicial Review' (2010) 60 UTLJ 41, 49–50.

5 Ben Saul, 'Australian Administrative Law: The Human Rights Dimension' in Matthew Groves and H. P. Lee (eds.), *Australian Administrative Law: Fundamentals, Principles and Doctrines* (Cambridge: Cambridge University Press, 2007), p. 50.

6 For present purposes, it is not relevant whether the power is expressly granted or assumed by courts.

sometimes by the people in a constituent assembly or plebiscite of some description, sometimes by constitutional amendment and sometimes by statute. Whichever method of entrenchment is chosen, 'the decision to enact a bill of rights undoubtedly involves an important delegation of power over the interpretation of rights from the ordinary political branches to the judiciary'.[7] Accordingly, as with the provisions of general statutes, such as freedom of information legislation, a standard of review of correctness should be applied in the review of decisions that allegedly infringe fundamental rights. Significant powers may be delegated to delegated decision-makers, but authority to interpret fundamental rights provisions conclusively[8] will not be: '[fundamental] rights are legal rights, and courts are constitutionally required to make up their own minds as to what the law requires'.[9] In administrative review, the legislature has taken a decision to delegate decision-making authority to a body other than a court. But in constitutional review, the protection of fundamental rights has been delegated to the courts themselves. It matters not how much power has been delegated to the delegated decision-maker in question; protection of fundamental rights has already been delegated to the courts.

This point was not lost on the House of Lords, which recently affirmed the distinction between administrative review and cases where the Human Rights Act 1998 is at issue. In *Miss Behavin'* v. *Belfast City Council*,[10] Baroness Hale of Richmond expressed the point in the following terms:

> The role of the court in human rights adjudication is quite different from the role of the court in an ordinary judicial review of administrative action. In human rights adjudication, the court is concerned with whether the human rights of the [applicant] have in fact been infringed, not with whether the administrative decision-maker properly took them into account.[11]

[7] David Erdos, *Delegating Rights Protection: The Rise of Bills of Rights in the Westminster World* (Oxford: Oxford University Press, 2010), p. 4.

[8] As opposed to preliminarily. See e.g. *Nova Scotia (Workers' Compensation Board)* v. *Martin* [2003] SCC 54; [2003] 2 SCR 504; J. M. Evans, 'Principle and Pragmatism: Administrative Agencies' Jurisdiction over Constitutional Issues' in Grant Huscroft and Michael Taggart (eds.), *Inside and Outside Canadian Administrative Law: Essays in Honour of David Mullan* (Toronto: University of Toronto Press, 2006), p. 377.

[9] Julian Rivers, 'Proportionality and Variable Intensity of Review' (2006) 65 CLJ 174, 191. See *Dickerson* v. *United States* (2000) 530 US 428 at 437; *R (Begum)* v. *Governors of Denbigh High School* [2006] UKHL 15; [2007] 1 AC 100 at 125–6.

[10] [2007] UKHL 19; [2008] LGR 127.

[11] *Ibid.*, p. 139. For some nuance, see p. 141 (Baroness Hale) and pp. 154–5 (Lord Neuberger); Thomas Poole, 'The Reformation of English Administrative Law' (2009) 68 CLJ 142, 160–4.

Baroness Hale's position follows quite naturally from the analytical distinction between decisions that have been delegated to the courts and decisions that have been delegated to other bodies.

This argument from 'constitutional competence' is strengthened if one holds the view that judges possess relative 'institutional competence' in protecting fundamental rights.[12] Believing that courts are, generally, better placed to determine issues pertaining to fundamental rights would strengthen the argument that their protection is to be delegated to courts.[13] But this position has not won universal support. In either case, judges must determine conclusively (subject to the possibility of subsequent constitutional or possibly legislative amendment) whether fundamental rights have been infringed and whether any infringement is justified. However, as I will suggest below,[14] this duty can be tempered by the development, if deemed appropriate, of doctrinal deference and the according of epistemic deference in constitutional review.

5.1.2 Protecting fundamental rights

One might also wonder what would happen if the distinction between administrative review and constitutional review were to be abolished. The point was the subject of discussion in *Multani* v. *Commission scolaire Marguerite-Bourgeoys*,[15] a case decided by the Supreme Court of Canada. At issue here was the decision of a school to prevent a Sikh student from wearing a kirpan – a sword or dagger which is worn for religious reasons. The basis for the decision was that the wearing of a kirpan at school would violate the section of the school's code of conduct that banned the carrying of weapons and dangerous objects. Charron J held that the student's challenge was directed at the decision, not at the school's code of conduct or any statutory provision. Moreover, because there was no question but that the school was acting within its general statutory authority, the challenge was of a constitutional nature, and should be dealt with accordingly. Ultimately, Charron J struck the

[12] Jeffrey Jowell, 'Of Vires and Vacuums: The Constitutional Context of Judicial Review' [1999] PL 448, 451–3.

[13] See e.g. Richard Fallon, 'The Core of an Uneasy Case for Judicial Review' (2008) 121 Harv LR 1693. For a succinct summary of the opposing view, see Jeremy Waldron, 'The Core of the Case against Judicial Review' (2006) 115 Yale LJ 1346.

[14] See below 5.1.5. [15] [2006] SCC 6; [2006] 1 SCR 256.

decision down as an unjustifiable infringement with the student's freedom of conscience and religion, guaranteed by s. 2(a) of the Charter.

Deschamps and Abella JJ concurred in the result, but disagreed with the approach taken by the majority. Instead, they urged:

> the administrative law approach must be retained for reviewing *decisions* and *orders* made by administrative bodies. A constitutional justification analysis must, on the other hand, be carried out when reviewing the validity or enforceability of a *norm* such as a law, regulation, or other similar rule of general application.[16]

They adduced two reasons in support of their preferred position. First, the proportionality test, applied under s. 1 of the Charter to ascertain whether infringements of fundamental rights are justified or not, is designed for application to general norms, not to individualised decisions. Here, Deschamps and Abella JJ relied in part on a comparison between the two versions of the Charter. The English version of s. 1 allows limitations to be imposed on certain Charter rights if they are 'prescribed by law' and satisfy the requirements of the proportionality test. The equally authoritative French version refers to 'restreints' imposed by a 'règle de droit',[17] the dictionary definition of which is a '[p]rinciple of a *general and impersonal* nature that determines a line of conduct'.[18] Thus, Deschamps and Abella JJ suggested, the proportionality test under s. 1 can be applied only to general rules, and not to individualised decisions.[19]

Secondly, Deschamps and Abella JJ alleged that confusion could result from permitting an individualised decision to be challenged on both administrative law and constitutional grounds. Parties to a case might not know in advance which grounds would be relied upon by the reviewing court. Instead, they argued, an administrative law analysis should be conducted whenever an individualised decision by a delegated decision-maker was challenged: 'If an administrative body makes a decision or order that is said to conflict with fundamental values, the mechanisms of administrative law are readily available to meet the needs of individuals whose rights have been violated.'[20]

[16] *Ibid.*, p. 307. Emphasis original.

[17] Additionally, the French text contains no equivalent to 'prescribed'.

[18] Hubert Reid, *Dictionnaire de droit québécois et canadien*, 2nd edn (Montreal: Wilson and Lafleur, 2001), p. 475. Emphasis added.

[19] The best treatment of this question is Danielle Pinard, 'Les Seules Règles de droit qui peuvent poser des limites aux droits et libertés constitutionnellement protégés et l'arrêt *Slaight Communications*' (1992) 1 National Journal of Constitutional Law 79.

[20] Above n. 15, p. 316.

Although these arguments have some merit,[21] the approach advocated by Deschamps and Abella JJ should not be followed. Consider the underlying logic. Anyone asserting that the proportionality test should not be applied to individualised decisions is left with two unpalatable options, one over-protective and the other under-protective. The over-protective option is to say that any infringement of a Charter right is unlawful.[22] Ordinarily, where infringement of a Charter right can be established, the focus shifts to s. 1 and whether the infringement satisfies the requirements of the proportionality test. But if s. 1 is not available to the delegated decision-maker, as Deschamps and Abella JJ would insist, then *any* infringement of a Charter right by a delegated decision-maker *must* be unlawful.[23] This position may be logical, but it is patently absurd. For example, under s. 2(b) of the Charter, extremely broad protection is given to freedom of expression, including the possession of child pornography. Regulation of possession of such material can be justified under s. 1 of the Charter.[24] However, if courts were to choose the over-protective option, a school board which, say, made an order prohibiting the possession of child pornography on the premises by a particular individual, would not be able to rely upon s. 1 of the Charter and its order would be unlawful. Moreover, the choice of the over-protective option would impose an impossible burden on legislatures and delegated decision-makers:

> From a practical point of view, it would be wrong to limit the application of section 1 to enacted laws or regulations. That would require the Crown to pass detailed regulations to deal with every contingency as a precondition of justifying its conduct under section 1. In my view, such a technical approach does not accord with the spirit of the Charter and would make it unduly difficult to justify limits on rights and freedoms which may be reasonable and, indeed, necessary.[25]

It is not surprising, considering its capacity to cause absurd and unrealistic results, that Deschamps and Abella JJ did not choose the over-protective option.

[21] For an excellent discussion, see Robert Leckey, 'Prescribed by Law/Une Règle de droit' (2007) 45 Osgoode Hall LJ 571.

[22] Naturally, what I say here about the Charter applies outside the confines of the (significant) Canadian landmass.

[23] Unless the infringement were expressly or impliedly authorised by statute, in which case the statute could be subjected to the proportionality test.

[24] See *R* v. *Sharpe* [2001] SCC 2; [2001] 1 SCR 45.

[25] *Committee for the Commonwealth of Canada* v. *Canada* [1991] 1 SCR 139 at 245, per McLachlin J.

Instead, they chose the second, under-protective option: to treat the infringement of the Charter right as a factor to be taken into account in assessing the unreasonableness of the impugned decision. However, this option is also unpalatable. Simply put, it is insufficiently protective of Charter rights. On the conventional understanding of review for unreasonableness, it is not permissible for a reviewing court to engage in any reweighing of the factors considered by the delegated decision-maker.[26] In *Multani*, Deschamps and Abella JJ considered the school board's decision to be unreasonable because it did not 'sufficiently consider' the right to freedom of religion (or the accommodation proposed by the student and his father).[27] With respect, however, that is not a basis for finding that the decision was unreasonable: failing to take a relevant factor into consideration, or even failing to give great weight to a relevant factor, may be an *indicium* of unreasonableness, but it is subject to the possibility of justification.[28] Against this, the assertion made by Deschamps and Abella JJ to the effect that 'it is difficult to imagine a decision that would be considered reasonable or correct even though it conflicted with constitutional values' is unconvincing.[29] As Charron J observed for the majority judges in *Multani*, abolishing the distinction between administrative review and constitutional review:

> could well reduce the fundamental rights and freedoms guaranteed by the Canadian Charter to mere administrative law principles or, at the very least, cause confusion between the two ... [T]he fact that an issue relating to constitutional rights is raised in an administrative context does not mean that the constitutional law standards must be dissolved into the administrative law standards. The rights and freedoms guaranteed by the Canadian Charter establish a *minimum* constitutional protection ...[30]

Writing for the Irish Supreme Court in *Clinton* v. *An Bord Pleanála (No. 2)*,[31] Geoghegan J echoed this concern: 'It would insufficiently protect constitutional rights if the court, hearing the judicial review application, merely had to be satisfied that the decision was not

26 See *Canada (Immigration and Citizenship)* v. *Khosa* [2009] SCC 12; [2009] 1 SCR 339.

27 *Multani*, above n. 15, p. 305.

28 Some support for their position can be garnered from *Baker* v. *Canada (Minister of Citizenship and Immigration)* [1999] 2 SCR 817, but that decision was subsequently heavily qualified by *Suresh* v. *Canada (Minister of Citizenship and Immigration)* [2002] SCC 1; [2002] 1 SCR 3.

29 *Multani*, above n. 15, p. 309.

30 *Ibid.*, pp. 270–1, per Charron J.

31 [2007] IESC 19; [2007] 4 IR 701.

[unreasonable].'[32] It is for this reason that abolishing the distinction between administrative review and constitutional review would jeopardise the protection of fundamental rights.

5.1.3 A constitutional potpourri: doctrinal deference and fundamental rights

However, the argument advanced by Charron J and Geoghegan J should not be pushed too far. A sweeping declaration that abolishing the distinction between administrative review and constitutional review would reduce the protection accorded to fundamental rights is not tenable. Despite the analytical difference between administrative review and constitutional review, there are overlaps between them. Henry Monagahan, for example, has noted how the rational-basis test often applied in constitutional adjudication in the United States bears a resemblance to the standard of review of unreasonableness in administrative law: 'What is striking, in the end, is that there is far less discontinuity between the role of judicial review in administrative law and constitutional law than one might suspect given the formal demands of the independent judgment rule [in constitutional review].'[33] Nevertheless, the tests are evidently analytically distinct: one is the result of judicial interpretation of various *constitutional* provisions; the other is the result of judicial interpretation of various *statutory* provisions. Just because the same results might be reached in administrative review or constitutional review does not mean that the distinction between administrative review and constitutional review ought to be abolished.

Confusion is apt to arise in this area because even the application of a standard of review of correctness is not as straightforward as it might seem on first sight.[34] For example, if a statutory provision were to provide that 'reasonable steps must be taken' or that 'the minister must have proportionate grounds for decision', then the *correct* interpretation of the statutory provision would be that 'reasonable steps' must be taken or 'proportionate grounds' must be present.[35] In some cases, then, a

[32] *Ibid.*, p. 723. [33] '*Marbury* and the Administrative State' (1983) 83 Colum LR 1, 33.

[34] For a similar perspective, see Tom Hickman, *Public Law after the Human Rights Act* (Oxford: Hart, 2010), pp. 99–101.

[35] See e.g. *R* v. *Monopolies and Mergers Commission, ex p. South Yorkshire Transport* [1993] 1 WLR 23, explained in Paul Daly, 'Deference on Questions of Law' (2011) 74 MLR 694.

standard of review of correctness may require review for unreasonableness, or proportionality.

As Scarman LJ explained in *Secretary of State for Education and Science* v. *Tameside*,[36] where the relevant statutory provisions[37] allowed the minister to intervene only if a local education authority had acted unreasonably:

> the [minister] cannot lawfully be satisfied that the local education authority is proposing to act unreasonably unless upon the information that was or ought to have been available to him the local education authority, acting reasonably, could not have acted, or proposed to act, as it in fact did. In other words, while it is not for the court to substitute its view for the minister's, *it is also the law that the Minister cannot substitute his view for that of the local education authority, provided always that an authority, acting reasonably, could have made the decision that in fact it made.*[38]

The correct interpretation, then, was that the minister could intervene only if the local authority had acted unreasonably.

Similarly, a variety of methods are employed by judges in enforcing constitutional limits on state action. In fact, judicial enforcement of fundamental rights protections is something of a potpourri. In the context of the Convention, the question whether Art. 8 has been infringed by state action has to be answered correctly. If that question is answered in the affirmative, however, a second question must be asked: was the infringement proportionate? The *correct* interpretation of Art. 8 is that once an infringement has been established, the infringement must be proportionate: 'The starting point is the right allegedly infringed by the exercise of discretionary power by the administrative authority. Next is the inquiry into whether the right has been reasonably or

[36] [1977] AC 1014.

[37] Section 68 of the Education Act 1944, provided as follows:

> If the Secretary of State is satisfied, either on complaint by any person or otherwise, that any local education authority or the managers or governors of any county or voluntary school have acted or are proposing to act unreasonably with respect to the exercise of any power conferred or the performance of any duty imposed by or under this Act, he may, notwithstanding any enactment rendering the exercise of the power or the performance of the duty contingent upon the opinion of the authority or of the managers or governors, give such directions as to the exercise of the power or the performance of the duty as appear to him to be expedient.

[38] *Tameside*, above n. 36, p. 1026. Emphasis added. See similarly, *ibid.*, p. 1064 (Lord Diplock).

justifiably limited in terms of the express qualifications on the right.'[39] Thus, proportionate limitations on rights enjoyed under Art. 8 must be tolerated. Claims under Art. 3[40] of the Convention are treated differently to claims under Art. 8[41] and other Articles.[42] However, the differential treatment results from the nature of the different Articles. Article 3 creates an absolute prohibition. Article 8 creates a prohibition which may be breached in a proportionate manner.

In the United States, so-called strict scrutiny, pursuant to which restrictions on certain rights must be narrowly tailored to further a compelling state objective, has been described as '"strict" in theory but fatal in fact'.[43] Whereas, where lesser rights or interests are infringed upon by state action, only a rational connection between the infringement and the objective need be established.[44] But these varying degrees of protection again result from judicial interpretation on a standard of review of correctness of constitutional guarantees.

To note that the standard of scrutiny varies as between these different provisions is simply to recognise that the provisions are constructed or have been interpreted differently.[45] Moreover, that similar values

[39] Michael Taggart, 'Re-inventing Administrative Law' in Nicholas Bamforth and Peter Leyland (eds.), *Public Law in a Multi-Layered Constitution* (Oxford: Hart, 2003), pp. 311, 325.

[40] *Soering* v. *United Kingdom* (1989) 11 EHRR 439; *Vilvarajah* v. *United Kingdom* (1991) 14 EHRR 248; *Chahal* v. *United Kingdom* (1996) 23 EHRR 413; *Saadi* v. *Italy* (2008) 49 EHRR 730.

[41] *Smith and Grady* v. *United Kingdom* (1999) 29 EHRR 493.

[42] *RB (Algeria)* v. *Secretary of State for the Home Department* [2009] UKHL 10; [2009] 2 WLR 512.

[43] Gerald Gunther, 'The Supreme Court, 1971 Term – Foreword: In Search of Evolving Doctrine on a Changing Court: A Model for a Newer Equal Protection' (1972) 86 Harv LR 1, 8. But contrast the views of Adam Winkler, 'Fatal in Theory and Strict in Fact: An Empirical Analysis of Strict Scrutiny in the Federal Courts' (2006) 59 Vand LR 793.

[44] See e.g. *United States* v. *Carolene Products* (1938) 304 US 144 at 152, per Stone J: 'regulatory legislation affecting ordinary commercial transactions is not to be pronounced unconstitutional unless, in the light of the facts made known or generally assumed, it is of such a character as to preclude the assumption that it rests upon some rational basis within the knowledge and experience of the legislators'.

[45] The foregoing analysis assists in rebutting Murray Hunt's argument that, because variable standards of review are employed in fundamental rights cases, the distinction between administrative review and constitutional review is unnecessary. Hunt, 'Against Bifurcation', above n. 4, p. 107. See also *R (Mahmood)* v. *Secretary of State for the Home Department* [2000] EWCA Civ 315; [2001] 1 WLR 840 at 853, per Laws LJ: 'at every turn [a reviewing court's applications of the proportionality test] will form part of a continuum with what the common law has already said'.

may be implicated or enforced,[46] at a high level of abstraction, ignores the analytical difference between administrative review and constitutional review.

Doctrinal deference may, then, play a role in fundamental rights adjudication.[47] The construction[48] of that doctrine may be influenced by considerations of expertise, complexity and legitimacy, democratic and procedural.[49] It would, after all, be 'extreme', 'implausible' and 'undesirable' to hold fast to a position that a 'court must adjudicate every challenge to satisfy itself as to its "correct" conclusion'.[50] But doctrinal deference can take different forms. Limitations of strict scrutiny or proportionality, rather than limitations of reasonableness, can be imposed upon delegated decision-makers. Below, I will compare the heightened level of scrutiny provided by the application of the proportionality test with the lower level provided by review for unreasonableness. It is the additional scrutiny provided by the application of the proportionality test that makes it a particularly acceptable tool in fundamental rights cases. Attaching the label of doctrinal deference to the proportionality test does not detract from its stringency. If, pursuant to both administrative review and constitutional review *all* decisions were subjected to a similarly lower level of scrutiny, the purpose of entrenching fundamental rights would be frustrated. Fundamental rights would

[46] Hunt, 'Against Bifurcation', above n. 4, pp. 105–6. See similarly Allan, 'Deference, Defiance, and Doctrine', above n. 4, 48–50; Geneviève Cartier, 'The *Baker* Effect: A New Interface between the *Canadian Charter of Rights and Freedoms* and Administrative Law – the Case of Discretion' in David Dyzenhaus (ed.), *The Unity of Public Law* (Oxford: Hart, 2004), pp. 61, 77.

[47] On occasion, the practical justifications for curial deference have caused courts to accord doctrinal deference to delegated decision-makers' fact-based decisions in respect of unknown future situations. See e.g. *Suresh*, above n. 28 and *RB (Algeria)*, above n. 42, both of which centred on risks of maltreatment of deportees. Such judicial reticence, however, risks undermining the protection of fundamental rights by making fundamental rights dependent on the accuracy of delegated decision-makers' factual assessments. See David Mullan, 'Administrative Tribunals and Judicial Review of *Charter* Issues after *Multani*' (2006) 21 National Journal of Constitutional Law 127. Courts need not relegate themselves to a secondary role in constitutional review just because difficult factual determinations have to be made about future events. According epistemic deference seems a more appropriate way of giving weight to the views of experts on complex questions, without weakening the protection for fundamental rights or causing reviewing courts to delve too deeply into murky waters.

[48] See Laurence Solum, 'The Interpretation-Construction Distinction' (2010) 27 Constitutional Commentary 95.

[49] See further below 5.1.5.

[50] Taggart, 'Proportionality', above n. 3, p. 456.

be weakly protected if they could always be interfered with on reasonable grounds, for they would have no greater status than the sort of interest that allows an individual to bring an application for judicial review. As long, however, as interference with fundamental rights remains generally more difficult to justify, doctrinal deference may be accommodated. As I will demonstrate below,[51] there are very real differences between the protections afforded by the proportionality test and the standards of review identified in Chapter 4.

5.1.4 Epistemic deference and fundamental rights

Whether a reviewing court must decide for itself whether a particular decision unjustifiably infringes upon a fundamental right, or must apply a test of unreasonableness or proportionality to an allegedly unjustifiable infringement, it may legitimately give weight to the decisions of other bodies. Epistemic deference is entirely appropriate in constitutional review. As Alison Young has recently argued, where a contestable issue concerning the definition and application of a fundamental right is before a court, the court may defer to the legislature or executive where the legislature or executive has greater knowledge or expertise than the court.[52] Young's suggestion is that courts are like individuals seeking advice from a doctor. Assuming that the doctor has greater competence to answer a medical question (an assumption that may be called into question, presumably, by whisky breath, trembling hands or a tendency to obfuscate important issues), the individual should defer to the views of the doctor:

> it is the role of the court to determine the scope and application of the Convention rights, but … in doing so it is to give weight to the opinions of the legislature and executive. It does so for epistemic reasons, when faced with contestable rights where there are reasons to believe that the executive or legislature may be better placed to determine the definition and application of the Convention right to the issue before the court.[53]

I would reverse the analogy. Judges are more akin to doctors than to patients. Judges are entrusted by constitutional instruments with the keeping of fundamental rights, just as doctors are entrusted with the keeping of patients' health. So, the question should be the extent to which the views of the patient should be considered by the doctor. The

[51] See below 5.2. [52] 'In Defence of Due Deference' (2009) 72 MLR 554.
[53] *Ibid.*, p. 573.

analogy is imperfect when reversed because the patient has a veto over the final decision, which is not always the case for a legislature or executive, but leaving the veto problem aside, Young's analogy provides a vehicle to explore the appropriate use of epistemic deference in constitutional review.

A doctor is obliged to take on board the considered views of a patient. But the weight to be given to the views of the patient will vary. The reason that 'doctors make the worst patients' is that the doctor-as-patient may have well-considered views about the appropriate course of treatment, to which great weight will have to be given (in a case of disagreement), thereby reducing the doctor's scope for decision-making. But it is not just doctors who might make bad patients in this sense. The views of the well-informed lay person, who has read and consulted widely on the relevant ailment, would also have to be given great weight. Less weight would have to be given to the views of less-well-informed patients. It is not difficult to appreciate how expertise, complexity and the procedural legitimacy of the patient's decision-making process would feed into the assessment of how much weight to accord to a patient's views. But the patient's expertise, or the extent to which the patient has consulted widely, does not justify according weight to *all* of his or her views. In fact, the decision-making process of a doctor – just like that of a judge – comprises many individual decisions. Thus, for example, a patient may be well-informed about survival rates for surgical treatment of cancer, but poorly informed on the consequences of chemotherapy. Epistemic deference could then only be accorded to a decision to perform surgery, not one to undergo chemotherapy.[54]

A useful legal example is the *Denbigh High School* case.[55] Here, the House of Lords strongly asserted that the questions whether Art. 9 of the Convention was infringed by a school board's uniform policy (which banned the jilbab, but not all Islamic dress) and whether any infringement was justified, were for the courts to resolve conclusively. However, multiple issues arose in considering whether the student's Art. 9 right to 'freedom of thought, conscience and religion' had been unjustifiably infringed. In the consideration of whether the infringement was

[54] 'Double counting' is not as significant an issue in this context as it was above 4.4.2.2. Here, judges are entitled to use all available tools to construe and apply constitutional provisions. I have not identified a declared constitutional principle which would prevent them from using the same tools at two different stages of the analysis.

[55] Above n. 9.

proportionate,[56] epistemic deference was accorded to the views of the school board on certain matters. For example, a relevant consideration for the House of Lords was that the policy would improve the educational environment of the school.[57] Because it was relevant whether the infringement of Art. 9 was to some extent justified by the improved educational environment and level of religious harmony occasioned by the uniform policy, it was also relevant to consider the educational environment and religious harmony which resulted from the policy. The school board was in a better position than the House of Lords to answer this question by virtue of the former's expertise and the consultative process it had engaged in with community representatives. On these questions, the school board's views prevailed. They were given great weight, and rightly so: 'The quality of the administrative process, insofar as it can be demonstrated, will enhance the court's confidence that the ultimate outcome (where there is scope for reasonable differences of judgment) falls within the permitted range.'[58] But nevertheless, the reviewing court has the final say as to whether or not the infringement is justifiable.

5.1.5 *The practical justifications for curial deference and fundamental rights*

It follows from the requirement of a standard of review of correctness in constitutional review that the role of the practical justifications for curial deference in constitutional review must be significantly more nuanced and less prescriptive than it is in administrative review. Nevertheless, expertise, complexity, democratic legitimacy and procedural legitimacy may figure in the analysis required to be conducted by a court in assessing whether or not a fundamental right was unjustifiably infringed. The practical justifications for curial deference may legitimately be called upon by courts in their decisions to accord doctrinal deference and their formulation of doctrinal deference.[59] In addition, epistemic deference may be accorded where, in reviewing the impugned decision for its compatibility with fundamental rights protections, the reviewing court concludes that decisions of the delegated decision-maker are relevant.

[56] In fact, a majority of the House of Lords held that there was no interference with Art. 9 and considered the proportionality of the infringement in the alternative.

[57] Above n. 9, pp. 116–17.

[58] Allan, 'Deference, Defiance, and Doctrine', above n. 4, p. 47.

[59] See e.g. *Turner* v. *Safley* (1987) 482 US 78 at 89.

However, given the delegation to courts of the determination of the scope of fundamental rights, it would be unduly prescriptive to limit reliance in constitutional review to the practical justifications for curial deference identified in Chapter 3. Other factors may be adjudged relevant in the delineation and enforcement of constitutional guarantees. Concerns about the separation of powers and judicial resources, for example, might motivate courts to circumscribe fundamental rights.[60]

Nonetheless, relying only on those practical justifications that can be linked to legislative intent in the manner suggested in Chapter 3 would have salutary effects. Most obviously, it would bring consistency to what can be a chaotic area. By limiting the considerations that are relevant in constitutional review, certainty would be enhanced. Moreover, proponents of according curial deference to delegated decision-makers in fundamental rights cases have treated the practical justifications for curial deference largely uncritically.[61] But as I detailed in Chapter 3, expertise, complexity, democratic legitimacy and procedural legitimacy are more troublesome than they appear at first sight. In situations like that presented in the *Denbigh High School* case, would there not be a risk that participatory processes engaged in by schools would function simply to accommodate competing interests along pluralist lines? If so, would that be an acceptable reason to defer to various aspects of the decision? What if the procedures were not significantly deliberative? What if local grandees were chosen to serve as delegated decision-makers, on the basis of their political or financial clout? How much experience did the delegated decision-makers really have in striking a balance between competing interests? Did the delegated decision-maker really understand the pupils' depth of religious sentiment? These problems did not seem to be present in the *Denbigh High School* case, but they may arise elsewhere. One way to avoid answering these difficult and potentially controversial questions is to adopt my position that the practical justifications are material only where it can plausibly be inferred from a proper consideration of the relevant statutory provisions that they influenced the legislative decision to delegate power to a body

[60] See e.g. David Wiseman, 'The *Charter* and Poverty: Beyond Injusticiability' (2001) 51 UTLJ 425 and, for a concrete example, *Sinnott* v. *Minister for Education* [2001] IESC 63; [2001] 2 IR 505.

[61] For a comprehensive study of the rationales offered by courts for curial deference in fundamental rights adjudication, see Brian Foley, *Deference and the Presumption of Constitutionality* (Dublin: Institute of Public Administration, 2008), pp. 74–126.

other than a court. Those provocative questions would have already been answered, by the legislature.

I have not set out to offer a theory of constitutional interpretation in this section. Any argument about the utility of the practical justifications in constitutional review must be largely pragmatic; there is no declared constitutional principle comparable to the one identified in Chapter 2 on which to rely. Accordingly, the role of the practical justifications in constitutional review is much more attenuated than is their role in administration review. It is inappropriate to insist that judges *must* have regard to expertise, complexity, democratic legitimacy and procedural legitimacy in interpreting and applying fundamental rights guarantees. However, it is legitimate to point out the utility of taking them into consideration, and interesting to draw comparisons and contrasts between administrative review and constitutional review.

5.2 Proportionality and unreasonableness

I do not wish to make the unrealistic claim that proportionality is the *sine qua non* of constitutional review.[62] As I have noted, protections of fundamental rights form something of a potpourri. However, proportionality has captured the global judicial imagination: final appellate bodies across the world have adopted it as the definitive test which infringements of fundamental rights must satisfy.[63] That is certainly true of two of the jurisdictions I have used for the purposes of comparison – England and Canada – and even in the United States some intrepid scholars have noted the similarities between proportionality and the various tests applied in constitutional review by the Supreme Court of the United States.[64] Therefore, the proportionality test provides a fruitful point of comparison with the variable standards of review identified in Chapter 4. For the purposes of the ensuing discussion, I will use the term 'review for unreasonableness' to cover what might be termed conventional administrative review.[65] This seems appropriate given my discussion of unreasonableness

[62] For such an argument, see David Beatty, *The Ultimate Rule of Law* (Oxford: Oxford University Press, 2004).

[63] See generally Alec Stone Sweet and Jud Mathews, 'Proportionality, Balancing and Global Constitutionalism' (2008) 47 Columbia Journal of Transnational Law 73.

[64] See generally Thomas Sullivan and Richard Frase, *Proportionality Principles in American Law: Controlling Excessive Government Actions* (Oxford: Oxford University Press, 2008).

[65] See above 1.2.

in Chapter 4. Also, in the interests of brevity, where I refer to review for unreasonableness, it can be taken as including manifest unreasonableness. My primary aim in this section is to demonstrate that the proportionality test is a more intrusive standard of review. Given that review for unreasonableness is itself more intrusive than review for manifest unreasonableness, everything that can be said about review for unreasonableness can be said *a fortiori* of review for manifest unreasonableness.

5.2.1 Proportionality and unreasonableness compared

Proponents of proportionality have occasionally maintained that it is no more intrusive or intensive a form of review than that provided by review for unreasonableness. Lord Hoffman, in an extrajudicial speech prior to the enactment of the Human Rights Act 1998, inclined towards this position, though he did not adopt it expressly:

> Whether the courts ride into battle with proportionality or rationality inscribed upon their banners, the weapons they carry to defend the citizen against the State are much the same ... Proportionality is not a new principle but another and sometimes better way of explaining how we apply our existing principles. It may or may not enable a court to give a more convincing explanation for the way it has applied established principles in the particular case.[66]

Similarly Jeffrey Jowell and Anthony Lester did 'not see proportionality as permitting intervention ... to an extent greater than' review for unreasonableness.[67] However, maintaining that proportionality is less intrusive is implausible. One of the primary reasons that proportionality came to occupy such a prominent place in English law is precisely because it is a more intrusive form of review.[68] Lord Steyn was characteristically clear in *R (Daly)* v. *Secretary of State for the Home Department*:[69]

66 'A Sense of Proportion' (1997) xxxii Irish Jurist 49, 60–1.

67 'Proportionality: Neither Novel nor Dangerous' in Jeffrey Jowell and Dawn Oliver (eds.), *New Directions in Judicial Review* (London, Stevens, 1988), pp. 51, 68. Here, my references to *Wednesbury* are to *Wednesbury* in the broader of the two senses mentioned above 1.2.3.

68 Ian Leigh, 'Taking Rights Proportionately: Judicial Review, the Human Rights Act and Strasbourg' [2002] PL 265, 272. The watershed case was *Smith and Grady* v. *United Kingdom*, above n. 41, where the ECHR held that review for unreasonableness was an insufficient remedy (and thereby a breach of Art. 13 of the Convention) where Art. 8 of the Convention had been breached by the government's policy on military service by homosexuals.

69 [2001] UKHL 26; [2001] 2 WLR 1622.

> There is a material difference between the *Wednesbury* … grounds of review and the approach of proportionality applicable in respect of review where Convention rights are at stake … Most cases would be decided in the same way whichever approach is adopted. *But the intensity of review is somewhat greater under the proportionality approach* … First, the doctrine of proportionality may require the reviewing court to assess the balance which the decision-maker has struck, not merely whether it is within the range of rational or reasonable decisions. Secondly, the proportionality test may go further than the traditional grounds of review inasmuch as it may require attention to be directed to the relative weight accorded to interests and considerations. Thirdly, even the heightened scrutiny test developed in [*Smith*][70] is not necessarily appropriate to the protection of human rights … [71]

However, the proportionality test does not necessarily equate to judicial imperialism.[72] In the sense that it permits delegated decision-makers to infringe upon fundamental rights as long as the infringements are proportionate, it can be described as doctrinal deference, albeit, as I hope to demonstrate, it is markedly less deferential than review for unreasonableness. Moreover, as Paul Craig has observed, epistemic deference may be accorded by judges in their application of the proportionality test:

> The fact that the ultimate decision as to compliance with proportionality resides with the court does not tell us how much weight will be accorded to the view of the initial decision-maker when the court is making its ultimate decision. This issue is itself one for the ordinary courts to decide. It is properly for the ordinary courts to determine how far the views of the initial decision-maker should be taken into account in this respect.[73]

Thus, as well as demonstrating that the proportionality test is less deferential to delegated decision-makers than the standards of review of unreasonableness or manifest unreasonableness, I will also note the possibility that epistemic deference can be accorded in the application of the proportionality test.

As a legal doctrine, proportionality wears many different clothes.[74] In most of its versions, however, the proportionality test is said to have four

70 *R* v. *Ministry of Defence, ex p. Smith* [1996] QB 517.

71 Above n. 69, pp. 1634–6. Emphasis added. See also Jeff King, 'Proportionality: A Halfway House' [2010] NZLR 327, 331–2.

72 The concerns of Richard Posner are worth noting. See *How Judges Think* (Cambridge, MA: Harvard University Press, 2008), pp. 354–63.

73 'Proportionality, Rationality and Review' [2010] NZLR 265, 288.

74 See e.g. Michael Fordham and Thomas de la Mare, 'Identifying the Principles of Proportionality' in Jeffrey Jowell and Jonathan Cooper (eds.), *Understanding Human Rights Principles* (Oxford, Hart, 2001), pp. 27, 28–9; Julian Rivers, 'Proportionality and

components. First, the court assesses whether the aim of the state action being reviewed is legitimate. For ease of reference, I shall refer to the first limb as the 'legitimacy limb'. Secondly, the court assesses whether the means used to achieve the aim are suitable to the achievement of the aim – the 'rational connection limb'. Thirdly, the court assesses whether the means used to achieve the aim are necessary to the achievement of the aim and whether alternative, less restrictive means exist of achieving the aim – the 'least restrictive alternative limb'. Fourthly, the court engages in a balancing test (sometimes called proportionality *stricto sensu*) to assess whether the effect of the state action is in proportion to the harm caused to the individual interest – the 'balancing limb'. The test adopted by the Supreme Court of Canada in *R* v. *Oakes*[75] contains these four limbs and I will treat it as paradigmatic for present purposes.

5.2.1.1 Important or legitimate objectives

First, 'the objective, which the measures responsible for a limit on a [fundamental] right or freedom are designed to serve, must be "of sufficient importance to warrant overriding a constitutionally protected right or freedom"'.[76]

To an extent, the requirement to establish that a delegated decision-maker attempted to attain an important or legitimate objective overlaps with review for unreasonableness. Conventionally, a delegated decision-maker who used a power for an improper purpose would be held to have committed a reviewable error: 'there is always a perspective within which a statute is intended to operate; and any clear departure from its lines or objects is just as objectionable as fraud or corruption'.[77] As a general rule, if the decision-maker is to avoid acting ultra vires – in the traditional sense of transgressing pre-defined boundaries by using the powers granted for improper purposes – the aim pursued must have been contemplated (implicitly or explicitly) by the parent legislation. Similarly, a delegated decision-maker attempting to meet the exigencies of the proportionality test will have to demonstrate that it has made an effort to give effect to the objective (or one of the objectives) contained in its parent statute. It has thus

Variable Standards of Review' (2006) 65 CLJ 174, 177–9; Walter van Gerven, 'The Effect of Proportionality on the Actions of Member States of the European Community: National Viewpoints from Continental Europe' in Evelyn Ellis (ed.), *The Principle of Proportionality in the Laws of Europe* (Oxford, Hart, 1999), pp. 37, 60.

75 [1986] 1 SCR 103. 76 *Ibid.*, p. 138. Internal citation omitted.

77 *Roncarelli* v. *Duplessis* [1959] SCR 121 at 140, per Rand J.

been suggested that, in its application to individualised decisions (as opposed to statutory or other general provisions), the legitimacy limb is otiose: 'The existence of a statutory authority that is not itself challenged makes it pointless to review the objectives of the act.'[78] In other words, the question whether the delegated decision-maker has pursued a legitimate objective is said to be subsumed by the standard inquiry into whether the delegated decision-maker pursued one of the objectives set out by its parent statute. Because, in challenges to individualised decisions, the parent statute itself is not being challenged – in which case the legitimacy of the objectives contained therein would be squarely at issue – then the legitimacy limb of the proportionality test does not fall to be considered by the reviewing court.

Nevertheless, the legitimacy limb should not be sawn off from the proportionality test in its application to individualised decisions. Its application is not pointless. Unlike with review for unreasonableness, the burden will be on the delegated decision-maker from the outset, to demonstrate that the impugned decision was made in pursuit of one of the delegated decision-maker's statutory objectives. To satisfy the legitimacy limb of the proportionality test, the delegated decision-maker will have to establish, first, that they actually chose an objective and, secondly, that the chosen objective was one envisaged by the parent statute. For example, in a case involving the compatibility of a local authority's housing decision with Art. 8 of the Convention, the onus would be on the delegated decision-maker to establish that it decided to seek the impugned order (say, an eviction order) in pursuit of one of its statutory objectives, perhaps to appropriately house vulnerable individuals falling within its jurisdiction.[79] By virtue of its imposition of a requirement that the delegated decision-maker prove that it actually had such an aim in mind and that such an aim fell within the objectives outlined by the parent statute, the legitimacy limb of the proportionality test has utility in its application to individualised decisions. Moreover, it requires more of the delegated decision-maker than does review for unreasonableness, where the onus is on the applicant to demonstrate that a power was not exercised for a proper purpose.[80]

[78] *Multani*, above n. 15, p. 324, per LeBel J.

[79] See Ian Loveland, 'The Shifting Sands of Article 8 Jurisprudence in English Housing Law' [2011] EHRLR 151, 163.

[80] The appropriateness of epistemic deference in the application of the legitimacy limb has been questioned in the context of constitutional review of statutory provisions. See Graham Mayeda, 'Between Principle and Pragmatism: The Decline of Principled Reasoning in the Jurisprudence of the McLachlin Court' in Sheila McIntyre and Sandra Rodgers (eds.), *The Supreme Court of Canada and the Achievement of*

5.2.1.2 Rational connection

Secondly, 'the measures adopted must be carefully designed to achieve the objective in question. They must not be arbitrary, unfair or based on irrational considerations. In short, they must be rationally connected to the objective.'[81]

As with the legitimacy limb, the rational connection limb overlaps with review for unreasonableness. In particular, it overlaps with review for unreasonableness and, especially, with one of the *indicia* of unreasonableness that I described: illogicality.[82] But as with the legitimacy limb, the overlap does not render the rational connection limb otiose in the context of individualised decisions. Again, the burden is on the delegated decision-maker to establish that there was a rational connection between the aim it sought to achieve and the means used to achieve it. One could say that the burden of justification that *might* be imposed on a delegated decision-maker accused of making an unreasonable decision (subject to the identification of *indicia* of unreasonableness) is already contained within the rational connection limb of the proportionality test. Therefore, more is required of the delegated decision-maker by the proportionality test than by review for unreasonableness.

That is not to say that epistemic deference will not be relevant. For example, in *Ross* v. *New Brunswick School District No. 15*,[83] where a school teacher was stripped of his teaching responsibilities because of public, constitutionally protected anti-Semitic remarks he had made while off duty, the Supreme Court of Canada held it 'sufficient' for the purposes of the proportionality test that the respondent school board had 'found it "reasonable to anticipate" that there was a causal relationship between the respondent's conduct and the harm – the poisoned educational environment'.[84] Evidently, the school board's decision tipped the balance in favour of finding a rational connection. Similarly, in *Miss Behavin'* v. *Belfast City Council*,[85] the House of Lords rejected a Convention challenge to a refusal to license a sex shop on the basis that 'the proximity of certain public buildings and shops of particular attraction to children, and of places of worship, appears to ... represent a rational ground for making and adhering to a nil determination: indeed it is *just the sort of assessment that a local authority is best able to judge*'.[86]

Social Justice: Commitment, Retrenchment or Retreat (Markham: LexisNexis Canada, 2010), p. 41.

81 Above n. 75, p. 139. 82 See above 4.3.1.1. 83 [1996] 1 SCR 825.

84 *Ibid.*, p. 881, per La Forest J. 85 Above n. 10.

86 *Ibid.*, p. 155, per Lord Neuberger. Emphasis added.

The differences between review for unreasonableness and the first two limbs of the proportionality test are primarily procedural. By placing the onus on the delegated decision-maker, the proportionality test imposes constraints tighter than those imposed by review for unreasonableness. However, there are also substantive differences between review for unreasonableness and the proportionality test, as the ensuing discussion of the necessity and balancing limbs will demonstrate.

5.2.1.3 Necessity

Thirdly, 'the means, even if rationally connected to the objective … should impair "as little as possible" the right or freedom in question'.[87] Jeff King has aptly summed up the more exacting nature of the necessity limb of the proportionality test, as compared to review for unreasonableness: 'The concept of "necessary" suggests that the *least*-restrictive option is either the only acceptable choice, or will be one of a very small number of acceptable alternatives.'[88] The decision-maker has to demonstrate that no less injurious means could have been employed to attain the desired objective. There is no equivalent in review for unreasonableness, the essence of which is to allow a delegated decision-maker a choice between alternatives, 'a margin of appreciation within the range of acceptable and rational solutions'.[89] Take again the example of a local authority's housing decision. Suppose that the delegated decision-maker's stated objective was to house a homeless family. Suppose further that other housing stock was available and could have been used to achieve that objective, perhaps with some renovations or modifications. In those circumstances, the decision would fail to satisfy the necessity limb of the proportionality test.

Much depends, admittedly, on the level of abstraction that the delegated decision-maker is permitted in framing its objectives. In my example, for instance, a local authority's aim in seeking an eviction order might be open to more than one plausible description: to give effect to the statutory requirement to move vulnerable people into appropriate housing, or to move family X into appropriate housing. It would be easier for the first version to satisfy the proportionality test than for the second: demonstrating the absence of similar housing which

[87] Above n. 75, p. 139. Internal citation omitted.

[88] 'Proportionality: A Halfway House' [2010] NZLR 327, 343–4. Emphasis original.

[89] *Dunsmuir* v. *New Brunswick* [2008] SCC 9; [2008] 1 SCR 190 at 220, per Bastarache and LeBel JJ.

would meet the needs of family X would be more difficult than demonstrating the presence of vulnerable individuals and the concomitant need for housing stock. In short, the more abstract the objective, the more likely it is that the means chosen will seem necessary to achieve the objective. Courts ought to be alive to this possibility and 'should not accept an unrealistically exacting or precise formulation of the government's objective which would effectively immunise the law from scrutiny at the minimal impairment stage'.[90]

Taken literally, however, the necessity limb would almost *never* be satisfied, for even the least creative reviewing court could conjure up alternative means, less restrictive of an individual's rights, of achieving an objective: 'A judge would be unimaginative indeed if he could not come up with something a little less "drastic" or a little less "restrictive" in almost any situation …'[91] In the local authority example, the alternative would be to build more houses, instead of evicting the tenant. It is hardly surprising that, despite its resounding statement in *Oakes*, the Supreme Court of Canada subsequently relaxed the requirements of the necessity limb:

> The tailoring process seldom admits of perfection and the courts must accord some leeway to the legislator. If the law falls *within a range of reasonable alternatives*, the courts will not find it overbroad merely because they can conceive of an alternative which might better tailor objective to infringement.[92]

But the perils of literalism should not compel courts to collapse the necessity limb into review for unreasonableness:

> To adopt a criterion of reasonable necessity is … to conflate the concept of necessity with the logically prior question whether the factors the decision-maker seeks to trade off against the right carry sufficient legitimacy as to be capable, in principle, of justifying the specific infringement.[93]

[90] *Alberta* v. *Hutterian Brethren of Wilson Colony* [2009] SCC 37; [2009] 2 SCR 567 at 597, per McLachlin CJ.

[91] *Illinois Elections Board* v. *Socialist Workers Party* (1979) 440 US 173 at 188–9, per Blackmun J, concurring.

[92] *RJR-MacDonald* v. *Canada (Attorney General)* [1995] 3 SCR 199 at 342. Emphasis added.

[93] Mark Elliott, 'Proportionality and Deference: The Importance of a Structured Approach' in Christopher Forsyth *et al.* (eds.), *Effective Judicial Review: A Cornerstone of Good Governance* (Oxford: Oxford University Press, 2010), pp. 264, 279.

Instead, epistemic deference can be employed 'to leaven the application of necessity, thereby enabling the views of the executive … to be taken into account when deciding whether the action was indeed necessary'.[94] Instead of simply assessing whether the delegated decision-maker acted reasonably, a reviewing court would examine whether the least injurious means of achieving the stated objective were employed, but with weight given to the delegated decision-maker's assessment of and choice between the available alternatives. The Supreme Court of the United States suggested as much in *Procunier* v. *Martinez*,[95] in the context of prison authorities' powers to censor inmates' mail: 'prison administrators [are not] required to show with certainty that adverse consequences would flow from the failure to censor a particular letter. Some latitude in anticipating the probable consequences of allowing certain speech in a prison environment is essential to the proper discharge of an administrator's duty.'[96] Lurking within this statement is the idea that weight should be given to the decisions of the prison authorities on such questions.

If reviewing courts are nevertheless concerned to be deferential in applying the necessity limb, they could adopt the reason and structure of unreasonableness described in Chapter 4. But it is better, from the point of view of protecting fundamental rights, to prefer epistemic deference in the application of the necessity limb to collapsing the necessity limb into review for unreasonableness. Crucially, it is only where the necessity limb is equated with review for unreasonableness that the proportionality test is rendered a less effective means of protecting fundamental rights. Where the necessity limb is applied literally, or even where its application is leavened by epistemic deference, it remains a more intrusive form of review, and therefore a more effective means of protecting fundamental rights, than review for unreasonableness.

5.2.1.4 Proportionality *stricto sensu*

Finally, 'there must be a proportionality between the *effects* of the measures which are responsible for limiting the Charter right or freedom, and the objective which has been identified as of "sufficient importance"'.[97] The utility of the balancing limb has been called into question by Peter Hogg, who has described it as 'redundant', asking

[94] Paul Craig, 'Proportionality, Rationality and Review' [2010] NZLR 265, 291.
[95] (1974) 416 US 396. [96] *Ibid*., p. 414, per Powell J.
[97] Above n. 75, p. 139. Internal citation omitted. Emphasis original.

rhetorically, '[i]f the objective of a law is sufficiently important to justify overriding a Charter right (first step), and if the law is rationally connected to the objective (second step), and if the law impairs the right no more than is necessary to accomplish the objective (third step), how could its effects then be judged to be too severe?'[98] However, the balancing limb can provide an important stopgap, especially in cases where other limbs of the proportionality test are applied – perhaps because of the according of epistemic deference – in a manner favourable to the delegated decision-maker. Moreover:

> Because the minimal impairment and proportionality of effects analyses involve different kinds of balancing, analytical clarity and transparency are well served by distinguishing between them. Where no alternative means are reasonably capable of satisfying the government's objective, the real issue is whether the impact of the rights infringement is disproportionate to the likely benefits of the impugned law. Rather than reading down the government's objective within the minimal impairment analysis, the court should acknowledge that no less drastic means are available and proceed to the final stage of [the proportionality test].[99]

Application of the balancing limb requires a reviewing court to subject a decision to greater scrutiny than does review for unreasonableness. Here, the delegated decision-maker has to demonstrate that the benefits of a decision outweigh the deleterious effects imposed on the individual against whose interests the decision was made. This sort of balancing of interests is entirely alien to review for unreasonableness. Once all relevant factors have been taken into consideration, 'it is entirely for the decision maker to attribute to the relevant considerations such weight as he thinks fit'.[100] In Canada, reviewing courts have been admonished not to 'reweigh the factors' considered by the delegated decision-maker.[101] Accordingly, as the English Court of Appeal commented in *R (Association of British Civilian Internees: Far East Region)* v. *Secretary of State for Defence*,[102] 'sometimes proportionality may require the reviewing court to assess for itself the balance that has been struck by

[98] Peter Hogg, *Constitutional Law of Canada*, 5th edn, 2 vols. (Scarborough: Carswell, 2007), II, p. 38.12.

[99] *Hutterian Brethren*, above n. 90, p. 606, per McLachlin CJ.

[100] *Tesco Stores* v. *Secretary of State for the Environment* [1995] 2 All ER 636 at 642, per Lord Keith of Kinkel.

[101] *Suresh*, above n. 28, pp. 23–4. See similarly *Canada (Citizenship and Immigration)* v. *Khosa* [2009] SCC 12; [2009] 1 SCR 339 at 378.

[102] [2003] EWCA Civ 473; [2003] QB 1397.

the decision-maker, and that may produce a different result from one that would be arrived at on an application of the *Wednesbury* test'.[103] To return once more to the local authority making a housing decision, the reviewing court would be concerned, in applying the balancing limb of the proportionality test, with whether the benefits to the local authority's housing programme would offset the effect on the evictee. Such an assessment would form no part of review for unreasonableness. That is not to say that epistemic deference is irrelevant in the application of the balancing limb. Indeed, the *Denbigh High School* case, discussed above, provides an excellent example of the appropriate according of epistemic deference at this stage of the proportionality test.[104]

5.2.2 *Proportionality or unreasonableness*

The test of proportionality, several commentators have argued, ought to be expanded to cover all judicial review of the substance of administrative action,[105] because it provides a more 'reasoned' and 'structured' form of judicial inquiry.[106] This goes much further than the suggestion I made in Chapter 4: that disproportionality should be considered an *indicium* of unreasonableness.[107] However, my analysis of how unreasonableness actually operates undercuts the argument that proportionality would represent a more reasoned and structured judicial inquiry. A focus on *indicia* of unreasonableness and the discharging of the burden of justification would itself require a more reasoned and structured judicial inquiry.

Paul Craig has argued that proportionality is a protean concept that is capable of being developed as a ground of review (though not necessarily the *only* ground of review[108]) which can be applied in a flexible manner depending on the subject matter of the decision being reviewed.[109] He accepts that proportionality should not 'bear the same meaning in

[103] *Ibid.*, p. 1413. [104] See above 5.1.4.

[105] See e.g. Paul Craig, 'Unreasonableness and Proportionality in United Kingdom Law' in Evelyn Ellis (ed.), *The Principle of Proportionality in the Laws of Europe* (Oxford, Hart, 1999), p. 85; Jeffrey Jowell and Anthony Lester, 'Proportionality: Neither Novel nor Dangerous' in Jeffrey Jowell and Dawn Oliver (eds.), *New Directions in Judicial Review* (London: Stevens, 1988), p. 51; Garreth Wong, 'Towards the Nutcracker Principle: Reconsidering the Objections to Proportionality' [2000] PL 92.

[106] Paul Craig, *Administrative Law*, 6th edn (London: Sweet and Maxwell, 2008), p. 637.

[107] See above 4.3.1.2.

[108] Craig, 'Proportionality, Rationality and Review', above n. 94, pp. 280–1.

[109] Craig, *Administrative Law*, above n. 106, pp. 637–40.

rights-based cases and non-rights-based cases'.[110] This is a sensible response to the need for a more intensive form of review of alleged infringements of fundamental rights. Drawing on the application of the proportionality test in Community law, which often falls below the level of intrusiveness of the proportionality test in fundamental rights adjudication, he has argued for variable standards of review within proportionality as a ground of review.[111] However, Craig's argument that there ought to be variable standards of review means that little of substance separates my analysis from his: 'The argument for adopting proportionality becomes little more than an argument about labels.'[112] Our views are 'united at their theoretical source'[113] for we agree that the standard of review ought to vary. How the variable standard of review should be characterised and developed is a secondary question.[114] My analysis of the potential variability of the burden of justification could apply, *mutatis mutandis*, to Craig's protean conception of proportionality.

Indeed, there may be costs to the adoption of proportionality as a general head of review. Applying a proportionality test to decisions that do not infringe fundamental rights would risk creating unnecessary confusion or even incoherence:

> One of the values of the proportionality analysis as a tool for the protection of human rights is its robustness and the fact that it imposes a hefty burden on the state to justify its decisions. However, if this discipline and this burden is not present in cases in which fundamental rights are not in issue, there is a real concern that this will infect the approach to proportionality in fundamental rights cases.[115]

Applying a robust proportionality test in constitutional review would further the goal of protecting fundamental rights and maintain the distinction between administrative review and constitutional review. A variable standard of review is appropriate in administrative review, but proportionality need not and should not be employed to that end.

110 'Proportionality, Rationality and Review', above n. 94, p. 280.

111 Paul Craig, *EU Administrative Law* (Oxford: Oxford University Press, 2006), pp. 655–715.

112 Tom Hickman, 'Problems for Proportionality' [2010] NZLR 303, 315.

113 *Toronto (City)* v. *Canadian Union of Public Employees, Local 79* [2003] SCC 63; [2003] 3 SCR 77 at 137, per LeBel J. See also Carol Harlow and Richard Rawlings, *Law and Administration*, 3rd edn (Cambridge: Cambridge University Press, 2009), p. 126.

114 See similarly King, 'Proportionality', above n. 71, p. 339; Dean Knight, 'A Murky Methodology: Standards of Review in Administrative Law' (2008) 6 NZJPIL 117, 153.

115 Hickman, 'Problems for Proportionality', above n. 112, p. 320.

5.3 Constraints imposed by statutory construction

It is also possible to employ rules of statutory construction to protect fundamental rights. In particular, the canon of constitutional avoidance that has been developed by the Supreme Court of the United States is apt to achieve this end. However, in doing so, it goes too far and, as a result, should not be employed by reviewing courts.

In *DeBartolo* v. *Florida Gulf Coast Building and Construction Trades Council*,[116] the National Labour Relations Board had concluded that hand-billing (the distribution of pamphlets) urging a customer boycott of an enterprise amounted to coercion such that it was an unfair labour practice on the part of a trade union. But the handing out of such pamphlets might well have been protected by the First Amendment to the United States Constitution. The union did not attack the substantive constitutionality of the Board's conclusion. Rather, it claimed that *Chevron* deference was inappropriate because the Board's conclusion raised serious constitutional problems. White J agreed: 'where an otherwise acceptable construction of a statute would raise serious constitutional problems, the Court will construe the statute to avoid such problems unless such construction is plainly contrary to the intent of Congress'.[117] Here, the Board's conclusion did raise serious constitutional problems because the union was engaged in 'expressive activity'.[118] White J held that the broad language in the National Labour Relations Act relating to coercion was 'open to a construction that obviates deciding whether a congressional prohibition of hand billing on the facts of this case would violate the First Amendment'.[119] Thus, the court concluded, the Board was not compelled to reach the question whether hand billing came within the terms of the statute.

The canon of constitutional avoidance developed by the Supreme Court of the United States in *DeBartolo* should not be adopted. First,

[116] (1988) 485 US 568.

[117] *Ibid.*, p. 575. Although I object to this formulation, I have no objection to the traditional use of the canon of avoidance, where a statute subject to challenge for unconstitutionality is ambiguous and a constitutional construction of the statute is available, or where a statute is ambiguous as to whether a constitutional right is infringed or not. In such cases, the canon of avoidance will apply such that the constitutional interpretation of the statute is adopted, or the statute is held not to infringe the constitutional right. See e.g. *Ashwander* v. *Tennessee Valley Authority* (1936) 297 US 288. Adrian Vermeule, 'Saving Constructions' (1997) 85 Geo LJ 1945, 1949, has described this as 'classical', as opposed to 'modern' constitutional avoidance.

[118] *DeBartolo*, above n. 116, p. 576.

[119] *Ibid.*, p. 578.

the principal rationale for the canon is comity: courts presume that the legislature legislates in accordance with constitutional constraints and wish for prudential reasons not to strike down statutes.[120] A presumption of constitutionality simply indicates that a court will not lightly strike down enacted legislation. An additional concern of the court has been to avoid offering what amount to advisory opinions of the constitutionality of indirectly impugned statutory provisions.[121] Whatever the merits of the presumption of constitutionality,[122] extending it to delegated decision-makers would be problematic. Because the allegedly unconstitutional decision is that of a delegated decision-maker, rather than that of the legislature, it is doubtful whether the same concerns about comity are relevant: respect for legislative enactments comes partly from the representative character of the legislature and the respect owed to a co-equal branch of government. It is difficult to justify saying the same of a delegated decision-maker.

Secondly, in the absence of an explicit direction to make decisions only within constitutional boundaries, it is doubtful that the legislature could be said to have any intent as to precisely how a delegated decision-maker is to fulfil its functions. Indeed, the intent imputed to the legislature by courts applying this canon of constitutional avoidance would not just be that the delegated decision-maker should render decisions only within constitutional boundaries, but that it should respect an amorphous zone – a 'judge-made constitutional "penumbra"'[123] – in which a decision might raise serious constitutional questions. A vague direction is given that serious constitutional problems should not be raised, but it is unclear what exactly a serious constitutional problem is; the boundaries are drawn by the reviewing court.[124] Such an implicit,

[120] 'This approach not only reflects the prudential concern that constitutional issues not be needlessly confronted, but also recognises that Congress, like this Court, is bound by and swears an oath to uphold the Constitution.' *DeBartolo*, above n. 116, p. 575.

[121] See e.g. *Ashwander*, above n. 117, pp. 345–8, per Brandeis J, concurring.

[122] See generally Brian Foley, *Deference and the Presumption of Constitutionality* (Dublin: Institute of Public Administration, 2008). See also Martha Jackman, 'Protecting Rights and Promoting Democracy: Judicial Review under Section 1 of the *Charter*' (1996) 34 Osgoode Hall LJ 661.

[123] Richard Posner, 'Statutory Interpretation in the Classroom and in the Courtroom' (1983) 50 U Chi LR 800, 816.

[124] See e.g. *Rust* v. *Sullivan* (1991) 500 US 173. The majority there upheld regulations against First Amendment challenge and also denied that the regulations at issue raised a serious constitutional problem, even though a dissenting opinion would have struck the regulations down on constitutional grounds!

subtle and detailed background assumption seems unrealistic. Henry Friendly's conclusion, albeit expressed in a slightly different context, seems apt: 'the idea that Congress must use strong language to show it wanted the Supreme Court even to consider the constitutional question – very likely just what Congress thinks the Justices are paid to do – seems rather fanciful'.[125]

Thirdly, as applied to delegated decision-makers, the canon of avoidance would allow consideration of a constitutional claim without the claim actually being argued. Although it is true that the canon ensures 'that certain rights and interests will not be compromised without explicit congressional instructions',[126] it amounts in practice to constitutional argument through the backdoor. A constitutional claim which is ultimately meritless, if not utterly so, can nonetheless be invoked against an otherwise perfectly legitimate decision. Indeed, for the purposes of applying the canon of avoidance the constitutional claim is generally assumed to be correct. Qualifications on fundamental rights, which may mean that an infringement is justifiable, would be ignored.[127] It would be more appropriate to require an individual faced by a decision of dubious constitutionality to challenge the substantive constitutionality of the decision.[128] As it has been developed by the Supreme Court of the United States, a canon of constitutional avoidance is inappropriate.[129]

5.4 Important interests and the standard of review

Should the alleged infringement of an important interest short of a fundamental right cause the intensity of review to be increased? Following the logic of my approach, the answer is 'no': the importance of an individual's interest is not a practical justification for curial deference. Consider the key passage of Lord Bridge of Harwich's leading speech in *Bugdaycay* v. *Secretary of State for the Home Department*,[130]

125 'Mr Justice Frankfurter and the Reading of Statutes' in *Benchmarks* (University of Chicago Press, Chicago, 1967), pp. 196, 210.
126 Cass Sunstein, 'Nondelegation Canons' (2000) 67 U Chi LR 315, 339.
127 But see *Symes* v. *Canada* [1993] 4 SCR 695 at 752.
128 See *Federal Communications Commission* v. *Fox Television Stations* (2009) 129 S Ct 1800 at 1811–12, per Scalia J.
129 For a more thoroughgoing critique, see Frederick Schauer, '*Ashwander* Revisited' [1995] Supreme Court Review 71. But see also Ernest Young, 'Constitutional Avoidance, Resistance Norms, and the Preservation of Judicial Review' (2000) 78 Tex LR 1549.
130 [1987] AC 514.

a case in which the applicant alleged that the minister's decision was unreasonable because he had failed to consider the threat to the applicant's life posed by the refusal of asylum:

> I approach the question raised by the challenge to the Secretary of State's decision on the basis … that the resolution of any issue of fact and the exercise of any discretion in relation to an application for asylum as a refugee lie exclusively within the jurisdiction of the Secretary of State subject only to the court's power of review. The limitations on the scope of that power are well known and need not be restated here. Within those limitations the court must, I think, be entitled to subject an administrative decision to the more rigorous examination, to ensure that it is in no way flawed, according to the gravity of the issue which the decision determines. The most fundamental of all human rights is the individual's right to life and when an administrative decision under challenge is said to be one which may put the applicant's life at risk, the basis of the decision must surely call for the most anxious scrutiny.[131]

Lord Bridge's reasoning does not establish a link between practical justifications for curial deference and legislative intent. Such a link could be established only if it can plausibly be inferred that the legislature delegated power because of advantages enjoyed by the delegated decision-maker relative to the legislature and the courts.[132] In *Bugdaycay*, power had not been delegated for the purpose of interfering with, or for that matter upholding, fundamental rights. It would be possible to impute an intention to the legislature that powers delegated should not be used to interfere with fundamental rights, but a proper consideration of the relevant statutory provisions would not identify a plausible link between the decision to delegate power and the presence of an important right.

Indeed, there are good reasons not to impute such an intention. First, the notion that a heightened standard of review ought to be applied to decisions which have allegedly infringed important interests emerged for particular historical reasons in England. Until the coming into force of the Human Rights Act 1998, fundamental rights were not entrenched in English law. However, the United Kingdom was a signatory to the Convention. Any individual who claimed that their fundamental rights had been infringed but was unable to gain relief from the English courts

[131] *Ibid.*, p. 531.

[132] Cf. T. R. S. Allan, 'Constitutional Dialogue and the Justification of Judicial Review' (2003) 23 OJLS 563, 570–1: 'Reference to Hansard may show all too clearly that the statute was intended to authorise executive action that would violate such rights.'

because review for unreasonableness was too narrow, could go to Strasbourg and lodge a claim with the European Court of Human Rights. A tension arose between the narrow grounds of judicial review in English law and the more expansive approach of the Strasbourg Court. One way of easing the tension was to follow the anxious scrutiny approach and increase the standard of review where necessary. But in jurisdictions where fundamental rights are entrenched, the need for an equivalent to anxious scrutiny is considerably diminished. It has faded from view in England and was only of utility to the House of Lords in the recent *Chagos Islands* litigation because, in the unusual circumstances of the case, the applicants could not rely upon the Convention.[133] Moreover, if a legal system has accorded the highest form of protection to a limited set of fundamental rights, it would seem to contradict the intent of the legislature, or the sovereign people, to allow judges to develop a new set of fundamental rights or interests that carry a higher level of protection than ordinary interests.[134]

Secondly, treating the importance of the individual interest at stake as a factor in ascertaining the appropriate degree of curial deference to accord could also be dangerous. If a fundamental right were misclassified as an important interest, an infringement would wrongly be subjected to a lower level of scrutiny. The risk of misclassification is always present where a distinction is maintained between administrative review and constitutional review, but it seems reasonable to suggest that the risk is heightened where there is a third category of right or interest.

Thirdly, it is also difficult to establish criteria for the identification of interests which are sufficiently important to attract a heightened standard of review but are nevertheless not sufficiently important to be protected at the constitutional level. What separates an important interest from an ordinary interest? What separates a fundamental interest from an important interest? Even if one were to say that the effect on the individual is the decisive factor, it would be necessary to develop some means of measuring the magnitude of the effect on the individual.

[133] *R (Bancoult)* v. *Secretary of State for Foreign and Commonwealth Affairs (No. 2)* [2008] UKHL 61; [2009] AC 453.

[134] Note too that the reluctance of the House of Lords to extend common law protections in the context of a claim of invasion of privacy in *Wainwright* v. *Home Office* [2003] UKHL 53; [2004] 2 AC 406 was partly based on the existence of remedies due to the incorporation of the Convention into domestic law. Cf. Human Rights Act 1998, s. 11; *Mahmood*, above n. 45, pp. 848–9, per Laws LJ.

Measuring magnitude is not a good means of differentiation.[135] Developing a spectrum of interests would be very difficult. It would also require judges to make difficult, and perhaps politically controversial, value judgements about which interests deserve more protection than others.[136]

5.5 Conclusion

I have argued that a standard of review of correctness should be applied in constitutional review, which should be kept separate from administrative review. Correctness is not a monolithic standard of review, however: some fundamental rights will be accorded a higher level of protection than others. Both epistemic deference and doctrinal deference may, if the judges deem it appropriate, be relevant; the question of relevance may usefully be answered, I have suggested, by reference to the practical justifications for curial deference. Accordingly, constitutional review could be placed in the correctness section of the visualisation offered at the end of Chapter 4. However, I feel that it would be unduly confusing to incorporate other subdivisions into my visualisation, particularly because the differences in the protection of fundamental rights result from the structure and interpretation of the provisions guaranteeing the fundamental rights, rather than from the delegation of power and the practical justifications for curial deference. In the final analysis, then, I do not urge that the doctrine of curial deference that I have developed should be applied to judicial review of alleged infringements of fundamental rights.

[135] See above 4.4.3.

[136] In the area of procedural fairness, courts by necessity have to develop a spectrum of interests, at the very least to allow them to differentiate between interests that attract the protections of procedural fairness and those that do not. But here, it is not necessary to develop a spectrum of interests. The Supreme Court of the United States has explicitly incorporated the importance of the interest at stake into its framework for analysis of the required level of procedural protection. See *Mathews* v. *Eldridge* (1976) 424 US 319. But its approach has been strongly criticised. See e.g. Jerry Mashaw, 'The Supreme Court's Due Process Calculus for Administrative Adjudication in *Mathews* v. *Eldridge*: Three Factors in Search of a Theory of Value' (1976) 44 U Chi LR 28, 38–9.

6

Jurisdiction, questions of law and discretion

In this chapter, I will argue that the doctrine of curial deference developed in Chapters 2 to 4 should be applied to the review of jurisdictional questions, questions of law, and exercises of discretion. Accordingly, I urge a marginalisation of concepts such as 'jurisdiction', 'questions of law' and 'discretion', in favour of a holistic approach. I focus once again on legislative intent. However, I will not argue in this chapter that it compels particular results. Rather, I will argue that attention to the extent of delegations of power and the practical justifications for curial deference casts significant doubt on reliance on concepts such as 'jurisdiction', 'questions of law' and 'discretion', and counsels instead a wide scope for a doctrine of curial deference with variable standards of review.

6.1 Jurisdiction

6.1.1 The concept of jurisdiction

'"Jurisdiction" competes with "right" as one of the most deceptive of legal pitfalls',[1] but as I use the term in this section, jurisdiction is synonymous with the authority to take a decision.[2] To say that a delegated decision-maker 'loses' or 'steps outside' its jurisdiction is simply to say that it takes a decision that it may not legitimately take and as a consequence a reviewing court can quash it, or takes a decision in such a way that a reviewing court can quash it. The real matter of interest is what precisely permits a reviewing court to intervene.

Although the doctrine of ultra vires and the orthodox uses of the concept of jurisdiction have come under sustained attack in recent

[1] *Yonkers* v. *United States* (1944) 320 US 685 at 695, per Frankfurter J.

[2] 'Power' would perhaps be a better term, but because I have already used it in a different sense I prefer 'authority' for present purposes.

decades,[3] they supply a strong justification for judicial review by anchoring it to legislative intent.[4] Thus, if a statute provides that a delegated decision-maker can do Y only if X is present, then the presence of X is a precondition to the doing of Y.[5] If a tribunal is delegated the power to make findings of discrimination in respect of the letting of self-contained dwelling units, then, that a given premises is a self-contained dwelling unit (X) is a precondition to making a finding of discrimination (Y).[6] X has been laid down in a statute by the legislature. If a delegated decision-maker does Y although X is not present, then it is defying the intention of the legislature, or in orthodox parlance, acting ultra vires: 'any grant of jurisdiction will necessarily include limits to the jurisdiction granted, and any grant of a power remains subject to conditions'.[7] Following this approach, to give effect to legislative intent a reviewing court will look closely at the decision to ensure that X is present:

> [Jurisdictional facts] were to be distinguished from facts on which findings were conclusive only by the legislature's having marked them out as condition-forming facts; that is statutory language must show that *these facts had actually to exist* before the tribunal whose powers were being defined could have conditional jurisdiction.[8]

As a result, 'the reviewing court must decide whether or not the fact exists; that is to say, the fact must exist in the opinion of the reviewing court'.[9] This is known as the collateral fact or jurisdictional question doctrine. The former term is unfortunately misleading, because the doctrine covers questions both of law and fact,[10] so I will employ the latter where possible.

[3] See generally Paul Craig, '*Ultra Vires* and the Foundations of Judicial Review' [1998] CLJ 63.

[4] Luc Tremblay, 'La Norme de retenue judiciaire et les "erreurs de droit" en droit administratif: une erreur de droit? Au delà du fondationalisme et du scepticism' (1996) 56 Revue du Barreau 141, 194–7.

[5] X need not be singular. There could be a set of such preconditions. I refer to X for ease of exposition.

[6] See *Bell* v. *Ontario Human Rights Commission* [1971] SCR 756. See also *R* v. *London Rent Tribunal, ex p. Honig* [1951] 1 KB 641; *R (A)* v. *London Borough of Croydon* [2009] UKSC 8; [2009] 1 WLR 2557.

[7] *Union des employés de service, local 298* v. *Bibeault* [1988] 2 SCR 1048 at 1086, per Beetz J.

[8] D. M. Gordon, 'Conditional or Contingent Jurisdiction of Tribunals' (1959–1963) 1 UBCLR 185, 197. Emphasis added.

[9] Peter Hogg, 'The Jurisdictional Fact Doctrine in the Supreme Court of Canada: *Bell* v. *Ontario Human Rights Commission*' (1971) 9 Osgoode Hall LJ 203, 210.

[10] *Ibid.*, p. 215.

6.1.1.1 The analytical problem

The first and primary problem with the doctrine is that, although 'categories are still analytically valid even if their borders are "fuzzy"',[11] no formula has ever been devised for distinguishing X from Y: 'No satisfactory test has ever been formulated for distinguishing findings which go to jurisdiction from findings which go to the merits.'[12] However, all statutory provisions can be cast in the basic form: if X is present, then the delegated decision-maker shall or may Y. The problem then becomes acute: 'The distinction ... was impossible to draw precisely because the two matters [X and Y] were inextricably interwoven.'[13] Because an X component may be identified in all statutory provisions, a court can invoke the doctrine to justify intervening whenever it so pleases, a risk borne out by the history of English administrative law: 'There was no predictability as to how a case would be categorised before the court pronounced on the matter. There was also no *ex post facto* rationality that could be achieved by juxtaposing a series of cases and asking why one case went one way and another was decided differently.'[14]

The analytical problem has also been recognised by the Supreme Court of Canada. The assessment of whether or not a question is jurisdictional in nature was subsumed by the pragmatic and functional analysis because of a growing disquiet on the Court about the risk that courts would exploit the difficulty of classifying questions as jurisdictional and non-jurisdictional to erode the autonomy of delegated decision-makers: 'The risk, of course, is that all a court need do to avoid the deferential standard of review ... is to classify a provision as one that goes to jurisdiction.'[15] As one commentator put it:

[11] Jonathan Adler and Nathan Sales, 'The Rest is Silence: *Chevron* Deference, Agency Jurisdiction, and Statutory Silences' [2009] U Illinois LR 1497, 1557.

[12] S. A. De Smith *et al.*, *Judicial Review of Administrative Action*, 5th edn (London: Sweet and Maxwell, 1995), p. 255. See similarly Louis Jaffe, 'Judicial Review: Constitutional and Jurisdictional Fact' (1957) 70 Harv LR 953, 959. For a more modest account of the difficulties, see David Mullan, 'The Jurisdictional Fact Doctrine in the Supreme Court of Canada: A Mitigating Plea' (1972) 10 Osgoode Hall LJ 440.

[13] Paul Craig, 'Jurisdiction, Judicial Control, and Agency Autonomy' in Ian Loveland (ed.), *A Special Relationship? American Influences on Public Law in the United Kingdom* (Oxford: Clarendon, 1995), pp. 173, 177.

[14] Paul Craig, *Administrative Law*, 6th edn (London: Sweet and Maxwell, 2008), p. 441. See similarly William Wade, 'Constitutional and Administrative Aspects of the *Anisminic* Case' (1969) 85 LQR 198, 210–11.

[15] *National Corn Growers Association* v. *Canada (Import Tribunal)* [1990] 2 SCR 1324 at 1345, per Wilson J, concurring.

> the concept of jurisdictional error in which the [court] was trading [in the mid-twentieth century] was so malleable as to be capable of justifying the conclusion within its reach of any question of law or mixed law and fact that a tribunal was called upon to decide in the exercise of its mandate.[16]

The difficulty of classification was noted by Dickson J in the *New Brunswick Liquor* case: 'The question of what is and is not jurisdictional is often very difficult to determine. The courts, in my view, should not be alert to brand as jurisdictional, and therefore subject to broader curial review, that which may be doubtfully so.'[17] Beetz J continued the attack in *Union des employés de service, local 298* v. *Bibeault*:[18]

> The concept of the preliminary or collateral question diverts the courts from the real problem of judicial review: it substitutes the question 'Is this a preliminary or collateral question to the exercise of the tribunal's power?' for the only question which should be asked, 'Did the legislator intend the question to be within the jurisdiction conferred on the tribunal?' The chief problem in a case of judicial review is determining the jurisdiction of the tribunal whose decision is impugned. The courts, including this Court, have often remarked on the difficulty of the task. I doubt whether it is possible to state a simple and precise rule for identifying a question of jurisdiction, given the fluidity of the concept of jurisdiction and the many ways in which jurisdiction is conferred on administrative tribunals.[19]

While Beetz J's opinion retained the language of jurisdiction, his embrace of the pragmatic and functional analysis largely removed the importance of the jurisdictional question doctrine.[20] The inquiry for a reviewing court would

16 David Mullan, 'The Supreme Court of Canada and Tribunals – Deference to the Administrative Process. A Recent Phenomenon or a Return to Basics?' (2001) 80 Can BR 399, 423. See also J. M. Evans, 'Developments in Administrative Law: the 1984–1985 Term' (1986) 8 Sup Ct LR 1, 27–8.

17 [1979] 2 SCR 227 at 233.

18 *Bibeault*, above n. 7. Cf. Beetz J's earlier position in *Syndicat des employés de production du Québec et de l'Acadie* v. *Canada Labour Relations Board and Canadian Broadcasting Corporation* [1984] 2 SCR 412 at 441.

19 *Bibeault*, above n. 7 at p. 1087.

20 In *Crevier* v. *Quebec (Attorney General)* [1981] 2 SCR 220, the Supreme Court of Canada held that the federal Constitution required judicial review to be available to keep delegated decision-makers within limits prescribed by legislatures. This has regularly been described as jurisdictional review. However, the term jurisdictional question came to refer to questions which, according to the pragmatic and functional analysis, are to be reviewed on a standard of review of correctness. Jurisdiction, then, became a label to describe the results of the pragmatic and functional analysis and not itself a key component in the analysis. See *Pushpanathan* v. *Canada (Citizenship and Immigration)* [1998] 1 SCR 982 at 1005. But see now *Smith* v. *Alliance Pipeline* [2011] SCC 7; [2011] 1 SCR 160.

instead focus solely on legislative intent and not on whether a particular question should be classified as jurisdictional in nature. It was said ultimately that the pragmatic and functional analysis 'must be applied even to those provisions which appear to limit a tribunal's jurisdiction'.[21]

Despite these difficulties, the concept of jurisdiction remains an attractive one. The risk of a delegated decision-maker, elected or otherwise, indulging in self-aggrandisement is ever-present, 'because a tribunal preoccupied with special problems or staffed by individuals of lesser ability is likely to develop distorted positions. In its concern for its administrative task it may strain just those limits with which the legislature was most concerned.'[22] It is an old justification for the jurisdictional question doctrine: 'It is a contradiction in terms to create a tribunal with limited jurisdiction and unlimited power to determine such limit at its own will and pleasure.'[23] The cunning rent tribunal administrator who has been delegated the power to set fair rents in respect of furnished premises might be tempted to take a relaxed view of whether premises are furnished or not in order to increase the power of the tribunal; or, tempted by notoriety and newspaper headlines, might conclude that the Albert Hall is a furnished tenancy after all. However, identifying when and where self-aggrandisement is occurring is extraordinarily difficult, because '[a]ny claim that a statute *permits* the adoption of a [decision] that it neither mandates nor proscribes is *pro tanto* an "interpretation" of the scope of the agency's authority'.[24] No firm line can be drawn between self-aggrandising decisions and non-self-aggrandising decisions. In addition, self-aggrandisement may occur where a delegated decision-maker *declines* to exercise a power that it does, or is intended to, possess: 'agency refusals to assert jurisdiction can serve agency interests and contravene [legislative] intent'.[25] Moreover, abolishing or marginalising the jurisdictional question doctrine would not necessarily result in the abolition or marginalisation of judicial review. Boundaries would still be policed by reviewing courts. The concept of jurisdiction, inasmuch as it suggests that

[21] *Canadian Union of Public Employees, Local 301* v. *Montreal (City)* [1997] 1 SCR 793 at 824 per L'Heureux-Dubé J.

[22] Jaffe, 'Constitutional and Jurisdictional Fact', above n. 12, p. 963. For an argument that self-aggrandisement by delegated decision-makers may give rise to constitutional concerns, see Timothy Armstrong, '*Chevron* Deference and Agency Self-Interest' (2003–2004) Cornell Journal of Law and Public Policy 203.

[23] *R* v. *Shoreditch Assessment Committee, ex p. Morgan* [1910] 2 KB 859 at 880, per Farwell LJ.

[24] Jerry Mashaw, Richard Merrill and Peter Shane, *Administrative Law: The American Public Law System: Cases and Materials*, 5th edn (St Paul: Thomson West, 2003), p. 818. Emphasis original.

[25] Adler and Sales, 'Silence', above n. 11, p. 1530.

delegated decision-makers do not have unlimited power, would still be operative.[26]

6.1.1.2 The grant of jurisdiction

The second, related problem arises from the concept of the grant of jurisdiction.[27] Because, within constitutional limits, the legislature can in theory delegate whatever power it wishes to, it may also delegate the power to a delegated decision-maker to determine X: 'the legislator may intend to give an administrative tribunal, expressly or by implication, the power to determine whether certain conditions of law or fact placed on the exercise of its power do exist'.[28] Even if a jurisdictional question exists, judicial intervention will not necessarily be justified, because the legislature may delegate the power of deciding the jurisdictional question to a body other than a court. In other words, instead of: if X, then Y, the formulation would be: if X (in the opinion of the delegated decision-maker), then Y. In the latter formulation, a standard of review of correctness would not be justified, although the decision would be reviewable according to the general principles of judicial review.[29] One can ascertain whether or not there is a grant of jurisdiction only by interpreting the statute.

The application of the concept of the grant of jurisdiction is well illustrated by *Tithe Redemption Commission* v. *Wynne*.[30] The legislation in question had the effect of extinguishing all tithe rent charges from a certain date and replacing them with annuities calculated as a percentage of the rent charges. The legislation also established a Tithe Redemption Commission and placed it under duties, inter alia, to determine which tithe rent charges had been extinguished by the legislation, to determine what annuities could be charged, to apportion annuities to be charged where land had two or more owners, to manage annuities and to keep a register. A question arose as to whether a particular property was in fact a rent charge at the relevant date. The Commission successfully argued that, although the question was a jurisdictional one, the legislation gave it the authority to answer it: '[the Act] indicates in clear language that the

[26] See Ch. 4.
[27] William Wade and Christopher Forsyth, *Administrative Law*, 10th edn (Oxford: Oxford University Press, 2009), pp. 216–17; *R* v. *Income Tax Special Commissioners, ex p. Cape Copper Mining Company* (1888) 21 QBD 313.
[28] *Bibeault*, above n. 7 at p. 1087, per Beetz J.
[29] See e.g. *R* v. *Secretary of State for the Home Department, ex p. Zamir* [1980] AC 930.
[30] [1943] KB 756.

Commission are intended by Parliament to decide all these matters on which the register, which they are directed to keep, depends'.[31] Similarly, in *R* v. *Secretary of State for the Home Department, ex p. Zamir*,[32] the applicant argued that a finding that an individual was an illegal entrant (for the purposes of immigration law) was a jurisdictional condition to a refusal to grant leave to enter. Lord Wilberforce held, however, 'that the whole scheme of the Act is against this argument … The nature and process of decision conferred upon immigration officers … is incompatible with any requirement for the establishment of precedent objective facts whose existence the court may verify'.[33] But the reasoning required by the concept of the grant of jurisdiction would actually undermine the jurisdictional question doctrine. In all cases, the reviewing court must examine the statute to determine whether a grant of jurisdiction was made. An exercise in statutory interpretation would have to be undertaken to determine whether the power to answer the jurisdictional question was delegated. The inquiry into jurisdiction would then become indistinguishable from an inquiry into the extent of the power delegated to the delegated decision-maker, along the lines suggested in Chapter 2.[34]

6.1.1.3 Limited review

The third problem is that there is a competitor to the jurisdictional question doctrine which holds that a grant of jurisdiction is automatically present whenever a delegated decision-maker has been delegated authority by the legislature. According to the limited review doctrine, reviewing courts should never interfere with a delegated decision-maker's decision as to the presence of X. They may quash a decision on jurisdictional grounds only if the delegated decision-maker was invalidly appointed or made an order it

[31] *Ibid.*, p. 762, per Scott LJ. [32] *Zamir*, above n. 29. [33] *Ibid.*, pp. 948–9.

[34] It has been objected that a delegated decision-maker cannot be exercising jurisdiction if it is trying to establish whether it has jurisdiction in the first place and in that sense its decision on the question cannot be conclusive because it was not a decision taken within jurisdiction. See B. C. Gould, '*Anisminic* and Jurisdictional Review' [1970] PL 358, 364–5. But that is to treat the question of 'jurisdiction' as dispositive. To the contrary, the relevant inquiry is into legislative intent: what is the extent of the power that has been granted to the delegated decision-maker, and are there practical justifications for curial deference? These are questions to be answered by a reviewing court, which will, albeit retrospectively, confirm or deny that the delegated decision-maker had the power to render a particular decision. That a reviewing court may assess the extent of the power that has been delegated by the legislature to the delegated decision-maker does not affect the extent of the power delegated.

had no power to make, such as ordering a civil sanction in a criminal case.[35] The theoretical argument underpinning limited review is that the legislature established the delegated decision-maker, the delegated decision-maker could not do Y without taking some view of X and for the court to intervene subsequently as to the existence of X would remove the delegated decision-maker's authority. A claim to be giving effect to legislative intent is again being made here: proponents of limited review suggest that there is an automatic grant of jurisdiction by virtue of the establishment of a delegated decision-maker and delegation of power to it.

Limited review is problematic in its own terms, however, because the delegated decision-maker can then make X whatever it wants X to be. The words enacted in a statute:

> would be empty vessels into which anything could be poured. The formal incantation of such words would suffice for the tribunal to remain within the scope of its authority. They could be applied to anything regardless of whether it was an Oxford College, or for that matter an oak tree or my dog.[36]

Permitting a delegated decision-maker to inscribe its decisions on a *tabula rasa* on all occasions, free from all but limited judicial oversight, would threaten to undermine if not destroy the principle that effect must be given by courts to legislative intent. Nonetheless, limited review may be lurking beneath the surface of judicial protestations that no jurisdictional question has been presented by a particular case. Unfortunately, confusion is the inevitable result because the legislature never identifies which approach ought to be followed in a particular case and because most cases do not present obviously jurisdictional questions (even without considering the problems raised by the application of the concept of the grant of jurisdiction) a reviewing court can rationalise following either approach.

This difficulty can be avoided, however, by requiring the undertaking of an inquiry in all cases into the extent of the power delegated to a delegated decision-maker. The appropriate allocation of decision-making authority as between a delegated decision-maker and a reviewing court can be determined by looking in the first instance to the extent of the delegation

35 See generally these articles by D. M. Gordon: 'The Relation of Facts to Jurisdiction' (1929) 45 LQR 459; 'Observance of Law as a Condition of Jurisdiction' (1931) 47 LQR 386 and 557; 'Conditional Jurisdiction', above n. 8; 'Jurisdictional Fact: An Answer' (1966) 82 LQR 515; 'What did the *Anisminic* Case Decide?' (1971) 34 MLR 1. See also Kent Roach, 'The Administrative Law Scholarship of D. M. Gordon' (1989) 34 McGill LJ 1.

36 Craig, *Administrative Law*, above n. 14, p. 443.

of power. Nevertheless, jurisdiction as a concept need not be jettisoned: some questions will seem obviously jurisdictional in nature.[37] As a relative, but not an absolute matter, account may be taken of a question's jurisdictional character: 'The jurisdictional aspect of the provision attracts less deference …'.[38] Moreover, the concept of jurisdiction would remain relevant, in the sense that delegated decision-makers could not exercise unlimited power; the boundaries of jurisdiction would be marked by the concept of unreasonableness. However, a court's decision to label a question as jurisdictional or non-jurisdictional should never fully answer the question of the appropriate degree of curial deference to accord. The concept of jurisdiction gives little guidance as to legislative intent. Conducting an inquiry into the extent of the power delegated would be more appropriate.

6.1.2 Jurisdiction and the practical justifications for curial deference

As I argued in Chapters 2 and 3, the second step for a court to take to attempt to give effect to legislative intent, having already considered the extent of the power delegated, is to consider the practical justifications for curial deference. A delegated decision-maker's expertise may be relevant in answering jurisdictional questions. It is likely that a delegated decision-maker will be more familiar than a reviewing court with the contours of the relevant regulatory domain and the areas in which the delegated decision-maker could usefully and appropriately exercise its powers:

> In many cases, an agency does not assert authority … solely to increase its authority; it does so because the assertion of jurisdiction furthers the policy of the act entrusted to the agency. The agency's expertise is highly relevant to this policy determination … [In respect of interpretations restricting the scope of its powers] [t]he agency's knowledge of where the resources will be most productive is extremely relevant in deciding how to allocate funding.[39]

37 See e.g. *R (A)*, above n. 6, where a duty imposed on local authorities to provide accommodation was limited to children in need within the local authority area.

38 *Alberta Union of Provincial Employees* v. *Lethbridge Community College* [2004] SCC 28; [2004] 1 SCR 727 at 741, per Iacobucci J. See also *Chieu* v. *Canada (Minister of Immigration and Citizenship)* [2002] SCC 3; [2002] 1 SCR 84 at 100–1.

39 Note, '*Chevron* Deference to Agency Interpretations that Delimit the Scope of the Agency's Jurisdiction' (1994) 61 U Chi LR 957, 981. See also Note, 'Judicial Deference to Agency Interpretations of Jurisdiction After *Mead*' (2005) 78 So Cal LR 1327.

Thus, in *Council of Canadians with Disabilities* v. *VIA Rail Canada*,[40] Abella J advised that courts should 'refrain from overlooking the expertise a tribunal may bring to the exercise of interpreting its enabling legislation and defining the scope of its statutory authority'.[41]

The decision of the Supreme Court of Canada in *ATCO Gas and Pipelines* v. *Alberta (Energy and Utilities Board)*[42] is also relevant. Bastarache J held that the respondent Board would not necessarily have more expertise than a reviewing court in determining the jurisdictional question that arose for resolution, namely whether the Board had the power to order the allocation of the proceeds of a sale of property by a public utility to the utility's customers: 'This question is undoubtedly one of law and jurisdiction. The Board would arguably have no greater expertise with regard to this issue than the courts.'[43] However, the reason for holding that deference was inappropriate was that the reviewing court was called upon 'to interpret provisions that have no technical aspect ... The interpretation of general concepts such as "public interest" and "conditions" ... is not foreign to courts and is not derived from an area where the tribunal has been held to have greater expertise than the courts.'[44] By negative implication, if reviewing the interpretation of narrow, technical concepts, a court should accord curial deference, even if the concepts were jurisdictional.

Complexity, as the Supreme Court of the United States has recognised, may also be relevant:

> even if we assume, for present purposes, that Enron is correct in its claim that the Federal Power Act gives the Federal Energy Regulatory Commission the authority to regulate the transmission component of a bundled retail sale, we nevertheless conclude that the agency had discretion to decline to assert such jurisdiction in this proceeding *in part because of the complicated nature of the jurisdictional issues*.[45]

Democratic legitimacy is relevant to an exception to the Supreme Court of Canada's usual scepticism about the jurisdictional question doctrine. *Nanaimo (City)* v. *Rascal Trucking*[46] extended the pragmatic and functional analysis to decisions taken by municipalities, but was concerned only with adjudicative decisions. Jurisdictional decisions have been held to be subject to correctness review because '[m]unicipalities do not

[40] [2007] SCC 15; [2007] 1 SCR 650. [41] *Ibid.*, p. 687.
[42] [2006] SCC 4; [2006] 1 SCR 140. [43] *Ibid.*, p. 162. [44] *Ibid.*
[45] *New York* v. *Federal Energy Regulatory Commission* (2002) 535 US 1 at 28, per Stevens J. Emphasis added.
[46] [2000] SCC 13; [2000] 1 SCR 342.

possess any greater institutional competence or expertise than the courts in delineating their jurisdiction'.[47] In *Rascal Trucking*, Major J offered three reasons not to defer to municipalities: first, they exercise plenary powers rather than perform limited adjudicative functions; secondly, they are political bodies, whose members are elected to further political aims, not on the basis of experience or proficiency in municipal or planning law; thirdly:

> council decisions are more often by-products of the local political milieu than a considered attempt to follow legal or institutional precedent. To a large extent council decisions are necessarily motivated by political considerations and not by an entirely impartial application of expertise.[48]

However, Major J's logic is questionable. Admittedly, the elected character of a municipality might raise the spectre of self-aggrandisement, but this risk is present in the case of every delegated decision-maker.[49] It could equally be said that the democratic legitimacy of local authorities may render them well placed to determine their own jurisdictional limits, in response to the needs of their constituents. Indeed, participation by interested parties in decisions about the limits of local authorities' powers (or those of any delegated decision-maker) may increase the procedural legitimacy of those decisions. In any such case the legislature has a variety of means for calling the municipality or delegated decision-maker to heel, including amending the empowering legislation. The power of amendment is also a reminder that the key factor in ascertaining the degree of curial deference that ought to be accorded to a delegated decision-maker is the statutory framework, which is created by the legislature. That municipal powers are plenary in nature urges caution, but any power will still have to be exercised within boundaries set down by reviewing courts. There is no justification for Major J's automatic assumption that local authorities' decisions on jurisdictional questions – or similar decisions of other delegated decision-makers – should be reviewed on a standard of correctness. The practical justifications for curial deference in fact suggest that a standard of review of correctness might not be appropriate, because it could well frustrate legislative intent.

[47] *United Taxi Drivers' Fellowship of Southern Alberta* v. *Calgary (City)* [2004] SCC 19; [2004] 1 SCR 485 at 492, per Bastarache J.

[48] *Rascal Trucking*, above n. 46, p. 356. [49] See above 6.1.1.1.

6.1.3 *Conclusion on jurisdiction*

A debate between two members of the Supreme Court of the United States is instructive. In *Mississippi Power and Light* v. *Mississippi, ex rel Moore,*[50] the majority of the court did not find it necessary to decide whether or not *Chevron* deference applied to the Federal Energy Regulatory Commission's determination that the applicant's participation in an ill-fated interstate electricity generation project pre-empted a state entity's attempt to punish the applicant company's stockholders. For Stevens J, the facts were 'not distinguishable' from a Supreme Court precedent.[51] However, Scalia J and Brennan J broached the question of the applicability of *Chevron* and clashed sharply. As framed by Scalia J, the question was whether the Commission had jurisdiction to determine the prudence of a particular company's participation in an electricity generation project. If the Commission, a federal body, had jurisdiction, then a state review board in Mississippi would have been prevented from determining whether the participation was prudent. A finding that participation was imprudent would have allowed a state review board to forbid the company from passing the cost of the wholesale project onto its consumers, but such a finding would have been precluded if the Commission had jurisdiction.

Scalia J in his concurring opinion, and Brennan J in his dissent, offered arguments in favour of and against the application of *Chevron* to jurisdictional questions. Brennan J rejected the applicability of *Chevron* to jurisdictional questions because, first, *Chevron's* applicability in this area would be at odds with the justification for its applicability in other areas: 'Our agency deference cases have always been limited to statutes the agency was "entrusted to administer" … Agencies do not "administer" statutes confining the scope of their jurisdiction, and such statutes are not "entrusted" to agencies.'[52] Secondly, the delegated decision-maker's expertise was not relevant, because:

> statutes confining an agency's jurisdiction do not reflect conflicts between policies that have been committed to the agency's care … but rather reflect policies in favour of limiting the agency's jurisdiction that, by definition, have not been entrusted to the agency and that may indeed conflict not only with the statutory policies the agency *has* been charged

50 (1988) 487 US 354.

51 *Ibid.*, p. 372. The previous case was *Nantahala Power and Light* v. *Thornburg* (1986) 476 US 953.

52 *Moore*, above n. 50, pp. 386–7. Internal citations omitted.

with advancing but also with the agency's institutional interests in expanding its own power.[53]

Thirdly, no presumption comparable to that made in *Chevron* of an implicit intention on the part of Congress to allow the agency 'to fill "gaps" in a statute' could be made in respect of a jurisdictional provision 'since by its nature such a statute manifests an unwillingness to give the agency the freedom to define the scope of its own power'.[54]

In response, Scalia J argued that it was both necessary and appropriate to apply *Chevron*. First, it was necessary to do so:

> because there is no discernible line between an agency's exceeding its authority and an agency's exceeding authorised application of its authority ... Virtually any administrative action can be characterised as either the one or the other, depending upon how generally one wishes to describe the 'authority'.[55]

Secondly, it was appropriate to do so:

> because it is consistent with the general rationale for deference: Congress would naturally expect that the agency would be responsible, within broad limits, for resolving ambiguities in its statutory authority or jurisdiction ... Congress would neither anticipate nor desire that every ambiguity in statutory authority would be addressed, *de novo*, by the courts.[56]

Thirdly, Scalia J denied 'that agencies can claim no special expertise in interpreting their authorising statutes if an issue can be characterised as jurisdictional'.[57]

Scalia J seems to have the better of the argument. It is perfectly plausible that a legislature would prefer the delegated decision-maker rather than a court to set the boundaries of the delegated decision-maker's jurisdiction. Decisions touching jurisdiction will for the most part, *contra* Brennan J, be just as much 'entrusted' to delegated decision-makers to 'administer' as those decisions which do not touch jurisdiction. At base, the question is one of legislative intent: 'when a reviewing court considers the scope of a decision-making power or the jurisdiction conferred by a statute, [it] *strives to determine what authority was intended to be given to the body in relation*

53 *Ibid.*, p. 387. Emphasis original.

54 *Ibid.*, p. 387. See also Thomas Merrill and Kristin Hickman, '*Chevron's* Domain' (2001) 89 Geo LJ 833, 910–11; William Eskridge and Kevin Schwartz, '*Chevron* and Agency Norm-Entrepreneurship' (2006) 115 Yale LJ 2623, 2628.

55 *Moore*, above n. 50, p. 381. 56 *Ibid.*, pp. 381–2. 57 *Ibid.*, p. 381.

to the subject-matter'.[58] If a delegation of a significant extent of power has been made by the legislature to an expert, democratically and procedurally legitimate delegated decision-maker in respect of a complex problem, it is plausible to infer that it intended the delegated decision-maker to have significant power to determine the boundaries of its jurisdiction. Equally, however, a non-expert, non-democratically and non-procedurally legitimate delegated decision-maker delegated a small extent of authority in respect of a non-complex area could well not have been intended to determine the scope of its jurisdiction. An overall analysis in terms of legislative intent is much more likely to give a satisfactory answer to a dispute about the authority of a delegated decision-maker than an attempt to distinguish jurisdictional from non-jurisdictional questions or self-aggrandising from non-self-aggrandising decisions. Jurisdiction should not be a central organising concept in judicial review.

6.2 Questions of law

6.2.1 Broad and narrow approaches

Two contrasting approaches, both of which themselves differ from the Canadian approach, have been taken to the judicial review of questions of law by the English and American courts: the narrow approach preferred by the Supreme Court of the United States and the broad approach preferred by the House of Lords. In the *Chevron* case the Supreme Court of the United States announced a rule of curial deference to some interpretations of law by delegated decision-makers.[59] In the instant case the question was the range of permissible interpretations of the term 'stationary source'.[60] Stevens J held that the term was ambiguous and went on to hold that in cases where 'the statute is silent or ambiguous with respect to the specific issue' a reviewing court must defer to the reasonable interpretation of a delegated decision-maker.[61] However, under *Chevron*, significant authority is retained by a reviewing court. Where a consideration of the statute evidences a clear legislative intent on a particular question, the reviewing court is obliged to give effect to that intent. In such cases the reasonableness of the delegated decision-maker's interpretation of law is irrelevant: there is only one permissible interpretation and it must be enforced by the reviewing court.

58 *Dunsmuir* v. *New Brunswick* [2008] SCC 9; [2008] 1 SCR 190 at 212, per Bastarache and LeBel JJ. Emphasis added.

59 *Chevron USA* v. *Natural Resources Defence Council* (1984) 467 US 837.

60 42 USC § 7502(b)(6).

61 *Chevron*, above n. 59, p. 843.

A broader approach has been preferred in England. The current default position in respect of questions of law was stated in simple terms by Lord Griffiths in *R* v. *Hull University Visitor, ex p. Page*:[62]

> In the case of bodies other than courts, in so far as they are required to apply the law they are required to apply the law correctly. If they apply the law incorrectly they have not performed their duty correctly and judicial review is available to correct their error of law so that they may make their decision upon a proper understanding of the law.[63]

Pursuant to the broad approach, a standard of review of correctness will be applied to all questions of law.[64] The Canadian approach, which applies a standard of review of unreasonableness to many interpretations of law, closely resembles my position. My advocacy of it starts with a critique of the broad and narrow approaches.

6.2.2 *Constitutional and analytical problems*

The underlying assumption of *Chevron* and *Page*[65] – that where the legislature lays down the 'general law of the land',[66] this law must be complied with by all delegated decision-makers – is deficient. It ignores the possibility that the legislature will delegate to delegated decision-makers the authority to answer questions of law and fact: 'in theory [a legislature] can give the task of determining the meaning of a term to, for example, a tribunal or inferior court'.[67] Lord Bingham of Cornhill, in *A* v. *Secretary of State for the Home Department*,[68] stated that as a general rule, 'under our constitution and subject to the sovereign power of Parliament it is the function of the courts and not of political bodies to resolve legal questions'.[69] Lord Bingham's formulation leaves open the possibility that the authority to

[62] [1993] AC 682. [63] *Ibid.*, p. 693.

[64] A modification to the narrow *Chevron* approach, which would have brought it closer to the broad English approach, was suggested by Stevens J in *Immigration and Naturalisation Service* v. *Cardoza-Fonseca* (1987) 480 US 421 at 446, to the effect that any 'pure question of statutory construction' should be resolved by the application of 'traditional tools of statutory construction'. *Chevron's* 'range of applicability would shrink substantially' under such an approach (Robert Anthony, 'Which Agency Interpretations Should Bind Citizens and the Courts' (1990) 7 Yale J on Reg 1, 21) but the approach of Stevens J has not generally been followed. See Linda Jellum, '*Chevron's* Demise: A Survey of *Chevron* from Infancy to Senescence' (2007) 59 Admin LR 725, 761–71.

[65] An assumption made quite baldly by B. C. Gould, above n. 34, pp. 365–6.

[66] *Page*, above n. 62, p. 702, per Lord Browne-Wilkinson.

[67] Craig, *Administrative Law*, above n. 14, p. 445.

[68] [2004] UKHL 56; [2005] 2 AC 68. [69] *Ibid.*, p. 102.

render interpretations of law can be delegated, but it tilts the balance in favour of the reviewing court. Although Lord Bingham cast it as a presumption, the default rule in favour of a standard of review of correctness is a strong one. While 'it remains possible, in theory, for Parliament to confer a decision-making power over questions of law on an administrative body, there is a strong presumption that it does not intend to do so'.[70] As I hope to demonstrate, adopting such a strong background presumption risks frustrating legislative intent. Moreover, the basis for such a strong default rule is not clearly stated.

6.2.2.1 The narrow approach

Even the narrow approach may frustrate legislative intent. Permitting the seeking of clarity in a statutory provision, when a reviewing court is permitted to conduct the seeking, vests strong discretion in the reviewing court. Judges might agree that a case raises a question of law. But even agreement that a question of law has been raised does not mean that the question of law has only one answer. Diligent, never mind ingenious, use of dictionaries and legislative history can conjure clarity where there appears to be none.[71] Equally, as an American appellate judge has observed, extrajudicially, 'virtually any phrase can be rendered ambiguous if a judge tries hard enough'.[72] Even when following the narrow approach to judicial review of questions of law, the 'search for meaning gives courts too much power to frustrate interpretative delegations when [the legislature] is likely to intend them and when they are likely to promote other normative values'.[73] Indeed, 'the question of clarity … is not binary; "clarity" and "ambiguity" are terms on a continuum that are meaningless without some implied threshold of certainty of meaning against which potential readings of the statute can be judged'.[74] A reviewing court is impelled to make a prima facie interpretation of the statute, which may colour its interpretative inquiry and lead it to insist upon clarity where in reality, none is present.

[70] T. R. S. Allan, 'Doctrine and Theory in Administrative Law: An Elusive Quest for the Limits of Jurisdiction' [2003] PL 429, 442.

[71] Thomas Merrill, 'Textualism and the Future of the *Chevron* Doctrine' (1994) 72 Wash U LQ 351, 372–3.

[72] Laurence Silberman, '*Chevron*: The Intersection of Law and Policy' (1990) 58 Geo Wash LJ 821, 826.

[73] Lisa Schultz Bressman, '*Chevron's* Mistake' (2009) 58 Duke LJ 549, 557.

[74] Note, '"How Clear is Clear" in *Chevron's* Step One?' (2005) 118 Harv LR 1687, 1698.

In fact, 'there might be multiple valid interpretations of a statutory provision or answers to a legal dispute'[75] and the legislature might have delegated a choice between different, valid interpretations of a statutory term to a delegated decision-maker. Such an aim could be frustrated by dogmatic judicial insistence that there is only one correct interpretation of a given statutory term.[76] Adopting the narrow approach as a default rule risks frustrating legislative intent, because the default rule may not reflect the intent of the legislature in a particular case. Moreover, if it is true that 'statutory provisions often do not yield a single, uniquely correct interpretation, but can be ambiguous or silent on a particular question, or couched in language that obviously invites the exercise of discretion',[77] then to search for a clear meaning is to attempt to grasp a mirage:

> in truth the High Court has a choice before it whether to interfere with an inferior court on a point of law. If it chooses to interfere, it can formulate its decision in the words: 'The court below had no jurisdiction to decide this point wrongly as it did'. If it does not choose to interfere, it can say: 'The court had jurisdiction to decide it wrongly, and did so'.[78]

It is perfectly possible, in theory, that a clear answer might exist; indeed, there surely are types of behaviour that are, say, clearly insulting for the purposes of the Public Order Act.[79] The difficulty is that no yardstick is available to measure the accuracy of an allegedly clear answer. Put simply, just because a court defines 'national security' as 'securing the freedom of individuals from terrorist attack' does not mean that the court is correct to do so. An *ex post* conclusion by a court does not settle the *ex ante* question of whether a clear answer exists. And for the purposes of the narrow approach, it is on the existence of a clear answer that the legitimacy of judicial

[75] *Dunsmuir*, above n. 58, p. 218, per Bastarache and LeBel JJ.

[76] Lord Cooke of Thorndon, writing extrajudicially, expressed uncharacteristic cynicism about judges insisting on 'true' interpretations of statutory provisions, '"true" being an adjective customarily used by judges to denote the interpretation which they prefer'. 'The Liberation of English Public Law' in *Turning Points of the Common Law* (London: Sweet and Maxwell, 1997), pp. 63, 69–70. As the argument in the text suggests, I agree with the sentiments expressed by Lord Cooke during his lapse into cynicism.

[77] J. M. Evans *et al*, *Administrative Law*, 3rd edn (Toronto: Edmond Montgomery, 1989), p. 414, quoted with approval by Wilson J in *National Corn Growers*, above n. 15, p. 1336. See also *National Railroad Passenger Corporation* v. *Boston and Maine Corporation* (1992) 503 US 407 at 418, per Kennedy J: 'Few phrases in a complex scheme of regulation are so clear as to be beyond the need for interpretation when applied in a real context.'

[78] *Pearlman* v. *Keepers of Harrow School* [1979] QB 56 at 70, per Lord Denning MR.

[79] *Brutus* v. *Cozens* [1973] AC 854. See Timothy Endicott, 'Questions of Law' (1998) 114 LQR 292, 316–21.

intervention depends. If the ability of a reviewing court to intervene depends on knowing *ex ante* that a clear answer exists, the sphere in which a court can legitimately intervene is greatly reduced.

An objector might at this juncture raise Ronald Dworkin's 'right-answer' thesis.[80] It is not clear that Dworkin intended that his thesis would be applicable in the administrative law context, for it is 'slanted to the concerns of private law'.[81] Indeed, Dworkin does not suggest that there is only one available answer to all legal questions. Rather, he argues that the role of the judge is to seek the best possible answer, given the characteristics of the particular legal system in question. Nonetheless, 'Dworkin's theory might appear to support the notion that every question of law has, in principle, a single correct answer which it is ultimately the preserve of the court to supply.'[82] However, even if one accepts a 'right-answer' thesis, its straightforward application to the review of delegated decision-makers is dubious:

> The courts might sensibly take the view that rather than seek to fit [a] standard into the jigsaw of legal materials in searching out the right interpretation, such matters should be regarded as discretionary to be settled by the authority to whom the power is delegated. A judge might justify this approach in terms of his wider legal and political theory; he might consider, as judges often do, that one might both subscribe generally to the right-answer thesis, and at the same time accept that, in matters of legislatively delegated powers, special considerations arise.[83]

In other words, the best possible answer, from a reviewing court's point of view, might be to defer to the delegated decision-maker. Indeed, if 'the existing legal materials, together with the background political principles, provide cogent reasons for two or more possible interpretations' and as a result 'the choice between them is … dependent upon

80 'Is There Really No Right Answer in Hard Cases?' in *A Matter of Principle* (Cambridge, MA: Harvard University Press, 1985), p. 119.

81 Margaret Allars, 'On Deference to Tribunals, with Deference to Dworkin' (1994) 20 Queen's LJ 163, 199.

82 T. R. S. Allan, 'The Rule of Law as the Foundation of Judicial Review' in Christopher Forsyth (ed.), *Judicial Review and the Constitution* (Oxford: Hart, 2000), pp. 413, 417. For an extensive development of Dworkin's theory in the context of judicial review of delegated decision-makers' interpretations of law, see Tremblay, 'Retenue judiciaire', above n. 4, pp. 173–89.

83 Denis Galligan, *Discretionary Powers: A Legal Study of Official Discretion* (Oxford: Clarendon, 1986), pp. 19–20. See also David Dyzenhaus, 'Form and Substance in the Rule of Law: A Democratic Justification for Judicial Review' in Christopher Forsyth (ed.), *Judicial Review and the Constitution* (Oxford: Hart, 2000), pp. 141, 165–7.

considerations of policy and an assessment of consequences',[84] a delegated decision-maker might be able to provide a better answer than the reviewing court.[85]

6.2.2.2 The broad approach

The critique of the narrow approach applies *a fortiori* to the broad approach because a default rule permitting a reviewing court to characterise some component of a decision as a question of law confers even more power on the reviewing court than the narrow approach, which allows the reviewing court to intervene only if a statutory provision has a clear meaning. The broad approach is also afflicted by additional problems. Not only does it rely on a difficult set of distinctions between questions of law, fact and application, but it is not clear what a question of law actually is.

Complications arise even where ostensibly neat questions of law present themselves. For example, a legal definition – 'necessary in order to meet the needs' of a person to whom s. 2 of the Chronically Sick and Disabled Persons Act 1970 applied – was apparently at issue in *R* v. *Gloucestershire County Council, ex p. Barry*.[86] However, their Lordships agreed that what appeared to be a question of law was actually quite hard to define. As Lord Clyde put it, '[t]he words "necessary" and "needs" are both relative expressions, admitting in each case a considerable range of meaning'.[87] Just how complicated the assessment of need could be emerges from a passage from Lord Nicholls of Birkenhead's speech:

> In setting the standards, or 'eligibility criteria' as they have been called, the local authority must take into account current standards of living, with all the latitude inherent in this concept. The authority must also take into account the nature and extent of the disability. The authority will further take into account the manner in which, and the extent to which, quality of life would be improved by the provision of this or that service or assistance, at this or that level: for example, by home care, once a week or more frequently. The authority should also have regard to the cost of providing this or that service, at this or that level … The relative cost will be balanced against the relative benefit and the relative need for that benefit.[88]

Some questions of law may be obvious, or appear obvious. Sometimes, 'the legal principle [will be] easily separable from the undisputed facts of the

[84] Galligan, *Discretionary Powers*, above n. 83, p. 18. [85] See further below 6.2.3.
[86] [1997] AC 584. [87] *Ibid.*, p. 610. [88] *Ibid.*, p. 605.

case'.[89] Choosing the legal instrument and subsequently construing it are questions of law. The selection and, in some cases, development of the relevant legal definitions from the relevant statute are also questions of law. In the famous *Anisminic* case,[90] the Foreign Compensation Commission chose the correct legal instrument (the Foreign Compensation (Egypt) (Determination and Registration of Claims) Order 1962), which was replete with legal definitions (e.g. who or what was a 'British national'?), but fatally misconstrued it. But as a consideration of the *Barry* example suggests, there is no reason to think that obviousness will be the norm. If obviousness is not the norm, a reviewing court can, by classifying a question as one of law, erode the power delegated by a legislature to a delegated decision-maker. The caution expressed by Abella J in *Lévis (City)* v. *Fraternité des policiers de Lévis*[91] seems appropriate: 'legal issues ought not to be declared readily extricable when they are legitimately and necessarily intertwined with the adjudicator's mandate and expertise'.[92]

It might be thought that these difficulties could be avoided by phrasing the question for review differently. For example, in *Barry*,[93] the House of Lords disposed of a narrow question: whether the resources of a local authority were relevant to the assessment of need under the statute. This means of avoidance becomes unavailing, however, when the possibility is allowed for that legal definitions can be effectively 'questions of degree'.[94] In these cases, the factors to be taken into account may have a 'quality of continuous variation'[95] or consist of 'two or more relevant factors',[96] the weight of which may vary from case to case. By phrasing the question in the manner it did in *Barry*, the House of Lords foreclosed the possibility that the proper interpretation of 'necessary in order to meet the needs' was that it was a question of degree, and whether financial resources should be taken into account or not was a matter for the delegated decision-maker. Adjusting the phrasing of the question would assume what is to be proved: that reviewing courts should answer questions of law.

Obstacles would also be present if the identification of questions of law were to be approached in a more negative fashion, by defining what questions of law are *not*. At least three categories of question can confidently be said to exist: questions of law, questions of fact and questions of

[89] *Pushpanathan*, above n. 20, p. 1018, per Bastarache J.

[90] *Anisminic* v. *Foreign Compensation Commission* [1969] 2 AC 147.

[91] [2007] SCC 14; [2007] 1 SCR 591. [92] *Ibid.*, p. 647. [93] *Barry*, above n. 86.

[94] W. A. Wilson, 'Questions of Degree' (1969) 32 MLR 361. [95] *Ibid.*, p. 365.

[96] *Ibid.*, p. 368.

application.[97] A fact is '[an] assertion that a phenomenon has happened or is or will be happening independent of or anterior to any assertion as to its legal effect'.[98] But there are also inferences of fact, which are 'conclusions drawn from primary facts, inferences deduced by a process of reasoning from them':[99] 'If the annual rate of depreciation of assets of a billion-dollar corporation is a "fact", it is nevertheless a very different kind of fact from the bigness of Cyrano's nose.'[100] There are also questions of application (sometimes described as questions of mixed law and fact) which the delegated decision-maker answers by ascertaining whether the facts as found (and the inferences from the facts) satisfy the relevant legal definition: 'Every exercise of regulatory powers, even where there is no legal dispute, involves the application of law to facts, a process which requires the exercise of reasoning powers.'[101] These questions of application lie in a grey area between law and fact.[102] One might then say that anything outside the grey area which is not a question of fact is a question of law.

A significant problem for an approach based on a distinction between questions of law, fact and application is that delegated decision-makers

[97] B. Smythe and C. T. Emery, 'Error of Law in Administrative Law' (1984) 100 LQR 612, 614–15.

[98] Louis Jaffe, 'Judicial Review: Questions of Law' (1955) 69 Harv LR 239, 241. Cf. John Dickinson, *Administrative Justice and the Supremacy of Law in the United States* (Cambridge, MA: Harvard University Press, 1927), p. 55: '"questions of law" and "questions of fact" ... are not two mutually exclusive *kinds* of question, based upon a difference of subject-matter. Matters of law grow downwards into roots of fact, and matters of fact reach upward, without a break, into matters of law. The knife of policy alone effects an artificial cleavage at the point where the court chooses to draw the line ...' Emphasis original. See also Paul Craig, 'Judicial Review, Appeal and Factual Error' [2004] PL 788.

[99] Jack Beatson, 'The Scope of Judicial Review for Error of Law' (1984) 4 OJLS 22, 39.

[100] Jaffe, 'Constitutional and Jurisdictional Fact', above n. 12, p. 979.

[101] Amnon Rubinstein, *Jurisdiction and Illegality: A Study in Public Law* (Oxford: Clarendon, 1965), p. 16. See similarly Clark Byse, 'Judicial Review of Administrative Interpretation of Statutes: An Analysis of *Chevron's* Step Two' (1988) 2 Admin LJ 255, 262.

[102] The English courts have tended to equate questions of application with questions of fact: often questions which clearly go beyond the limited ambit of assertions of fact and factual inferences are described as factual questions. See e.g. *R* v. *Hillingdon London Borough Council, ex p. Puhlhofer* [1986] AC 484 (the meaning of 'accommodation'); *RB (Algeria)* v. *Secretary of State for the Home Department* [2009] UKHL 10; [2009] 2 WLR 512 (the risk of mistreatment on *refoulement* and the reliability of assurances as to treatment). The tendency is understandable. Applying a standard of review of correctness to questions of application or fact would be inappropriate, because it would allow the reviewing court to substitute judgment on questions delegated to the decision-maker. This can be avoided by characterising questions as factual rather than legal in nature. Beatson, 'Scope', above n. 99, pp. 41–2.

rarely reason in these terms: 'It will be immediately apparent that the three "stages" of the process do not in practice occur consecutively or even separately.'[103] Nor do courts themselves reason in these terms and 'it would be strange if reviewing courts insisted on the division being rigidly maintained by administrative tribunals when it is not maintained by superior courts presided over by highly skilled lawyers'.[104]

As a classic extract from De Smith's treatise suggests, the set of distinctions is difficult to maintain:

> Perplexing problems may … arise in analysing the nature of the process by which a tribunal determines whether a factual situation falls within or without the limits of a category or standard prescribed by a statute or other legal instrument. Every finding by a tribunal postulates a process of abstraction and inference, which may be conditioned solely by the adjudicator's practical experience and knowledge of affairs, or partly or wholly by his knowledge of legal principle. He hears evidence and, by satisfying himself as to its reliability, finds what were the 'true' facts; it may then be necessary for him to draw a series of inferences from these primary findings in order to determine what were the material facts on which he has to base his decision; in order to draw certain of these inferences correctly he may need to apply his knowledge of legal rules. At what point does an inference drawn from facts become an inference of law? Is the application of a statutory norm to the material facts always to be classified as the determination of a question of law? And where in this spectrum lie questions of policy?[105]

In the midst of the likely confusion, it is the reviewing court that takes the ultimate decision on how to classify the question; its discretion may not be unbounded, but it is certainly very strong. Following the broad approach, it would be quite easy for a court to characterise a question as one of law and therefore to require judicial intervention on a standard of review of correctness. Yet, as the *Barry* example and the extract from De Smith's treatise suggest, neat questions of law rarely bound freely into judicial view. Indeed, in determining the meaning of a statutory provision, assessments of the context presented by a particular case will invariably influence the decision-maker: 'in many cases, the application of the act would have a retroactive impact on the ascertainment of the meaning of the legal rule it contains'.[106]

[103] Smythe and Emery, 'Error of Law in Administrative Law', above n. 97, p. 615.

[104] Beatson, 'Scope', above n. 99, p. 40.

[105] De Smith *et al.*, *Judicial Review*, above n. 12, p. 277.

[106] Stéphane Beaulac, *Handbook on Statutory Interpretation: General Methodology, Canadian Charter and International Law* (Markham: Lexis Nexis, 2008), pp. 14–15. See also James Corry, 'Administrative Law and the Interpretation of Statutes' (1936) 1

The malleable nature of the distinction between law and fact has prompted significant judicial scepticism in Canada: 'There is no clear line to be drawn between questions of law and questions of fact, and, in any event, many determinations involve questions of mixed law and fact.'[107] As Iacobucci J recognised in *Canada (Director of Investigation and Research)* v. *Southam*, 'the distinction between law on the one hand and mixed law and fact on the other is difficult. On occasion, what appears to be mixed law and fact turns out to be law, or *vice versa*.'[108] If the lines between law, fact and application cannot be drawn clearly and confidently, it is doubtful that the distinction between 'law' and 'fact' is an appropriate means of allocating decision-making authority between delegated decision-makers and reviewing courts. It is more likely that 'law' and 'fact' are used as labels, affixed *ex post facto* to conclusions reached on other grounds: 'distinctions between law, fact, and policy, acquire a concrete content only in relation to specific instances of administrative action, where they reflect the court's conclusions about the most appropriate division of responsibility between court and agency in all the circumstances'.[109] If this is the case, then it would presumably be preferable that the court should explain what justifies the allocation of decision-making authority: an inquiry into the extent of the power delegated would, it is submitted, be much more appropriate. Simply put, the difficulty of distinguishing questions of law from questions of fact from questions of application supports an argument against the broad approach.

In short, a decision to follow either the narrow or broad approach carries with it the risk of frustrating legislative intent, with the additional problem in the case of the broad approach that it requires concrete reliance on an abstract concept ('law') and a difficult and malleable distinction between law and fact. A holistic approach is preferable, pursuant to which 'the crucial judicial question is the scope of the authority delegated to the agency'.[110]

An inquiry into whether the legislature intended the delegated decision-maker or the reviewing court to answer a particular question, whether it is

UTLJ 286, 290–1; Peter Hogg, 'Judicial Review: How Much Do We Need?' (1974) 20 McGill LJ 157, 163. See e.g. *R* v. *Skoke-Graham* [1985] 1 SCR 106.

107 *Pushpanathan*, above n. 20, p. 1010, per Bastarache J. See also *Baker* v. *Canada (Immigration and Citizenship)* [1999] 2 SCR 817 at 853–4.

108 [1997] 1 SCR 748 at 767.

109 T. R. S. Allan, 'Constitutional Dialogue and the Justification of Judicial Review' (2003) 23 OJLS 563, 570. See also Mark Aronson, 'Unreasonableness and Error of Law' (2001) 24 UNSWLJ 315; Gamini Peiris, 'Jurisdictional Review and Judicial Policy: The Evolving Mosaic' (1987) 103 LQR 66, 94.

110 Henry Monaghan, '*Marbury* and the Administrative State' (1983) 83 Colum LR 1, 26. Internal citation omitted.

one of law, fact or an inhabitant of the grey area, will be more appropriate, with any interpretation then subject to the relevant standard of review.[111]

6.2.3 *Practical justifications*

The foregoing analysis suggests that the narrow or broad approach has to rely for support on something other than an assumption that there is a 'general law of the land' which reviewing courts ought to enforce. Perhaps practical justifications for the narrow or broad approach can be identified.

6.2.3.1 Expertise

Ivan Hare's argument that expertise justifies the broad approach begins with a reference to the separation of powers: 'It seems an obvious distribution to give to the judicial branch the decision on what the law means in order to serve the principle of separating the functions of law-making (the legislative), and law enforcement (the executive) from legal interpretation ...'[112] In addition, the High Court is the 'only part of the judicial branch which is sufficiently independent of the legislature and the executive to be able to impose any meaningful check or balance upon them'.[113] Inasmuch as it is based on the separation of powers, Hare's argument is deficient because it does not address why the three functions need to be separated and whether lawmaking and law-interpreting powers can be vested in bodies other than courts.[114] In reality, Hare's argument relies not on the separation of powers but on the expertise of the High Court: 'this is the area in which the judicial branch can claim a special expertise'.[115] The argument based on expertise was recently echoed by Rothstein J of the Supreme Court of Canada: 'appellate and

[111] It follows that the categorical approach adopted by the Supreme Court of Canada in *Smith* v. *Alliance Pipeline* [2011] SCC 7; [2011] 1 SCR 160, which relies heavily on the distinction between law and fact, ought to be rejected.

[112] 'The Separation of Powers and Judicial Review for Error of Law' in Christopher Forsyth and Ivan Hare (eds.), *The Golden Metwand and Crooked Cord: Essays on Public Law in Honour of Sir William Wade* (Oxford: Hart, 1998), pp. 113, 131.

[113] *Ibid*., p. 132.

[114] Indeed, one might ask if a tripartite division between the powers can be maintained, especially in the modern administrative state, where they are so often enmeshed. An example, perhaps extreme, is the Panel on Takeovers and Mergers, which 'combines the functions of legislator, court interpreting the Panel's legislation, consultant, and court investigating and imposing penalties in respect of alleged breaches'. *R* v. *Panel on Takeovers and Mergers, ex p. Datafin* [1987] QB 815 at 841, per Sir John Donaldson MR.

[115] Hare, 'Separation of Powers', above n. 112, p. 131.

reviewing courts have greater law-making expertise relative to trial judges and administrative decision-makers'.[116]

It may well be the case, however, that the delegated decision-maker has greater familiarity with the purposes of the statute than a reviewing court. The best answer to a question of law might come from a delegated decision-maker more familiar than a court with the particular area of law. In her concurring reasons in the *National Corn Growers* case,[117] Wilson J of the Supreme Court of Canada suggested that the forerunner to *Page*,[118] and a similar Canadian case,[119] were evidence of:

> a lack of sympathy for the proposition that if administrative tribunals are to function effectively and efficiently, then we must recognise (1) that their decisions are crafted by those with specialised knowledge of the subject-matter before them; and (2) that there is value in limiting the extent to which their decisions may be frustrated through an expansive judicial review.[120]

However, Wilson J noted that Canadian courts came to realise that they were, relative to delegated decision-makers, inexpert in many fields. Moreover – a point of critical importance for present purposes – '[c]ourts have also come to accept that they may not be as well-qualified as a given agency to provide interpretations of that agency's constitutive statute that make sense given the broad policy context within which that agency must work'.[121] Some complex questions are best resolved by expert decision-makers.

A practical risk is that by permitting courts to follow the narrow or broad approach, deleterious consequences may follow. 'Administrative law is not for sissies',[122] was Scalia J's pithy, extrajudicial means of drawing attention to the difficulties faced by reviewing courts: applying the general principles of judicial review to the output of the modern administrative state requires judges to grapple with abstract principles and with various substantive areas of law. Environmental law, employment law, planning law and immigration law, to name but several, are discrete but huge silos of rules and regulations. To fully comprehend

116 *Canada (Citizenship and Immigration)* v. *Khosa* [2009] SCC 12; [2009] 1 SCR 339 at 394.

117 *National Corn Growers*, above n. 15.

118 *Anisminic*, above n. 90.

119 *Metropolitan Life Insurance* v. *International Union of Operating Engineers, Local 796* [1970] SCR 425. See also David Mullan, 'Judicial Deference to Administrative Decision-making in the Age of the Charter' (1986) 50 Sask LR 203, 204–5.

120 *National Corn Growers*, above n. 15, p. 1335.

121 *Ibid.*, p. 1336. See similarly Evans, 'Developments', above n. 16, pp. 27–9.

122 'Judicial Deference to Administrative Interpretations of Law' [1989] Duke LJ 511.

such great volumes of law and the regulatory creatures who inhabit these silos requires concentration of almost Herculean qualities. When the informal components of, say, employment law and the accompanying dynamics of the relationships between employers and employees are added to the mix, the need for delegated decision-makers, better able than courts to comprehend the intermingling of law and custom, becomes more pressing: 'the "correct" interpretation of a term may be directed by the mandate of the [delegated decision-maker] and by the coherent body of jurisprudence it has developed'.[123] Ossification of regulation is accordingly a risk attendant upon judicial intervention in the administrative sphere: 'When a court finds that the statutory text has a specific meaning, it forecloses future changes, even if flexibility is part of why [the legislature] created the agency in the first place.'[124]

The case for curial deference will be all the stronger where the delegated decision-maker is democratically legitimate and has engaged in a procedurally legitimate delegated decision-making process.[125] In short, wide-ranging judicial review on questions of law could cause reviewing courts to frustrate legislative intent. An analysis of the extent of the power delegated and the practical justifications for curial deference seems a much more appropriate means of ascertaining legislative intent than either the narrow or broad approach to judicial review of questions of law.

6.2.3.2 Uniformity and equity

It has also been suggested that uniform interpretation is equitable. This seemed to be the suggestion of Lord Denning MR in *Pearlman* v. *Keepers of Harrow School*:[126]

> The High Court has, and should have, jurisdiction to control the proceedings of inferior courts and tribunals by way of judicial review. When they go wrong in law, the High Court should have power to put them right. Not only in the instant case to do justice to the complainant. But also so as to secure that all courts and tribunals, when faced with the same point of law, should decide it in the same way. It is intolerable that a

123 *Canada (Attorney General)* v. *Mossop* [1993] 1 SCR 554 at 599–600, per L'Heureux-Dubé J, dissenting. See generally H. Wade MacLauchlan, 'Administrative Interpretations of Law: How Much Formalism Can We Reasonably Bear?' (1986) 36 UTLJ 343, 357–9.

124 Bressman, '*Chevron's* Mistake', above n. 73, p. 566. See also Scalia, 'Deference', above n. 122, pp. 517–19; See also *National Bank of Greece (Canada)* v. *Bank of Montreal* [2001] 2 FC 288 at 293.

125 In Ch. 3, I gave examples of cases in which curial deference was accorded to interpretations of law on these bases. I will not labour the point here.

126 *Pearlman*, above n. 78.

> citizen's rights in point of law should depend on which judge tries his case, or in which court it is heard.[127]

Lord Denning MR may simply have been suggesting that fairness requires equitable treatment, which may be satisfied just as well by review in the manner outlined in Chapter 4:[128] if differential treatment is justifiable, it is acceptable. However, Rothstein J of the Supreme Court of Canada has made the equity argument in blunter terms: 'Divergent applications of legal rules undermine the integrity of the rule of law.'[129] Rothstein J cited in support of his argument one of the components of Lon Fuller's 'inner morality' of law: congruence between official action and declared rule.[130] But, in his well-known discussion of a hypothetical ordinance banning vehicles from a park, Fuller took a position which seems to conflict with that imputed to him by Rothstein J:

> the proper interpretation of the ordinance will depend on the meaning attributed to the institution 'park' by the practices and attitudes of the society in question. In some countries – in the cooler latitudes, for example – a park tends to be a place of quiet and repose, where the citizen may escape the tumult of the city. In the warmer latitudes it may be a place of music and gaiety, to which the citizen will betake himself after his need for repose has been satisfied by a siesta. Now this difference in the meaning of the institution may have an important bearing on the interpretation of the word 'vehicle'. A steam calliope may be welcomed to one kind of park, for example, as a contribution to its merriment; indeed, an ingenious police sergeant might justify a ruling that it may come in by reasoning that the calliope is not really a 'vehicle' at all, since it carries nothing but itself, being a musical instrument mounted on wheels. By the same token a hearse – with its sinister burden – would be definitely excluded. *In another clime, where parks mean something quite different, these rulings might be reversed.*[131]

It is, in any event, not clear that the cited section from *The Morality of Law* supports Rothstein J's position. Fuller's point (as relied upon by Rothstein J) is that inability to conform to the stated requirements of a

[127] *Ibid.*, p. 70.

[128] I am grateful to Amanda Perreau-Saussine for prompting this point. But for a fuller development of the approach suggested by Lord Denning MR, see Tremblay, 'Retenue judiciaire', above n. 4, pp. 202–9.

[129] *Khosa*, above n. 116, p. 394. See also *Abdoulrab* v. *Ontario (Labour Relations Board)* [2009] ONCA 491, (2009) 95 OR (3d) 641 at 653–4; Yves-Marie Morissette, 'Le Contrôle de la compétence d'attribution: thèse, antithèse et synthèse' (1986) 16 RDUS 591.

[130] *The Morality of Law*, rev. edn (New Haven: Yale University Press, 1969), pp. 81–91.

[131] *Anatomy of the Law* (New York: Praeger, 1968), p. 58. Emphasis added.

rule, due to, for example, vagueness or lack of clarity in the rule, is damaging to the 'inner morality' of law. But nothing in *The Morality of Law* suggests that legal rules cannot diverge in meaning or application, geographically or otherwise. The key point for Fuller was that the rule must be capable of being followed by the citizen in a particular context. It does not matter, then, if the rule is promulgated by the legislature, or a delegated decision-maker, as long as it is sufficiently clear to be followed. It does not matter either if a rule is applied in different ways in different areas or contexts.

Moreover, Rothstein J takes an unrealistically absolutist view of the desirability of consistent decision-making:

> The requirement of consistency in the application of the law is unquestionably a valid objective and so a persuasive argument. For litigants to receive diametrically opposite answers to the same question, depending on the identity of the members of administrative tribunals, may seem unacceptable to some and even difficult to reconcile with several objectives, including the rule of law. Yet, as the courts have held, consistency in decision-making and the rule of law cannot be absolute in nature regardless of the context. So far as judicial review is concerned, the problem of inconsistency in decision-making by administrative tribunals cannot be separated from the decision-making autonomy, expertise and effectiveness of those tribunals.[132]

Indeed, it could be said that deferential judicial review of delegated decision-makers' interpretations of law could actually serve the value of congruence, because the delegated decision-maker may well be more responsive to the context presented by a particular case. When a delegated decision-maker:

> develops a regime of rules to implement a statutory scheme, those rules have immediate nationwide application, are likely to be coherent with one another, and are able to address issues with greater clarity and precision than either [the legislature] could accomplish through legislation or the … courts could accomplish through lengthy case-by-case adjudication.[133]

This is all the more likely where the delegated decision-maker has developed 'internal mechanisms … to ensure the consistency of [its] own decisions'.[134]

132 *Domtar* v. *Quebec (Commission d'appel en matière de lesions professionelles)* [1993] 2 SCR 756 at 787–8, per L'Heureux-Dubé J.

133 William Eskridge and Lauren Baer, 'The Continuum of Deference: Supreme Court Treatment of Agency Statutory Interpretations from *Chevron* to *Hamdan*' (2008) 96 Geo LJ 1083, 1169. But see Guido Calabresi, *A Common Law for the Age of Statutes* (Cambridge, MA: Harvard University Press, 1982), pp. 44–58.

134 *Domtar*, above n. 132, p. 798, per L'Heureux-Dubé J.

It has also been suggested that the precedential value of the answer given to a particular question may, if sufficiently high, suggest a legislative intent to vest its resolution in the courts.[135] But it is not clear why the precedential value of a question would favour vesting its resolution in a court: would it not be equally plausible that the legislature intended a delegated decision-maker to resolve the question, if the delegated decision-maker could do so more effectively? Moreover, the legislature could if it wished provide a right of appeal on questions of law, which would indicate an intention to have certain questions resolved by courts:[136] the provision of a statutory appeal would be a factor to be taken into account in determining the extent of the power delegated.[137] Or it could simply vest the resolution of the question in a court.

In general, uniformity cannot support a narrow or broad approach to judicial review of questions of law. However, in cases where two delegated decision-makers come into conflict about the appropriate scope of their respective authority, uniformity may require the intervention of a reviewing court to resolve the conflict. A situation may arise where 'the need for an authoritative ruling [is] acutely felt'.[138] However, even here, legislative intent and curial deference may play a role. A decision of the Supreme Court of Canada is instructive. In *British Columbia Telephone* v. *Shaw Cable Systems*,[139] an apparent conflict had arisen between a decision of the telecommunications regulator, which required a telephone company to allow cable companies to install equipment on the telephone company's property, and a decision of a labour arbitrator, pursuant to which the telephone company was obliged under a collective agreement to permit only union employees to carry out installation work on its property.

L'Heureux-Dubé J held that if neither of the decisions should be quashed, the court would have to rely on a 'doctrine of paramountcy', a concept borrowed from constitutional law, where it mediates between provincial and federal legislation covering the same area. In administrative law, an analogous doctrine would have to be developed:

[135] See e.g. *Canada (Deputy Minister for National Revenue)* v. *Mattel Canada* [2001] SCC 36; [2001] 2 SCR 100; *Harvard College* v. *Canada (Commissioner of Patents)* [2002] SCC 76; [2002] 4 SCR 45.

[136] See *Chieu* v. *Canada (Minister of Citizenship and Immigration)* [2002] SCC 3; [2002] 1 SCR 84.

[137] See above 2.3.3.3. [138] Peiris, 'Mosaic', above n. 109, p. 93. [139] [1995] 2 SCR 739.

> where a legislature enacts two statutes whose provisions appear to be in operational conflict (i.e., where compliance with one necessitates violation of the other), the courts will attempt to interpret the statutes so as to eliminate the operational conflict. Similarly, it is my view that where the legislature creates two administrative tribunals which reach decisions that are in operational conflict, the 'presumption of legislative coherence' requires the courts to abandon policies of curial deference and attempt to reconcile the conflict.[140]

Although the rationale for introducing a 'presumption of legislative coherence' was essentially pragmatic ('it is better that this determination ... be made by the courts ... as opposed to by individuals'[141]), an analogy with the pragmatic and functional analysis underpinned it with principle. For the first step was to consider 'the legislative purpose behind the establishment of each administrative tribunal. The more important a tribunal's purpose, the more likely the government would have intended that tribunal's decision to take precedence over that of another tribunal.'[142] Secondly, the reviewing court should consider 'the extent to which an administrative tribunal's decision is central to the purpose of that tribunal';[143] the more central, the better for that tribunal in the paramountcy stakes. Thirdly, also relevant was 'the degree to which an administrative tribunal, in reaching a decision, is fulfilling a policy-making or policy implementation role';[144] again the more policy-laden the decision, the more likely that the tribunal will outrank the other. In the instant case, the telecommunications regulator's decision, 'being an expression of the broad policy-making role accorded to it by Parliament, should take precedence over the decision of the labour arbitration board to the extent of the inconsistency'.[145] Giving effect to legislative intent was a prominent theme in L'Heureux-Dubé J's reasoning and uniformity was relegated in importance. Her approach to deciding which interpretation to favour in cases of regulatory overlap seems sound.[146] Achieving uniformity does not necessarily require a reviewing court to answer the relevant question of law.

Even in cases where jurisdictional overlaps render uniformity of great importance, deference may yet be appropriate. In *Collins* v. *National Transportation and Safety Board*,[147] the Court of Appeals for the District

[140] *Ibid.*, pp. 769–70. [141] *Ibid.*, p. 771. [142] *Ibid.*, p. 771. [143] *Ibid.*, p. 771
[144] *Ibid.*, p. 771. [145] *Ibid.*, p. 779, per McLachlin J.
[146] See similarly *Martin* v. *Occupational Safety and Health Review Commission* (1991) 499 US 144 at 150–7.
[147] (2003) 351 F 3d 1246.

of Columbia Circuit was faced with divergent interpretations of the International Regulations for Preventing Collisions at Sea. The key problem was whether to prefer the interpretation of the Coast Guard, the primary delegated decision-maker, or the Board, which had an appellate jurisdiction,[148] but an underlying difficulty was that the regulations at issue were enforced by three different bodies – the Coast Guard, the Navy and the relevant state authority – depending on the identity of the mariner:

> Even if every pilot knows what is expected of him, it is likely to be helpful – in some cases perhaps vital – that he also know the obligations of other pilots. Vessels whose masters behave in accord with well-established common rules are more likely to communicate clearly with each other, and thus avoid accidents across the enforcement agencies' jurisdictions, than if a variety of rules creates a Babel. When vessels under Navy, Coast Guard and state supervision converge, five whistle blasts should mean the same thing.[149]

The court deferred to the interpretation of the Coast Guard. It did not consider it necessary to engage in a *de novo* consideration of the best interpretation of the regulations. Curial deference thus may be appropriate even where uniformity is of great importance.[150]

[148] This question was resolved following the approach of the Supreme Court of the United States in *Martin*, above n. 146.

[149] *Collins*, above n. 147, p. 1253, per Williams J.

[150] Tremblay, 'Retenue Judiciaire', above n. 4, pp. 209–13, has argued inventively that uncertainty and insecurity, which undermine the fundamental principles of individual autonomy and freedom, are caused by adoption of a doctrine of curial deference. In Tremblay's view, deference is inimical to foreseeability and predictability. However, for Tremblay's argument to be truly convincing, he would have to demonstrate either that current practices in statutory interpretation lead to a high level of foreseeability and predictability or that his preferred approach to statutory interpretation would lead to a high level of foreseeability and predictability. He does not demonstrate the former (which in any event seems unrealistic) and his preferred approach is the constructive interpretation associated with Ronald Dworkin; even Dworkin does not claim that following his approach will lead to the development of a high level of foreseeability and predictability. If such *ex ante* foreseeability and predictability does not exist, then there is no argument against decisions being vested in delegated decision-makers, rather than in courts. The exigencies of foreseeability and predictability can be satisfied just as well by delegated decision-makers. Moreover, the fact that judicial review is available ensures that a delegated decision-maker cannot, without justification, reach a decision that contradicts the text of a statute (thereby reducing foreseeability and predictability). See above 4.3.1.3.

6.2.3.3 'Major questions'

A loose quotation from Scalia J's opinion in *MCI Telecommunications Corporation* v. *A T & T*,[151] is often invoked in support of a so-called 'major questions' exception to the *Chevron* doctrine, pursuant to which a reviewing court will presume that certain questions are of such importance that the legislature could not possibly have intended to delegate their resolution:

> It is *highly unlikely* that Congress would leave the determination of whether an industry will be entirely, or even substantially, rate-regulated to agency discretion – and *even more unlikely* that it would achieve that through such a subtle device as permission to 'modify' rate-filing requirements.[152]

But the outcome in *MCI* had nothing to do with the presence of a major question per se. The case turned on the interpretation of the statutory term 'modify'[153] and the court simply rejected the suggestion that the term 'modify' could permit a fundamental change to the statutory requirement to file rates: 'Since an agency's interpretation of a statute is not entitled to deference when it goes beyond the meaning that the statute can bear … the Commission's permissive detariffing policy can be justified only if it makes a less than radical or fundamental change in the [legislation's] tariff-filing requirement.'[154] The best reading of *MCI*, then, is that the agency interpretation was clearly foreclosed by the statute, although the interpretation would also have been unreasonable under *Chevron* step two because it 'greatly understate[d] the extent to which its policy deviates from the filing requirement, and greatly undervalue[d] the importance of the filing requirement itself'.[155]

The leading case on 'major questions' is *Food and Drug Administration* v. *Brown and Williamson Tobacco Corporation*.[156] The FDA had asserted jurisdiction to regulate tobacco products on the basis that nicotine was a 'drug' and cigarettes (and smokeless tobacco) were 'drug delivery devices' and that nicotine is intended to have deleterious effects, knowledge of which could be imputed to a reasonable cigarette manufacturer.[157] O'Connor J accepted that *Chevron* was the appropriate framework within which to assess the FDA's assertion of jurisdiction, but was 'guided to a degree by common sense as to the manner in which Congress is likely to delegate a

[151] (1994) 512 US 218. [152] *Ibid.*, p. 231. Emphasis added. [153] 47 USC § 203(b)(2).
[154] *MCI*, above n. 151, p. 229. [155] *Ibid.*, p. 229.
[156] (2000) 529 US 120. See also *Carcieri* v. *Salazar* (2009) 129 S Ct 1058 at 1069, per Breyer J, concurring.
[157] 21 USC § § 321(g) and (h).

policy decision of such economic and political magnitude to an administrative agency'.[158] O'Connor J held that the structure of the legislation precluded the agency from asserting jurisdiction, because if cigarettes were to be regulated, they would have to be banned, but Congress had elsewhere 'foreclosed the removal of tobacco products from the market'.[159] The conclusion was bolstered by legislative and agency history: the FDA had repeatedly disclaimed any authority to regulate cigarettes, a backdrop against which Congress had legislated for decades. Ultimately, she concluded:

> In *extraordinary* cases ... there may be reason to hesitate before concluding that Congress has intended such an implicit delegation ... This is hardly an ordinary case ... [W]e are confident that Congress *could not have intended to delegate a decision of such economic and political significance* to an agency in so cryptic a fashion.[160]

Whether *Brown and Williamson* created a major questions exception or not, it has yet to produce any progeny.[161] Even without such limited authority for an exception, it would be foolish to create one. First, it would introduce an unclear and malleable distinction between major and minor questions of law. Secondly, a major questions exception sits uneasily with the delegation argument. A legislature might well intend to delegate a major question for resolution by a delegated decision-maker: 'The court may allow matters of great importance to rest within the agency's discretion, and if the reading of the law justifies that result they should be left to agency discretion.'[162] It may not be preferable for important questions of policy to be determined otherwise than in the legislature,[163] but most modern legislatures do delegate major questions of policy, within constitutional boundaries, and this choice ought to be respected by a judiciary mindful of its obligation to give effect to legislative intent. Thirdly, a major questions exception sits uneasily with the practical justifications for curial deference. Expertise might very well be relevant to the resolution of major questions of policy, for example, whether genetically modified foods should be permitted or not.

[158] *Brown and Williamson*, above n. 156, p. 133. [159] *Ibid.*, p. 137.
[160] *Ibid.*, pp. 159–60. Emphasis added.
[161] For a rejection of an argument based on *Brown and Williamson*, see *Massachusetts* v. *Environmental Protection Agency* (2007) 549 US 497 at 530–1.
[162] Louis Jaffe, *Judicial Control of Administrative Action* (Boston: Little Brown, 1965), p. 585.
[163] See e.g. Theodore Lowi, *The End of Liberalism: The Second Republic of the United States* (New York: Norton, 1979); David Schoenbrod, *Power Without Responsibility: How Congress Abuses the People Through Delegation* (New Haven: Yale University Press, 1993).

Complexity, similarly, might be relevant: the question of how to regulate tobacco products and how any regulation would interact with existing regulatory regimes, is a polycentric question which might call for resolution by a procedurally flexible expert body. Complexity and expertise, however, while important, are by no means dispositive. It might be particularly relevant in respect of genetically modified foods to allow public participation in the delegated decision-making process.[164] Procedural legitimacy, then, may be another reason to allow major questions to be determined by delegated decision-makers. Finally, if the delegated decision-maker is an elected office-holder, a legislature might have decided to vest a decision on a major question of policy in her rather than in a delegated decision-maker who was relatively lacking in democratic legitimacy.

6.2.3.4 Other considerations

Practical justifications, in general, counsel *against* a narrow or broad approach to judicial review of questions of law. The practical justifications even undercut the broad and narrow approaches, because delegated decision-makers might be better than reviewing courts at giving effect to the purposes of a statute: 'As far as information is concerned, specialised agencies are closer to the statute, its legislative history, and its original purposes and compromises than are generalist judges.'[165]

In addition, several commentators have identified the difficulties in defining questions of law as leaving open the possibility of ideological differences intruding into administrative law doctrine. For example, at the conclusion of his study of legal pluralism in nineteenth-century England, Harry Arthurs discussed the rise of error of law as a ground of review and commented that it leaves:

> [no] assurance that the distinctive norms of administrative law, or of other elements of our pluralistic legal system, will be respected. And since the ordinary courts are able to impose ordinary law on all disputants that come before them, they may effectively disrupt or suppress other special legal systems [because] the last word belongs to the ordinary courts.[166]

[164] Alan Irwin, 'Expertise and Experience in the Governance of Science: What is Public Participation For?' in Gary Edmond (ed.), *Expertise in Regulation and Law* (Aldershot: Ashgate, 2004), p. 32.

[165] Adrian Vermeule, *Judging under Uncertainty: An Institutional Theory of Legal Interpretation* (Cambridge, MA: Harvard University Press, 2006), pp. 209–10.

[166] *Without the Law: Administrative Justice and Legal Pluralism in Nineteenth-Century England* (Toronto: University of Toronto Press, 1985), p. 209.

In considering the possible dangers of judicial review of questions of law a cynic might also point to the avowed willingness of some judges more readily to find a clear statutory meaning.[167] The cynic's view is possibly borne out by an empirical study carried out by Cass Sunstein and Thomas Miles. Their 'simplest finding' in a study of applications of *Chevron* by the Supreme Court of the United States and the Federal Circuit Courts of Appeals was that 'the application of the *Chevron* framework is greatly affected by the judges' own convictions. Whatever *Chevron* may say, the data reveal a strong relationship between the justices' ideological predispositions and the probability that they will validate agency determinations.'[168] In other words, if the judge agreed with the delegated decision-maker, *Chevron* step two was applied; if the judge did not agree, then a clear answer was insisted upon. The empirical study suggests that ideological hostility to the aims of delegated decision-makers may be a driving force in judicial review of questions of law, which if true would provide a strong argument against following the narrow or broad approaches. At a deeper level, the finding that statutory interpretation can vary according to the interpreter's political preferences recalls the earlier suggestion that clarity cannot be measured by any yardstick and most of the time a genuinely clear answer will not exist.[169] That the answer can apparently vary according to the interpreter's political preferences indicates that the question does not have one clear answer.

6.2.4 *The scope of curial deference on questions of law*

A legislature may have intended to delegate decisions on questions of law to delegated decision-makers; at least, there is no good reason to presume that it would not have so intended. In some instances, it will not be appropriate to defer on questions of law, because the legislature may have intended to delegate the power of interpretation of the question of law at issue to a court. For example, interpretations of general statutes which cover a wide range of delegated decision-makers, such as freedom of information legislation, may properly be reviewed on a standard of review of correctness.[170] There is, perhaps, a hint of the concept of jurisdiction here. Nonetheless, jurisdictional boundaries marked out by

[167] See e.g. Scalia, 'Deference', above n. 122, p. 521.
[168] 'Do Judges Make Regulatory Policy? An Empirical Investigation of *Chevron*' (2006) 73 U Chi LR 823, 825–6. See also Richard Pierce, 'Two Problems in Administrative Law: Political Polarity on the District of Columbia Circuit and Judicial Deterrence of Rule-making' [1988] Duke LJ 300.
[169] See above 6.2.2.1. [170] See above 2.3.1.

statutes *in toto* seem more workable, and more likely to give effect to legislative intent, than a jurisdictional question doctrine marked out by particular parts of particular statutory provisions.

However, an approach, narrow or broad, that leads to a default rule which permits delegated powers to be circumscribed at the instance of a reviewing court might frustrate legislative intent:

> such an approach is based upon the presumption that the courts' particular interpretation of phrases such as 'employee', 'course of employment', 'boat' or 'resources' is necessarily to be preferred to that of the agency; *and* that substitution of judgment is the only way to exercise control over such agency interpretations. Neither of these assumptions is well founded. The courts' particular interpretation of such terms may not necessarily be better than that of the agency, *and* adequate control may be maintained [through a different standard of review].[171]

The argument for curial deference on questions of law is all the stronger where multiple interpretations of a statutory provision are reasonable and possible. This may often be the case. Most if not all statutory terms will admit of more than one definition: 'certain questions that come before administrative tribunals do not lend themselves to one specific, particular result. Instead, they may give rise to a number of possible, reasonable conclusions.'[172] However, the possibility of multiple answers is not a precondition of curial deference. While it is difficult to reject the suggestion that courts ought to defer where more than one interpretation is possible, curial deference requires more than that. What matters is whether the decision on a particular question was delegated by the legislature. If reviewing courts remain mindful of their obligation to give effect to legislative intent, the application of a standard of correctness to interpretations of law might in many cases prove to be inappropriate.

6.3 Exercises of discretion

6.3.1 The distinction between law and discretion

It is not novel to question the distinction between statutory interpretation and the exercise of delegated powers.[173] Writing for a unanimous

[171] Craig, *Administrative Law*, above n. 14, p. 448. Emphasis original.

[172] *Dunsmuir*, above n. 58, p. 220, per Bastarache and LeBel JJ.

[173] Admittedly, such questioning may simply not be relevant in the context of the United States, where the Administrative Procedure Act seems to require a distinction between judicial review of interpretations of law and exercises of discretion. See e.g. Jack

Supreme Court of Canada on the point in *Baker* v. *Canada (Immigration and Citizenship)*,[174] L'Heureux-Dubé J held that extending the pragmatic and functional analysis to the control of discretionary powers was not only appropriate, but compelled by logic. L'Heureux-Dubé J considered that the justifications for the traditional doctrines governing judicial review of exercises of discretion:

> incorporate two central ideas – that discretionary decisions, like all other administrative decisions, must be made within the bounds of the jurisdiction conferred by the statute, but that considerable deference will be given to decision-makers by courts in reviewing the exercise of that discretion and determining the scope of the decision-maker's jurisdiction.[175]

Once it is accepted that power to render interpretations of law can be delegated in the same manner as discretionary powers can be delegated, the 'two central ideas' referred to by L'Heureux-Dubé J are relevant both to interpretations of law and exercises of discretion. As a result, it is difficult to ascertain any reason to treat review of exercises of discretion and review of interpretations of law separately.

First, both discretionary powers and the power to render interpretations of law may be delegated by legislation. If so, they will be delegated and limited by means of statutory provisions:

> there is no bright line distinction between the determination of questions of law and the exercise of discretionary decision-making powers. The resolution of questions of law will involve almost invariably elements of judicial discretion, and the exercise of discretion is just as invariably constrained in some measure by legal principles. As in many other aspects of administrative law, there is a range or a spectrum characterised at one end by extremely broad, unstructured discretion, the only non-constitutional limits on which are those that might be discerned from the overall purpose of the Act. At the other end of this spectrum, there are provisions that depend upon the application of legal terms sharply defined either in the statute itself or by clear common law principle.[176]

Secondly, just as a delegated decision-maker to which a discretionary power has been delegated may exercise it in different ways, the process of interpreting and applying statutory provisions will often require a delegated decision-maker to choose between alternative, reasonable interpretations and outcomes: 'there is no easy distinction to be made

Beerman, 'End the Failed *Chevron* Experiment Now: How *Chevron* Has Failed and Why it Can and Should Be Overruled' (2010) 42 Conn LR 779, 805.

174 *Baker*, above n. 107. 175 *Ibid.*, p. 853.

176 David Mullan, *Administrative Law*, 2nd edn (Toronto: Irwin Law, 2001), p. 108.

between interpretation and the exercise of discretion; interpreting legal rules involves considerable discretion to clarify, fill in legislative gaps, and make choices among various options'.[177] As Michael Taggart put it, 'in interpreting particular words in statutes and divining the limits of broadly-conferred discretionary powers, lawyers and judges are involved in the same interpretative exercise'.[178] The House of Lords in the *South Yorkshire Transport* case suggested that the application of the vague statutory term at issue 'left a meaning broad enough to call for the *exercise of judgment* rather than an exact quantitative measurement'[179] by the delegated decision-maker, but it would hardly be jarring to replace the word 'judgment' with 'discretion'.[180]

Thirdly, the delegation argument and the argument based on practical justifications for curial deference seem equally applicable in determining the appropriate degree of curial deference to accord to an exercise of discretion or an interpretation of law. Hence the decision of the Supreme Court of Canada in *Baker* to extend the pragmatic and functional analysis from the review of interpretations of law to the review of exercises of discretion: 'the standard of review of the substantive aspects of discretionary decisions is best approached within this framework, especially given the difficulty in making rigid classifications between discretionary and non-discretionary decisions'.[181]

At the very least, it must be accepted that the distinction between law (and fact) and discretion is not a clear one: 'the concepts of discretion, law and fact each shade into the others, and clear demarcation is impossible'.[182] Thus, fourthly, a strong argument in favour of incorporating exercises of discretion into a doctrine of curial deference is that the unclear, and hence malleable, distinction between 'law' and 'discretion' should not play a major role in determining the allocation of decision-making authority between delegated decision-makers and reviewing courts. Moreover, as I will argue in the next subsection, the primary doctrinal means of maintaining a distinction between 'law' and 'discretion' – the employment of grounds of

[177] *Baker*, above n. 107, p. 854, per L'Heureux-Dubé J.

[178] Michael Taggart, 'The Tub of Public Law' in David Dyzenhaus (ed.), *The Unity of Public Law* (Oxford: Hart, 2004), pp. 455, 469.

[179] *R* v. *Monopolies and Mergers Commission, ex p. South Yorkshire Transport* [1993] 1 WLR 23 at 32, per Lord Mustill. Emphasis added.

[180] See also Lord Diplock's definition of discretion in *Secretary of State for Education* v. *Tameside Borough Council* [1977] AC 1014 at 1064 as 'a right to choose between more than one possible course of action upon which there is room for reasonable people to hold differing opinions as to which is to be preferred'.

[181] *Baker*, above n. 107, pp. 854–5. [182] Hogg, 'Jurisdictional Fact', above n. 9, p. 216.

review, rather than a doctrine of curial deference to regulate judicial review of exercises of discretion – is inappropriate.

6.3.2 *The distinction between grounds and standards of review*

The Supreme Court of Canada discussed the distinction between grounds and standards of review in *Canada (Citizenship and Immigration)* v. *Khosa.*[183] The first question for the court in the instant case was whether s. 18.1(4) of the Federal Courts Act displaced the general principles of judicial review. On the face of it, the provision is phrased in comprehensive terms:

> (4) The Federal Court may grant relief [on an application for judicial review] if it is satisfied that the federal board, commission or other tribunal
> (a) acted without jurisdiction, acted beyond its jurisdiction or refused to exercise its jurisdiction;
> (b) failed to observe a principle of natural justice, procedural fairness or other procedure that it was required by law to observe;
> (c) erred in law in making a decision or an order, whether or not the error appears on the face of the record;
> (d) based its decision or order on an erroneous finding of fact that it made in a perverse or capricious manner or without regard for the material before it;
> (e) acted, or failed to act, by reason of fraud or perjured evidence; or
> (f) acted in any other way that was contrary to law.

The court was not faced with a full conflict between the pragmatic and functional analysis and s. 18.1(4). Jurisdictional questions and questions of procedural fairness, the court had previously held, are reviewable on a standard of correctness.[184] Because to this extent no conflict arises between the pragmatic and functional analysis and s. 18.1(4), a standard of review of correctness could be applied to jurisdictional and procedural fairness questions.

However, there was an apparent conflict between s. 18.1(4)(c) and (d) and the pragmatic and functional analysis. Section 18.1(4)(c) appears to prescribe a standard of review of correctness for the review of questions of law but the court had held that, where unreasonableness is the appropriate standard of review, reasonable interpretations of law must be upheld by a

[183] *Khosa*, above n. 116.

[184] *Dunsmuir*, above n. 58, pp. 222 (jurisdictional questions) and 251 (procedural fairness).

reviewing court.[185] Also, s. 18.1(4)(d) appears to take a more restrictive line than did the pragmatic and functional analysis: errors of fact can apparently only be corrected where the manner of making the decision was 'perverse or capricious' or the decision was made 'without regard for the material' before the delegated decision-maker, a pair of standards which prima facie seem higher than the generally-applicable standard of review of unreasonableness.

To address the apparent conflicts, Binnie J invoked a distinction between 'grounds' and the 'standard' of judicial review.[186] A *ground* of review is an error on the part of a delegated decision-maker which permits judicial intervention: judicial intervention may be provided for by a legislative provision or by the general principles of judicial review. On this reading, s. 18.1(4) provides a number of grounds for judicial intervention: jurisdictional errors, breaches of procedural fairness, errors of law, errors of fact and fraud. However, except in the case of s. 18.1(4)(d), none of the grounds of review specifies the *standard* of review.[187] Would a decision containing one of the specified grounds have to be 'patently unreasonable', 'unreasonable', 'perverse or capricious' or simply 'wrong' before the court could intervene? On these matters the statute is almost entirely silent. In Binnie J's view, for a conflict between the statute and the pragmatic and functional analysis to have arisen, both a ground and standard of review would have to be specified. Here, only s. 18.1(4)(d) specified a standard of review and, Binnie J held, was 'quite consistent with' precedent.[188] In respect of s. 18.1(4)(c), no standard was specified and thus no conflict arose: 'if the interpretation is by an expert adjudicator interpreting his or her home statute or a closely related statute',[189] an answer to a question of law would have to be unreasonable before a reviewing court could intervene.

Neither the facts nor the reasoning of *Khosa* are of particular relevance but the distinction between grounds and standards of review is a useful one. Such a distinction is unknown to the English law of judicial review. In England, control of discretionary powers is exercised by reference to the various grounds of judicial review. A decision may be quashed for: absence of a condition precedent;[190] impermissible delegation of power;[191] error of

[185] *Ibid.*, pp. 220–2. [186] *Khosa*, above n. 116, p. 374. [187] *Ibid.*, pp. 370–5.
[188] *Ibid.*, p. 372. [189] *Ibid.*, p. 371.
[190] *R* v. *Secretary of State for the Home Department, ex p. Khawaja* [1984] AC 74.
[191] *Lavender* v. *Minister for Housing and Local Government* [1970] 1 WLR 1231.

law;[192] material error of fact;[193] failure to consider all relevant factors, or taking into account irrelevant factors;[194] using a statutory power for an improper purpose;[195] fettering the exercise of a discretionary power;[196] bad faith;[197] basing a decision on insufficient evidence;[198] breaching one of the two rules of natural justice;[199] failing to fulfil a legitimate expectation;[200] unreasonableness;[201] or giving insufficient reasons for a decision.[202]

None of these grounds of review permits a reviewing court to substitute its decision for that of the delegated decision-maker. In that sense, they can perhaps be described as constituting an example of doctrinal deference in their own right. However, these grounds of review are reviewable on a standard of review of correctness. It is for the court to decide, in the final analysis, what are the relevant considerations, the proper purposes of a statute are and so on. As Lord Hoffman put it in the *Tesco Stores* case, the question of what factors are relevant is 'a question of law':[203]

> It is for the courts, if the matter is brought before them, to decide what is a relevant consideration. If the decision-maker wrongly takes the view that some consideration is not relevant, and therefore has no regard to it, his decision cannot stand and he must be required to think again.[204]

That a standard of review of correctness is to be applied does not necessarily mean that reviewing courts will use the grounds of review in an interventionist fashion. Epistemic deference is capable of being applied,[205] and is in practice: 'If you look at what judges do, as well as at what they say, there is a good deal of deference. As the broad principles of administrative law are applied to particular parts of the variegated administrative landscape,

192 *Page* above n. 62. I accept that some commentators have claimed that error of law is *the* organising principle of judicial review, but along with the other grounds of review, it provides a reason for striking down an exercise of discretion.
193 *E* v. *Secretary of State for the Home Department* [2004] EWCA Civ 49; [2004] QB 1044.
194 *Tesco Stores* v. *Secretary of State for the Environment* [1995] 2 All ER 636.
195 *R* v. *Foreign Secretary, ex p. World Development Movement* [1995] 1 WLR 386.
196 *British Oxygen* v. *Minister of Technology* [1971] AC 610.
197 *Smith* v. *East Elloe Rural District Council* [1956] AC 736 at 770.
198 *R* v. *Bedwellty Justices, ex p. Williams* [1997] AC 225.
199 *R* v. *Bow Street Stipendiary Magistrate, ex p. Pinochet Ugarte (No. 2)* [2000] 1 AC 119; *McInnes* v. *Onslow-Fane* [1978] 1 WLR 1520.
200 *R (Bancoult)* v. *Secretary of State for Foreign and Commonwealth Affairs (No. 2)* [2008] UKHL 61; [2009] AC 453.
201 *Associated Provincial Picture Houses* v. *Wednesbury Corporation* [1948] 1 KB 223.
202 *R* v. *Secretary of State for the Home Department, ex p. Fayed* [1998] 1 WLR 763.
203 *Tesco Stores*, above n. 194, p. 657.
204 *Ibid.*, p. 642, per Lord Keith of Kinkel.
205 See above 4.1.

accommodations of various sorts are made. *Ad hoc* deference in this process is common.'[206] However, as Stratas JA recently observed, using grounds of review raises the spectre of courts interfering 'much more readily with tribunal decisions'; they can 'fasten onto a certain type of error, such as a failure to take into account a consideration that the reviewing court itself deems relevant, and then use that error to quash a tribunal decision'.[207] Grounds of review are tools that can be used to chip away at the autonomy of delegated decision-makers: 'Judicial judgment of what constitute relevant and irrelevant factors allows for a wide degree of interference in the merits of tribunal decisions.'[208] Briefly put, the delegated decision-maker, rather than the reviewing court, may be in the best position to assess what the relevant factors are, the extent to which a rule is required to further statutory objectives, the extent to which delegation will be appropriate and so on due to its expertise and democratic legitimacy, the complexity of the decision and the procedural legitimacy of its delegated decision-making process. Legislative intent may thus be frustrated in the sense that grounds of review do not give adequate effect to the relevant statutory provisions.

Moreover, the grounds of review which have been developed by the courts bear little or no resemblance to the relevant statutory provisions. Lord Phillips, albeit in a dissenting opinion, put the point rather well in *Lumba* v. *Secretary of State for the Home Department*,[209] a case in which, inter alia, it was held to be unlawful for the respondent not to apply its published policy to the applicant: 'It would be *totally unrealistic* to postulate that when Parliament passes an Act conferring a discretionary power it does so with the intention that if the decision-maker publishes a policy in relation to the exercise of that power he will abide by that policy unless he has good reason not to do so.'[210] If reviewing courts are serious about their obligation to give effect to legislative intent, reliance on

[206] Michael Taggart, 'Lord Cooke and the Scope of Review Doctrine in Administrative Law' in Paul Rishworth (ed.), *The Struggle for Simplicity in the Law: Essays for Lord Cooke of Thorndon* (Wellington: Butterworths, 1997), pp. 189, 202–3. Internal citations omitted. See similarly Peter Hogg, 'The Supreme Court of Canada and Administrative Law: 1949–1971' (1973) 11 Osgoode Hall LJ 187, 221.

[207] *Kane* v. *Canada (Attorney General)* [2011] FCA 19, 328 DLR (4th) 193 at 223.

[208] David Mullan, 'The Jurisdictional Fact Doctrine in the Supreme Court of Canada: A Mitigating Plea' (1972) 10 Osgoode Hall LJ 440, 446. See similarly Grant Huscroft, 'Judicial Review from *CUPE* to *CUPE*: Less is Not Always More' in Grant Huscroft and Michael Taggart (eds.), *Inside and Outside Canadian Administrative Law: Essays in Honour of David Mullan* (Toronto: University of Toronto Press, 2006), pp. 296, 307.

[209] [2011] UKSC 12. [210] *Ibid.*, [304]. Emphasis added.

grounds of review rather than analysis of the relevant statutory provisions is a poor way to go about fulfilling it.

Rather than having an unruly group of grounds of review that run into one another, the judicial focus should be on overall compliance with the terms of the statute, rather than a narrow inquiry into, say, whether relevant factors were considered or a power was used for an improper purpose. Grounds of review may still be useful. Whether, say, a discretion was fettered, or irrelevant factors taken into account may function as *indicia* of unreasonableness in a particular case: 'The nominate grounds, language of jurisdiction, and ossified interpretations of statutory formulae, *while still useful as familiar landmarks*, no longer dictate the journey.'[211] For example, in *Kane* v. *Canada (Attorney General)*,[212] Evans JA considered it to be 'prima facie unreasonable' for a decision-maker 'to base an exercise of discretion on incorrect fact'.[213] In other words, a factual error was an *indicium* of unreasonableness, and would permit a finding of unreasonableness, subject to the possibility of the delegated decision-maker adducing cogent reasons or reasoning or sufficient evidence to justify its decision.

6.3.3 *Democratically-legitimate delegated decision-makers*

Once the distinction between grounds and standards of review is appreciated, the use of a standard of review of correctness with the traditional grounds of review seems inapt. One might nonetheless protest that the decisions of elected officials or bodies should be treated with a high degree of curial deference, and that a reduced number of grounds of review should be available. However, there is no good reason to exclude decisions of high-ranking elected officials from the scope of a doctrine of curial deference.

The leading decision in Canada is *Baker* v. *Canada (Immigration and Citizenship)*,[214] where a decision taken by the minister not to grant an exemption was reviewed according to the pragmatic and functional analysis. The popular mandate of the minister, albeit acting through delegates,[215] did not prevent the pragmatic and functional analysis from being applied. L'Heureux-Dubé J treated the minister's greater knowledge about when to grant exemptions to applicants as relevant to the expertise factor in

211 *Dr Q* v. *College of Physicians and Surgeons of British Columbia* [2003] SCC 19; [2003] 1 SCR 226 at 237, per McLachlin CJ. Emphasis added.

212 *Kane*, above n. 207. 213 *Ibid.*, p. 198. 214 *Baker*, above n. 107.

215 Though of course, in classic theory, still constitutionally accountable for their actions. See *Carltona* v. *Commissioners of Works* [1943] 2 All ER 560.

determining the appropriate standard of review, which was unreasonableness, not patent unreasonableness. Perhaps mindful of the political sensitivity of review of such decisions, Binnie J suggested in a subsequent case that the 'highest standard of deference' was presumptively appropriate when reviewing exercises of discretion by high-level executive officers. In *Mount Sinai Hospital Centre* v. *Quebec (Minister of Health and Social Services),*[216] the minister's remit to regulate in the public interest favoured:

> a high degree of deference, as does the expertise of the minister and his advisors, not to mention the position of the minister in the upper echelon of decision makers under statutory and prerogative powers. The exercise of the power turns on the minister's appreciation of the public interest, which is a function of public policy in its fullest sense.[217]

As Binnie J's formulation suggests, the democratic legitimacy of the minister will often be a reason for a delegation of power and a practical justification for curial deference.

However, extending the pragmatic and functional analysis to review of exercises of discretion by elected representatives has not been uncontroversial in Canada. The impugned decision in *Chamberlain* v. *Surrey School District No. 36*[218] was the refusal by the respondent to approve the use for pedagogical purposes of books depicting same-sex parented families. Although constituted by statute, the delegated decision-maker in question was an entirely elected body. In his concurring reasons, LeBel J advocated a more limited form of judicial review of the respondent's decisions than that envisaged in the pragmatic and functional analysis:

> Courts must respect the responsibility of such bodies to serve those who elected them, and will, as a rule, interpret their statutory powers generously … The decisions or actions of an administrative body of this kind will be invalidated *if they are plainly contrary to the express or implied limitations on its powers*. The mechanical application, in this context, of a test which was developed with a quite different kind of administrative body in mind is not only unnecessary, but may also lead both to practical difficulties and to uncertainties about the proper basis of judicial review.[219]

LeBel J argued that the pragmatic and functional analysis would simply be inappropriate in the context of reviewing the exercise of discretion by an elected school board:

[216] [2001] SCC 41; [2001] 2 SCR 281.
[217] *Ibid.*, p. 316.
[218] [2002] SCC 86; [2002] 4 SCR 710.
[219] *Ibid.*, p. 822. Emphasis added.

> The full set of factors included in the standard-of-review formula does not translate well into this context. Consider, for example, the presence or absence of a privative clause. One would not expect to find a privative clause in connection with the Board's decisions, and the absence of one in the statute in no way signals that the legislature expected intervention by the courts in the Board's day-to-day business to be possible. Expertise is another factor which is more apposite in the adjudicative context than it is here. Trustees are authorised to make decisions not because they have any special expertise, but because they represent the community. Their level of expertise does not indicate anything about the extent of their discretion.[220]

In the context of the pragmatic and functional analysis, LeBel J's criticisms are valid. However, they are met by my doctrine of curial deference. Taking LeBel J's criticisms in turn, the elected character of the delegated decision-maker goes to democratic legitimacy, one of the practical justifications for the delegation of decision-making power and for a doctrine of curial deference. Although a privative clause – or right of appeal – may rarely be present in such circumstances, the delegated decision-maker will nonetheless be exercising statutory powers and the extent of the powers delegated can be ascertained by reference to the relevant statutory provisions. *Pace* LeBel J, the delegated decision-maker's expertise may be relevant here: if the delegated decision-maker's powers are broad enough to permit it to consider the social mores of the locality, its greater knowledge of those mores justifies a measure of deference, as McLachlin CJ suggested: 'As elected representatives, it is [the Board members'] job to bring community views into the educational decision-making process. The Board is better placed to understand community concerns than the court.'[221] Alternatively if social mores are not relevant to the question at hand or if the relevant social mores are universal or national and not specific to the locality, then the delegated decision-maker might have no greater expertise than the reviewing court.

The importance here of democratic legitimacy should also be clear. Although disparaging the possibility of identifying relevant expertise for the purposes of the pragmatic and functional analysis, LeBel J went on to argue that the respondent would have been entitled to a high degree of curial deference had it been acting within its statutory powers:

> What kind of educational materials are best suited to realising the province's pedagogical objectives and to reflecting the preferences of the particular community served by the Board is a question on which courts are singularly

[220] *Ibid.*, p. 823. [221] *Ibid.*, p. 825.

> ill-equipped to impose their views. Review of this decision on a reasonableness standard, in my respectful view, fails to give due recognition to the Board's role as a local government body accountable to the electorate. [222]

LeBel J did not mention complexity, but how difficult the question of resolving the balance between – to name but a few considerations – free expression, pedagogical interests and the wishes of local parents may be relevant to determining the appropriate degree of curial deference. Similarly, this would be an area in which the extent of consultation and deliberation engaged in by the delegated decision-maker would be highly relevant to determining the appropriate degree of curial deference to accord. In short, there is no reason not to apply a doctrine of curial deference with variable standards of review to the decisions of elected officials or elected bodies.

6.4 Conclusion

The strongest attraction of a doctrine of curial deference with a wide scope is that it removes the difficulties of identifying a distinction between jurisdictional and non-jurisdictional questions, defining questions of law, or identifying a distinction between 'law' and 'discretion'. Beyond this, an 'unduly court-centred view of the universe' is to be guarded against.[223] Retaining the power to intervene when a delegated decision-maker has made a jurisdictional error, or an error in answering a question of law, pits reviewing courts against delegated decision-makers in an all-or-nothing fashion, when following a more nuanced approach might be more appropriate. Varying the standard of scrutiny permits a reviewing court to operate with a scalpel rather than a sledgehammer, sensitive to the statutory context rather than reacting to the formal classification of a question as jurisdictional, legal or the exercise of a discretion. Moreover, a focus on the extent of the power delegated to the delegated decision-maker and, in particular, the practical justifications for curial deference, could reduce the risk 'that judges, whether consciously or unconsciously, will impose their own standards of rationality on the administrative process'.[224]

[222] *Ibid.*, pp. 825–6. [223] *Dunsmuir*, above n. 58, p. 250, per Binnie J.

[224] David Dyzenhaus, 'The Politics of Deference: Judicial Review and Democracy' in Michael Taggart (ed.), *The Province of Administrative Law* (Oxford: Hart, 1997), pp. 279, 307.

Notwithstanding these features, an understandable concern would be that delegated decision-makers might not be kept in check. Even if the reader agrees that curial deference is possible on questions of law, and that the difficulties in defining questions of law or searching for clear answers gives reviewing courts too much power, the nagging fear that the Albert Hall will be declared to be a furnished tenancy might still remain. The fear is unfounded: curial deference does not mean judicial abstention. Impugned decisions may in many cases be reviewed on a standard of review of correctness. Even in cases where a great deal of power has been delegated, judicial scrutiny will take place, and reasoning will have to be adduced in support of a defective decision. Certain voices, perhaps a chorus of voices, might remain unconvinced.[225] However, the American and Canadian legal systems have suffered no obviously deleterious effects from abandoning the old orthodoxy that judges must keep delegated decision-makers firmly in check.

Finally, it should be noted that no presumption in favour of delegated decision-makers or reviewing courts is necessary, even though 'a presumption in favour of administrative interpretations [would be] a modest counterbalance to the natural reluctance of courts to deny their own superiority'.[226] My approach is neutral: a proper consideration of the relevant statutory provisions will determine the appropriate allocation of decision-making authority as between delegated decision-makers and reviewing courts.

225 '[I]n the common law system, judges at base still consider themselves to be the bulwarks against Leviathan.' Ian Holloway, '"A Bona Fide Attempt": Chief Justice Sir Owen Dixon and the Policy of Deference to Administrative Expertise in the High Court of Australia' (2002) 54 Admin LR 687, 698. See also Scalia, 'Deference', above n. 122, p. 514.

226 MacLauchlan, 'Formalism', above n. 123, p. 376.

7

Deference and political questions

In this chapter, I am again occupied by a question of the appropriate scope of the doctrine of curial deference developed in Chapters 2 to 4. Again, I will argue for an expansive field of application for the doctrine. In particular, I will suggest that any concerns that the review of delegated decision-making in sensitive areas would tend to interfere unduly with the machinery of government can be assuaged by a reduction, where appropriate, in the standard of review.

7.1 Justiciability

There is a tangle of terminology in the literature, which is liable to lead to confusion,[1] so I ought to be clear about the way in which I am using the term justiciability. As employed here, justiciability refers to two distinct things: the jurisdiction (in the sense of ability) of a court to hear a case and what I initially call the 'political question' doctrine or, in classic terminology, the jurisdiction of a court to hear a case as distinct from the suitability of a matter for judicial resolution.[2] Jurisdiction will not be canvassed here, save to list some examples: where a litigant fails to establish *locus standi*, or where the *lis* is moot or not ripe for judicial resolution. If a litigant fails at this preliminary stage,

[1] 'The word "justiciable" will be largely avoided, because in its broadest sense it is legitimately capable of denoting almost any question.' Melville Weston, 'Political Questions' (1925) 38 Harv LR 296, 299.

[2] See also Geoffrey Marshall, 'Justiciability' in A. G. Guest (ed.), *Oxford Essays in Jurisprudence (First Series)* (Oxford: Clarendon, 1961), pp. 265, 266–9. I should note, in terms of decisions being suitable for judicial resolution, that – with one minor exception – I do not consider questions of justiciability that arise in the consideration of tort cases (see e.g. Jeff King, 'The Justiciability of Resource Allocation' (2007) 70 MLR 197), because I am concerned solely with judicial review.

the applicability of a doctrine of curial deference will not fall to be considered by a court.[3]

Of interest for present purposes is that courts invoke so-called 'political question' doctrines, ostensibly to avoid considering the merits of a particular case which has come before them. The word 'political' should not be taken literally. It will never be the case that a decision will be unreviewable simply because a decision has implications that are likely to bear on government policy. For good or ill, policy pervades the legal arena, and if it were nonjusticiable then judges would be forced to exit almost entirely: 'the subject-matter of a putative judicial review cannot be consigned outside the court's jurisdiction on the footing that the merits of the decision under challenge are politically controversial'.[4]

No definition of the 'political question' doctrine has common currency,[5] which makes discussion difficult and increases the risk of attacking a straw man. Several commentators have argued that there should be no 'political question' doctrine at all, on the basis that there is an unconscionable 'moral cost' to allowing a potential legal violation to go inevitably unpunished.[6] It is more common to hear praise of the doctrine, although even its supporters have recognised the force in the argument that it 'can cause the courts to fall short of upholding the ideal of the rule of law'.[7] My argument is that there may be areas where the intensity of judicial review ought to be reduced but that there

[3] For broader discussion, see Jonathan Siegel, 'A Theory of Justiciability' (2007) 86 Tex LR 73; Lorne Sossin, *Boundaries of Judicial Review: The Law of Justiciability in Canada* (Scarborough: Carswell, 1999).

[4] Sir John Laws, 'Law and Democracy' [1995] PL 72, 76.

[5] See e.g. *Baker* v. *Carr* (1962) 369 US 186; *Council of Civil Service Unions* v. *Minister for the Civil Service* [1985] AC 374; Rachel Barkow, 'More Supreme than the Court? The Fall of the Political Question Doctrine and the Rise of Judicial Supremacy' (2002) 102 Colum LR 237; Jesse Choper, 'The Political Question Doctrine: Suggested Criteria' (2005) 54 Duke LJ 1457; Bruce Harris, 'Judicial Review, Justiciability and the Prerogative of Mercy' (2003) 62 CLJ 631.

[6] Martin Redish, 'Judicial Review and the "Political Question"' (1984–1985) 79 Nw U LR 1031, 1060. See also T. R. S. Allan, *Constitutional Justice: A Liberal Theory of the Rule of Law* (Oxford: Oxford University Press, 2001), pp. 161–99; Aharon Barak, *The Judge in a Democracy* (Princeton: Princeton University Press, 2006), pp. 177–89; Erwin Chemerinsky, 'Who Should Be the Authoritative Interpreter of the Constitution? Why There Should not Be a Political Question Doctrine' in Nada Mourtada-Sabbah and Bruce Cain (eds.), *The Political Question Doctrine and the Supreme Court of the United States* (Lexington; Plymouth, 2007), p. 181.

[7] Harris, 'Justiciability', above n. 5, p. 633.

are at most only two related categories of decision where review can be automatically excluded.

I will not draw a sharp distinction between judicial review of powers delegated by statute and executive or prerogative powers. The general trend has been to permit review of all powers, including executive or prerogative powers. If these powers are reviewable, then it is *a fortiori* the case that powers delegated by statute are reviewable, because powers delegated by statute are inherently limited,[8] whereas executive or prerogative powers need not be.

7.1.1 *The concepts of primary and secondary justiciability*

Bruce Harris has usefully distinguished primary from secondary justiciability. Primary justiciability refers to the category of decision.[9] Secondary justiciability refers to the grounds of judicial review or to the standard of review applied by a reviewing court, which may be reduced due to concerns that a court might not have the necessary tools at its disposal to review the impugned decision effectively, perhaps because of the complex nature of the decision.[10]

On the one hand, judges speak of categories of 'political question' or justiciability, suggesting that matters falling within these categories are beyond the remit of the courts, as a matter of primary justiciability. An example may be found in the speech of Lord Roskill in the *GCHQ* case:

> Prerogative powers such as those relating to the making of treaties, the defence of the realm, the prerogative of mercy, the grant of honours, the dissolution of Parliament and the appointment of ministers as well as others are not, I think susceptible to judicial review because their nature and subject-matter are such as not to be amenable to the judicial process. The courts are not the place wherein to determine whether a treaty should be concluded or the armed forces disposed in a particular manner or Parliament dissolved on one date rather than another.[11]

On the other hand is the secondary justiciability position that, despite judicial protestations to the contrary, no category of decision is *a priori*

[8] See above 2.3.3.2.

[9] Following Harris, I generally use the label of 'primary justiciability' rather than that of 'nonjusticiable', or 'nonjusticiability'; for my purposes, primary justiciability equates to nonjusticiability.

[10] Harris, 'Justiciability', above n. 5, p. 644.

[11] *Council of Civil Service Unions*, above n. 5, p. 418, per Lord Roskill. See however, Barkow, 'Fall and Rise', above n. 5; Caroline Neenan, 'Reviewing Prerogative Powers: Roskill's List Revisited' [1998] JR 36.

beyond the scope of review, although various considerations may decrease the standard of review.[12]

The definition of primary justiciability warrants clarification. Sometimes it is tempting to talk of primary justiciability where a court has refused to grant a remedy, but it is only where a court refuses to review a decision on the basis of the decision's subject matter that one can properly talk of primary justiciability. On the occasions that courts ostensibly determine a power exercised by another branch of government to be unreviewable, one of two things has occurred. Either the court has in fact reviewed the power and found judicial intervention to be inappropriate, or the court has refused to exercise a review jurisdiction and has not considered the substance of the matter. The distinction is subtle, but important. In the first scenario, review has been exercised, even though the litigant has gone home unhappy. Often in the first scenario, it will be obvious from the court's decision that review was not being ruled out in principle, although the circumstances in the instant case did not warrant judicial intervention; but on occasion judicial rhetoric may be misleading. In the second scenario, areas of decision have been hived off from judicial review, a process which incurs the moral cost of not subjecting potentially illegal state actions to judicial scrutiny. There is a difference then between an unreviewable power and an unfettered power.[13]

Any confusion can be teased out by considering the speech of Lord Rodger of Earlsferry in the *Chagos Islands* litigation.[14] Here, an Order in Council had been issued to prevent individuals from visiting the outer islands of the British Indian Ocean Territory without specific permission. Lord Rodger was prepared to accept in principle the possibility of review of the exercise of the prerogative power to make laws for the 'peace, order and good government' of British overseas territories, but held that he could not second-guess the use of the power in an individual case, 'simply because such questions are not justiciable. The law cannot resolve them: they are for the determination of the responsible ministers rather than judges. In this respect, the legislation made for the colonies

[12] See e.g. Adrian Vermeule, 'Our Schmittian Administrative Law' (2008) 122 Harv LR 1095.

[13] See e.g. *Adegbenro* v. *Akintola* [1963] AC 614 for an apparent example of the latter.

[14] *R (Bancoult)* v. *Secretary of State for Foreign and Commonwealth Affairs (No. 2)* [2008] UKHL 61; [2009] AC 453.

is in the same position as legislation made by Parliament for this country ...'.[15]

Despite the use of the term justiciable – in the sense of primary justiciability – Lord Rodger's reasoning does not actually support a position that certain categories of decision are beyond judicial review. In fact, Lord Rodger accepted in principle that the decision was reviewable, but found that the power of the Queen in Council to pass colonial legislation was coextensive with the power of the Queen in Parliament to pass primary legislation. On the most plausible reading of his speech, Lord Rodger simply found that the power of the Queen in Council was very broad indeed and amounted to plenary lawmaking power.[16] If this interpretation is accurate, the power *was reviewed* by Lord Rodger. However, because of the sheer breadth of the power, the Order in Council was perfectly lawful and no relief could be afforded to the Chagossians.

The best reading is that a ground of relief was not established, not that the exercise of the power was not reviewed.[17] As Chris Finn has noted, 'there will simply be considerable pragmatic difficulties in showing that the purpose for [the prerogative's] exercise was truly improper, that a matter upon which weight was placed was "irrelevant" or that one not taken into account was "relevant" in the necessary legal sense'.[18] It is usually the case, when judges invoke 'nonjusticiability' or 'political questions', that the applicant has simply failed to establish the existence of a reviewable error, or an enforceable legal right.[19] How difficult would it be, one might ask rhetorically, to demonstrate that a declaration of war was irrational[20] or would infringe fundamental rights?[21]

However, to say that a particular decision is justiciable if a legal right is established would be to beg the question.[22] For, it will not be possible to

15 *Ibid.*, p. 504. Emphasis added.

16 See similarly *ibid.*, pp. 485–6 (Lord Hoffman) and 508 (Lord Carswell).

17 For further discussion, see Mark Elliott and Amanda Perreau-Saussine, 'Pyrrhic Public Law: *Bancoult* and the Sources, Status and Content of Common Law Limitations on Prerogative Power' [2009] PL 697.

18 'The Justiciability of Administrative Decisions: a Redundant Concept?' (2002) 30 FLR 239, 260–1.

19 Allan, *Constitutional Justice*, above n. 6, p. 173.

20 *R* v. *Jones (Margaret)* [2006] UKHL 16; [2007] 1 AC 136 at 172–3.

21 *Operation Dismantle* v. *The Queen* [1985] 1 SCR 441; *R (Gentle)* v. *Prime Minister* [2008] UKHL 20; [2008] 1 AC 1356.

22 See Timothy Endicott, 'The Reason of the Law' (2003) 48 *American Journal of Jurisprudence* 83, 98–9.

establish a legal right in the first place unless the decision is reviewed. It would, surely, be nonsensical to say of a statutory provision interpreted by a court as not giving rise to enforceable rights that it was nonjusticiable. Consider the treatment of the justiciability of the exercise of the prerogative power to grant honours by the Ontario Court of Appeal in *Black* v. *Chrétien*.[23] The Canadian prime minister had advised the British government not to bestow honours upon publishing magnate, Lord Black, whose newspapers had continually lambasted the prime minister's stewardship of the ship of state. Lord Black's claim was for negligent misrepresentation and declaratory relief; the prime minister's defence consisted of, inter alia, a claim of primary justiciability. The prime minister prevailed. The court held that exercises of the prerogative are reviewable only where rights, and not privileges, of the individual are engaged.[24] Here, it was impossible for Lord Black to establish a 'right' because the grant of honours was a privilege, and hence beyond the purview of the courts. As such, the court assumed that which was to be proved: that Lord Black had no legal rights. However, Lord Black's claim was precisely that, had the power been exercised appropriately, he would have, in effect, had a legal right. Unfortunately for him, the claim was precluded by the court's reliance on a distinction between rights and privileges. However dubious the distinction,[25] it at least demonstrates that it is only truly possible to speak of primary justiciability where review of a power has been entirely excluded, and the merits of an applicant's claim have not been considered at all.

7.1.2 Primary justiciability

7.1.2.1 The scope of primary justiciability

One might consider Brennan J's well-known elaboration of the 'political question' doctrine in *Baker* v. *Carr*[26] to inadvertently prove the point that primary justiciability is not actually embraced by courts:

> Prominent on the surface of any case held to involve a political question is found a textually demonstrable constitutional commitment of the issue to a coordinate political department; or a lack of judicially discoverable and manageable standards for resolving it; or the impossibility of

[23] (2001) 199 DLR (4th) 228. [24] *Ibid.*, pp. 249–50.

[25] See Lorne Sossin, 'The Rule of Law and Justiciability of Prerogative Powers: A Comment on *Black* v. *Chrétien*' (2002) 47 McGill LJ 435, 445–7.

[26] *Baker*, above n. 5.

> deciding without an initial policy determination of a kind clearly for non-judicial discretion; or the impossibility of a court's undertaking independent resolution without expressing lack of the respect due coordinate branches of government; or an unusual need for unquestioning adherence to a political decision already made; or the potentiality of embarrassment from multifarious pronouncements by various departments on one question.[27]

Despite the force of his exposition of the doctrine, just a handful of lines below it, Brennan J noted 'the impossibility of resolution by any semantic cataloguing' and the 'necessity for discriminating inquiry into the precise facts and posture of the particular case',[28] a pair of admissions which undercut any argument in favour of primary justiciability. The message of Brennan J's opinion is that various considerations may militate against applying the normal standard of judicial review but that there are no categories of decision that are beyond judicial review.

For example, an oft-cited example of a 'political question' is the conclusion of treaties by the executive arm of the state. However, one might consider the questions of, for example, whether the signing of the treaty took the legally prescribed form, or went through the correct procedure, apt for judicial review. Leaving aside any questions as to jurisdiction, if a minister off on a frolic of his own were to sign a treaty, a court might well, as a matter of domestic law, regard the signing as a nullity, on procedural grounds.[29] The grounds of review invoked or standard of review sought, rather than the subject matter of the power sought to be reviewed, will be the critical variables.

[27] *Ibid.*, p. 217. [28] *Ibid.*, p. 217.

[29] As an English Divisional Court commented, *obiter*, in *R (Wheeler)* v. *Prime Minister* [2008] EWHC 1409 (Admin), [55]:

> That ... a decision [to ratify a treaty] is not altogether outside the scope of judicial review is illustrated by the fact that section 12 of the European Parliamentary Elections Act 2002 makes statutory approval a condition precedent to the ratification of any treaty which provides for an increase in the powers of the European Parliament: [counsel] realistically conceded that a decision to ratify without such approval would be amenable to review.

Contrast the surprising conclusion of the British Columbia Court of Appeal in *Ganis* v. *Canada (Minister of Justice)* [2006] BCCA 543 at [24–6] that the existence of a treaty is not justiciable. One would expect deference to be paid to the executive's assessment of whether or not a treaty is in place, on the basis that it is much better placed than a reviewing court to judge the subtleties of relationships between states, but it seems unnecessary to rule out any and all judicial review.

In addition, the source of the power relied upon no longer seems a promising basis for primary justiciability: 'Judicial review has developed to the point where it is possible to say that no power – whether statutory or under the prerogative – is any longer inherently unreviewable.'[30] In the *GCHQ* case, the House of Lords accepted that, in principle, the exercise of prerogative powers by the executive is reviewable.[31] As the Supreme Court of Canada has put it, '[i]t is for the executive and not the courts to decide whether and how to exercise its powers, but the courts clearly have the jurisdiction and the duty to determine whether a prerogative power … does in fact exist and, if so, whether its exercise infringes [constitutional provisions]'.[32] In respect of statutory powers, as Lord Bingham of Cornhill has observed, 'the ordinary if not the invariable rule'[33] governing the courts' treatment of claims of primary justiciability is as stated by Lloyd LJ in the *Datafin* case: 'If the source of power is a statute, or subordinate legislation under a statute, then clearly the body in question will be subject to judicial review.'[34] The Supreme Court of Canada has put the point quite firmly:

> All decision-making powers have legal limits, derived from the enabling statute itself, the common or civil law or the Constitution. Judicial review is the means by which the courts supervise those who exercise statutory powers, to ensure that they do not overstep their legal authority. The function of judicial review is therefore to ensure the legality, the reasonableness and the fairness of the administrative process and its outcomes.[35]

However, a solid foundation for the legitimacy of judicial review of statutory powers has been identified in the Canadian constitution.[36] Accordingly, an even better example is provided by the House of Lords' recent review of a decision of the Director of the Serious Fraud

30 Harry Woolf, Jeffrey Jowell and Andrew Le Sueur, *De Smith's Judicial Review*, 6th edn (London: Sweet and Maxwell, 2007), p. 15.

31 *Council of Civil Service Unions*, above n. 5, pp. 407 (Lord Scarman), 410–11 (Lord Diplock) and 417–18 (Lord Roskill).

32 *Khadr* v. *Canada (Prime Minister) (No. 2)* [2010] SCC 3; [2010] 1 SCR 44 at 61, per *curiam*.

33 *Mohit* v. *Director of Public Prosecutions of Mauritius* [2006] UKPC 20; [2006] 1 WLR 3343 at 3354.

34 *R* v. *Panel on Takeovers and Mergers, ex p. Datafin* [1987] QB 815 at 847.

35 *Dunsmuir* v. *New Brunswick* [2008] SCC 9; [2008] 1 SCR 190 at 211, per Bastarache and LeBel JJ. See also David Mullan, 'Judicial Deference to Executive Decision-making: Evolving Concepts of Responsibility' (1993) 19 Queen's LJ 137, 164–75.

36 See *Crevier* v. *Quebec (Attorney-General)* [1981] 2 SCR 220 at 234.

Office to discontinue a fraud investigation on the basis of a threat to national security.[37]

The director has been delegated broad power to 'investigate any suspected offence which appears to him on reasonable grounds to involve serious or complex fraud', and 'institute and have the conduct of any criminal proceedings which appear to him to relate to such fraud'.[38] The Attorney-General is to supervise the director in the discharge of the latter's functions.[39] In the instant case, the director was investigating an alleged bribe paid by a company which was the main contractor on a deal between the British and Saudi Arabian governments concerning the supply of military equipment. However, the Saudi Arabian government issued an explicit threat that if the director continued his investigations, Saudi Arabia would withdraw from bilateral counterterrorism arrangements, cease to co-operate with Britain's strategic objectives in the Middle East and pull out of negotiations about the purchase of military aircraft. After representations from the British ambassador to Saudi Arabia – who warned that 'British lives on British streets' would be endangered if the threats were followed through on – and the prime minister – who also expressed concerns about the national interest – the director, having consulted with the Attorney-General, agreed to discontinue the aspect of the investigations that concerned the Saudi Arabian government.

The House of Lords took the view that the director's statutory authority was analogous to that of the Director of Public Prosecutions and accepted that the courts would be 'very slow' to interfere with the exercise by the director of his various discretions for several reasons: the relevant powers were vested in the director, not the courts; the decision had a polycentric character; and the statutory powers were broadly phrased. However:

> the discretions conferred on the Director are not unfettered. He must seek to exercise his powers so as to promote the statutory purpose for which he is given them. He must direct himself correctly in law. He must act lawfully. He must do his best to exercise an objective judgment on the relevant material available to him. He must exercise his powers in good faith, uninfluenced by any ulterior motive, predilection or prejudice.[40]

[37] *R (Corner House Research and Campaign Against Arms Trade)* v. *Director of the Serious Fraud Office* [2008] UKHL 60; [2009] AC 756.

[38] Criminal Justice Act 1987, s. 1(3) and (5). [39] *Ibid.*, s. 1(2).

[40] *Corner House Research*, above n. 37, p. 841, per Lord Bingham of Cornhill. See similarly *Unison Networks* v. *Commerce Commission* [2007] NZSC 74; [2008] 1 NZLR 42.

In the instant case, the House of Lords accepted that the threat to national security was a factor which the director could lawfully take into account in exercising his discretion to discontinue the investigation. Despite the broad discretion of the director, and the sensitive nature of the decision, the possibility of primary justiciability preventing a review of the director's decision was not seriously countenanced.[41]

Another example is the decision of the Court of Appeal of New Zealand in *Curtis* v. *Minister for Defence*.[42] Here, the applicant was one of a number of concerned citizens who challenged the minister's decision to disband the air combat force of the Royal New Zealand Air Force; the Air Force would remain, though shorn of its combat division. The decision was taken pursuant to the minister's 'power of control' of the army, granted to him by s. 7 of the Defence Act 1990. In the view of the applicant, however, the disbanding of the air combat force would leave New Zealand without the air force which was expressly required by the Act. In particular, s. 11(2) provided that the 'armed forces ... shall continue to comprise ... (c) the Royal New Zealand Air Force'. That being the case, the applicant submitted, the minister could not exercise his power in such a way as to remove one of the constituent elements of the armed forces.

The Court of Appeal found in favour of the minister. Although there are references in the judgment to the nonjusticiable character of decisions about the level at which the armed forces should be armed, the disposition of the case did not turn on primary justiciability. The court could easily have invoked primary justiciability, on the basis that the national defence was at issue. However, it addressed thoughtfully the claims raised by the applicant. First, it rejected the suggestion that the minister's decision abolished the air force and therefore contravened s. 11(2) of the Act. The court took into consideration the evidence of the Chief of Air Staff as to the continuing air operations of the army and concluded that no contravention of the Act had been effected by the minister: 'It has no doubt become a different sort of air force from that which has hitherto existed but it nevertheless remains an air force.'[43] Secondly, the court suggested that while the army as a whole – being the navy, ground force and air force – would have to be armed, it would not be necessary for all of these individual components to be armed: 'It is

[41] See also *R (Purdy)* v. *Director of Public Prosecutions* [2009] UKHL 45; [2009] 3 WLR 403.
[42] [2002] 2 NZLR 744. [43] *Ibid.*, p. 750.

sufficient if it can fairly be said that the New Zealand Defence Force as a whole is an armed force.'[44]

Thirdly, the court refused to be drawn on the question of the appropriate level at which the air force ought to be armed, describing it as 'a political not a legal issue';[45] the claim that the air force was insufficiently armed was, in the court's view, 'par excellence a nonjusticiable question'.[46] But one should not be fooled by the use of the term nonjusticiable. In the court's view, the Act required that the army had to be armed to some degree but did not require its components to be armed to any particular level. The Act provided a baseline below which the minister could not go, but provided him with a discretionary power to choose a level above the baseline. The court decided the threshold question as to whether the army remained 'armed', as the Act required, leaving the decision whether to maintain a small or large number of armed forces to the minister. To describe the decision as nonjusticiable is simply to state that the applicant could not identify a legal impediment to the minister's decision. Had the minister abolished the air force *tout court*, then presumably the court would have held such a decision to be unlawful, regardless of the sensitive, political nature of the decision. In view of its willingness to engage in a thorough review of the statutory language, despite the sensitive nature of the impugned decision, the court's reasoning can safely be described as exemplary.

7.1.2.2 Exceptions: textual commitments and constitutional rules

I alluded earlier to the existence of two linked exceptions to my argument that no category of decision is *a priori* nonjusticiable as a matter of primary justiciability. The first exception may be found in the first line of Brennan J's definition: primary justiciability might be said to exist where there is a textually demonstrable commitment of a particular power to a particular branch of government.[47] There is one category of case in the United States which has developed from the relatively obscure clause of the federal Constitution that guarantees a 'republican form of government',[48] where review is automatically precluded, because the protection

[44] *Ibid.*, p. 751. [45] *Ibid.*, p. 751. [46] *Ibid.*, p. 752.

[47] Even a trenchant critic of the 'political question' doctrine will be forced to admit the textually demonstrable commitment exception. See e.g. Michael Tigar, 'Judicial Power, the "Political Question Doctrine", and Foreign Relations' (1970) 17 UCLA LR 1135, 1163–4.

[48] Article IV, § 4.

of the guarantee has been held to have been vested in the political branches of government.[49] Similarly, an English Divisional Court refused to order that a bill initiating a referendum be introduced in Parliament partly on the basis that to do so would 'be to order [parliamentarians] to do an act within Parliament in their capacity as Members of Parliament and would plainly be to trespass impermissibly on the province of Parliament'.[50]

On the same plane as textually demonstrable commitment, and very similar in character, is the second exception: where a constitutional rule or rules excludes review.[51] For example, a provision of the Irish Constitution prevents the exercise of discretionary powers by the president from being called into question in courts of law. A court would not be able to adjudicate on any claim that the president had acted irrationally, or even in bad faith: the Constitution would bar it.[52] In and of itself, a rule of this nature does not amount to a doctrine in any meaningful sense.[53]

7.1.2.3 Primary justiciability and the rule of law

Caution should be exercised, however, before permitting textually demonstrable commitment or constitutional rules as exceptions, thereby permitting areas of primary justiciability, for there are strong arguments against primary justiciability. A judicial finding of primary justiciability is a 'nuclear option' which renders entire areas of the law judicially uninhabitable.[54] Moreover, even if a textually demonstrable commitment or constitutional

[49] See *Pacific States Telephone and Telegraph* v. *Oregon* (1912) 223 US 118 at 142–3. Of course, it is possible that the courts will overrule the line of reasoning that excludes judicial review. See e.g. Erwin Chemerinsky, 'Cases under the Guarantee Clause Should be Justiciable' (1994) 65 U Colo LR 849.

[50] *Wheeler*, above n. 29, [49]. See also *Te Runanga o Wharekauri Rekohu* v. *Attorney General* [1993] 2 NZLR 301; *New Zealand Maori Council* v. *Attorney-General* [2007] NZCA 269; [2008] 1 NZLR 318.

[51] The difference between the two exceptions is that the constitutional rules *preclude* judicial review by their own terms; but demonstrable commitments *commit* decisions to a particular branch.

[52] Art. 13.8.1° makes this pellucidly clear: 'The President shall not be answerable … *to any court* for the exercise and performance of the powers and functions of his office or for any act done or purporting to be done by him in the exercise and performance of these powers and functions.' Emphasis added.

[53] Louis Henkin, 'Is There a "Political Question" Doctrine?' (1975) 85 Yale LJ 597, 609.

[54] Jeff King, 'Institutional Approaches to Judicial Restraint' (2008) 28 OJLS 409, 421. See also Roger Masterman, *The Separation of Powers in the Contemporary Constitution: Judicial Competence and Independence in the United Kingdom* (Cambridge: Cambridge University Press, 2011), pp. 90–3.

rule can be found, it may yield to deeper concerns. On the one hand, it can be tempered by the possibility of an extreme case: 'if the constitutional limitations on majoritarian power are to mean anything, at some point the judiciary must be able to question the political branches' assertion of factual necessity'.[55] Hence Souter J's suggestion that the US Supreme Court would, despite the textually demonstrable commitment of the matter to the political branches, quash an impeachment verdict reached on the toss of a coin.[56] Hence, similarly, Lord Hoffman's insistence that Orders in Council cannot be used to authorise extraordinary rendition from or to British overseas territories.[57] Even the possibility of decisions repugnant to the shared values of a society being taken under the cloak of primary justiciability should be enough to prevent judges from making the cloak available in the first place.[58]

On the other hand, the likelihood of finding a textually demonstrable commitment or constitutional rule will be tempered by the need for judicial intervention when fundamental rights are infringed: 'it is now common ground that if a [fundamental rights ground] requires the court to examine and adjudicate upon matters which were previously regarded as nonjusticiable, then adjudicate it must'.[59] The delegation of the protection of fundamental rights to the courts would be undermined, perhaps even rendered ineffective, if primary justiciability were permitted.

If access to judicial review itself is conceived of as a fundamental right, the mere possibility of textually demonstrable commitments or constitutional rules is highly problematic.[60] Leaving that possibility aside, acceptance of the need for judicial intervention to protect fundamental rights is the thin end of the reviewability wedge. Textually demonstrable commitments or constitutional rules are 'likely to be inconsistent with the rule of law. Whenever there is a plausible claim that such action has infringed established rights ... there cannot properly be a form of

[55] Redish, '"Political Question"', above n. 6, p. 1051.

[56] *Nixon* v. *United States* (1993) 506 US 224 at 253–4, per Souter J, concurring. See also *ibid.*, p. 239, per White J, concurring. Admittedly, the majority did determine that there was a clear textual commitment of the impeachment process to the political branches, which rendered it a category of decision free from judicial intervention.

[57] *Bancoult*, above n. 14, pp. 482–3.

[58] See also *Andrews* v. *Mitchell* [1905] AC 78.

[59] *Gentle*, above n. 21, p. 1382, per Baroness Hale of Richmond. See also *Webster* v. *Doe* (1988) 486 US 592 at 603; *Operation Dismantle*, above n. 21.

[60] See generally Douglas Edlin, 'A Constitutional Right to Judicial Review: Access to Courts and Ouster Clauses in England and the United States' (2009) 57 *American Journal of Comparative Law* 67.

deference to governmental decisions that precludes ordinary legal analysis.'[61] Even where no infringement of fundamental rights can be established, as Jeffrey Jowell has urged, '[t]here is a minimum level of scrutiny in which any court should engage, irrespective of the subject-matter';[62] the rule of law would be compromised if those affected by unlawful action could not bring their claims before a court.

Admittedly, claims that the state has acted unlawfully do not necessarily have the same entrenched status as fundamental rights.[63] One might suggest that, then, they ought to be treated differently from the point of view of justiciability. However, a two-tiered system in which the same unreasonable action would be subject to judicial review only if it infringed a fundamental right would be incongruous. More intrusive review will usually be appropriate where fundamental rights are not engaged, but it does not follow that no review at all would be appropriate. It is difficult to see why the absence of a fundamental right would justify an unreasonable decision, never mind one taken in bad faith. Indeed, to permit the interests of the citizenry to be determined by unreasonable government action would surely be deeply troubling, even to those who hold fast to a thin conception of the rule of law. As the Supreme Court of Canada has observed, '[a]t its most basic level, the rule of law vouchsafes to the citizens and residents of the country a stable, predictable and ordered society in which to conduct their affairs. It provides a shield for individuals from arbitrary state action.'[64] Accordingly, primary justiciability should be considered as 'a limit, if not an affront, to the rule of law'.[65]

7.1.3 Secondary justiciability

Thus, it is submitted, formal, *a priori* classifications which would entirely exclude certain categories of decision from review must be rejected, and

[61] Allan, *Constitutional Justice*, above n. 6, p. 163.

[62] 'The Democratic Necessity of Administrative Justice' [2006] Acta Juridica 13, 21.

[63] One might say, however, that individuals, both *qua* individuals and collectively, have a fundamental right to non-arbitrary decision-making. See e.g. Lorne Sossin, 'The Unfinished Project of *Roncarelli* v. *Duplessis*: Justiciability, Discretion, and the Limits of the Rule of Law' (2010) 55 McGill LJ 661, 672–3.

[64] *Reference re Secession of Quebec* [1998] 2 SCR 217 at 257.

[65] Chris Finn, 'The Concept of "Justiciability"' in Matthew Groves and H. P. Lee (eds.), *Australian Administrative Law: Fundamentals, Principles and Doctrines* (Cambridge: Cambridge University Press, 2007), pp. 143, 156. The importance of political accountability should not be forgotten, however: 'justiciability should be seen as a point of departure for rule of law accountability, albeit an incomplete and sometimes inadequate response to the challenge'. Sossin, 'Unfinished Project', above n. 63, p. 675.

possible exceptions must be regarded with the greatest suspicion. However, a more nuanced approach can be taken to justiciability. According to the concept of secondary justiciability judges should not open their judicial review toolboxes fully on all occasions, because of prudential concerns. First, there is 'the anxiety, not so much that the judicial judgment will be ignored, as that perhaps it should but will not be';[66] courts may lack competence, by dint of cognitive limitations or the restrictions of the adjudicative process, to resolve certain matters. Secondly, there are the considerations outlined by Brennan J in the passage quoted earlier from *Baker*; for example, the need for comity between the branches of government and the necessity to maintain an appearance of unity. Thirdly, exercise of the general principles might require the release of sensitive information.[67]

Apart from the third, which can be addressed by rules governing the admissibility of evidence,[68] these prudential concerns are indistinguishable in character from the practical justifications for curial deference: the complexity of the decision under review and the delegated decision-maker's expertise and legitimacy, democratic and procedural.

Various conceptions of secondary justiciability are available or have been mooted. Lorne Sossin has recently suggested that the development of a 'general distinction ... between merits-based review, which looks to whether the exercise of authority was correct or reasonable, and an ultra vires-based review, which looks to whether the authority was exercised in good faith and for proper purposes, may be a sensible point of departure'.[69] Two problems with Sossin's approach are immediately apparent. First, it would require reviewing courts to police an ill-defined (and perhaps undefinable) boundary between merits and jurisdiction. Reliance on an abstract concept such as jurisdiction is neither necessary nor desirable.[70] Secondly, it relies on a formal, *a priori* classification between merits and jurisdiction which will surely render some decisions

[66] Alexander Bickel, *The Least Dangerous Branch: The Supreme Court at the Bar of Politics*, 2nd edn (New Haven: Yale University Press, 1986), p. 184.

[67] See e.g. *Savage and McOwen* v. *Director of Public Prosecutions* [1982] ILRM 385.

[68] See above 3.3.2.

[69] Sossin, 'Unfinished Project', above n. 63, p. 664. In Sossin's defence, he is operating within the framework developed in *Black*, above n. 23, and a distinction between merits and jurisdiction seems something of an advance on a distinction between rights and privileges, which one thought had been consigned to the dustbin of judicial review history long before it was fished back out by the Ontario Court of Appeal.

[70] See above 6.1.

unreviewable, giving teeth to the concept of primary justiciability, at the expense of the rule of law.

Another possibility is exemplified by the English approach. The English courts have reduced the intensity of judicial review of various sensitive matters – such as the substance of a medical expert's judgement,[71] the decision of a public prosecutor to initiate a prosecution[72] and the allocation of scarce resources[73] – by reducing the available grounds of review.[74] It is notable, for example, that in the *Corner House* case discussed above,[75] no mention was made by Lord Bingham of Cornhill of the possibility of review on the ground of *Wednesbury* unreasonableness.[76] However, the choice of which grounds of review to remove from consideration must be an arbitrary one. It is difficult to perceive a rational basis for removing some grounds of review rather than others. Moreover, no criteria seem to be available to judge which grounds of review should be removed, and when. For example, it is hard to identify the difference between review for bad faith and review for irrelevancy of considerations or review for unreasonableness that would justify including the first and excluding the others. As Lord Greene MR put it in the *Wednesbury* case, 'all these things run into one another'.[77] If such arbitrariness is inherent in the removal of certain grounds of review, then it ought not to be hard-wired into judicial review doctrine.

A better approach was developed and followed by the Canadian courts.[78] Put briefly, the Canadian pragmatic and functional analysis concentrated on the appropriate standard of review and the English approach on the appropriate grounds of review. According to the pragmatic and functional analysis, the standard of judicial review increased or decreased depending on the application of a four-factor test to the decision under review: either a standard of correctness, unreasonableness or patent unreasonableness would apply. Notably, the Canadian

[71] *R* v. *Cambridge Health Authority, ex p. B* [1995] 1 WLR 898.

[72] *R* v. *Director of Public Prosecutions, ex p. Kebilene* [2000] 2 AC 326.

[73] *R* v. *Secretary of State for the Environment, ex p. Hammersmith and Fulham London Borough Council* [1991] 1 AC 521; *Nottinghamshire County Council* v. *Secretary of State for the Environment* [1986] AC 240.

[74] See above 1.2.3. See also *Axa General Insurance* v. *Scottish Ministers* [2011] Scot CS CSIH 31 at [89]; *Mercury Energy* v. *Electricity Corporation of New Zealand* [1994] 2 NZLR 385 at 391; *Air New Zealand* v. *Wellington International Airport* [2009] 2 NZLR 713 at 736.

[75] See above 7.1.2.1.

[76] See Jeffrey Jowell, 'Caving In: Threats and the Rule of Law' [2008] JR 273, 274.

[77] *Associated Provincial Picture Houses* v. *Wednesbury Corporation* [1948] 1 KB 223 at 229.

[78] See above 1.2.1.

system was also capable of being applied to the review of sensitive decisions.[79] Although the pragmatic and functional analysis is now defunct, it remains a pertinent example of secondary justiciability.

For present purposes, the key point is that a doctrine of curial deference such as the pragmatic and functional analysis allows the intensity of judicial review to be reduced in appropriate cases:

> due respect for the court's limited capacity to engage in intensive review does not require the court to abdicate its review function. The court will fashion the mode of control that suits the occasion and is capable of a more nuanced approach than that of all or nothing: that unless it is intensive there can be no review at all.[80]

Indeed, the concept of secondary justiciability underpins the doctrine of curial deference developed in Chapters 2 to 4. Where the practical justifications for curial deference suggest that a higher degree of curial deference ought to be accorded, the standard of review can be decreased accordingly. After the fashion of the Canadian pragmatic and functional analysis, my doctrine of curial deference can also accommodate secondary justiciability:

> It is the variable standard of deference which allows the courts to afford a degree of respect to the decisions of elected bodies and which has come to mean that while action taken at what might have been called the fringes of justiciability may be reviewable *per se*, it may not necessarily be subject to intensive review in practice.[81]

No floodgates would be burst open by such an approach: applicants would have to demonstrate the presence of *indicia* of unreasonableness and delegated decision-makers would have the opportunity to discharge any resulting burden of justification. I submit that my approach can accommodate the concerns of secondary justiciability while, by its rejection of primary justiciability, ensuring that review of delegated decision-makers will, in principle, always be available.

David Dyzenhaus has eloquently expressed the concern that what he terms grey holes, where the general principles of judicial review are not applied with full force, may be more offensive to the rule of law than

[79] See above 6.3.3.
[80] *Air New Zealand*, above n. 74, p. 749, per Baragwanath J, dissenting, but not on this point.
[81] Masterman, *The Separation of Powers in the Contemporary Constitution*, above n. 54, p. 104.

black holes of primary justiciability, where the general principles of judicial review are not applied at all. Grey holes are even worse than black holes, because in his view they permit the executive to fall short of the rule of law while simultaneously pretending to comply with it: 'they give to official lawlessness the façade of legality'.[82] Grey holes have been identified with variable standards of review.[83] But Dyzenhaus's critique is aimed at judges who do not properly apply the general principles of judicial review, not at variable standards of review. These should be perfectly acceptable if, as I have suggested, they form part of the general principles of judicial review. It would be strange to suggest (and in my view Dyzenhaus does not) that Canada was in violation of the rule of law when patent unreasonableness was a standard of review, or that the rule of law is violated by the use by English courts of the super-*Wednesbury* standard of review.

7.1.4 Conclusion

Analogues to textually demonstrable commitments and constitutional rules excluding review are contained in the American Administrative Procedure Act. The approach of the Supreme Court of the United States to these provisions is instructive and provides an appropriate point of conclusion to the discussion of justiciability. Section 701(a) of the APA provides that judicial review will be generally available 'except to the extent that (1) statutes preclude judicial review; or (2) agency action is committed to agency discretion by law'.[84] The presence of these clauses gives rise to the same incoherence that is created by the presence of a privative clause in a statute. Indeed, the situation created by the APA is indistinguishable from the situation created by an individual privative clause, for the APA only legitimates the exclusion of review; that exclusion is, in the final analysis, effected by privative language in the statute. Where language in the relevant statutory provisions satisfies the two clauses in the APA, it has a privative effect. Such language is permitted, but not mandated, by the APA. The incoherence could be removed by treating the satisfaction of the two clauses as factors going to the choice of the appropriate standard of review.

82 *The Constitution of Law: Legality in a Time of Emergency* (Cambridge: Cambridge University Press, 2006), p. 207.
83 See Vermeule, 'Our Schmittian Administrative Law', above n. 12, pp. 1121, 1131.
84 5 USC § 701(a).

Perhaps for this reason, the exceptions, the first of which resembles a constitutional rule barring review and the second of which allows for textually demonstrable commitments, have been narrowly construed: 'clear and convincing evidence' of a legislative intent to restrict access to judicial review must be demonstrated.[85] The court 'will not lightly interpret a statute to confer unreviewable power on an administrative agency',[86] such that 'judicial review of a final agency action by an aggrieved person will not be cut off unless there is persuasive reason to believe that such was the purpose of Congress'.[87] In particular, a narrow construction has been given to the mysterious s. 701(a)(2), which has been characterised as a 'very narrow exception' applicable only in cases where there is 'no law to apply'.[88]

A retrograde step was taken in *Heckler* v. *Chaney*,[89] however. Here, Rehnquist J held that decisions of the Food and Drug Administration not to initiate enforcement proceedings 'should be presumed immune from judicial review'.[90] Such decisions were committed to agency discretion under s. 701(a)(2), because of the complicated balancing required in taking such decisions, the fact that a decision not to initiate enforcement proceedings does not involve the use of coercive powers (in contrast to decisions to exercise authority) and the analogy to prosecutorial discretion of executive branch officers, where a decision not to indict 'has long been regarded as the special province of the executive branch'.[91] The presumption of unreviewability could be rebutted 'where the substantive statute has provided guidelines for the agency to follow in exercising its enforcement powers',[92] but was not in the instant case.

The reasoning is unconvincing. The complex nature of the decision not to initiate an enforcement action could be taken account of in determining the appropriate standard of review. If appropriate, a lower standard of review could be applied. In short, an application of the concept of secondary justiciability could address the concerns of the court about the complex nature of the decision. Inasmuch as the court suggested that all decisions not to initiate enforcement proceedings

85 *Rusk* v. *Cort* (1962) 369 US 367 at 380, per Stewart J.

86 *Southern Railway Company* v. *Seaboard Allied Milling* (1979) 442 US 444 at 454, per Stevens J.

87 *Abbott Laboratories* v. *Gardner* (1967) 387 US 136 at 140, per Harlan J.

88 *Citizens to Preserve Overton Park* v. *Volpe* (1971) 401 US 402 at 410, per Marshall J, quoting in the second instance Senate Report No. 752, 79th Congress, First Session (1945), p. 26.

89 (1985) 470 US 821. 90 *Ibid.*, p. 832. 91 *Ibid.*, p. 832. 92 *Ibid.*, p. 833.

would be presumptively unreviewable, its reasoning was surely overbroad. As Brennan J suggested in his concurring opinion, it should not be taken to cover 'nonenforcement decisions made for entirely illegitimate reasons, for example, nonenforcement in return for a bribe'.[93] But by its terms, the majority's reasoning was not so limited.

A more convincing and more narrowly drawn approach is provided by Marshall J's concurring opinion. Drawing on the concept of secondary justiciability, Marshall J held that the court should accord 'substantial deference' to the agency's choice as to an allocation of finite enforcement resources because 'the choice among valid alternative enforcement policies is precisely the sort of choice over which agencies generally have been left substantial discretion by their enabling statutes'.[94] On the merits, no relief would be forthcoming. However, Marshall J objected to the breadth of the approach taken by Rehnquist J, whom he accused of moving from 'asserting that agencies must be given substantial leeway in allocating enforcement resources among valid alternatives to suggesting that agency enforcement decisions are presumptively unreviewable no matter what factor caused the agency to stay its hand'.[95] He found the analogy with prosecutorial discretion to be inapt because the '*sine qua non* of the APA was to alter inherited judicial reluctance to constrain the exercise of discretionary administrative power',[96] and he regarded as 'simply untenable'[97] the attempt to draw a line between coercive and negative agency action.[98] Ultimately, 'Congress should not be presumed to have departed from principles of rationality and fair process in enacting the APA.'[99]

Traces of the normative arguments outlined above can be discerned in Marshall J's reasoning, which both exposes and resolves the incoherence created by the privative provisions of the APA.[100] Because the concept of secondary justiciability allows the stringency of judicial review to be reduced in appropriate cases, the concern that courts may represent inappropriate forums for the resolution of complex issues can be assuaged. The unpalatable alternative is the carving out of whole areas from judicial oversight.

[93] *Ibid.*, p. 839. [94] *Ibid.*, p. 842. [95] *Ibid.*, p. 843. [96] *Ibid.*, p. 848.
[97] *Ibid.*, p. 851.
[98] '[A]ny distinction, as such, between "negative" and "affirmative" orders, as a touchstone of jurisdiction … serves no useful purpose …' *Rochester Telephone Corporation* v. *United States* (1939) 307 US 125 at 143, per Frankfurter J.
[99] *Chaney*, above n. 89, pp. 852–3. [100] See above 7.1.2.3.

Conclusion

Elena Kagan has suggested that '[t]he delegation of power to an agency to administer a statute, even when manifested in explicit rule-making and adjudicatory authority, does not necessarily entail a delegation of power to the agency (rather than the courts) to answer any and all interpretive questions to which the statute may give rise'.[1] The problem is that, in the modern administrative state, some means of allocating decision-making authority between the political and judicial branches must be developed. The relevant legislation will generally be silent on the specific question of the allocation of decision-making authority and, even where legislation does purport to address the question of the allocation of decision-making authority, it will have to be interpreted. Silence alone does not justify intrusive judicial review any more than it does deferential judicial review. My argument has been that a proper consideration of the relevant statutory provisions will indicate that the legislature has given some guidance as to how decision-making authority should be allocated as between delegated decision-makers and reviewing courts. Variable delegations of power and the variability of the practical justifications for curial deference will indicate that a variable standard of review is the most appropriate means of allocating decision-making authority. A variable standard of review can be developed by reference to the concept of unreasonableness, and can be applied to all delegated decision-making. If a variable standard of review were required by statute, then courts would be obliged to develop and implement a variable standard of review. Where a proper consideration of the relevant statutory provisions leads to the conclusion that a variable standard of review is appropriate, then the judicial obligation to give effect to legislative intent strongly suggests, if not requires, that courts must develop and implement a doctrine of curial deference with variable standards of review.

[1] Elena Kagan, 'Presidential Administration' (2001) 114 Harv LR 2245, 2379.

Giving effect to a doctrine of curial deference with variable standards of review

I have developed a doctrine of curial deference with variable standards of review in the nature of an ideal-type, 'a rational, coherent and abstract mental representation of a thing … which appears in a confused and incoherent form in the world'.[2] I recognise that adopting my ideal-type in its entirety may not be immediately feasible, but courts may be able to accommodate it partially, within existing judicial review doctrine. My argument prompts three general recommendations for reviewing courts in Canada, the United States and England which could be implemented with immediate effect. First, where existing judicial review doctrine requires the application of a variable standard of review, the variable standard of review should be applied to as wide a range of decisions as possible: jurisdictional questions, interpretations of law, exercises of discretion and 'political questions'. Secondly, any variable standard of review should contain three standards of review: correctness, unreasonableness and manifest unreasonableness. If necessary, existing standards of review could be reformed to reflect the three standards that I have proposed. Thirdly, the appropriate standard of review should be calculated by reference to the extent of delegations of power and the practical justifications for curial deference. I also have three specific recommendations: Canadian courts should reintroduce a third standard of review, American courts should adopt a holistic approach to determining the appropriate standard of review and English courts should begin to accord curial deference to interpretations of law rendered by delegated decision-makers.

Whether courts are deferential in practice – and therefore need not adopt a doctrine of curial deference – is an empirical question that I have not set out to answer. It may be that significant degrees of deference are accorded to delegated decision-makers by reviewing courts, even though the language of curial deference is not used. But if it is the case that theory and practice are not consistent, then adopting a doctrine of curial deference with variable standards of review would help to achieve consistency between theory and practice.[3]

[2] Luc Tremblay, *The Rule of Law, Justice, and Interpretation* (Montreal and Kingston: McGill-Queen's University Press, 1997), p. 137.

[3] I would also suggest that the doctrine of curial deference I have developed would have provided an appropriate means of resolving the issues raised before the United Kingdom Supreme Court in *R (Cart)* v. *Upper Tribunal* [2011] UKSC 28; [2011] 3 WLR 107. There, the court relied on judicial discretion and considerations of proportionality in the use of

The ultra vires debate

For many years the orthodox English position was that the ultra vires principle was the keystone of judicial review. The legislature delegated authority within certain parameters which the courts would police, thereby giving effect to the intentions of the legislature: the judiciary was faithfully imposing on the executive limitations laid down by the legislature in statutes. However, as the 'common law' theorists pointed out, in reality judges were fashioning 'principles of good administration'.[4] They were doing so of their own volition, independent of legislative intent,[5] and the ultra vires principle was merely a 'fig-leaf'.[6] Defenders of the orthodox position, although agreeing that the ultra vires principle was a fig leaf, considered it a vital one, hiding the immodesty of the courts' challenge to parliamentary sovereignty.[7] For, if courts were fashioning independent principles of good administration, these were, surely, fetters on the sovereignty of Parliament:

> If ... the maker of an administrative decision complies with all the requirements for validity, express or implied, laid down in the relevant statute, the common law cannot add any additional requirement ... without challenging the power of Parliament to specify the requirements of validity.[8]

Nonetheless, the orthodox account remained deficient. The ultra vires principle needed to be reconceptualised to accommodate the intentions of Parliament and the creative role of the courts in developing principles of good administration. Grasping the nettle, the defenders of orthodoxy argued that Parliament, save where it clearly indicates otherwise,

judicial resources to limit judicial review of the Upper Tribunal. The court suggested that the traditional grounds of review would in principle be applicable, but that due to considerations of proportionality they would be available only where an important point or principle was raised or some other compelling reason for intervention could be demonstrated. However, the court put the cart before the horse, in that it did not address the logically prior question, on which I have focused, of what sorts of decision or error should *in principle* be reviewable. Doing so might have allowed the court to reach a similarly thrifty conclusion, but on the basis of principle rather than pragmatism.

4 Denis Galligan, 'Judicial Review and the Textbook Writers' (1982) 2 OJLS 257, 261.

5 Paul Craig, '*Ultra Vires* and the Foundations of Judicial Review' (1998) 57 CLJ 63.

6 Sir John Laws, 'Law and Democracy' [1995] PL 72, 79.

7 Christopher Forsyth, 'Of Fig Leaves and Fairytales: The *Ultra Vires* Doctrine, Sovereignty of Parliament and Judicial Review' (1996) 55 CLJ 122.

8 William Wade and Christopher Forsyth, *Administrative Law*, 10th edn (Oxford: Oxford University Press, 2009), p. 34.

'intends to legislate in conformity with the rule of law'[9] and must be taken to legitimate the courts' role in developing the principles of good administration: 'even the most dim-witted legislator, or officious back-bencher, will, if asked, say that in legislating they intend that the powers granted should be fairly exercised':[10]

> While the details of the principles of review are not attributed to parliamentary intention, the judicially-created principles of good administration are applied consistently with Parliament's general intention that the discretionary power which it confers should be limited in accordance with the requirements of the rule of law.[11]

Because descriptive accuracy is sacrificed for theoretical consistency, even its supporters admit that this 'modified ultra vires doctrine' has a 'wholly formal and (admittedly) conclusionary character'.[12] But if the ultra vires principle can be relied upon to justify any decision reached by a reviewing court, the judicial obligation to give effect to legislative intent may be dissolved in an elixir of judicial creativity. For the 'common law' theorists, the development of judicial review is almost entirely divorced from legislative intent. Only where the legislature affirmatively specifies grounds or standards of judicial review is legislative intent said to be relevant. Judicial review would develop, on this approach, in splendid isolation from statutory language, limited only by the principle that it must 'reflect the considered judgment of the courts at that time that this was the best reading of the rule of law'.[13]

My approach to legislative intent has charted a middle course between two extremes: the common lawyers discount statutory provisions save for those extremely rare instances in which the legislature affirmatively specifies clear rules for the conduct of judicial review; and the traditionalists identify legislative intent with doctrines developed by judges. In fact, once it is accepted that judicial review is legitimate, legislative intent can play an important role in shaping the general principles of judicial review, suggesting, in particular, the development of a doctrine of curial

[9] Mark Elliott, *The Constitutional Foundations of Judicial Review* (Oxford: Hart, 2001), p. 110.

[10] Christopher Forsyth, 'Heat and Light: A Plea for Reconciliation' in Christopher Forsyth (ed.), *Judicial Review and the Constitution* (Oxford: Hart, 2000), pp. 393, 401.

[11] Elliott, *Constitutional Foundations*, above n. 9, p. 110.

[12] T.R.S. Allan, 'Legislative Supremacy and Legislative Intent: A Reply to Professor Craig' (2004) 24 OJLS 563, 572.

[13] Paul Craig, 'The Common Law, Shared Power and Judicial Review' (2004) 24 OJLS 237, 251.

deference with variable standards of review. The principles of good administration need not be marginalised and will be relevant to determining whether or not a decision survives the appropriate standard of review. Following my approach, the fundamental insight of the common law theorists – that it is for judges to develop the general principles of judicial review – is incorporated, but the judicial role is relocated in such a way as to give more prominence to legislative intent, thus avoiding the 'substantial implausibility which is involved in the assertion that the complex principles of good administration simply spring from Parliament's legislative silence'.[14] In short, legislative intent need not be treated as marginal, or as an empty vessel into which judicial review doctrine can be poured.

Curial deference and the rule of law

Safeguarding the rule of law

In the introduction, I addressed T. R. S. Allan's assertion that a doctrine of curial deference is necessarily empty. I hope that by now I have also assuaged concerns that a doctrine of curial deference is necessarily pernicious. Nonetheless, in the event that concerns have persisted, it seems worthwhile to venture a few thoughts on the relationship between the rule of law and curial deference. The content of the rule of law will invariably be contested,[15] but an exposition which is satisfying and relevant to the present discussion has been provided by Matthew Kramer. The rule of law is a 'juristic phenomenon' which describes the 'fundamental conditions that have to be satisfied for the existence of any legal system', but in the context of 'liberal-democratic societies' the rule of law 'is a morally cherishable expression of commitments to the dignity and equality of individuals'.[16] It is the latter sense that is relevant here. In particular:

> Central to the liberal-democratic tradition has been an emphasis on the liberty and autonomy and dignity of the individual, on the fundamental legal and political equality of persons, on equality of opportunity, on the

[14] Mark Elliott, 'Legislative Intention versus Judicial Creativity? Administrative Law as a Cooperative Endeavour' in Christopher Forsyth (ed.), *Judicial Review and the Constitution* (Oxford: Hart, 2000), pp. 341, 351.

[15] See e.g. Paul Craig, 'Formal and Substantive Conceptions of the Rule of Law: An Analytical Framework' [1997] PL 467; Jeremy Waldron, 'Is the Rule of Law an Essentially Contested Concept (in Florida)?' (2002) 21 *Law and Philosophy* 137.

[16] *Objectivity and the Rule of Law* (Cambridge: Cambridge University Press, 2007), p. 102.

> responsibility of governments to protect the lives and basic well-being of their citizens, on the importance of reasoned deliberation and justification in the domain of public power, on opportunities for adults to participate in elections and in other forms of political activity, and on the separation of powers of government.[17]

Without addressing them individually (and noting that some are not germane) I think it is reasonable to claim that such of these values as are relevant are comfortably satisfied by my doctrine of curial deference. In particular, the rule of law is safeguarded by requiring delegated decision-makers to act reasonably:[18] 'Courts retain the authority to control administrative abuses of power; deferential review simply recasts the question of "law" as whether the agency's interpretation is "reasonable".'[19] Requiring delegated decision-makers to keep within boundaries of unreasonableness gives content to the value of ensuring that exercises of public power are justifiable, by making judicial review available to individuals who have had adverse decisions rendered against them. Indeed, '[i]t is difficult to see how the rule of law may be upheld unless courts are prepared to wade into vaguely and broadly defined discretions to delineate the boundaries of lawful conduct'.[20]

The dynamism of deference

In addition, unreasonableness – central to the doctrine of curial deference that I have developed – is not static. If understood in the way that I have suggested, unreasonableness is a dynamic concept. The set of *indicia* of unreasonableness is not closed. According to changes in judicial and social attitudes, *indicia* may be added or subtracted from the set identified above. Jeffrey Jowell's description of constitutional principles captures the essence of the idea:

> New principles emerge by a process of accretion reflecting a constitution's changing imperatives and shifting settlements. These are based upon altering notions of the proper scope of governmental power as well

[17] *Ibid.*, p. 144.

[18] Constitutional requirements are also respected. See e.g. *Dunsmuir* v. *New Brunswick* [2008] SCC 9; [2008] 1 SCR 190; Henry Monaghan, '*Marbury* and the Administrative State' (1983) 83 Colum LR 1, 27.

[19] Colin Diver, 'Statutory Interpretation in the Administrative State' (1985) 133 U Pa LR 549, 569.

[20] Lorne Sossin, 'Empty Ritual, Mechanical Exercise or the Discipline of Difference? Revisiting the Standard of Review in Administrative Law' (2003) 27 Advocates' Quarterly 478, 504.

> as upon other fundamental social values which become endorsed over time.[21]

Felix Frankfurter's advice, rendered in the general context of statutory interpretation, seems apposite: 'In those realms where judges directly formulate law because the chosen lawmakers have not acted, judges have the duty of adaptation and adjustment of old principles to new conditions.'[22] Whether the rule of law, principles of good administration or some conception of justice supplies the *indicia* is important, and judges ought to be clear about the source from which they are drawing. But of the utmost importance for present purposes is that unreasonableness is sufficiently dynamic to be responsive to changes in context, and is legitimate because it reflects judicial and social attitudes.

Curial deference and a culture of justification

Moreover, the rule of law may actually be enhanced by a doctrine of curial deference with variable standards of review, because a 'culture of justification' is incorporated in the necessary conception of unreasonableness. Deference need not amount to abdication, and deferential courts may continue to play a major role in developing principles of good administration and requiring public justification of state action.

Curial deference and the administrative state

I might claim, perhaps grandiosely, that the incorporation of practical justifications into the overall argument in favour of a doctrine of curial deference is important because it begins to offer a deeper rationale for the legitimacy of the administrative state, responding to Jerry Mashaw's argument that:

> the normative demands of administrative law are at war with our understanding of the practical necessities of administration. We have failed to construct a normative model of administration that fits its realities, or more properly, a normative model that builds on best practices in an administrative world beset by inadequate budgets, legislative imperatives, public resistance, as well as real scientific uncertainties.[23]

[21] Jeffrey Jowell, 'Of *Vires* and Vacuums: The Constitutional Context of Judicial Review' [1999] PL 448, 455–6. Internal citation omitted.

[22] 'Some Reflections on the Reading of Statutes' (1947) 47 Colum LR 527, 535.

[23] 'The Story of *Motor Vehicle Manufacturers Association of the United States* v. *State Farm Mutual Automobile Insurance Company*: Law, Science and Politics in the Administrative State' in Peter Strauss (ed.), *Administrative Law Stories* (New York: Foundation Press, 2006), pp. 334, 394.

The practical justifications I have offered, and in particular the way in which I have offered them, are capable of underpinning a general theory of administrative law and administration. Expertise, complexity, democratic legitimacy and procedural legitimacy are reasons for respecting the autonomy and importance of the administrative state, because they justify delegations of power to delegated decision-makers. Asking why delegations of power have been made is valuable because it requires courts to engage with delegated decision-makers and attempt to understand the delegated decision-making process. My argument also addresses David Dyzenhaus's suggestion that declared constitutional principle (what he called formalism) and the practical justifications (substance) could not peacefully coexist: 'formalism without substance is futile. But the relationship between formalism and substance is such that the latter inevitably undermines the former.'[24] If the two are as closely interrelated as I have argued, neither can undermine the other. They are complements, not competitors.

Moreover, solid foundations for continued peaceful coexistence between the judicial and political branches are laid: my doctrine of curial deference is rooted in legislative intent, but the role of the judiciary in elaborating the doctrine is retained, giving effect to the suggestion that 'it would be much better if judges did not think they had either to stoop or to conquer'.[25] The relationship between unreasonableness and legislative intent that I have argued for goes beyond recognising 'that the precise content and impact of the principles of good administration must always ultimately be determined by reference to, *inter alia*, the legislative framework giving rise to the administrative discretion in question'.[26] Appreciating the judicial obligation to give effect to legislative intent opens up a space which a dynamic conception of unreasonableness, with its variable standard of review, can occupy.

Dialogue is also facilitated. Permitting delegated decision-makers to justify the presence of *indicia* of unreasonableness in their decisions in turn permits delegated decision-makers to engage (through counsel) in an actual dialogue with reviewing courts about the appropriate content of the principles of good administration. A similar dialogue is permitted

[24] David Dyzenhaus, 'The Politics of Deference: Judicial Review and Democracy' in Michael Taggart (ed.), *The Province of Administrative Law* (Oxford: Hart, 1997), pp. 279, 298.

[25] David Dyzenhaus, 'The Logic of the Rule of Law: Lessons from Willis' (2005) 55 UTLJ 691, 714.

[26] Elliott, 'Cooperative Endeavour', above n. 14, p. 355.

in respect of all impugned decisions, helping to ensure that a balance is maintained between the requirements of the principles of good administration and the effective and efficient dispatch of administrative business.

Proponents of curial deference should welcome the linking of curial deference to legislative intent. Any doctrine of curial deference or indeed any other means of developing the general principles of judicial review that does not rest on the foundation of a declared constitutional principle is on relatively shaky ground compared to one that does. It is true that recalcitrant judges can always subvert a scheme of curial deference by relying on allegedly clear expressions of legislative intent, but it is not clear that the solution requires the abandonment of legislative intent. A doctrine of curial deference based on a proper consideration of the relevant statutory provisions will be stronger than an entirely judge-made doctrine. Such a doctrine might ostensibly be based on abstract concepts such as the rule of law or the principles of good administration, but really would be tethered to a background theory that is likely to be controversial and unlikely to achieve widespread acceptance. On what basis, a judge might ask, should a free-standing principle be allowed to interfere with the traditional judicial task of statutory interpretation? Once curial deference is seen to have its basis in legislative intent, an answer is readily available to this barbed question.

INDEX

For EU product safety concerns, contact us at Calle de José Abascal, 56–1°, 28003 Madrid, Spain or eugpsr@cambridge.org.

www.ingramcontent.com/pod-product-compliance
Lightning Source LLC
LaVergne TN
LVHW011526200926
848484LV00001B/166